# Oracle API Management 12c Implementation

Learn how to successfully implement API Management using Oracle's API Management Solution 12c

Luis Augusto Weir

Andrew Bell

Rolando Carrasco

Arturo Viveros

BIRMINGHAM - MUMBAI

# Oracle API Management 12c Implementation

Copyright © 2015 Packt Publishing

All rights reserved. No part of this book may be reproduced, stored in a retrieval system, or transmitted in any form or by any means, without the prior written permission of the publisher, except in the case of brief quotations embedded in critical articles or reviews.

Every effort has been made in the preparation of this book to ensure the accuracy of the information presented. However, the information contained in this book is sold without warranty, either express or implied. Neither the authors, nor Packt Publishing, and its dealers and distributors will be held liable for any damages caused or alleged to be caused directly or indirectly by this book.

Packt Publishing has endeavored to provide trademark information about all of the companies and products mentioned in this book by the appropriate use of capitals. However, Packt Publishing cannot guarantee the accuracy of this information.

First published: September 2013

Second edition: September 2015

Production reference: 1250915

Published by Packt Publishing Ltd.
Livery Place
35 Livery Street
Birmingham B3 2PB, UK.

ISBN 978-1-78528-363-5

www.packtpub.com

# Credits

**Authors**
Luis Augusto Weir
Andrew Bell
Rolando Carrasco
Arturo Viveros

**Reviewers**
Jorge Quilcate
Chintan Shah

**Acquisition Editor**
Vivek Anantharaman

**Content Development Editor**
Athira Laji

**Technical Editor**
Edwin Moses

**Copy Editors**
Dipti Mankame
Kevin McGowan

**Project Coordinator**
Bijal Patel

**Proofreader**
Safis Editing

**Indexer**
Priya Sane

**Production Coordinator**
Shantanu N. Zagade

**Cover Work**
Shantanu N. Zagade

# Foreword

**Application Programming Interfaces (APIs)** are not new — we have heard about them, exposed them, and used them for decades. In the early days of APIs, they were little more than method calls made to functions exposed by developers for developers within a limited scope and to a very specific audience. Over the years, with the emergence of protocols, such as **SOAP**, **Web Services** established themselves as the standard to extend and leverage existing systems via interfaces exposed — arguably an evolution from APIs themselves.

As Web Services and **Service Oriented Architecture (SOA)** went through the lifecycle from hype to reality, managing these services became extremely important, giving birth to the concept of **SOA Governance**. SOA Governance has evolved over the past few years as a rich, mature, and extensive approach to manage your service lifecycle from seed to runtime and analytics. SOA Governance has been used in several successful SOA projects around the world providing the much needed framework of well-defined roles, processes, and tools to manage and extend massive SOA projects across enterprises on the planet.

In the meanwhile, the **Digital** revolution continues to grow at a pace like never before. As we see every industry in the world being disrupted by technology — mobile, music, media, payments, hotels, and even the 300-year-old taxi industry — the importance of this revolution being grounded with a strong Integration layer becomes even more important. The promise of digitalization must invariably be backed by applications being able to discover and talk to each other while exposing themselves securely with an elevated user experience. This interactivity could be between applications residing in the same environment, across the planet in a cloud or on smart devices worn by you and me; there is no better way to expose and manage these than through a simple yet sophisticated **API Management** methodology and platform. API Management is no longer simply a buzzword in the technical world but a real strategic investment for businesses — exposing, leveraging, and even monetizing their APIs, whether for business or community — it is a reality today.

In many ways, API Management is an evolution of SOA Governance, but at the same time, a clearly independent approach. Yes, there is a strong overlap, and yet it does not undermine the importance of having a clear co-existence strategy with both.

In this book, the authors bring together these two exciting and extremely important paradigms in the application, services, and API space to the concept of **Application Services Governance**. I am confident that you will enjoy and be stimulated on this journey with Luis, Rolando, Arturo, and Andy as much as I have, through this book and through knowing Luis for years as a thought leader in the SOA Governance, API Management, and now the Application Services Governance space.

While all these concepts rely on your drive and vision to bring them to reality in your world, I hope that the knowledge you gain from this book enables you further to envision, lead, and execute your technology initiatives, whichever industry you are in, to the next level of innovation and success.

**Vikas Anand**
Vice President of Product Management, Oracle Service Integration & Oracle iPaaS, Oracle Corp.

# About the Author

**Luis Augusto Weir** is an Oracle Ace director and a principal architect for HCL technologies. In addition, he currently leads the global OFM and Oracle PaaS solutions offerings in the Modern Apps and Integration Practice (MAPI) at HCL. With several years of experience implementing IT solutions across the globe, he has successfully delivered several large and complex Service Oriented Architecture (SOA) and API solutions for Fortune 500 companies. He has led SOA and other middleware capabilities for different renowned SIs, such as CSC, Cognizant, and Capgemini. He is currently focusing on creating digital solutions and strategies to key global HCL customers and helps them adopt and realize the full benefits that technologies, such as APIs, mobile frameworks, cloud integration platforms, and IoT, can bring to the business.

Having had a natural talent for software, computers, and engineering in general, Luis' career in software started from an early age. Even before starting university, Luis's entrepreneurial spirit led him to start several ventures, including the very first social media website in his country of origin (Venezuela) as well as a small software development firm. Although none of these ventures turned into a multimillion corporation, the experience and knowledge gained during this period led him to develop the passion for distributed software computing, which inevitably led to SOA.

Luis is very passionate about technology. He is a published author, a blogger, and also a regular speaker in major conferences and events. Being a well-known industry expert, especially when it comes to Oracle middleware technologies, he is an Oracle Technology Network (OTN)-certified SOA black belt.

# Acknowledgments

First of all, I would like to thank my coauthors Rolando, Arturo, and Andy for their efforts and hard work in making this title a reality.

Second, I would like to thank our Packt editors Vivek Anantharaman and Gaurav Sharma for their support in publishing this title. I also thank our Packt reviewers and specially to Jorge Quilcate for his excellent feedback! Finally, also thanks to Claudio Ivaldi and Lalitha Hari Priya for their valuable inputs.

Third, I would like to thank Kiran Somalwar, Ram Mangati, and Anil Balwanti, from HCL and Jürgen Kress, Bob Bhubart, Yogesh Sontakke, Peter Belknap, and Mark Dutra from Oracle Corporation for their help in publishing and promoting this title. Special thanks to Jürgen and Bob for their outstanding support throughout the entire process.

Finally, but by no means least, I would like to thank my beautiful family, my mom, dad, and siblings, but most importantly infinite thanks to my beautiful wife, Elena, and our two gorgeous daughters, Helena and Clara. You are what matter most and the real reason I do what I do.

# About the Author

**Andrew Bell** works at CSC where he is the Lead SOA/BPM solution architect for the Oracle Global Practice. He has more than 28 years experience in the IT industry covering a wide range of software products and industry verticals.

Andrew has more than 23 years experience working with Oracle products and toolsets, including 10 years working with Oracle SOA Suite and Oracle BPM. He first started working in the SOA space 12 years ago and has successfully delivered many challenging and complex Oracle Middleware projects for large blue chip clients.

Andrew is well respected for his depth of knowledge in the areas of SOA and BPM. He has strong team lead and communication skills and a deep all-round technical knowledge, which covers both the Oracle stack and Java.

> I would like to thank my wonderful girlfriend Alison for her patience and support while I spent many hours locked away working on this book and also my boys James, Christopher, and George. I would also like to thank my good friend Luis for giving me the opportunity to write this book with him. Much appreciated.

# About the Author

**Rolando Carrasco** is a Fusion Middleware director for S&P Solutions, a consulting firm focused in Oracle Fusion Middleware.

Rolando has been working with Oracle Middleware for more than 13 years. Since the old days of Oracle AS, Oracle Interconnect, he's been working with Oracle Integration Products.

Rolando is an Oracle ACE and also one of the leaders/coordinators of the Oracle Users Group—ORAMEX—in Mexico.

Rolando has been implementing SOA with major companies of the telecom, finance, manufacturing, and retail industry for a long time. He has also been guiding them in governing their SOA implementation.

Rolando has strong presentation skills that have helped him to present at different forums throughout Latin America. He's been a constant speaker at the Oracle Technology Tour Latin America.

His blog is one of the most read in the Spanish-speaking community (`http://oracleradio.blogspot.in/`). He is a constant contributor in the OTN in Spanish section of Oracle.com. Together with Arturo Viveros, he is a creator of the SOA myth busters' blogs (`https://soamythbusters.wordpress.com/`).

Rolando worked for Oracle from 2002 to 2010. From 2005 to 2010, he worked for Oracle Corporation as a part of the outbound product management team for Fusion Middleware.

His background is a mix of presales, consulting, and product management. He's been working with XML, web services, SOA, and Integration technologies since 2000.

During the past 2-3 years, Rolando has been focused on cloud technology and the concepts of API Management. Those are the two topics where he has found a new interest, and they are pretty much related with his strong SOA background.

# Acknowledgments

First and foremost, I thank my Lord Jesus Christ for being my Savior and giving me the strength to work as hard as I can.

I thank my wife and my daughter for being so patient during all these months of writing this book. It's been quite a long journey. Also, I thank my mom, dad, and brother, who are always there to support me.

I also thank my company S&P Solutions, and especially, Marcos Schejtman, for helping me with the *Oracle API Gateway Implementation Overview* chapter, without whom it would have been difficult to write.

A special mention to Arturo Viveros, who is my colleague and friend. With him, I've written a lot about technology. He is very enthusiastic and one of my greatest supporters.

Also, I thank Ricardo González for being my business partner for all these years.

I would like to thank Leonardo González because, besides being one my closest teammates, he is a great friend.

I also would like to thank Luis W. He was the one who invited me to work with him. He is one of the most talented persons I have ever met.

# About the Author

**Arturo Viveros** is an outstanding professional currently based in Mexico City with 11 years of experience in the development, design, architecture, management, and delivery of IT projects for a variety of industries, including banking, financial, telecom, insurance, government, construction, manufacture, healthcare, and retail. He is also an entrepreneur and a technology enthusiast, always looking to be in the cutting edge of technological innovation by attending multiple events and conferences worldwide, as well as by networking and collaborating constantly with some of the top IT professionals in the world. He is also adept at producing highly specialized technical articles, blogging and speaking regularly in technology-related forums, both in Mexico and abroad.

Arturo has several IT certifications, including Oracle IT Architecture SOA, Java Programmer, and Web Component Developer, and has been recently recognized as an Oracle ACE. He has also obtained the SOA Architecture and Cloud Architecture Certifications by Arcitura Inc. with honors, and is a certified trainer for both, having already delivered courses both in Spanish and English in Mexico, Colombia, and Peru.

Arturo is also a regular contributor for *SOA Magazine*, *Service Technology Magazine*, and *OTN*, as well as part of the Mexican Oracle User Group's (ORAMEX) directive board. He currently works in S&P Solutions, a 100 percent Mexican company with presence in all of Latin America, which specializes in providing advanced consultancy services related to Oracle Fusion Middleware technologies.

> First of all, I would like to thank my very good friends, Luis Weir and Rolando Carrasco, to invite me to collaborate with them in this exciting project. It has been a great honor for me and a lot of fun working with you guys.
>
> Also, I would like to thank my beloved family, especially my beautiful wife, Jessica, who is always by my side, as well as my mom, Luly, my dad, Arturo, and my brother, Daniel, for always supporting and cheering me. I love you all very much.

# About the Reviewers

**Jorge Quilcate** is a developer, consultant, and speaker who mainly focusses on Java EE and Integration, recognized as Oracle ACE Associate specializing in SOA and Middleware.

He is certified as a specialist in WebLogic Server, SOA/BPM Suite, and Java. He also implements and supports open source projects related to DevOps tools and Java EE. He tweets at `@jeqo89`.

**Chintan Shah** is a well-versed expert in Oracle Fusion Middleware (FMW) and has been working on FMW technologies for over 12 years. He is a hands-on architect. He is an active member of the FMW community and maintains a highly accessed blog at `http://chintanblog.blogspot.in/`.

# www.PacktPub.com

## Support files, eBooks, discount offers, and more

For support files and downloads related to your book, please visit www.PacktPub.com.

Did you know that Packt offers eBook versions of every book published, with PDF and ePub files available? You can upgrade to the eBook version at www.PacktPub.com and as a print book customer, you are entitled to a discount on the eBook copy. Get in touch with us at service@packtpub.com for more details.

At www.PacktPub.com, you can also read a collection of free technical articles, sign up for a range of free newsletters and receive exclusive discounts and offers on Packt books and eBooks.

https://www2.packtpub.com/books/subscription/packtlib

Do you need instant solutions to your IT questions? PacktLib is Packt's online digital book library. Here, you can search, access, and read Packt's entire library of books.

## Why subscribe?

- Fully searchable across every book published by Packt
- Copy and paste, print, and bookmark content
- On demand and accessible via a web browser

## Free access for Packt account holders

If you have an account with Packt at www.PacktPub.com, you can use this to access PacktLib today and view 9 entirely free books. Simply use your login credentials for immediate access.

## Instant updates on new Packt books

Get notified! Find out when new books are published by following @PacktEnterprise on Twitter or the *Packt Enterprise* Facebook page.

# Table of Contents

| | |
|---|---|
| **Preface** | **v** |
| **Chapter 1: Application Services Governance** | **1** |
|   **SOA Governance** | **1** |
|   **API Management** | **4** |
|   **SOA Governance and API Management Convergence** | **8** |
|   **Delving into Application Services Governance** | **10** |
|     ASG implementation | 11 |
|     The ASG framework | 12 |
|     ASG framework scope | 13 |
|       Strategy | 14 |
|       People | 17 |
|       ASG design-time | 22 |
|       ASG runtime | 24 |
|       DevOps | 26 |
|       Tools | 28 |
|   **Summary** | **28** |
| **Chapter 2: Implementation Case Study** | **29** |
|   **Case study description** | **29** |
|   **Discovery and readiness assessment** | **34** |
|   **Gap analysis** | **37** |
|   **Recommendations** | **39** |
|   **Roadmap** | **47** |
|   **Summary** | **49** |

*Table of Contents*

## Chapter 3: Oracle API Catalog Implementation — 51
### An overview of Oracle API Catalog — 51
#### Architecture and functional overview — 52
- The OAC core platform — 52
- The OAC application — 53
- OAC roles and user interfaces — 64
### Implementation use case — 66
### Implementing OAC — 67
#### Basic configuration — 68
- Logging in to OAC — 68
- Setting up departments — 69
- Setting up users — 72
#### Changing system settings — 76
### Bootstrapping OAC — 77
#### Bootstrapping Oracle SOA Suite with the command-line Harvester — 82
#### Bootstrapping Oracle Service Bus with the command-line Harvester — 86
- Manually bootstrapping WSDLs and WADLs with the command-line Harvester — 90
### SDLC harvesting using the Ant Harvester — 91
#### Using the SOA Suite Ant Harvester — 91
- Using the OSB Ant Harvester — 95
### Discovering APIs — 97
#### Using the OAC console to discover APIs — 98
#### Viewing and editing API metadata — 99
#### My APIs and API rating — 104
#### Setting up and using the JDeveloper plug-in for OAC — 106
- Installing the OER JDeveloper plug-in — 106
- Using the OER JDeveloper plug-in with OAC — 110
#### Exporting and importing configuration and assets — 118
- Exporting assets using the Import/Export utility — 119
- Importing assets using the Import/Export utility — 121
#### The REX API — 122
- Using the REX API to find and update an API — 123
### Summary — 137

## Chapter 4: Oracle API Manager Implementation Overview — 139
### Understanding API Management — 140
### Oracle API Manager overview — 142
#### Introduction — 142
#### Architecture and functional overview — 144
#### Oracle API Manager capabilities and components — 145
#### Oracle API Manager roles — 146
### API Manager case study background — 148

| | |
|---|---|
| Performing administrative tasks prior to the use of Oracle API Manager | 149 |
| Publishing APIs from the OSB Console as an API curator | 155 |
| Accessing the Oracle API portal as an administrator | 159 |
| Working with Oracle API Manager as a consumer | 166 |
| Using API Manager to work with JSON/REST-based APIs | 177 |
| Summary | 179 |
| **Chapter 5: Oracle API Gateway Implementation Overview** | **181** |
| OAG overview | 181 |
|    OAG features | 182 |
| API security with OAG | 183 |
|    OAG architecture overview | 184 |
| Implementing use cases | 189 |
| Implementing OAG | 192 |
|    Service discovery | 193 |
|    API registration in OAG | 193 |
|    Implementing OAG policies | 198 |
|       Creating a policy to handle authentication and authorization using LDAP and OAuth | 199 |
|       Adding throttling filters to an existing policy | 211 |
|       Applying a policy to a web service | 213 |
|       Deploying a policy | 215 |
|       Creating a REST/JSON API | 216 |
| Summary | 233 |
| **Chapter 6: Installation Tips and Techniques** | **235** |
| Explaining the installation topology | 236 |
| Installation overview | 237 |
| Installing OAC | 238 |
|    Installing the database | 239 |
|    Temporary disk space requirements | 239 |
|       Installing WebLogic 12c | 240 |
|    Installing OAC Software | 241 |
|    Creating the OAC domain | 244 |
| Installing the Oracle API Manager software | 252 |
|    Creating the Oracle API Manager 12c WebLogic domain | 257 |
|    Installing Oracle API Gateway | 271 |
| Summary | 279 |
| **Index** | **281** |

# Preface

Digital transformation is at the core of every business strategy regardless of what type of business an organization is in. Companies that embark on a digital transformation journey are able to create innovative and disruptive solutions that are capable of delivering a much richer, unified, and personalized user experience at a lower cost. They are able to engage the customer in a seamless fashion through many channels, such as mobile apps, responsive websites, and social media. Organizations that adopt innovative digital business models gain considerable competitive advantage over those that don't.

The fundamental driver for digital transformation is the ability to unlock key information assets and business functionality, which is often hidden inside an organization's enterprise systems, and also services built following traditional Service Oriented Architecture (SOA) approaches.

Especially in regard to SOA, although many organizations have succeeded in the implementation of traditional SOA solutions, it has been broadly acknowledged that traditional SOA (meaning SOA implemented using traditional SOA tools, standards, and skills) did not deliver all of the capabilities required to fully unlock and also materialize an organizations' enterprise information and functional assets.

Moreover, new technology trends, such as multi-device mobile applications, Internet of Things (IoT), and API Management, have all introduced new ways of thinking about how technology can deliver benefits to the business. Although these technologies are in fact broadly based on SOA principles, they introduce their own flavor of architectures, implementation approaches, and integration patterns.

Here are some examples:

- Creation of lightweight APIs that typically implement REST as a binding protocol and JSON as a message format, to facilitate the following:
    - Integration of mobile apps with backend systems
    - Exposing key information and functionality to third parties
    - Pay-per-use APIs that generate additional revenue
- Cloud integration via Integration Platform as a Service (iPaaS) solutions, therefore giving birth to what is known today as hybrid architectures
- Sensors built into devices and/or machines using embedded Java (or equivalent) that connect to other systems and/or machines using lightweight protocols, such as MQTT, which can also participate in broader business processes
- Strong inter-business collaboration becomes a common practice in development teams, which allows broader process flows that are more customer-centric

Unfortunately, given the potential benefits that these new technologies bring to businesses and customers alike, many organizations rushed to adopt such technologies often at a tactical level without a clear strategy and with almost no governance in place. This approach has resulted in similar integration challenges to those experienced in the past, such as with early SOA adoption. However, the scale of these problems is much greater in nature as the spectrum of integration now also extends beyond on-premise systems into the cloud and mobile applications to name a few.

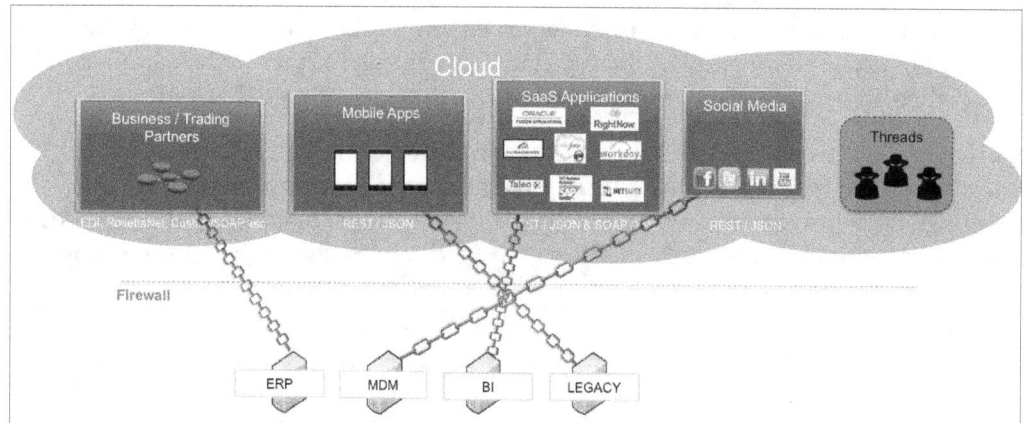

We can conclude that tactically implementing these new technologies without a robust governance framework drastically increases the complexity of integration, which in turn increases program costs both in terms of capital projects and runtime support. Although this might not be apparent initially, in the mid and long term this will likely become a roadblock to continue on the digital journey.

So, how do we define governance in relation to SOA and now API, mobile, and cloud? Although a very common question among practitioners, one is likely to be presented with many different answers depending on who is asked. However, the real question is not really what it is, but what it means to an organization and what benefits it can bring to a business. How can it be successfully implemented and which tools and processes are required to achieve it?

SOA Governance is a commonly misunderstood term and is often confused with other disciplines, such as Software Development Lifecycle (SDLC), Development Operations (DevOps), and/or Standards. In practice, although SOA Governance covers all of these concepts, its scope is broader still and covers everything from planning, analysis, service discovery and design, building, and testing stages of an SOA solution (design-time governance) to live operations and monitoring (runtime governance).

This book defines SOA Governance as the interaction between policies (what), decision makers (who), and processes (how) that are needed in order to successfully deliver SOA solutions (*SOA Governance: Framework and Best Practices - An Oracle Whitepaper*: `http://www.oracle.com/us/technologies/soa/oracle-soa-governance-best-practice-066427.pdf`).

In the context of APIs and mobile applications, SOA Governance has evolved into a new discipline known as API Management. This book defines API Management as the adoption and adaptation of SOA Governance principles and tools in the context of managing the end-to-end lifecycle of an API and the personas (actors) around it.

If we think of new technologies and trends, such as cloud, B2C, and B2B collaboration, market place and APIs as dimensions of a cube and superpose SOA Governance with API Management, we give rise to a more holistic approach; this book refers to this approach as Application Services Governance (to read more on Application Services Governance, refer to *Govern Your Services and Manage Your APIs With Application Services Governance* at `https://www.gartner.com/doc/2239615/govern-services-manage-apis-application`).

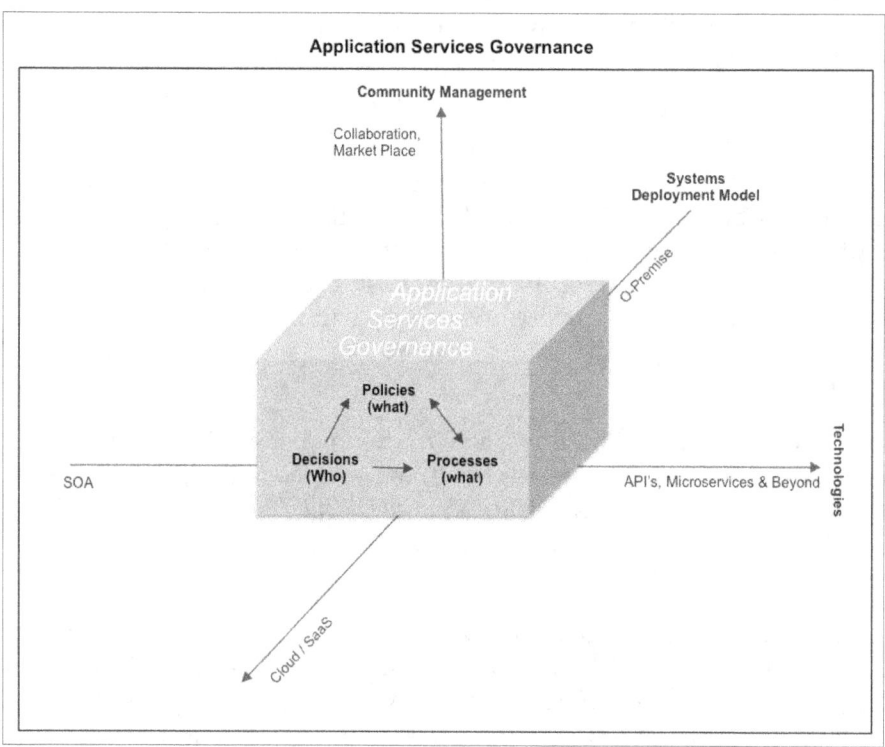

Application Services Governance implementations can only be successful in business terms if they can realize measurable benefits and provide a Return on Investment (ROI) or important nontangible benefits. Failing to apply this principle means that these solutions will be seen as complex and expensive technologies, rather than architecture and solutions that deliver business benefits.

While reading this book, SOA practitioners and API developers will embark on the journey of implementing Application Services Governance using Oracle API Management solution. The book will discuss the common problems that different organizations face when implementing SOA and APIs. It also explains how the implementation of best-practice processes, standards, and other techniques, along with appropriate Oracle toolsets, can solve these key architectural issues.

*Preface*

The components that build up the Oracle API Management solution are depicted in the following diagram:

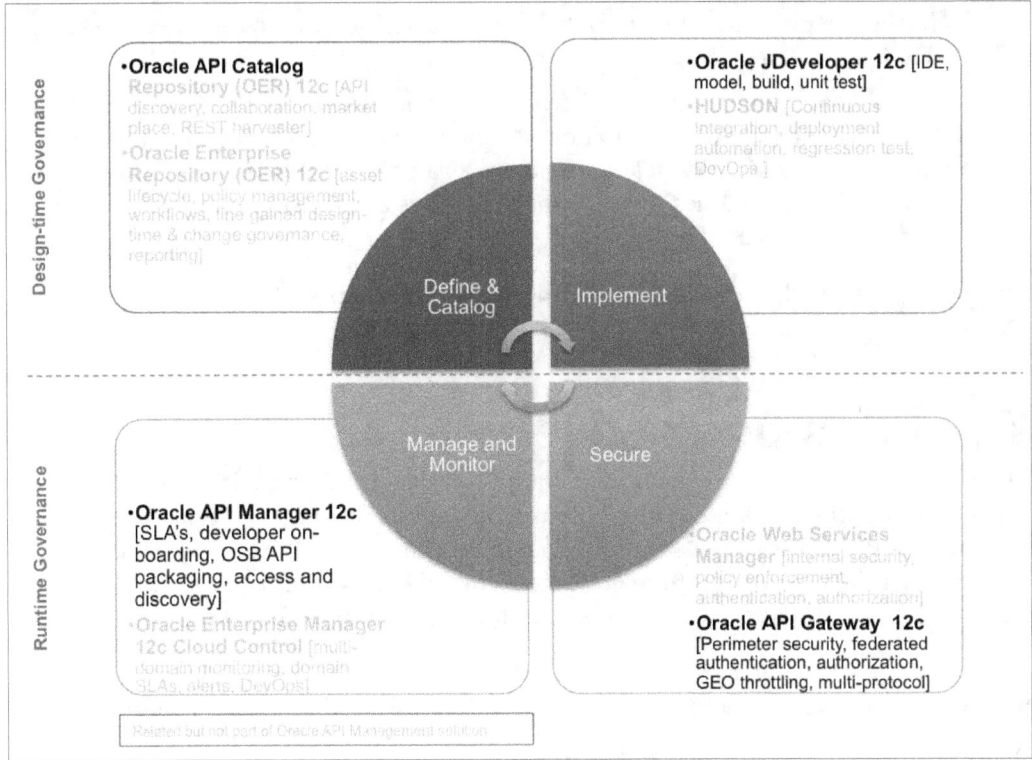

Here are the components:

- Oracle API Catalog (OAC): This is aimed at design-time governance. This tool is very simple to implement and allows the quick collection and publication of APIs (WSDL-based or WADL-based) from Oracle and non-Oracle environments, hence allowing APIs to be visible and reused. The tool comes with a rich user interface and provides capabilities, such as API discovery, collaboration capabilities (for example, My APIs and ratings), and API metadata.
- Oracle API Manager (OAPIM): This is built on top of Oracle Service Bus (OSB) 12*c*. This tool facilitates a runtime environment for the management of APIs through their life cycle. Using the OAPIM portal, different personas, such as architects and developers, can discover, consume, and monitor APIs running on the Oracle Service Bus.

- **JDeveloper**: This is Oracle's preferred integrated development environment (IDE) for the development of software solutions using Java, OSB, SOA Suite, and other technologies, such as SQL, PLSQL, XML, and PHP, among others. JDeveloper offers a wide variety of plugins to integrate with other products, such as OER and OAC.

- **Oracle API Gateway (OAG)**: Formerly Oracle Enterprise Gateway, OAG is a standalone product to implement robust security polices and apply these to services. OAG is typically deployed as a policy enforcement point (PeP) in demilitarized zones (DMZ) where services are consumed or exposed by applications located in untrusted networks.

This book presents the concepts, guidelines, and tips required for successful API Management using the Oracle API Management solution.

# What this book covers

The main objective of this book is to explain key concepts along with presenting practical guidelines on how to implement Application Services Governance using the Oracle API Management solution. The initial chapters of the book are focused on implementing the design-time governance, while subsequent chapters deal with runtime governance and focus on more advanced features of the toolset.

*Chapter 1, Application Services Governance,* describes in detail the key concepts around SOA Governance, API Management, and the Oracle API Management solution.

*Chapter 2, Implementation Case Study,* introduces a realistic use case of an organization that needs to implement API Management. The chapter highlights the steps followed by the organization as well as key critical success factors for the implementation.

*Chapter 3, Oracle API Catalog Implementation,* covers fundamental concepts and an implementation of OAC based on a realistic use case, including topics such as bootstrapping and harvesting, tool usage to classify and search APIs, and also how to extend OAC for richer functionality.

*Chapter 4, Oracle API Manager Implementation Overview,* provides an overview of the product and its capabilities and then describes how to implement the tool to solve a realistic use case.

*Chapter 5, Oracle API Gateway Implementation Overview,* provides an overview of the product and its capabilities and then describes how to implement the tool to solve a realistic use case.

*Chapter 6, Installation Tips and Techniques,* covers the Oracle API Management solution deployment topology and installation tips and steps for Oracle API Catalog (OAC), Oracle API Manager (OAPIM), and Oracle API Gateway (OAG).

# What you need for this book

This book makes use of the following software:

- JDeveloper 12*c* R1 (12.1.3)
- Oracle Enterprise Repository 12*c* R1 (12.1.3)

>  Note that Oracle API Catalog installation binaries are the same as Oracle Enterprise Repository.

- Oracle API Gateway 11*g* R2 (11.1.2.3.0)
- Oracle SOA Suite 12*c* R1 (12.1.3)
- Oracle Service Bus 12*c* R1 (12.1.3)

# Who this book is for

This book is mainly intended for enterprise architects, solution architects, technical architects, and SOA consultants who have implemented, or wish to implement SOA Governance or API Management using the Oracle API Management solution and toolsets.

It is essential that the reader has previous experience or knowledge of the following subjects:

- JDeveloper 12*c*
- Oracle SOA Suite 12*c*
- Oracle Service Bus 12*c*
- XML technologies in general

# Conventions

In this book, you will find a number of text styles that distinguish between different kinds of information. Here are some examples of these styles and an explanation of their meaning.

# Preface

Code words in text, database table names, folder names, filenames, file extensions, pathnames, dummy URLs, user input, and Twitter handles are shown as follows: "Each schema can reference definitions in other schemas by making use of the xsd:import directive."

A block of code is set as follows:

```
./harvest -url http://localhost:7101/oer -user
admin -password <password> -file ./test/samples
```

When we wish to draw your attention to a particular part of a code block, the relevant lines or items are set in bold:

```
<soapenv:Body>
  <wbcv:getSubscriberBalance>
    <subscriberID>${http.querystring.attribute}
    </subscriberID>
  </wbcv:getSubscriberBalance>
</soapenv:Body>
```

Any command-line input or output is written as follows:

**PATH=<JAVA_HOME>/bin:$PATH**

**export PATH**

**New terms** and **important words** are shown in bold. Words that you see on the screen, for example, in menus or dialog boxes, appear in the text like this: "Finally, review the entered installation details using the summary screen and hit the **Create** button when you are happy."

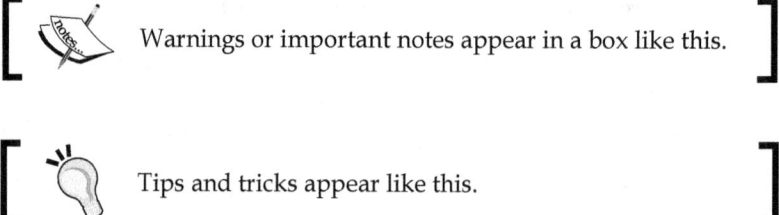

Warnings or important notes appear in a box like this.

Tips and tricks appear like this.

# Reader feedback

Feedback from our readers is always welcome. Let us know what you think about this book—what you liked or disliked. Reader feedback is important for us as it helps us develop titles that you will really get the most out of.

To send us general feedback, simply e-mail `feedback@packtpub.com`, and mention the book's title in the subject of your message.

If there is a topic that you have expertise in and you are interested in either writing or contributing to a book, see our author guide at `www.packtpub.com/authors`.

# Customer support

Now that you are the proud owner of a Packt book, we have a number of things to help you to get the most from your purchase.

# Downloading the color images of this book

We also provide you with a PDF file that has color images of the screenshots/diagrams used in this book. The color images will help you better understand the changes in the output. You can download this file from `http://www.packtpub.com/sites/default/files/downloads/OracleAPI_Management_12c_Implementation_ColorImages.pdf`.

# Errata

Although we have taken every care to ensure the accuracy of our content, mistakes do happen. If you find a mistake in one of our books—maybe a mistake in the text or the code—we would be grateful if you could report this to us. By doing so, you can save other readers from frustration and help us improve subsequent versions of this book. If you find any errata, please report them by visiting `http://www.packtpub.com/submit-errata`, selecting your book, clicking on the **Errata Submission Form** link, and entering the details of your errata. Once your errata are verified, your submission will be accepted and the errata will be uploaded to our website or added to any list of existing errata under the Errata section of that title.

To view the previously submitted errata, go to `https://www.packtpub.com/books/content/support` and enter the name of the book in the search field. The required information will appear under the **Errata** section.

## Piracy

Piracy of copyrighted material on the Internet is an ongoing problem across all media. At Packt, we take the protection of our copyright and licenses very seriously. If you come across any illegal copies of our works in any form on the Internet, please provide us with the location address or website name immediately so that we can pursue a remedy.

Please contact us at `copyright@packtpub.com` with a link to the suspected pirated material.

We appreciate your help in protecting our authors and our ability to bring you valuable content.

## Questions

If you have a problem with any aspect of this book, you can contact us at `questions@packtpub.com`, and we will do our best to address the problem.

# Application Services Governance

This chapter will introduce the main concepts surrounding SOA Governance and API Management, and how they relate, differentiate and converge into a discipline known as **Application Services Governance**. The chapter elaborates on how to set out the goals and aspirations for the governance effort; it will discuss the objectives and benefits of Application Service Governance and will also elaborate on the necessary steps required for its implementation.

## SOA Governance

A **Service Oriented Architecture (SOA)** is a strategy for constructing business-focused software systems from loosely coupled, interoperable building blocks (called services) that can be combined and reused quickly, within and between enterprises to meet business needs.

Oracle defines SOA Governance as an agile and efficient decision and accountability framework, to effectively direct and assist in realizing the benefits of SOA, while encouraging a cultural evolution in how an organization delivers SOA to the enterprise.

SOA Governance defines the interaction between policies (what), decision makers (who), and processes (how). This is shown in the following diagram:

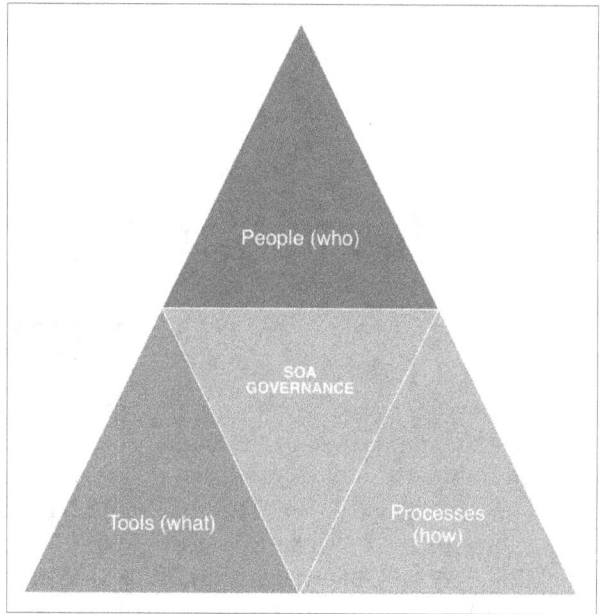

In order to implement successful SOA Governance, organizations need to understand how to align processes, people, and tools in order to maximize business benefits.

But what does it mean to deliver business benefits? In simplistic terms, it means creating reusable assets and eliminating liabilities.

In SOA terms, **assets** are electronic artifacts such as APIs, XML documents (XSDs, WSDLs, or XSLTs), documents (requirements, designs, and so on), systems, and services that add measurable value to the business. For example, a service that supports multi-channel submission of sales orders delivers value in the form of cost savings by way of reuse. Should a new channel be introduced at a later date, let's say mobile apps, the existing service can potentially be reused thus avoiding the costs of defining, designing, building, and testing a service specific to the new channel.

Assets are usually electronically stored in a repository and can be associated with other assets. Throughout the chapters of this book, assets will be elaborated on further and concepts such as asset types and asset taxonomies will be described.

Liabilities, on the other hand, are duplicated, deprecated, redundant, or unused assets that no longer deliver business benefits and potentially introduce additional cost. For example, having several services delivering identical functionality represents a liability since the total cost of supporting and running each service exceeds the cost of having a single consolidated service.

It is not common to use the term liability when talking about SOA Governance. However, we felt that if there is a description to describe what adds value to the business, there should be another one to define what takes the value away from it.

Challenges that prevent organizations from realizing the benefits of SOA can also be considered a liability. The following table lists some of the most common challenges and their consequences to the business:

| Challenge | Consequence |
| --- | --- |
| Lack of visibility of the existing assets and their performance characteristics | No asset reuse <br> More duplication (increased liabilities) <br> Higher costs |
| Tactical projects over strategic solutions | Projects deliver *short-term* benefits, but bring no *enterprise-wide* value or long term benefits |
| Poor decision-making and lack of accountability | No sense of ownership makes decision-making, policy enforcement, and accountability almost impossible |
| Low quality assets which becomes difficult to maintain and change | Assets are difficult to change and their cost is high. Changing an asset is considered risky and costly, which prevents new and innovative solutions from being introduced |
| Poor estimation techniques and inaccurate planning | Project overruns, ending up costing more than originally budgeted |

For SOA Governance to deliver real business benefits, it is imperative to establish the goals and objectives of the SOA Governance effort. These need to be aligned with the goals of the business and its I.T strategy. Without clearly aligned objectives, an SOA implementation can be perceived as failing to deliver any meaningful business benefit.

All such objectives should be supported by clearly defined success factors that are achievable and measurable prior, during, and after the implementation.

*Application Services Governance*

The following principles should be followed when defining the objectives of an SOA Governance implementation:

- **Business value**: Ensuring that the project investments yield business value
- **Alignment**: Keeping the SOA aligned with the business and architecture, and in compliance with the business and IT policies
- **Business agility**: Gaining visibility into your SOA for more rapid decision-making
- **Risk reduction**: Controlling dependencies, managing the impact of change, and enforcing policies
- **Cost savings**: Promoting consolidation, standardization, and reuse

Once the objectives have been defined, these should be well documented and presented to the key stakeholders within the business and IT departments to obtain the desired level of sponsorship. This sponsorship is critical to achieve the required level of assistance from different departments in order to develop the maturity assessment and roadmap, and to secure any extra funding, if needed.

# API Management

Before elaborating further on this topic we would like to describe more accurately what an API actually is. **Application Programming Interface**, or **API** for short, is a type of SOA asset that characterizes itself by:

- Making use of lightweight data transport and data formats such as REST and JSON

>
> **Representational State Transfer** (**REST**) is a an architectural style for the creation of web services using native methods or verbs (GET, POST, PUT, DELETE, and others) within the **Hypertext Transfer Protocol** (**HTTP**) to access resources via fully qualified **uniform resource identifiers** (**URIs**).
>
> For further reading, go to the following URL:
>
> http://en.wikipedia.org/wiki/Representational_state_transfer
>
> **JavaScript Object Notation** (**JSON**) is a lightweight data format based on the JavaScript language. For further reading, go to http://www.json.org/.

- Stateless (meaning there is no session or persistence of state; a request is received and a response is sent as part of the same thread)
- Being highly scalable

- Being **public** (accessible via public Internet) or **private** (accessible only via private channels such as virtual private networks—VPNs, corporate wide area networks—WANs and/or a companies' extranet)
- An API technical contract (basically its interface) may or may not be declared; however if done so, a variety of notations (many of which are still evolving) can be used. For example:
    - **Web Application Description Language (WADL):** http://www.w3.org/Submission/wadl/
    - **RESTful API Modeling Language (RAML):** http://raml.org
    - **Swagger:** http://swagger.io
    - **API Blueprint:** https://apiblueprint.org

> A bit of history: APIs actually predate SOA by far. APIs (or a least the notion of creating application interfaces to interact with other applications) existed even in the mainframe days. However, the term API as we know it today really refers to web APIs as the term gained popularity during the mobile app revolution, especially as mobile app developers in their search for a lightweight alternative to the then popular SOAP/WSDL-based web services, started creating services using REST and JSON which eventually became known as RESTful APIs.

A basic definition of **API Management** is the adoption and adaptation of SOA Governance principles and tools in the context of managing the end-to-end lifecycle of an API and the community around it.

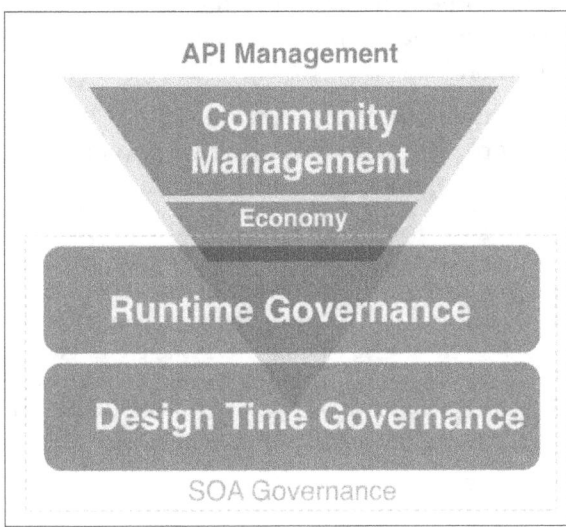

From the diagram (which is an extended version of Gartner's Application Services Governance) the following fundamental similarities and differences can be noted:

- The concept of **Community Management** is central to API Management, whereas in SOA Governance, although it was present, it was never a fundamental pillar.

> By community, we mean all the **personas** (actors) that participate in the API ecosystem, from consumers of an API (app developers for example) to the creators of the API (developers) and administrators of the API platform.

- More focus has been given to the runtime management of the API. For this reason, API Management tools tend to provide a lot of insight into API runtime analytics.
- There is a lot more flexibility around how an API is defined and built. This is reflected by the fact that several notations are available to define an API (some of them listed earlier in the chapter).
- The notion of **API economy** becomes very relevant to the business as it provides an opportunity to monetize APIs' usage. This means that the business sees an API as another revenue stream.

Having said that, we can conclude that API Management extends SOA Governance objectives by focusing on:

- **Productizing and externalizing information assets and business functionality via APIs**: APIs should be handled as products in their own right that offer information assets and business functionality to customers (known and unknown).
- **Community management**: Management of the API community (external and internal) by providing a facility where different people (developers, designers, architects, operators, business partners) can collaborate.

> One of the key tenets of API Management is the ability to manage a community of known and unknown people alike via a web portal that is usually publicly available (meaning via public Internet access). While this principle might not be true in all scenarios (that is, a company might want to make APIs available only to partners via an extranet), this is a generally accepted definition among API practitioners.

- **Runtime lifecycle management**: End-to-end management of an API through all of its phases. The API lifecycle starts during the creation of the API and ends when the API is retired. The typical phases are: creation, publishing, deprecation, and retirement.
- **Runtime analytics and metering**: Robust runtime analytics focused as much on consumer usage — metering (that is, total API calls, consumer SLAs, and others) and analytics as on platform statistics (API status, throughput, latency, and others).
- **Continuous delivery**: Having the ability to rapidly build, test and make APIs available for general use, and most importantly the continuous improvement of the API is fundamental in any API Management strategy and therefore API Management tooling. Having said that, adopting disciplines such as **Development Operations (DevOps)** as the main method to deliver APIs becomes a fundamental objective.

This book will not cover DevOps in great detail as other books and articles are dedicated explicitly to this topic. This book, however, will touch on areas that are related to DevOps but in the context of SOA Governance and API Management.

- **Global deployment models**: APIs (or more specifically web APIs) were born in support of scalable and flexible mobile and web architectures. Web and mobile applications respect no geographical boundaries; however, resources that can be globally accessible via the Internet are exposed to issues such as network latency, bottlenecks, a single point of failure and language localizations, to name a few. Having said that, an objective of API Management should be to provide cloud-based multi-geography deployments with localized capabilities such as localized language and throttling.
- **Web security**: The topic of security is a broad and complex one as it is relevant for every layer of a technology stack. However, when talking about APIs one should not try to boil the ocean. The focus should be on threads that apply web and mobile applications such as the one listed in the **Open Web Application Security Project (OWASP)** Top 10 project.

Refer to:

OWASP top 10: `https://www.owasp.org/index.php/Top10#OWASP_Top_10_for_2013`

OWASP top 10 mobile risks: `https://www.owasp.org/index.php/OWASP_Mobile_Security_Project#tab=Top_10_Mobile_Risks`

- **Monetization**: Give the business the ability to monetize APIs. The objective should be making APIs a new revenue stream for the business.

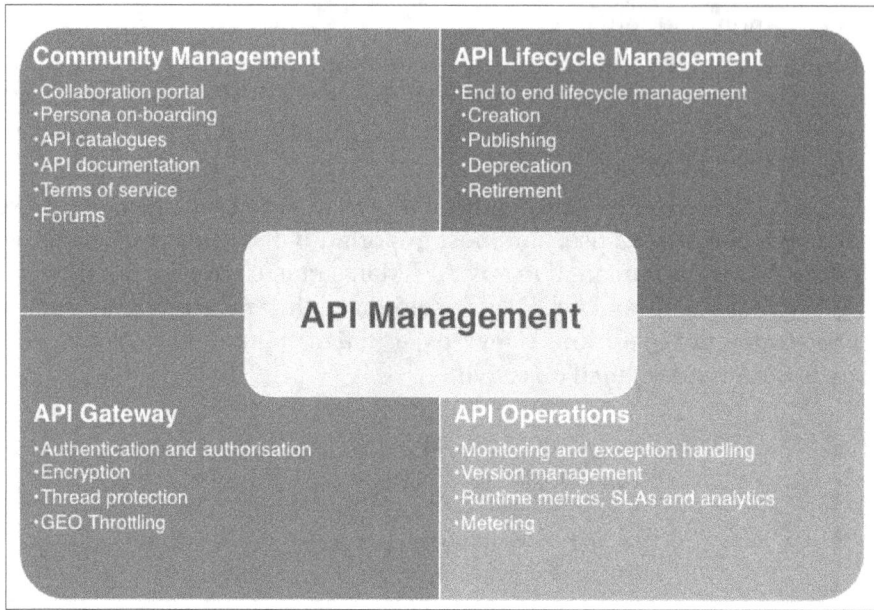

# SOA Governance and API Management Convergence

Understanding how and where SOA Governance and API Management converge is as important as understanding each separately. Although this book defines API Management as an extension of SOA Governance, the truth is that the former takes taking SOA Governance to a completely different level. APIs have become the default mechanism to expose business functionality and information assets, not only to mobile apps and web applications but also to business partners and even things (any devices such as watches, TVs, and so on). With different renowned analysts concurring in their prediction that by 2020 there will be some 26 billion connected devices and at least 6 billion smartphones, it doesn't require a mathematician to estimate that the number of APIs to be built will grow almost at the same pace.

Having said that, it is also natural that to expect that disciplines such as API Management and SOA Governance, rather than evolving separately, will converge and eventually evolve as a single discipline. We are already seeing evidence of this. Many product vendors (including Oracle) have adapted (or are adapting) their SOA offerings to provide full support for API development and API Management. However, this evolution has only just started in recent years and more changes are expected to come.

The following diagram aims to provide a view of where both disciplines differ and converge:

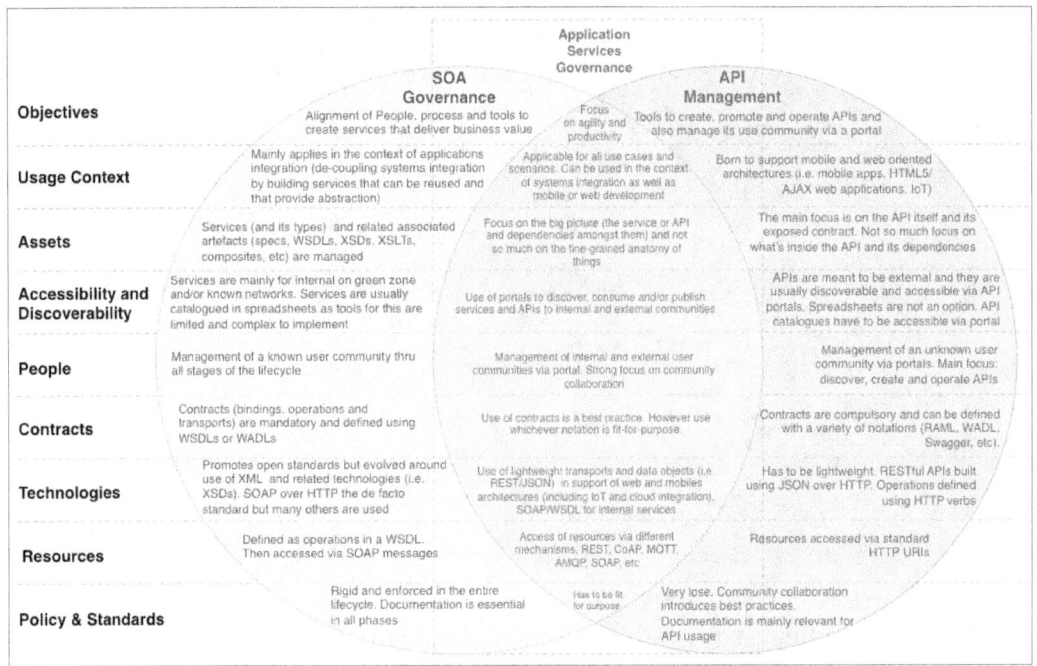

As can be seen from the diagram, the convergence of SOA Governance and API Management gives birth to a new discipline known as **Application Services Governance (ASG)**. The objectives of ASG are visible in the center, where SOA Governance and API Management overlap.

# Delving into Application Services Governance

As explained in the previous section, ASG was born as a result of the convergence of SOA Governance and API Management. ASG combines the best of both worlds and disregards the worst. It can be used in any context where APIs and services are involved with application integrations (in the cloud, on-premise or both), mobile architectures, web architectures, and **Internet of Things (IoT)**, to name a few.

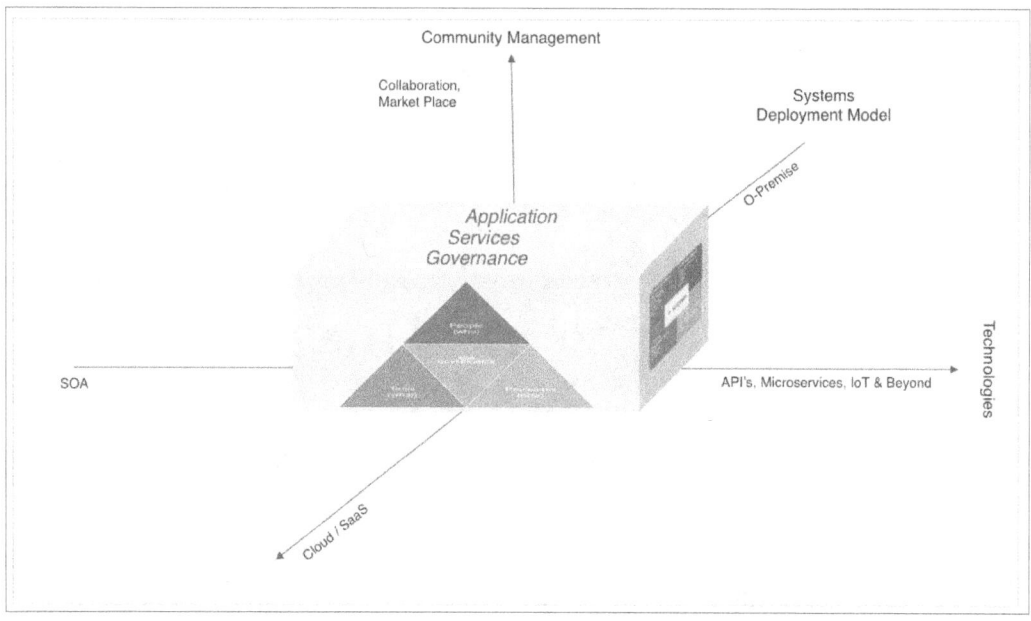

For those more familiar with traditional SOA, ASG will seem a simplified version of SOA Governance that has been augmented with all of the nice features available in API Management (community support, metering and monetization, and contract management all via a web portal) and features that didn't deliver (for example, UDDI registries and its integration with asset repositories). For those coming from a mobile or API development background, the impact will probably be more notable given that design time is very lightweight in API Management but in the convergence it should get more rigorous.

## ASG implementation

Understanding what ASG is, its relation to SOA Governance and API Management as well as its objectives, is an important step forward; however, it is not a guarantee for success. A successful governance implementation must tick several boxes and answer several questions, such as:

- **What artifacts are required to deliver governance?** It is vital for the success of a governance implementation to have a clear understanding of the artifacts to be delivered, what their purpose is, and what value they add to the overall governance implementation. The main artifacts are:
    - **Governance strategy**: It defines the goals and objectives for adopting ASG in the enterprise. Moreover, it defines the success criteria needed to ensure that the business benefits are realized by the adoption of SOA.
    - **Reference architecture**: It defines the core building blocks for SOA and API implementation.
    - **ASG policies and standards**: Guidelines such as patterns, anti-patterns, conventions, and best practices are considered or adopted when designing solutions.

> Policies define principles and assertions to be evaluated when making decisions. Standards define clear guidelines on what is or isn't allowed. Policies are usually but not exclusively created to enforce standards.

    - **Assets and taxonomies**: Define all the assets available in the enterprise, their description, and type.

- **How can it be delivered?** All of the necessary tools, processes, and procedures required when delivering governance and its objectives. The key artifacts that should be created or influenced are:
    - **ASG Implementation Roadmap**: it defines the activities required to deliver an ASG strategy and milestones for the implementation. This topic will be covered in more detail later in the chapter.

> A roadmap must set realistic targets, ones that are achievable based on the organizations' current maturity state. Not doing so means that wrong expectations will be set to the business, inevitably leading to failure.

○ **Design-time and runtime governance**: These two fundamental concepts will be described in detail later in the chapter.

- **Who is responsible for delivering it?** A description of all the participants required to deliver the artifacts previously listed, including their roles and responsibilities.

# The ASG framework

The answers to these questions, together with the concepts and tooling outlined in this book, provide the foundation for implementing a robust **governance framework** that underpins an end-to-end SOA and API ecosystem.

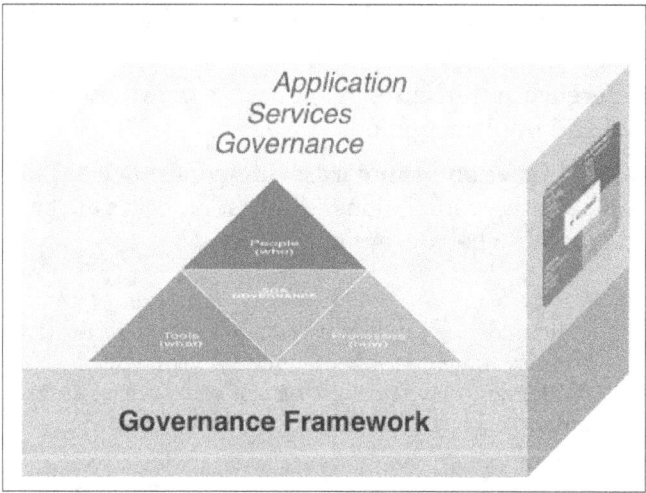

A governance framework defines the approach, artifacts, processes, tools, and people required to implement governance.

Having an effective and strong governance framework in place is extremely important as it delivers a common and consistent language for the enterprise to define and manage semantics, processes, standards, and accountability for the entire SOA and API lifecycle.

Indeed, without a well-defined governance framework, it is highly likely that the members of an organization, or its partners, will have their own understanding of what SOAs, APIs, and ASGs actually mean and how they are best implemented, leading to misalignment and duplication of effort across departments and between the collaborating organizations. In large and complex ASG implementations, this situation leads to poor implementations and almost inevitably, failure to deliver meaningful solutions.

# ASG framework scope

A governance framework defines the roles, responsibilities, processes, and procedures (what-how-who) that are needed to enforce the governance of all aspects of the service and API lifecycle (what-how-who). It also defines the standard tools that should be used on each phase (this is particularly relevant in API Management for the community management aspects of it).

This book sets out to discuss the tooling and concepts provided by Oracle Corporation to achieve successful ASG. The following diagram depicts in more detail what a governance framework would look like when put into the context of the Oracle SOA Governance and API Management solutions. We will explore the concepts illustrated in this diagram throughout this chapter showing how each contributes to the overall framework.

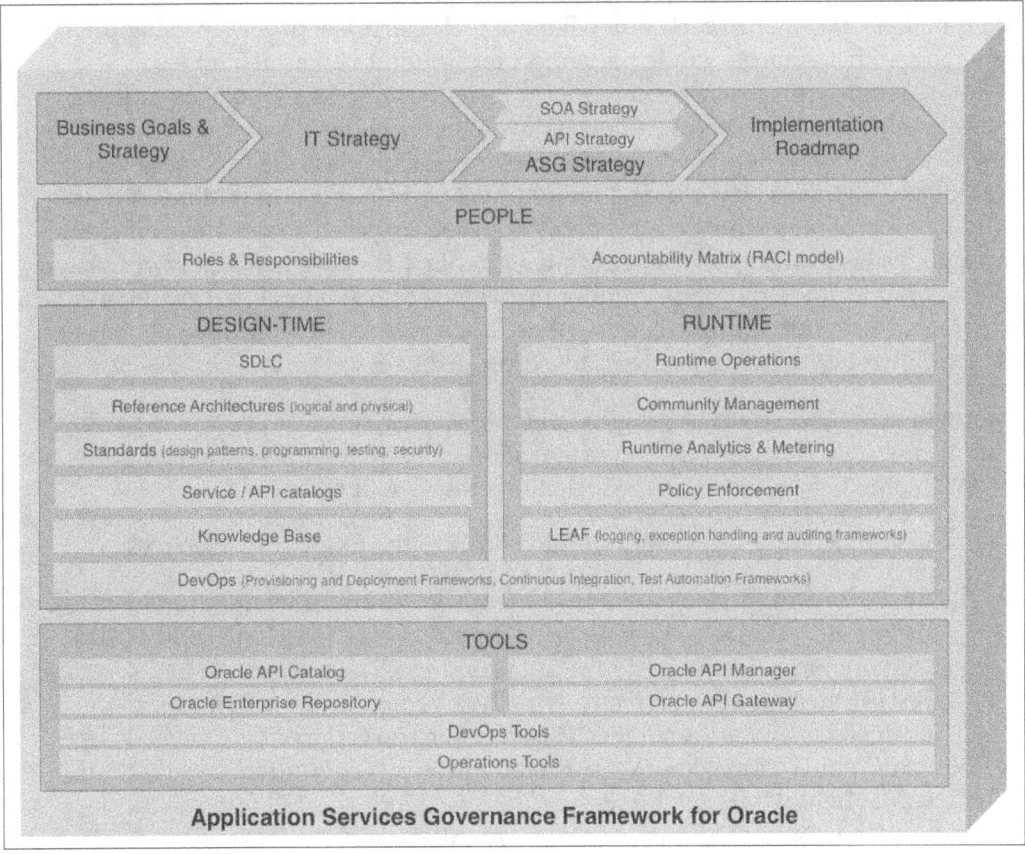

*Application Services Governance*

The preceding diagram shows how the business objectives and strategy are the fundamental drivers of an ASG implementation. Without a clear focus on the business drivers and on how SOA and API solutions can help achieve these business goals, an ASG implementation will most likely fail to deliver and end up being perceived by the management as yet another expensive technology that adds little value. To avoid this, the governance framework should define metrics that can demonstrate how SOA solutions and APIs are being effectively utilized to deliver tangible benefits to the business.

The sections to come elaborate further on the building blocks that constitute an ASG framework.

## Strategy

Not having an ASG strategy of some sort means that SOA and API solutions are being built ad-hoc by projects somewhere in the enterprise, probably using their own tools and standards. While the project itself might benefit from these ad-hoc solutions, this is not good news for the enterprise as a whole, as running and operating non-standard solutions tends to become more and more complex in time, therefore increasing the total cost of ownership. This issue becomes even more evident as companies start moving their applications to the cloud. Many end up building tactical point-to-point interfaces between on-premise systems and cloud applications because there wasn't a strategy in place to advise on what approach to take or what technology to use. Similar problems occur when departments rush into building ad-hoc mobile apps. Because these apps were built tactically they tend to use their own middleware solutions to expose APIs.

Elaborating an ASG strategy is a good place to start to solve or prevent many of these and other issues. This is a very important start as it sets the foundation and direction on which other governance framework deliverables will be based.

Having said that, an ASG strategy should consider the following objectives:

- **Business and IT strategy requirements**: Without understanding what the organization as a business is trying to achieve (the goals) and what IT strategy has been derived in support of these, it is impossible to deliver an ASG strategy that can effectively deliver value that is meaningful to the business and IT stakeholders. It is therefore imperative that the business goals and IT strategies are translated into a set of requirements that can subsequently be used to measure the success of an ASG framework implementation. A simple yet meaningful example is this table:

| Business Requirement | IT strategy | Derived ASG requirements |
|---|---|---|
| Increase digital sales (mobile, web, and social networks) by 50 percent in the next 5 years | Modernize all legacy systems into modern platforms that deliver the required digital capabilities | • Deliver a suitable digital platform that can deliver omni-channel support via APIs<br>• A framework/solution to monetize APIs |
| Reduced IT total cost of ownership by 50 percent in the next 5 years | Move as many systems as possible to the cloud in the reduced TCO | Cloud integration capabilities to enable the business to move systems to the cloud |

- **Use case discovery**: Based on the derived ASG requirements, organize a series of workshops with business and IT stakeholders from different parts of the business to identify:
    - If SOA and/or API related solutions are being used?
    - If yes, for what purpose?
    - If no, would SOA and/or API solutions be of any use?

> In order for this activity to be successful, ensure that you engaged stakeholders that have very good understanding of the relevant business processes. As important as this is one's ability to effectively articulate what SOA and APIs are, and why it can help them

- **Maturity assessment**: This consists of evaluating the current state of an SOA and API adoption within an organization using a maturity model as a reference to evaluate maturity. The ideal outcome of the assessment should be to understand:
    - How your organization's SOA and API maturity level compares with other similar organizations in the industry
    - Where are the weak points and what can be done to improve them
    - The gap between the as-is and the to-be and what has been done to bridge that gap (the implementation roadmap)

>  *Chapter 1, Application Services Governance*, of the book Oracle SOA Governance *11g* implementation (`https://www.packtpub.com/application-development/oracle-soa-governance-11g-implementation`) has a section that discusses in detail the elaboration of a maturity assessment.

- **Reference capability model**: A capability model is a vendor-agnostic conceptual architecture that depicts the different components and capabilities that build up a particular platform and/or solution. The more ASG requirements derived from the business, the more robust the capability model will be, as each component in the model should be targeted at addressing a particular requirement rather than just being there for the sake of having a capability without any view on whether the business actually needs it or not. As depicted in the following sample model, capabilities that should normally be considered API Management tools are mobile integration support, cloud and on-premise integration capabilities, in-memory caching, to name a few.

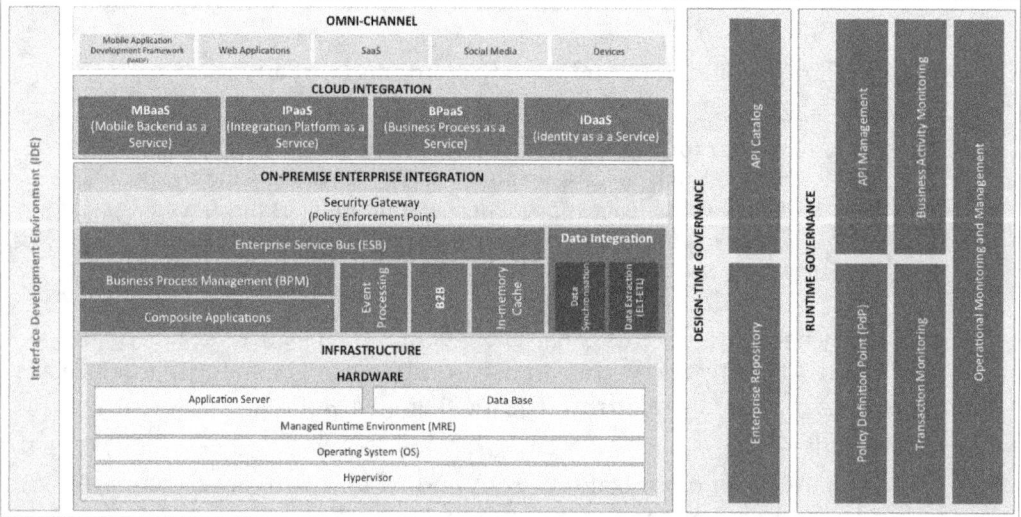

- **Implementation roadmap**: A roadmap is a high-level plan depicting what capabilities will be delivered and when. A roadmap should ideally commence with the elaboration of the strategy (as has been previously recommended), then be processed with a foundation phase. The purpose of the foundation phase is to provide a solid base for the entire ASG implementation by delivering the design-time and runtime artifacts of the framework. The foundation should also be responsible for identifying the teams that will support the ASG initiative going forward and also ideally deliver a limited set of use cases that provide high business value but aren't very complex (quick wins). The subsequent phases consist of the broader rollout of the solution to other departments and/or geographies.

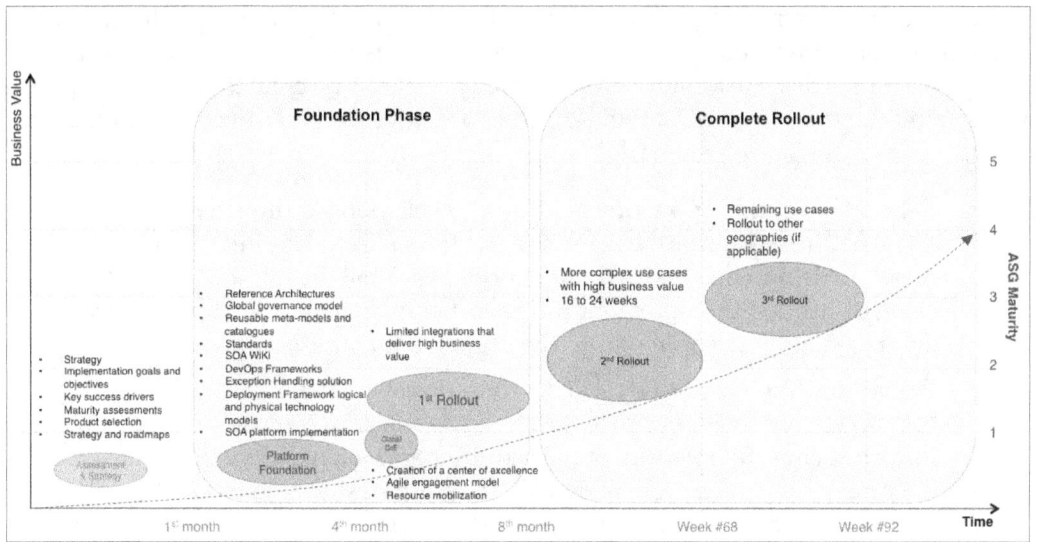

## People

One of the greatest challenges to successfully implement ASG-related solutions has, in fact, nothing to do with the intrinsic complexity behind their technology platforms. It is widely recognized that the real difficulty lies in dealing with people and processes from different parts of business and aligning them with the sole objective to deliver enterprise-wide solutions. This is not only true in the case of SOA and API architectures but also a challenge faced in systems design in general.

>  The people challenge and the consequence it has for IT has been nicely put in Conway's law:
>
> *"Organizations which design systems ... are constrained to produce designs which are copies of the communication structures of these organizations."*
>
> - http://en.wikipedia.org/wiki/Conway's_law

There is no simple solution or answer to the people challenge in an SOA. However, a good place to start is by defining an accountability framework to bring clarity to the roles required in an ASG initiative and their responsibilities. A very efficient way to represent such a matrix is by creating a RACI model. In a RACI model, all activities and deliverables are listed and mapped against responsible, accountable, consulted, and informed parties. However, before such a model can be created, one must first understand the roles in an SOA and API software development lifecycle and their relevance in an ASG implementation:

- **C-Level executive sponsors**: Having C-level sponsorship (that is, CIO and CTO) in an ASG initiative is imperative for success. Having the right level of sponsorship will ensure that the organizational, behavioral, and cultural changes needed to implement the governance processes and procedures are embraced by the people within the organization and not ignored or rejected.

- **Functional/Business analyst**: This role consists of experts in the organization's business processes. In general terms, he/she is responsible for producing suitable functional requirements such as functional design documents, a future process model, and/or a business rules catalog. The functional analyst should, among other things, engage with the business to ensure that all the functional requirements are well understood by the technical and solution architects to ensure that the requirements are presented in an appropriate format. The role of the analyst in an ASG implementation is to assist in the identification of relevant use cases where SOA and API solutions can add value to the business. This can be accomplished by sustaining a series of workshops with the relevant analysis with the sole purpose of identifying where the main pain points in the business processes are and catalog if potential SOA solutions could be built to address them.

- **Enterprise architect**: An enterprise architect is responsible for ensuring that the solution being delivered by the project not only delivers the desired business goals and can be successfully traced back to its original requirements, but also ensures that the overall solution aligns with the wider enterprise strategies and standards. The role of the enterprise architect in an ASG initiative is to help deduce the correct ASG requirements from the business and IT strategies and any other business domain-specific need.
- **ASG Solution architect**: He/she is responsible for producing solution architectures, capturing the non-functional requirements and also ensuring that the functional requirements are consistent with the solution as defined in the solution architecture. The solution architect may also participate and/or influence the definition of detailed designs, and may take part in the approval or rejection of these documents. The ASG solution architect is the **subject matter expert (SME)** in the technologies in question. Some of the responsibilities of the solution architect include:
    - Analyzing project requirements and ensuring that these conform to the expected level of quality
    - Identifying and cataloging the SOA and API assets and ensuring that these are discoverable and reused when appropriate
    - Providing technical leadership and guidance to the design and development teams (in development activities as well as support)
    - In an ASG implementation, the solutions architect is responsible for elaborating the ASG strategy, the accountability framework, design-time artifacts (with support from designers) and the development of runtime artifacts and implementation of the relevant ASG tools

The role of an ASG solutions architect should be as much about integrating people as it is about integrating systems. Dealing with people from different departments, backgrounds, and agendas is a huge challenge that must not be underestimated. The ASG solutions architect role requires someone that not only has a sound architectural and technological background but also has charisma, interpersonal skills, and can communicate to the business and technical teams equally. In a nutshell, it requires someone that can connect people and is capable of selling solutions which address different points of view.

- **ASG designer**: He/she is responsible for providing suitable detailed designs that successfully deliver all of the desired business and technical functionality. The designer is also responsible for providing further clarification and guidance to the development teams. An ASG designer will also create the XML assets such as WSDLs and schemas, and define the unit test scripts that should be executed by the developer. In an ASG implementation, the designer will support the solutions architect in the delivery of design-time artifacts.

- **ASG developer**: He/she is responsible for building and unit testing SOA services. The developer is also responsible for packaging the code ready for release, and for producing any relevant documentation that is required to support the deployment of the code (such as release notes). The SOA developer may partially contribute to the deployment and monitoring of services. In an ASG implementation, the designer will support the solutions architect in the delivery of run-time artifacts.

- **ASG testers**: Test teams are responsible for defining and executing the test scripts to support different testing stages (for example, system test, system integration test, user acceptance test, performance test, among others). In the context of the ASG implementation, the ASG tester should contribute towards the creation of a testing strategy and subsequently the implementation of the relevant DevOps tooling.

- **ASG middleware engineer**: He/she is responsible for installing and configuring the ASG infrastructure. He/she is also responsible for the deployment of services and APIs between different environments and also monitoring of the SOA and API infrastructures. Once a service or API has gone live, the support specialist is also responsible for monitoring the platform, conducting root cause analysis exercises when needed, and performing bug fixes and regression testing on the code.

- **DevOps engineer**: He/she is responsible for the installation and configuration of the DevOps-related tools (for example, version control systems, continuous integration, and packing tools) and also for helping define DevOps processes and enforcing them in the SOA and API lifecycles.

- **DevOps manager**: Owner of the DevOps solution, his/her role is to define and implement DevOps and also enforce its adoption. The success of this role should be measured by its ability to make the developers' lives easier by automating tasks such as deployments, installation, and configuration, but should also be responsible for bridging the gaps between development and operations teams.

The following RACI model provides a comprehensive view of the accountability matrix when implementing ASG:

| Deliverable | Responsible | Accountable | Consulted | Informed |
|---|---|---|---|---|
| Business strategy | CEO | CEO | CIO/CFO/COO | Everyone |
| IT strategy | CIO | CIO | CTO / Enterprise architects | Everyone |
| EA strategy | Enterprise architect | Chief enterprise architect | ASG solution architects | All architecture groups |
| ASG strategy | Solution architect | Lead solution architect | Enterprise architects | All architecture groups |
| ASG RACI | Solution architects | Lead solution architect | Enterprise architects | ASG architecture groups |
| ASG design-time | Solution architects and designers | Lead solution architect | Enterprise architects | ASG groups |
| ASG runtime | Developers and middleware engineers | Lead solution architect | Solution architects and designers | ASG groups |
| DevOps | DevOps manager | DevOps manager | DevOps engineer | All architecture groups |
| ASG tools | Middleware engineers | Lead solutions architect | Solution architects and designers | ASG groups |
| DevOps tools | DevOps engineer | DevOps manager | DevOps engineer | All Architecture groups |

## ASG design-time

ASG design-time focuses on the inception, discovery, cataloging, harvesting, design and testing of services throughout its lifecycle. The purpose of ASG design-time is to provide mechanisms to ensure that these phases can be achieved as efficiently as possible without compromising on quality and delivering as much business value as possible. One of the key concerns of ASG design-time is to make sure that services and APIs can be properly cataloged and/or harvested with the right level of metadata. It is equally concerned with ensuring that services and APIs can be discovered and reused. For this purpose, ASG leverages the strong community management capabilities that API Management portals usually come with.

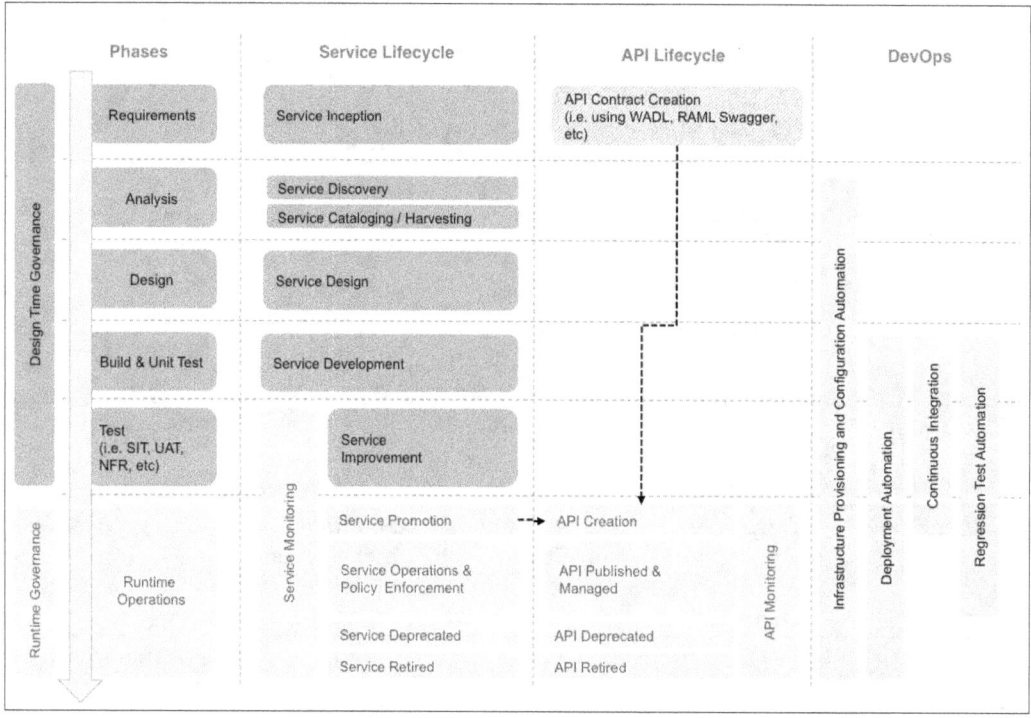

The API lifecycle focuses on ASG runtime, as can be seen from the preceding diagram. However, it is important to understand that SOA Governance and API lifecycles overlap and are complimentary methodologies that can be executed in parallel.

A key concern of ASG design-time governance is the ability to deliver a fit for purpose reference architecture and overarching standards. In ASG there is a lot of emphasis on collaboration and communication. It is therefore necessary that any architecture and/or standards produced in support of ASG design-time governance are the result of interactions between different groups and that supporting processes are in place to allow these to be modified and improved with time.

Some of the key deliverables of ASG design-time are:

- **ASG SDLC**: ASG **software development lifecycle (SDLC)** defines the end-to-end software development lifecycle for the delivery of services and APIs. Development standards should cover in some detail the end-to-end software development lifecycle including all the different assets that should be produced throughout the different phases of the lifecycle. The diagram shown earlier is a lightweight version of an ASG SDLC.
- **Logical reference architecture**: This architecture materializes the conceptual capability model by defining vendor-specific products that can be utilized to deliver the different capabilities required.
- **Physical reference architecture**: This defines a deployment topology for the products within the logical architecture that is capable of addressing all non-functional requirements such as high availability, security, compliance, among others.
- **ASG design standards**: This document describes the service taxonomy and a design patterns language that the designers and architects should consider when producing designs for SOA and API-related solutions.
- **ASG programming standards**: These provide developers with coding best practices and sample recipes to cook common solutions to common problems. These standards also provide guidance on how to leverage reusable code components such as exception handling, deploying, and monitoring frameworks.
- **ASG information standards**: These provide developers with best practices and samples to create data schemas using the notation of choice such as JSON or XSDs.
- **Security standards**: These define guidelines that should be considered when defining and applying security policies for services and APIs. Note that these standards will be dependent on how the runtime security framework is implemented.

- **Monitoring and SLA standards**: These define guidelines on the implementation of sensors and business activity, monitoring dashboards, composites and proxy services. These standards become particularly important at runtime as they enhance the search and monitoring capabilities of SOA instances once a service becomes operational.
- **Service and APIs catalog**: This contains the one and only version of the truth regarding services and APIs available in the enterprise. Building a catalog can be a very complex task and many organizations end up using spreadsheets. ASG opposes the use of such methods and recommends the use of tools such as API catalogs that can be used to dynamically or manually maintain an accurate inventory of all services and APIs available. The focus of this deliverable is to define what this catalog should look like in terms of metadata and make sure that the chosen tool can deliver it.
- **Service and APIs catalog**: ASG promotes the use of tools such as Wikis or content management systems for the publication of ASG-related information. This is a lesson learned from traditional SOA Governance implementations where several documents were usually created only to be outdated and ultimately forgotten. Instead, by using tools such as Wikis, not only will all information be available by just using a browser, but an entire community can contribute towards keeping the content updated.

# ASG runtime

ASG runtime focuses on the runtime operations lifecycle (promotion, operation, deprecation, and retirement), also including community management, runtime analytics and metering, enforcement of runtime policies, and LEAF (logging, exception handling, and auditing frameworks). Note that, in contrast to ASG design-time, API Management is mainly focused on runtime and therefore, from an ASG standpoint, the framework should be able to address not only traditional SOA runtime governance requirements but extend beyond and support all features expected of an API Management solution.

The key areas of focus are:

- **Runtime operations**: This runtime deliverable consists of a tool capable of supporting the runtime lifecycle of services and APIs from the moment they are promoted into production and subsequent stages. It is essential for any tool to be able to create and publish APIs from exposed services, to monitor the runtime characteristics of an API, and to manage the API lifecycle, ultimately to retirement.

- **Community management**: ASG runtime should have the capability to manage a community of known and unknown people (or actors). The solution should be able to support the following personas at a minimum:
    - **API developer**: This creates and publishes an API so others can discover it and use it
    - **API consumer**: He/she is a registered user that is capable of browsing the API catalog and generating API keys in order to consume APIs
    - **API administrator**: He/she is responsible for operating the platform
- **Runtime analytics and metering**: This is the ability to keep track of consumer-specific usage and to be able report on it in real time or historically.
- **Policy enforcement**: This is the ability to enforce policies at runtime. Policies can be about security (authentication and authorization), but also contractual (for example set and enforce restrictions based on usage).
- **LEAF: Logging, exception handling and auditing frameworks (LEAF)** delivers a robust framework that can be leveraged by developers to standardize the way logs are generated, exceptions are handled, and business transactions are monitored:
    - **Deployment framework**: Creating a framework of components that standardize the way code is promoted to different environments is extremely important, not only from a configuration management perspective but also from a project point of view. Applications such as Oracle SOA Suite *12c* or OSB *12c* do come with services exposed by the external systems within a BPEL or a pipeline flow. These external systems are expressed in the form of URLs which change from environment to environment and should therefore not be hardcoded into applications.

Promoting code using IDE tools such as JDeveloper and/or Eclipse is highly undesirable and not recommended, as this approach requires a high degree of manual intervention, which can introduce human error.

A runtime deployment framework should standardize and centralize the way code is promoted between all environments. Oracle API Gateway and Oracle API Manager come with utilities (for example, the ANT utilities or the WSLT scripts) that can be used and extended in order to create a robust deployment solution.

- **Exception handling framework**: One of the key success factors of an ASG implementation is the ability of the **business as usual** (**BAU**) team or the operations team to be able to support the solution once it has gone into production. Although this depends on many factors (for example, infrastructure, networks, storage, external systems, and so on), it is essential that errors are reported to the appropriate teams quickly and efficiently in order to minimize the risk of disruption to a business. The team running productions systems must be able to conduct root cause analysis and search for errors and logs in order to rapidly diagnose errors.

    An exception-handling framework is a set of runtime components that are built with the sole purpose of standardizing the way exceptions of all types (business faults, systems faults, remote faults, binding faults, among others) are handled, reported, and diagnosed. By providing a consistent way of handling exceptions in different scenarios and for different message interaction patterns (for example, synchronous request/reply, asynchronous fire and forget, asynchronous call back, and so on) the complexity of supporting services and APIs in production systems can reduce dramatically.

- **Auditing framework**: In distributed environments where transactions can jump across several systems it becomes extremely difficult to keep track not only of the number of business transactions processed but also their success ratios. This lack of visibility creates discomfort among business users and harms the perception business has of ASG-related solutions. Implementing a solution (either commercial off the shelf or built from scratch) that can deliver user-friendly dashboards with statistics on business transaction success ratios and statuses can dramatically increase business confidence.

## DevOps

**Development Operations** (**DevOps**) is a relatively new discipline that brings together development and operations throughout the entire ASG lifecycle and therefore avoids the issues that can result from both teams not collaborating. Some of the issues that DevOps aims to address are:

- Environmental issues due to a discrepancy in the configuration of the production, test, and development systems
- Issues resulting in the manual deployment of artifacts into different environments

- Lack of agility as it takes too long to regress test service and APIs
- Operational related issues as support teams don't know how to monitor and troubleshoot services and APIs

The key deliverables of DevOps are:

- **Continuous integration framework**: Ensuring that the code stored in the code repositories is always working and testable is one of the golden rules of continuous integration. By implementing tools such as **Jenkins** (http://jenkins-ci.org/) or **Hudson** (http://hudson-ci.org/) to support continuous integration efforts in the ASG development lifecycle, the quality of the code, and the speed of delivery can improve dramatically. Having such components in an ASG framework means that projects delivering services and APIs have to align with the practices and guidelines specified, resulting in better quality solutions and a faster delivery.

- **Testing framework**: As the amount of services and APIs increase and their interdependencies grow, the process of unit testing and regression testing can become a challenge. Testing teams are not necessarily subject matter experts in SOA or API development and, therefore, it is imperative that they are able to utilize standardized solutions to test the web services. There are several tools available that can help automate the testing of SOA services.

- **Provisioning framework**: Manually installing and configuring an entire SOA and API platform can be very complex and can take several days. Furthermore, all installations are manually executed, increasing the chance of human error. Furthermore, ideally, the installation should be easily reproducible for creating further environments with identical topologies. Human error and configuration problems can be the cause of severe delays when testing code, as it becomes extremely difficult to identify the root cause of issues. To avoid such issues and the many others that can result in a poor infrastructure configuration management, a framework should be constructed to automate software installation and configuration across all environments. Automating installation and configuration tasks using tools such as Puppet Labs (https://puppetlabs.com/), Chef (https://www.chef.io/chef/) or Ansible (http://www.ansible.com/home) represent a much better option than doing this manually. The investment is minimal compared to the cost of issues that can result due to environment inconsistencies and misconfigurations.

## Tools

The tools to be covered in this book have already been described in the *Preface*. However, because ASG is broader than the Oracle toolset covered in this book, the following diagram illustrates a set of tools that the authors believed to be best of bread for implementing ASG:

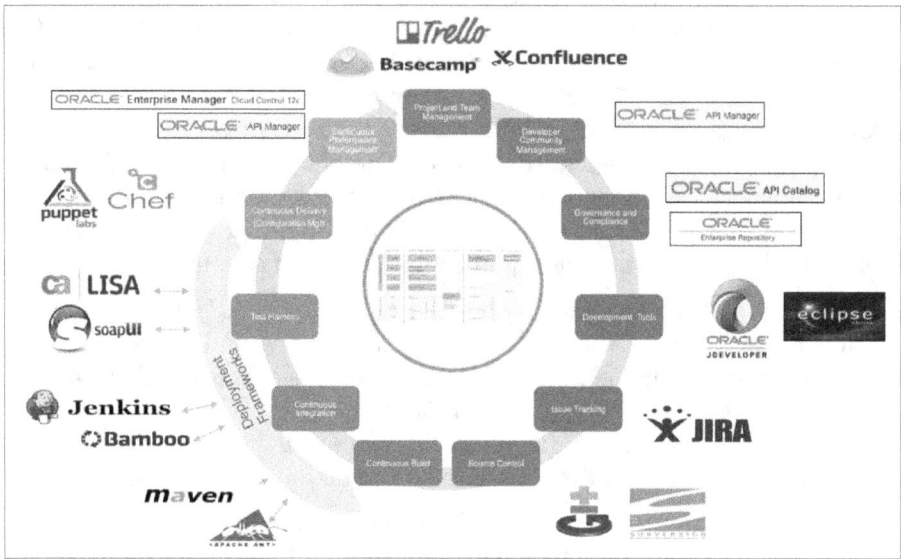

## Summary

Through the different sections of this chapter, we have introduced the fundamental concepts around SOA Governance, API Management and how these two converge, giving birth to ASG. The chapter continued by elaborating further on the objectives of ASG and why implementing an ASG framework ensures that business benefits are realized. On this same topic, the people, ASG design-time and ASG runtime aspects of the ASG framework were described to a good degree of detail. Examples of the ASG roles and responsibilities and RACI models were provided, the main artifacts of ASG design-time and runtime were listed and described with examples and diagrams. The discipline of DevOps was defined including the problems it aims to solve and what deliverables it encompasses.

The chapter concluded by providing the author's choice of tooling to support an end-to-end ASG implementation.

The following chapters of this book will make use of these concepts, but will delve deeper into the steps needed to implement the ASG using the Oracle API Management solution.

# 2
# Implementation Case Study

This chapter introduces a case study that will be further developed throughout this book. The case study is designed to help the reader to understand the concepts presented throughout this book and how to apply them to implement an Oracle API Management solution. It describes a fictitious company that has previously introduced SOA and SOA Governance into the organization and that are now looking to expand this with API Management. It details many of the typical problems faced by organizations wishing to introduce APIs and how the benefits derived from their introduction must be tangible and measurable.

The case study is based on actual scenarios experienced by the authors and therefore should provide a realistic view of the key challenges faced when implementing API Management and how they can be overcome.

## Case study description

WBCV Telecom is a manufacturer and retailer of mobile phones and devices. It has a very strong lineup of products that are considered niche and that result in high profit margins. WBCV has experienced rapid growth in the last six years but this has started to slow in recent months due to the emergence of new startup organizations employing dynamic business models and digital operations. Such companies are able to penetrate the market quickly by offering low cost and innovative products that are very disruptive in nature. These companies have low overheads and a high degree of automation and are challenging less agile and established businesses.

WBCV Telecom's CIO realized that in order to compete with organizations employing disruptive and dynamic business models, they too had to transform their operations and modernize their IT systems in order to become a true digital organization. In other words, the WBCV CIO realized that in order to compete with organizations that were born digital, they had to be reborn digital.

*Implementation Case Study*

WBCV Telecom's CIO and a team of enterprise architects began this journey, or rebirth, by creating an inventory of their existing IT systems to form a complete as-is view of the organization. They then reclassified all of their systems following a PACE-layered application strategy and subsequently moved away from big commercial off the shelf products (such as traditional ERP products) to smaller best-of-breed solutions on the cloud, which were integrated using best-of-breed integration products. This is shown here:

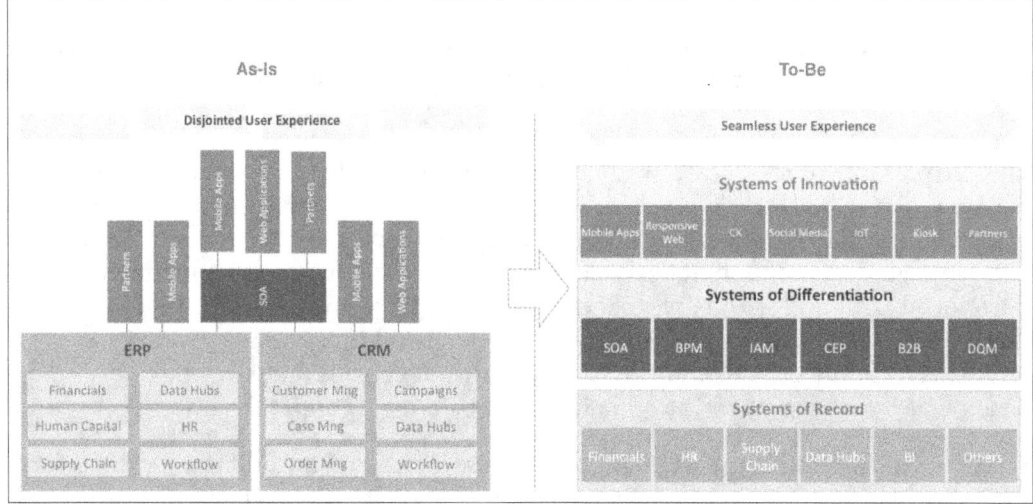

 For further information on PACE layer application strategy, refer to the following URL:
https://www.gartner.com/doc/1890915/accelerating-innovation-adopting-pacelayered-application

While conducting this analysis, WBCV's enterprise architects began to realize that many departments, in a desperate attempt to come up with more innovative products and customer-centric services that could fight off the fierce competition, had already started implementing their own tactical solutions using a variety of **software as a service** (**SaaS**) applications. Furthermore, they had in some instances also started to build and expose their own mobile applications without following any sort of enterprise standard. Although it was acknowledged that the intention behind building these ad-hoc solutions was genuine, the end result of doing this was negative to WBCV as a whole. Not only did they end up being locked into specific vendors and products, but also the user experience delivered by these different applications and mobile apps was very disjointed. Rather than providing a positive differentiator, this confusing approach resulted in many of these consumers moving to competitors instead.

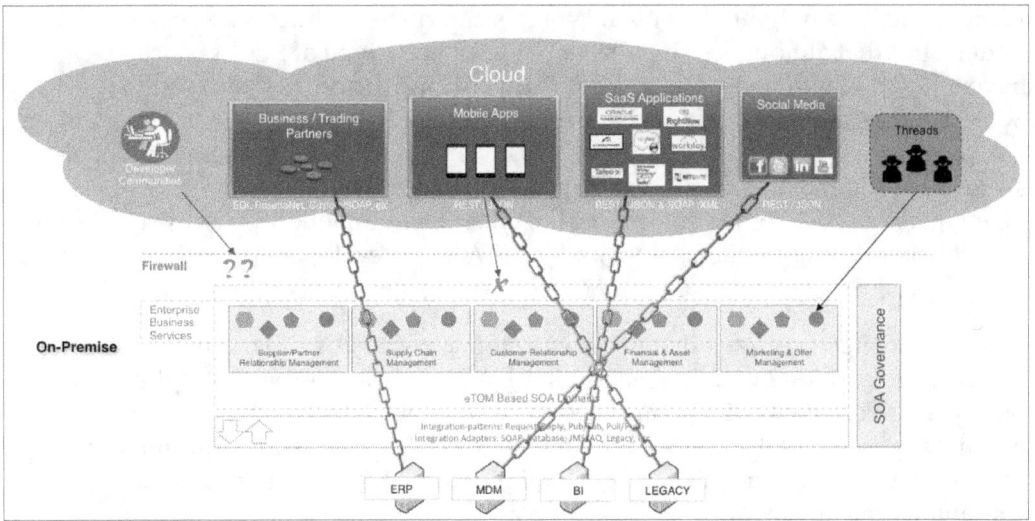

WBCV has already got a fairly mature SOA architecture in place as it implemented a SOA Governance strategy a few years back. This means that, although departments have built their own ad-hoc solutions, many of the interfaces that connect the on-premise systems to the cloud-based applications or mobile applications were brokered by business services implemented in the SOA layer.

For further info on how WBCV implemented SOA Governance go here:
`https://www.packtpub.com/application-development/oracle-soa-governance-11g-implementation`

For this reason, despite the overall complexity of the current WBCV technology landscape, the enterprise architects saw an opportunity to leverage their existing SOA investment by extending it with a new API Management layer on top. WBCV could therefore leverage its existing investment in their SOA infrastructure while adding more capabilities such as integration to cloud-based systems and exposure of web APIs to support new mobile applications.

*Implementation Case Study*

With further research into this area, WBCV's enterprise architects began to understand that although web APIs were in essence a type of SOA service, they have unique requirements that are not really taken into account with traditional SOA solutions and are therefore better served using API Management. For example, the fact that web APIs are usually accessible via the Internet means that stronger security is required and also the management of an unknown community of developers requires some sort of portal to allow them to not only discover APIs but also collaborate among themselves and with WBCV developers (who are exposing the APIs).

WBCV's architects realized that in order to implement SOA Governance and API Management consistently, they had to implement a new approach, **Application Services Governance (ASG)** combines both strategies into a single solution capable of handling traditional system integration and service orientation requirements as well as new requirements such as cloud integration, mobile integration, and community management.

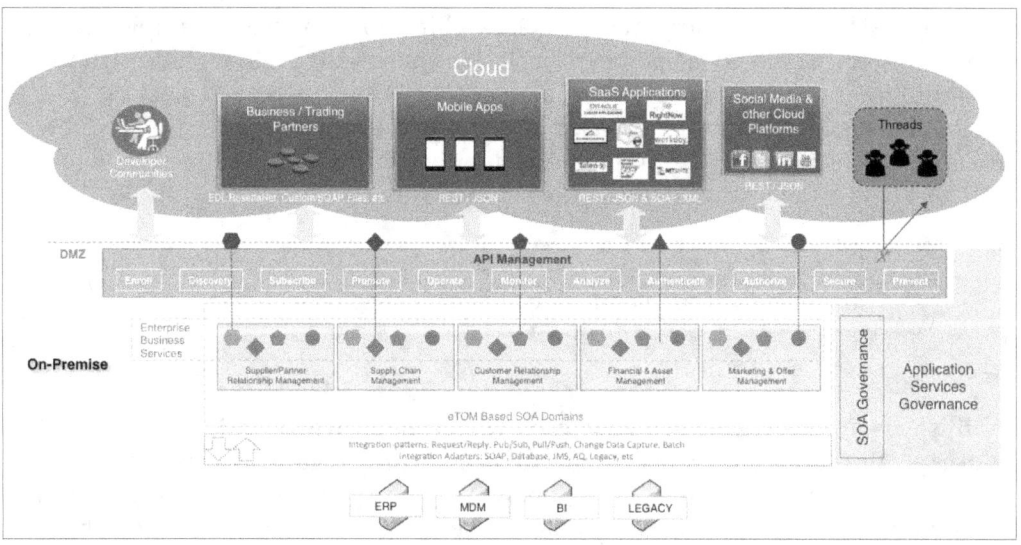

Once they understood at a high level what an ASG strategy consisted of, WBCV's architects needed to gain a more detailed understanding of API Management and what it entailed. Furthermore, they needed to understand what capabilities were missing from the current SOA stack in order to deliver it. In order to achieve this, they knew that some sort of maturity assessment was required. WBCV subsequently employed 4APPmigos, who are highly specialized in the implementation of ASG and API Management, to undertake a nine week time-boxed consultancy exercise with the following objectives in mind:

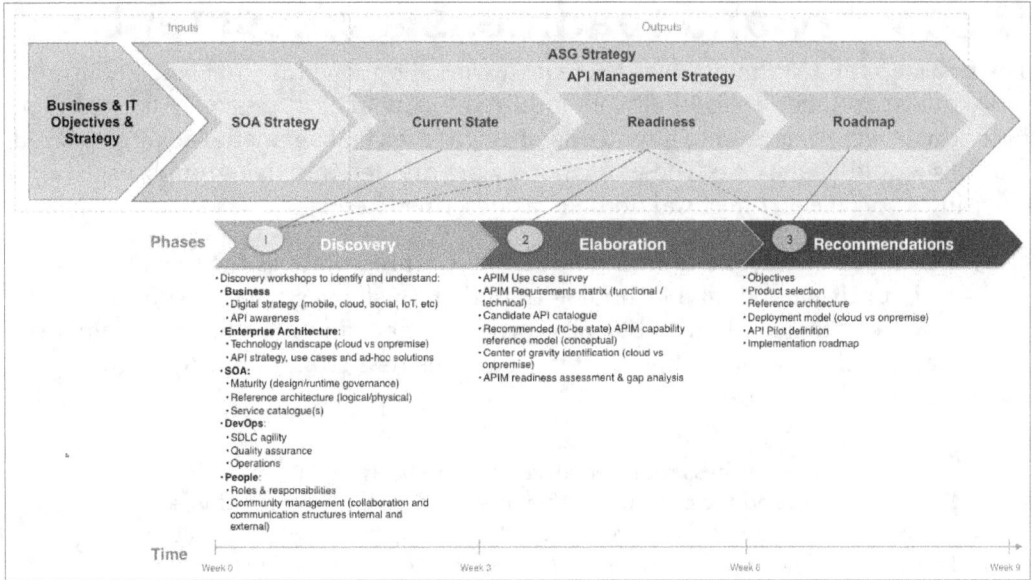

- **Discovery**: Conduct a series of time-boxed workshops, the objective of which was to gather enough information to elicit a view of WBCV digital strategy (if any), a view of its current IT landscape and of its organizational architecture.
- **Readiness assessment**: Assess and benchmark (against others in the industry sector) WBCV's readiness to embark on an API Management implementation journey. To this end, 4APPmigos needed to evaluate the key domains relevant when implementing APIs such as business, architecture, SOA, DevOps, and people.
- **Gap analysis and recommendations**: Identify potential gaps for each domain and make a series of recommendations that would fill these gaps from a people, technology and processes point of view
- **Implementation roadmap**: This indicates a high-level plan showing the different phases and objectives of the program of work, indicating when delivery would be fulfilled

*Implementation Case Study*

# Discovery and readiness assessment

The first step for 4APPmigos was to create a workshop schedule that listed all the individuals (and their roles) that were required to attend each session. All identified individuals were expected to attend and strong senior management backing ensured that this would be the case. The workshops were divided into five groups, each covering a specific architectural domain, as described here:

- **Business**: Understand from key business representatives the role of disruptive and digital technologies in their business strategy. APIs are exposed to help digitize business processes and supply chain management and without proper alignment with the business strategy, an ASG strategy is doomed to failure.

> The business representatives need to be aware of what APIs are and the critical role they play in digital transformation, so 4APPmigos had prepared a short, comprehensive presentation that described, in business language terms, what APIs are, why they are important to a digital strategy and what benefits the business would gain from their adoption. A 30-minute slot was reserved in the first session to cover this presentation.

- **Enterprise architecture**: The role of enterprise architecture is crucial in any large organization. Enterprise architects act as a bridge between the business, IT, and business units within an organization. They provide domain expertise and business knowledge, both of which are crucial when contextualizing IT solutions. As a result of their extensive domain knowledge, they are able to proactively suggest situations where implementing APIs can add value to the business. Understanding the maturity of enterprise architecture within an organization by, for example, evaluating how successfully an EA framework such as TOGAF has been adopted, will indicate whether implementing a true enterprise-wide solution is truly viable.

> A good description of the TOGAF enterprise architecture frameworks is available at the following link:
> `http://www.opengroup.org/soa/source-book/togaf/entsoa.htm`

- **SOA**: As described in *Chapter 1, Application Services Governance*, an API is effectively a type of service. For this reason, an API strategy without an SOA strategy is incomplete and vice-versa; this is the main driver behind ASG. Understanding the maturity of SOA within an organization will indicate whether building APIs will be as simple as REST-enabling existing known SOAP services or a much more complex affair. Moreover, it will indicate if governing an API Management initiative will require a considerable effort in workforce education or merely up-skilling staff, which will likely be the case if an organization is already fairly mature in terms of SOA.

- **DevOps**: As described in Chapter 1, *Application Services Governance*, DevOps is a relatively new discipline that aims to bring together development and operational teams to prevent issues in areas such as configuration management, testing, and operations. This is achieved by integrating both teams very early in the lifecycle and promoting strong communication between them. If an organization lacks maturity in this space, it can result in several issues that will ultimately result in the lack of agility, poor quality of products, and slow speed to market. APIs should be treated as products in their own right and therefore this communication is important when exposing APIs.

- **People and Organization**: One of the greatest challenges to implementing IT solutions is the lack of collaboration and communication between different teams. This is particularly true in disciplines such as SOA Governance and API Management since the cross-functional nature of these disciplines requires the involvement of many individuals from different parts of the business. For this reason, understanding the communication and collaboration structures within an organization will indicate how easy or challenging it will be to get a consensus and feedback on requirements and solutions.

Conway's law suggests this:

"Organizations which design systems ... are constrained to produce designs which are copies of the communication structures of these organizations."

- M. Conway (http://en.wikipedia.org/wiki/Conway's_law)

*Implementation Case Study*

Before the workshops took place, 4APPmigos prepared a questionnaire aimed at measuring capability and maturity in each of the aforementioned areas. Based on the outcomes of the workshops and other information available from the industry sector, the results of this questionnaire were quantified in order to get a view of:

- **Current** maturity level for each of the mentioned areas
- **Needed** maturity level based on the maturity level of other similar organizations of comparable size that have succeeded in implementing API Management
- **Ideal** maturity state depicting a target or future maturity state after API Management was implemented and stable

The gap between the current and needed maturity levels dictated the short term activities needed in each area prior to starting API Management. Once these gaps had been plugged, the remaining gaps to achieve the ideal maturity state would dictate the activities required to implement full API Management strategy.

At the end of the workshops, 4APPmigos was able to produce the following results:

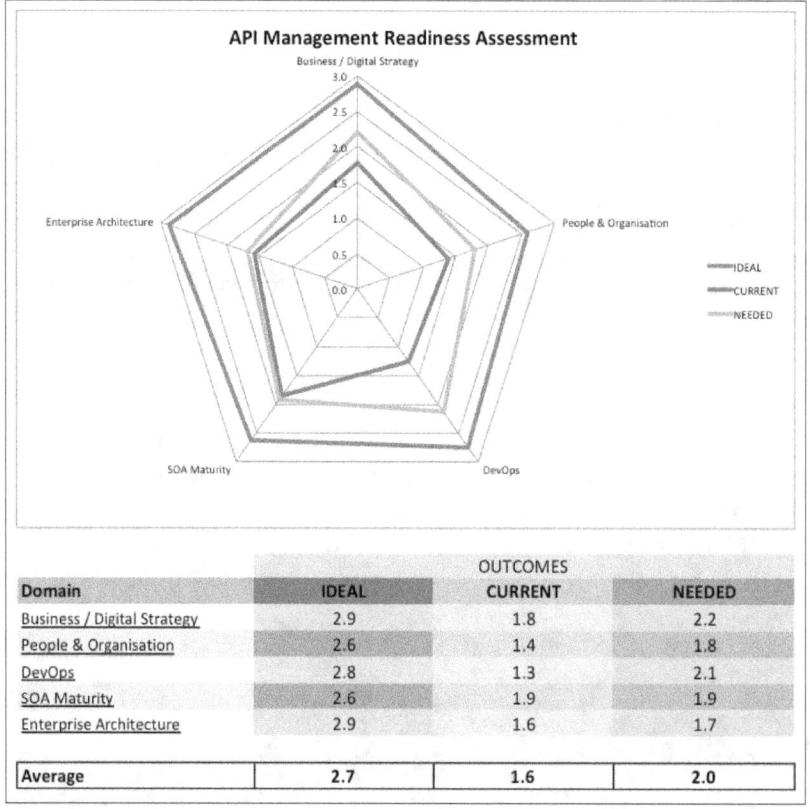

| Domain | IDEAL | OUTCOMES CURRENT | NEEDED |
|---|---|---|---|
| Business / Digital Strategy | 2.9 | 1.8 | 2.2 |
| People & Organisation | 2.6 | 1.4 | 1.8 |
| DevOps | 2.8 | 1.3 | 2.1 |
| SOA Maturity | 2.6 | 1.9 | 1.9 |
| Enterprise Architecture | 2.9 | 1.6 | 1.7 |
| Average | 2.7 | 1.6 | 2.0 |

The results should be read as follows:

- **Zero (0)**: This is the lowest possible score, meaning that no capability or maturity was available in the respective area.
- **One (1)**: This indicates that some capability and maturity was available in the respective area but only on an ad-hoc and fragmented basis. This would be the case when departments or different teams had created their own tactical solutions.
- **Two (2)**: This indicates that a good capability and/or maturity are in place and being rolled out across the enterprise.
- **Tree (3)**: This is the highest possible score, meaning an established and mature enterprise-wide capability.

## Gap analysis

The results of the capability analysis indicated that WBCV was reasonably mature in SOA. This was to be expected given that WBCV had already made a significant investment in maturing its SOA implementation and had already started to see the fruits of that investment. Likewise, WBCV's enterprise architecture team had been implementing **The Open Group Architecture Framework** TOGAF for the past few years and, although they were still facing some challenges rolling it out across the entire organization, they were in fairly good shape in this discipline.

For further information on **TOGAF** please refer to this:
http://www.opengroup.org/subjectareas/enterprise/togaf

Furthermore, given that WBCV's CIO had already created a digital strategy and initiated a digital transformation process, WBCV scored well in this domain also. However, the conclusion was that the digital strategy didn't give enough relevance to APIs and their role in delivering a seamless customer experience across multiple channels.

The domains where WBCV faired the lowest were on the DevOps and People domains. Several reasons were attributed to this low score. Among the most significant ones were:

- The development and operations teams were often disconnected and had completely different views and expectations of one another's roles. The gap between these two teams was evident given the nature of the issues WBCV were experiencing in areas such as:
    - **Configuration management**: The development, test, and production environments all had discrepancies in terms of configuration, which had resulted in delays and higher project costs as issues were inconsistently identified, often late in the project lifecycle when fixes were more expensive to implement.
    - **Testing**: The support team had no input or involvement in this phase, meaning that an opportunity was missed to give support teams early exposure to potential issues and their resolutions.
    - **Operations support and maintenance**: Because the knowledge transfer between development and support teams occurred after the solution was deployed into production, the support teams had little time and exposure to cover all the potential fault scenarios and their resolutions. The lack of exposure to code also meant that they didn't have time to learn in detail how to enhance the code. This resulted in major issues as BAU staff could not support the solution on their own and they required expensive consultants to help them solve issues and perform enhancements.
- On a large project, teams are often segmented by technology. This segmentation imposes many overheads and boundaries in terms of communication between the teams. Ultimately, these communication gaps resulted in silos that were further magnified once the solutions were deployed into production. Given the complexity of the solutions and inter-dependencies among the different technologies (hence different teams), the process of supporting code, especially as a result of major incidents was very chaotic and time-consuming.

*Chapter 2*

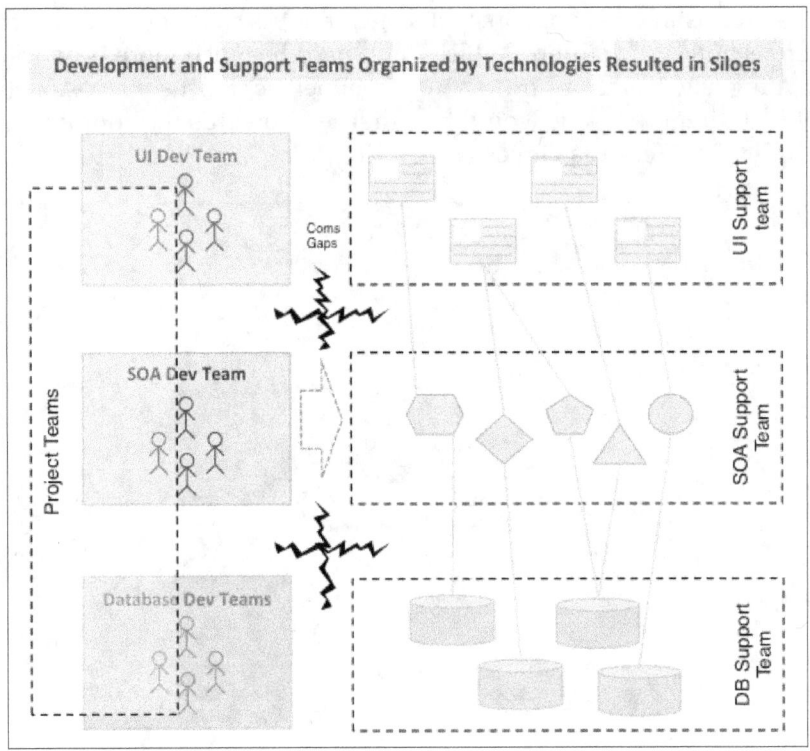

# Recommendations

In order to address the identified gaps in terms of people, processes, and tools, 4APPmigos made the following recommendations in their report:

- **People and organization**: New business capabilities (for example an order management service or sales order service) should be delivered by a single multi-disciplinary team containing all skills required. This model implies smaller team sizes, with all the necessary skills to develop and support a business capability co-located. As a result, communication gaps and management overheads would be avoided. Also, because these capabilities would be delivered following ASG principles, solutions should in principle be modular and integrate cohesively.

*Implementation Case Study*

Upskill existing personnel responsible for SOAs so that they can further define, build, and support APIs. This would be much more beneficial than creating new teams or hiring new personnel just for the purpose of handling API requirements. This would be a first step towards the adoption of **Application Services Governance (ASG)**.

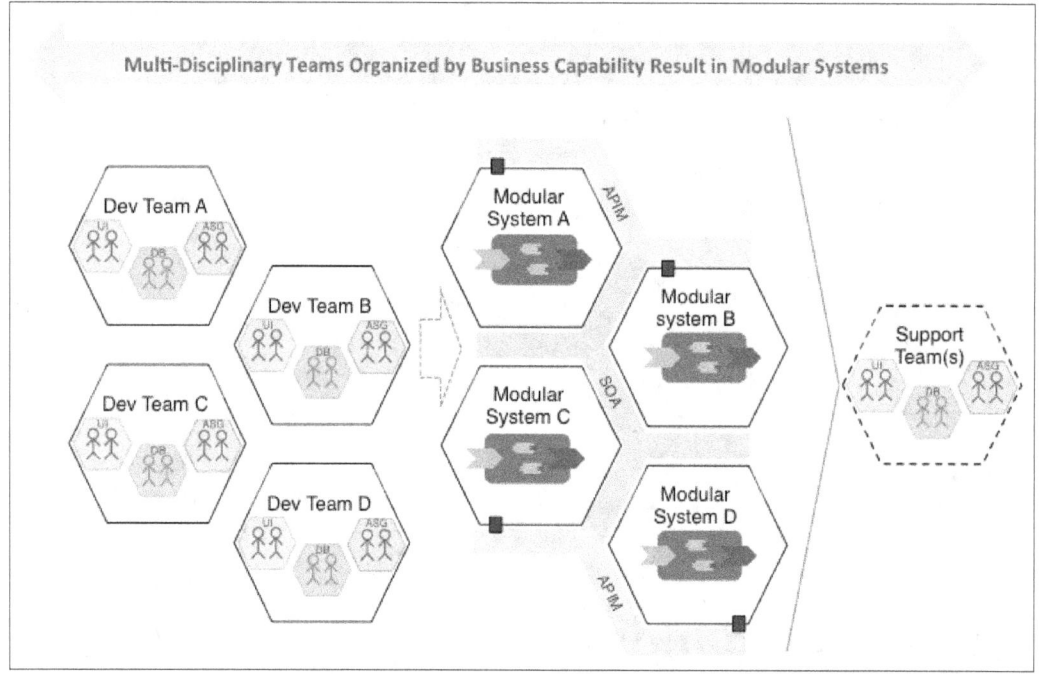

 Refer to *Chapter 1, Application Services Governance*, for further details on what implementing ASG entails.

- **Technology**: Having understood all the capabilities required to deliver the derived business requirements, as well as existing capabilities, 4APPmigos created a digital reference capability model. The model divided the capabilities into three layers following a PACE layering architecture approach. Those capabilities that were available and those missing were both highlighted — those available in light blue and those missing in red marked with an X.

Middleware capabilities such as SOA, BPM, API Management and data integration, which are considered to be enablers of omni-channel and seamless user experiences, were classified as systems of differentiation. Traditional capabilities that are responsible for the storage of operational, transactional and reference data (such as financial systems, supply chain, and MDM data hubs) were classified as systems of records. The uppermost layers contain those capabilities that make use of leading edge technologies such as **mobile application development frameworks** (**MADP**), IoT platforms, responsive web technologies, and others. These are necessary to deliver the promised disruptive business solutions and a seamless user experience regardless of the channel used by customers. These were the systems of innovation.

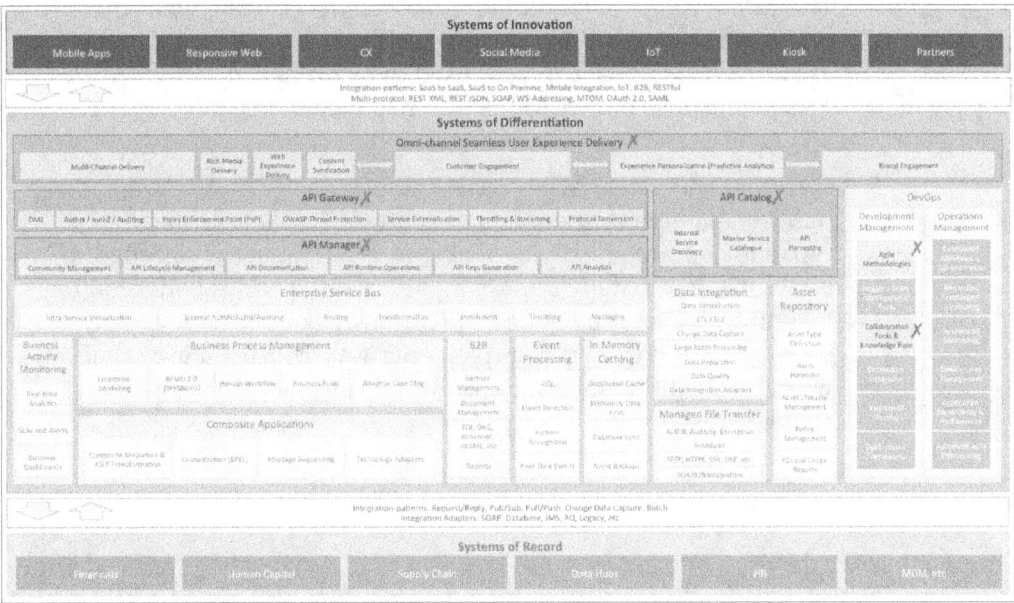

From the preceding model, it can be seen that WBCV had already invested in SOA and SOA Governance capabilities, among others. However, 4APPmigos identified that the following API Management capabilities were lacking.

- **API gateway**: A set of capabilities needed to externalize web services as web APIs in a **demilitarized zone** (**DMZ**) and in a highly secure fashion. This layer acts as a **policy enforcement point** (**PeP**), enforcing policies for robust authentication (AuthN), authorization (AuthZ), auditing, and thread protection. Other capabilities such as throttling, protocol conversion (that is, REST/JSON or CoAP to SOAP/XML and vice-versa) should also be provided by the API gateway

- **API manager**: A set of capabilities such as API portals for API community management (developer on-boarding and self-service) and API lifecycle management including API documentation capabilities, robust runtime management and analytics capabilities, and API key generation.

- **API catalog**: This consists of capabilities needed to continuously harvest existing SOA and API platforms to create a master view of existing APIs or candidate APIs (basically internal SOAP services). The API catalog is aimed at internal architects, designers, and developers that require an online facility to search for and discover existing services that can be reused or externalized as web APIs. This facility also allows for useful metadata to be added to services and APIs

- **DevOps**: These consist of capabilities to rapidly create, test, publish, manage, deprecate, and retire APIs. Some of these capabilities were already available in WBCV, but they needed to be augmented to deliver more agility. This provides better tooling that brings development and operations teams closer together. 4APPmigos felt that, by complementing WBCVs existing capabilities with the identified missing ones, application services governance could be realized.

Having clearly understood the missing capabilities from an API Management point of view, the next step for 4APPmigos was to evaluate all the major vendors of API Management products. By formulating a detailed **API Management product evaluation** model, tailored specifically for WBCV requirements, they could recommend the product or suite that would best fit the requirements of WBCV. Based on the requirements, the model evaluated four principle core capabilities: API gateway, API manager, API catalog, and DevOps. Each core capability accounted for 25% of the total score. Within each core capability, several other more granular capabilities were evaluated and weighted based upon WBCV's requirements.

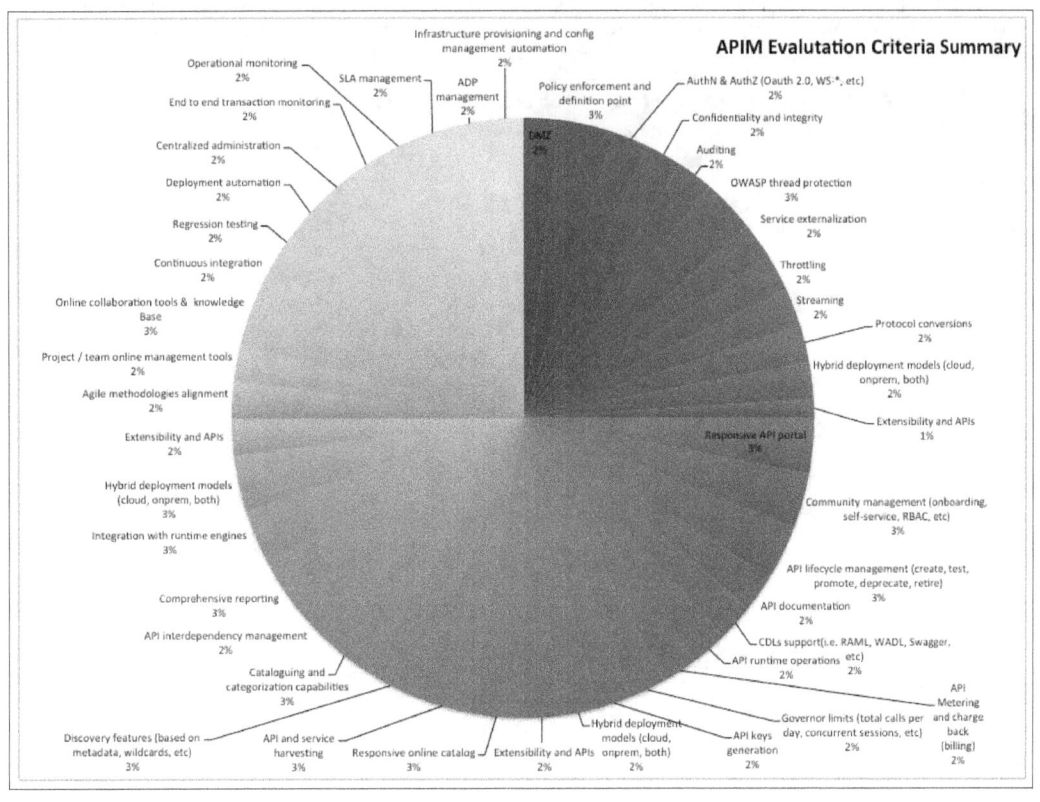

*Implementation Case Study*

In order to select the products and vendors to evaluate, 4APPmigos first looked at the Gartner's Magic Quadrant for Application Services Governance (https://www.gartner.com/doc/2571325/magic-quadrant-application-services-governance) and from it identified the top two leaders in this area. Secondly, cognizant of the fact that Oracle had recently launched a series of products focused on API Management (the recent nature meant that they did not appear in the quadrant at the time that the evaluation took place), 4APPmigos decided to also evaluate the **Oracle API Management** solution. This decision was also influenced by the fact that WBCV had already implemented several other Oracle products for their SOA solution; the most relevant being **Oracle SOA Suite** and **Oracle Enterprise Repository**. It was thought likely the new Oracle API products would integrate better with existing products since they are from a single vendor.

So, in total, 4APPmigos evaluated three vendors and, after careful consideration, the Oracle API Management solution, consisting of Oracle API Gateway, Oracle API Manager, and Oracle API Catalog was selected. Many factors contributed to this decision and, even though Oracle didn't have the highest score in some core capability areas such as API manager (as this was a fairly new product at the time the evaluation took place), overall Oracle did provide better support for all the required capabilities for WBCV. Furthermore, Oracle had also recently launched their Oracle Cloud Services for PaaS (https://cloud.oracle.com/home) meaning that the solution could be delivered entirely on the cloud, thereby fully supporting a hybrid model. Also, the weaknesses in the Oracle API Management solution were compensated for by the strong capabilities presented in terms of Gateway, Catalog and DevOps, especially in terms of the cataloging capabilities, in which Oracle's solution was by far ahead of the competition.

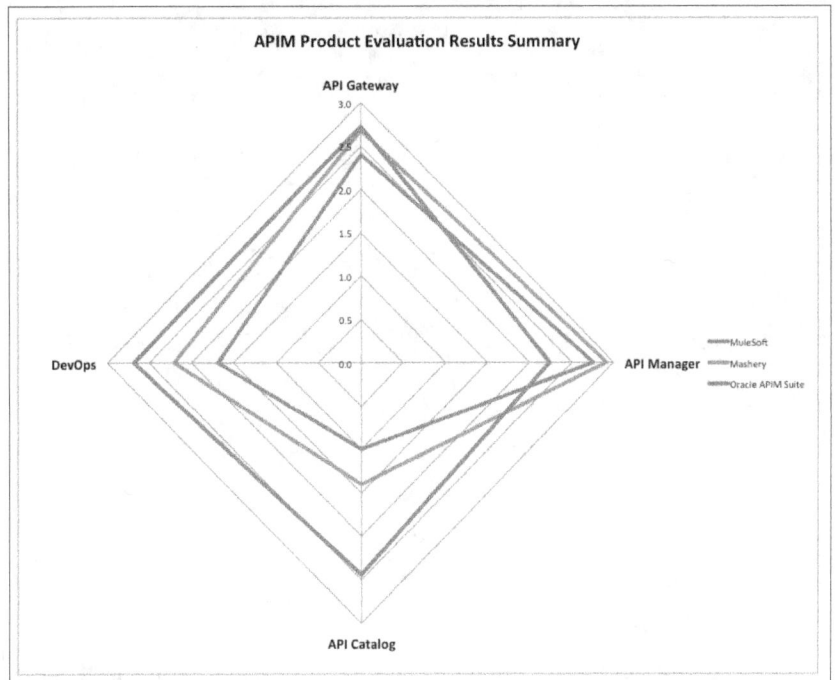

 At the time of writing, only Oracle API Manager was available as an option within the SOA Cloud Service. However the Oracle Cloud **Infrastructure as a Service** (**IaaS**) offering provided a suitable alternative to deploy Oracle API Gateway and Oracle API Manager in a virtual machine within the Oracle Cloud.

*Implementation Case Study*

With the capability gaps identified and specified in a reference model and the recommendation of a product suite that best fitted WBCVs requirements in place, 4APPmigos proceeded to elaborate the technology architecture to depict how the entire solution would hang together. The architecture looked as follows:

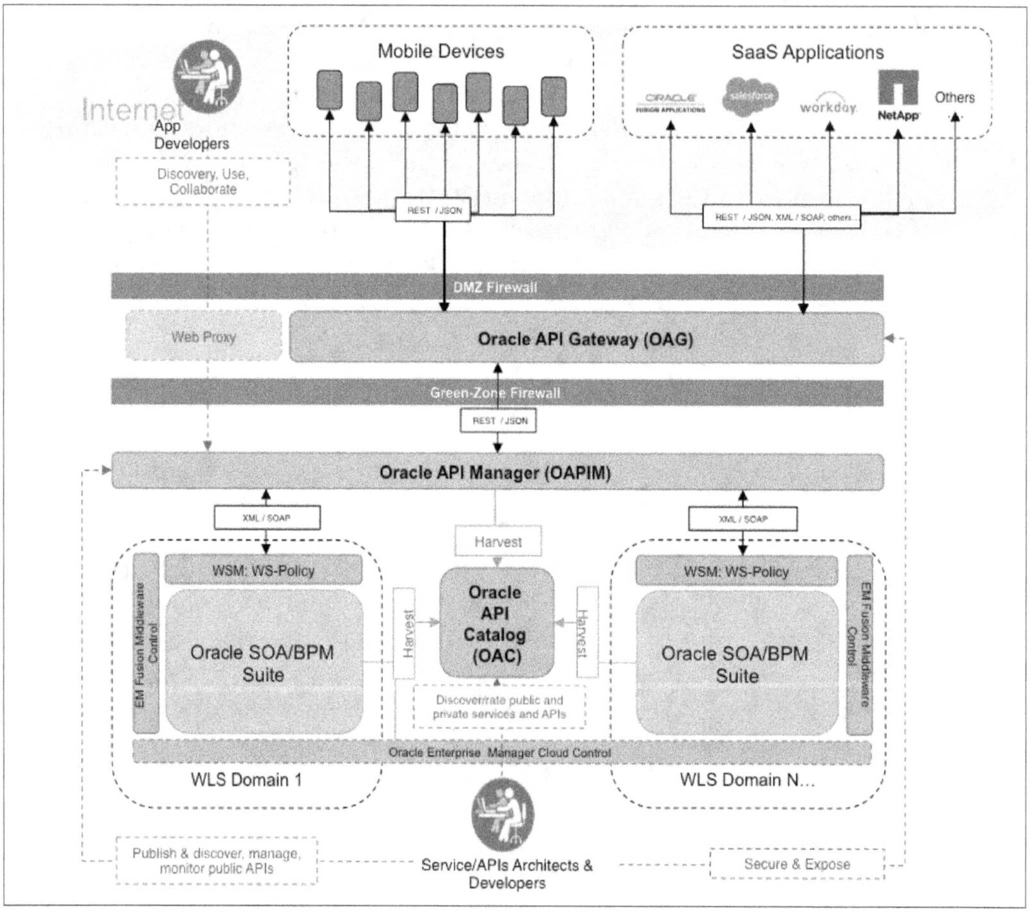

The specifics of how to implement each of the products within the Oracle API Management solution and their use will be covered in subsequent chapters of this book.

*Chapter 2*

# Roadmap

Having defined a digital reference capability model, evaluated, and selected the right set of API Management products and also created a technical architecture for the solution, the next step in the process was to create a high-level plan describing the different phases and milestones required to deliver all aspects of the solution. To this end, 4APPmigos developed the following implementation roadmap. The roadmap is straightforward and simple to follow; its objective was to raise awareness of the journey of implementing API Management to senior managers and to the relevant teams. The intention was to depict, on one page, the phases, objectives, milestones, and timelines needed to deliver the overall solution.

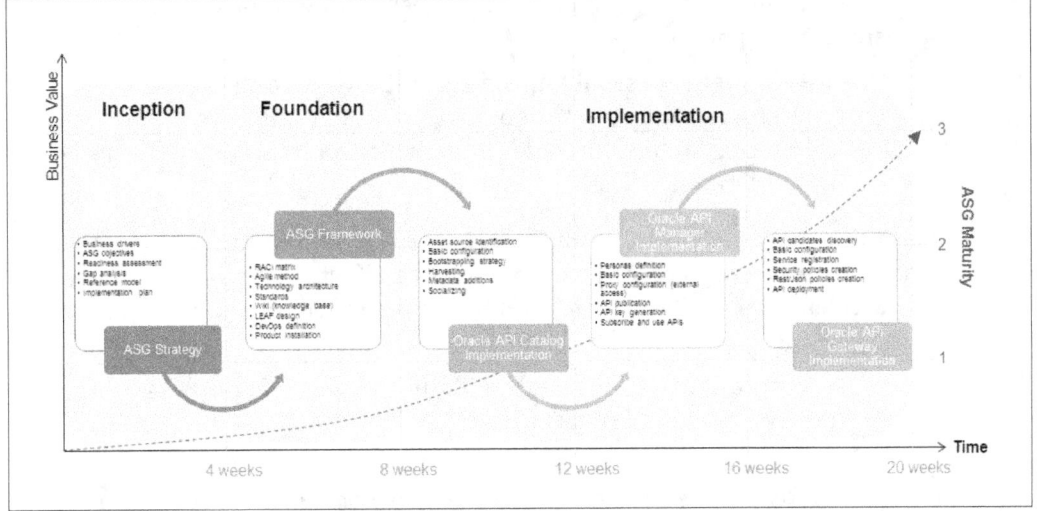

 4APPmigos also delivered a detailed plan and an estimated cost for the implementation of the API Management solution. This level of detail, however, is not provided in this book as project planning and estimating are part of the project management discipline which is not specific to API Management.

The roadmap was broken down into three phases, each with different objectives, which had to be delivered within a twenty week period. These timelines were based on previous discussions with the business, which had identified which capabilities were most critical for the business, based on its digital strategy, and when these capabilities should be delivered into production.

*Implementation Case Study*

The projects teams decided to deliver capabilities in sprints of four weeks as opposed to delivering the whole solution in one big bang, which would be the case with the waterfall approach. This would ensure that the business remained engaged and that progress could be clearly demonstrated. This in turn would ensure that the budget was firmly in place for the initiative.

The phases and milestones were as follows:

- **Inception**: The objective of this phase is to deliver the ASG strategy and all artifacts therein. Although this phase was already completed by the time 4APPmigos presented the roadmap, the purpose of showing it was to raise awareness that progress had already been made and a considerable amount of work had already been put into place. The key milestone of this phase was:
    - **ASG strategy**: Basically, this deals with the readiness assessment report, capability reference model, product evaluation report, technology architecture and implementation roadmap delivered by 4APPmigos

- **Foundation**: This concerns with the delivery of a solid foundation for the rest of the project by creating all framework artifacts that would simplify and accelerate the delivery of subsequent phases. The key milestone of this phase was:
    - **ASG framework**: This deals with the delivery of an ASG governance framework and all of its artifacts

> Refer to the ASG framework section in *Chapter 1, Application Services Governance*, for further information on what an ASG framework is and the implementation details.

- **Implementation**: This deals with the iterative delivery of the Oracle API Management products: Oracle API Catalog, Oracle API Manager, and Oracle API Gateway. The implementation of these products will be covered in subsequent chapters.

> Refer to the *Preface* for a brief description of what each of these products is and what capabilities they deliver. You may also refer to Oracle's API Management website for further information at http://www.oracle.com/us/products/middleware/soa/api-management/overview/index.html.

# Summary

This chapter started by describing how WBCV telecom struggled to keep pace with its competition and how it was rapidly losing market share due to the innovative and disruptive nature of the products and offerings being launched by its smaller, agile competitors. It introduced a realistic case study to illustrate the key concepts being conveyed. The chapter goes on to describe how WBCV's CIO realized that the key to halting this trend of declining market share was to dramatically enhance the customer user experience, engaging with its customers in a seamless fashion through multiple delivery channels. It described how WBCV Telecom transformed itself into a digital organization capable of fighting off competitors, allowing them to not only deliver an omni-channel user experience, but also to adopt the same level of agility and disruptiveness as its competitors.

This chapter described how WBCV's CIO, working together with a team of enterprise architects, elaborated a PACE-layered applications model that would subsequently help it to initiate a digital modernization of all systems without losing focus on what mattered most: the customer experience. In the process of doing so, WBCV enterprise architects realized the importance of having an API Management layer, built on top of their existing SOA infrastructure, that could present information assets in such a way that innovative and disruptive business solutions (such as mobile apps, responsive web pages, wearable devices, and IoT) could be created and launched rapidly. To this end, WBCV commissioned a niche consultancy firm, named 4APPmigos who specialize in the implementation of **Application Services Governance** (**ASG**), to assist them on their journey.

The chapter then went on to describe in detail how 4APPmigos executed an API Management readiness assessment, which was then followed by the creation of a digital capability reference model that highlighted the gaps in capabilities. We described how 4APPmigos tailored the API Management product selection model for WBCV which helped them to select the Oracle API Management solution. This was the best fit for WBCV telecom needs.

In the final sections of the chapter, we demonstrated the API Management technology architecture that was recommended by 4APPmigos and the implementation roadmap that was put forward for its implementation.

The subsequent chapters of this book will talk about how to implement the different products of the Oracle API Management solution.

# 3
# Oracle API Catalog Implementation

This chapter will provide an architectural and functional overview of **Oracle API Catalog (OAC)**. It will discuss the different components and layers that build up the product architecture and then provide a short overview of the product functionality. Subsequently, an implementation use case is described which is then followed up by a series of hands-on and step-by-step recipes that illustrate how to implement the product to address the use case requirements. The chapter covers both simple recipes and also more complex ones, showing for example how to configure and use the Ant Harvester and also how to consume the REX API to extend OAC functionality.

## An overview of Oracle API Catalog

As briefly discussed in the *Preface* of this book, the name API Catalog suggests that OAC is a product whose main purpose is to help organizations create a catalog of all available APIs thereby unlocking functionality and information which would have been previously hidden. Web API catalogs allow app and/or mobile developers and architects to discover and reuse assets rather than recreating them from scratch. This, in turn, delivers benefits to the business and IT since cost and time to market can be significantly reduced.

How can OAC achieve this? How are APIs loaded into OAC? How is the product implemented? How rich is the functionality? Are there limitations and if so can I extend the functionality? These are some of the questions that a systems implementer needs to ask. This chapter aims to address these questions and go beyond just the theory by providing several hands-on examples on how OAC can be implemented to address real world business requirements.

## Architecture and functional overview

OAC is implemented in a four-tier architecture style as illustrated in the following diagram:

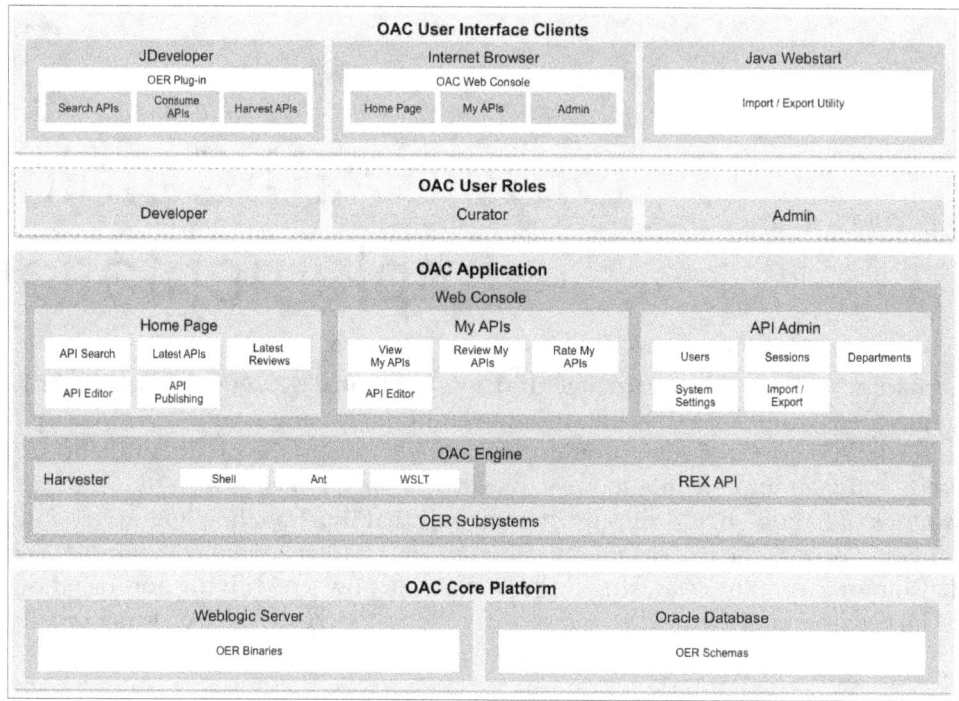

## The OAC core platform

At the bottommost layer, the core platform consists of an Oracle database that holds the OAC/OER database schemas (data, lob, and index), and also a WebLogic application server that hosts the OAC installation binaries.

 OAC uses the same binaries as **Oracle Enterprise Repository** (**OER**), hence the diagram shows **OER Binaries** in the core platform.

 For exact versions of the products used in this book you may refer to *Chapter 6, Installation Tips and Techniques*, or for the latest versions of the product you may refer to the OER Oracle download page: `http://www.oracle.com/technetwork/middleware/repository/downloads/index.html?ssSourceSiteId=ocomen`.

# The OAC application

OAC is a JEE application that runs on a WebLogic server. It can be summarized into two main components: the web console and the OAC engine.

The web console delivers a web user interface, whereas the OAC engine delivers server-side functionality to support the console as well as other user interfaces such as the JDeveloper plug-in and the Import/Export utility.

## The OAC web console

The web console delivers the following views:

- **API Catalog Home Page**: This is the landing page for an authenticated user. The home page allows the user to visualize recently published APIs and latest reviews added to them, search for APIs based on different criteria and even export APIs' metadata directly from the search results. In addition, from the home page the user can navigate to the **My APIs** and **Admin** pages. The following screenshot shows the OAC home page following a new installation of OAC:

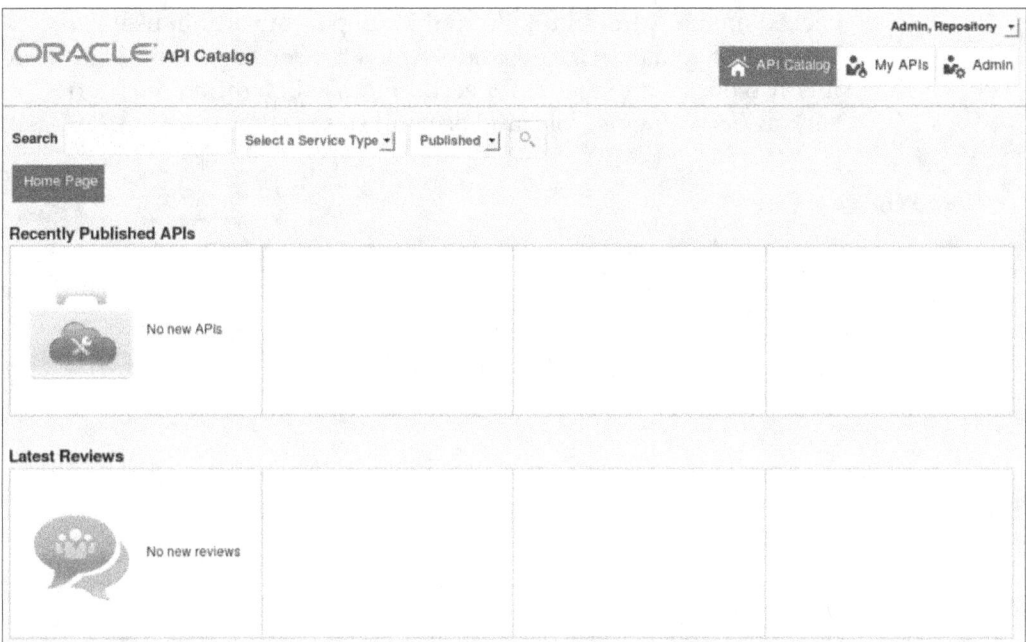

- **My APIs**: In the API pages a user (typically a developer) can visualize the APIs that they have marked as being part of their *My APIs*. Details on how to achieve this will be covered later on in the section **My APIs** and API rating. The following screenshot shows the **My APIs** page after a new install of OAC:

- **Admin**: This consists of the following subpages:
    - **Users**: This subpage is the landing page for an admin user that has clicked on the **Admin** link. From this subpage an admin user can create, edit, delete, activate, and deactivate user accounts. In addition, it is also possible to search for accounts based on different criteria such as departments, role, and account status.

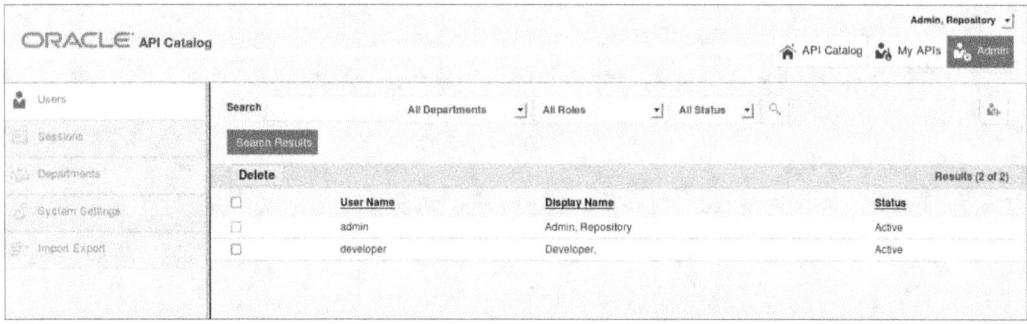

- **Sessions**: This subpage shows any active sessions in the OAC console. From this screen it is possible to delete an existing session; this might be useful in scenarios when, for example, OAC access has been revoked for a particular user. However, as the user still may have an active session, this should also be terminated.

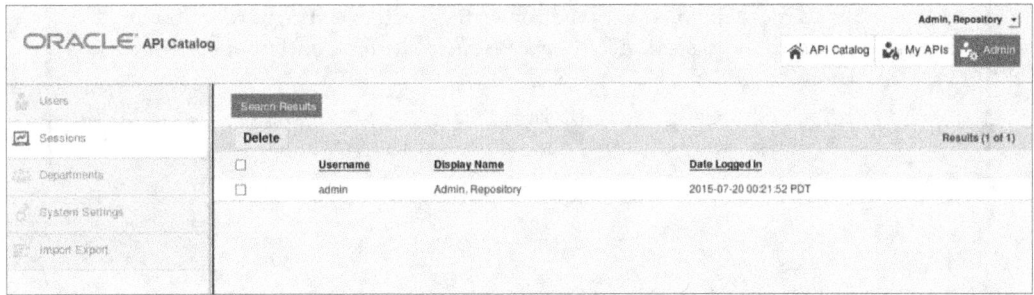

- **Departments**: From this subpage, an admin user can search, create, edit and delete departments. Configuring departments is optional in OAC although it is recommended to logically group users.

 Departments do not drive any behavior or access restrictions in OAC. Users that belong to different departments but have the same role(s) will have access to the same information and functionality. This can't be said about roles. Different roles will provide different type of access and information.

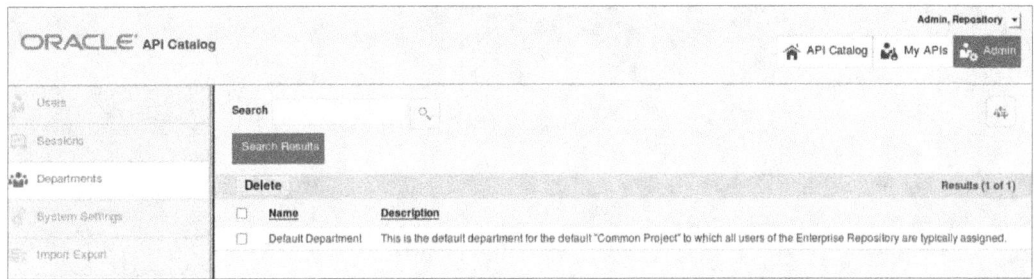

*Oracle API Catalog Implementation*

- ° **System Settings**: In this page an admin user can search and modify internal OAC settings. Settings can also be moved to a database by clicking on the **Move settings to database** link; this is only required when setting up OAC in a cluster.

> For a more detailed explanation of the **System Settings** functionality, please refer to section *3 System Settings Overview* of the *Administrator's Guide for OAC*:
>
> http://docs.oracle.com/middleware/1213/oac/administer-cat/syssettings.htm#CATCG989

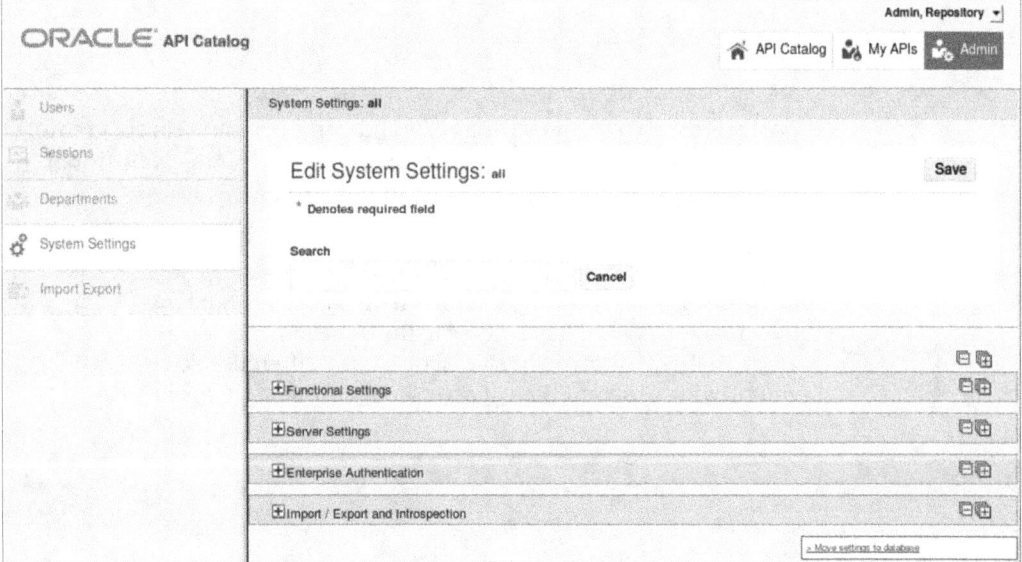

OAC settings are grouped into four main categories:

- **Functional Settings**: These are settings related to **search** and **PDF exports** capabilities within OAC.

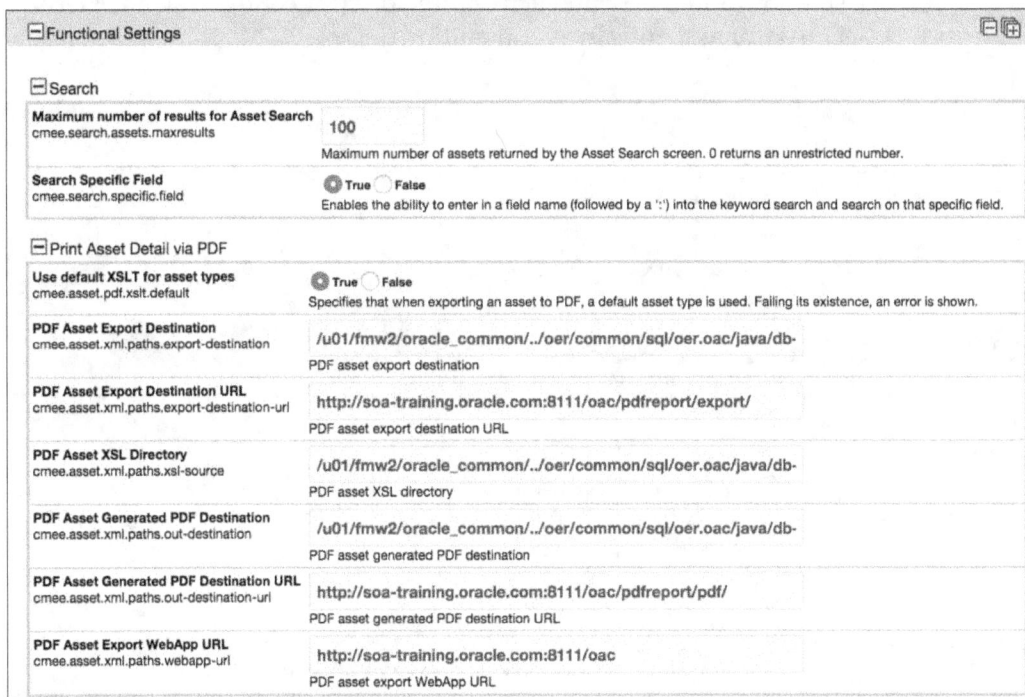

- **Server Settings**: These are settings related to HTML embedding in the descriptor.

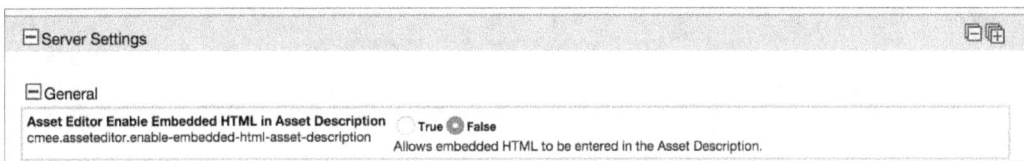

## Oracle API Catalog Implementation

- **Enterprise Authentication**: These are settings related to user login and authentication / authorization. This category has three groups of settings: **General** (for basic login settings), **Plugin Login Settings** (for custom login modules — for example if implementing a single-sign on solution) and LDAP and active directory (for configuring an external LDAP for authentication and authorization).

### Enterprise Authentication

#### General

|  |  |  |
|---|---|---|
| **Unapproved User Login**<br>enterprise.security.unapproveduser.allowlogin | ● True ○ False | Enables unapproved users to log in to the system. This is useful for LDAP or container-managed authentication. |
| **Enable LDAP Login**<br>enterprise.authentication.ldap.enabled | ○ True ● False | Enables the LDAP Login Module for authentication. |

#### Plugin Login Settings

|  |  |  |
|---|---|---|
| **Plug-in Login Module Class Name**<br>enterprise.loginmodules.pluggableloginmodule.classname | com.flashlir + | Class name of the plug-in login module |

#### LDAP and Active Directory Settings

|  |  |  |
|---|---|---|
| **LDAP Server Host Name**<br>ldap.host | | Host name for the LDAP server; required |
| **LDAP Server Port Number**<br>ldap.port | 389 | LDAP server port number; defaults to 389; optional |
| **LDAP Mask**<br>ldap.mask | uid=^, ou=yourOrganizationalUnit, o=yourDomain.com | The LDAP mask, either the authentication bind or search criteria; required |
| **Creation of Unapproved User Accounts**<br>ldap.allow-user-creation | ● True ○ False | Determines if unapproved user accounts can be created; defaults to true; optional |
| **Assign default roles to users**<br>ldap.assign-default-roles | ● True ○ False | Determines if users shall be assigned default roles |
| **Auto create missing roles**<br>ldap.auto-create-missing-roles | ● True ○ False | Determines if should auto create missing roles |
| **Auto create missing departments**<br>ldap.auto-create-missing-depts | ● True ○ False | Determines if should auto create missing departments |
| **LDAP Version**<br>ldap.version | 3 | The LDAP version used, which can be either 2 or 3; defaults to 2; optional |
| **Administrator Account Distinguished Name** | | |

*Chapter 3*

There are numerous settings available for LDAP and Active Directory configuration; more than can be captured in a single screenshot. For detailed information on how to set up OAC to use an external LDAP for authentication and authorization, please refer to section *7 Configuring Oracle API Catalog to use External Authentication Tooling* of the Administrator's Guide for OAC at `http://docs.oracle.com/middleware/1213/oac/administer-cat/extauth.htm#CATCG205`.

- **Import/Export and Introspection**: These are associated with the import/export utility. As more and more APIs are loaded into OAC, it becomes more relevant to fine-tune these settings to ensure a smooth import/export.

| Import / Export and Introspection | |
|---|---|
| **Import / Export** | |
| Import/Export job monitor max idle (msecs). cmee.extframework.impexp.monitor.maxidle | 600000 |
| | Maximum time (in msecs) that an import/export job can be idle before it is automatically killed by the job monitor. |
| Import/Export job monitor max idle for Rex transactions(msecs). cmee.extframework.impexp.monitor.rex.maxidle | 600000 |
| | Maximum time (in msecs) that a rex transaction can be idle before it is automatically killed by the job monitor. |
| Import/Export job monitor max runtime (msecs). cmee.extframework.impexp.monitor.maxruntime | 0 |
| | Maximum time (in msecs) that an import/export job can run before it is automatically killed by the job monitor. |
| Import/Export job monitor period (msecs). cmee.extframework.impexp.monitor.period | 5000 |
| | Time (in msecs) between scans for the job monitor. |
| Import/Export job proxy period (msecs) cmee.extframework.impexp.proxy.period | 5000 |
| | The time (in msecs) between checks by job proxies for job status on other cluster nodes. |
| Import/Export job proxy timeout (msecs) cmee.extframework.impexp.proxy.timeout | 60000 |
| | The time (in msecs) before a job proxy stops monitoring status of remote jobs on other clustered nodes. |

*Oracle API Catalog Implementation*

- **Import Export**: This is a link to the import/export utility.

This utility requires Java Web Start to be enabled to run in your browser. Refer to the following link for further instructions on how to do this:

http://docs.oracle.com/middleware/1213/oac/administer-cat/basic.htm#CATCG13804

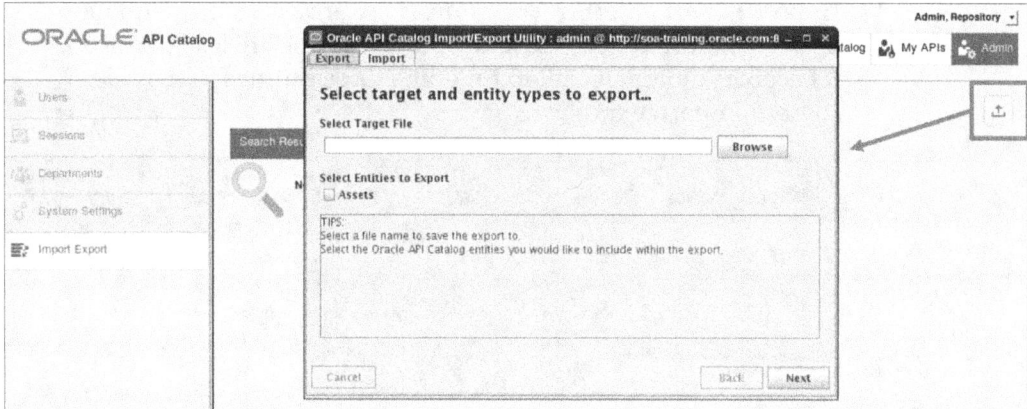

For a more detailed overview of the OAC web console, you may refer to the section *Getting Started with the OAC Console* in the OAC Developer's guide at the following link:

http://docs.oracle.com/middleware/1213/oac/develop-cat/using-web.htm#CATIN376

To finalize this section, the following diagram provides a good overview of the relationship between key entities in OAC.

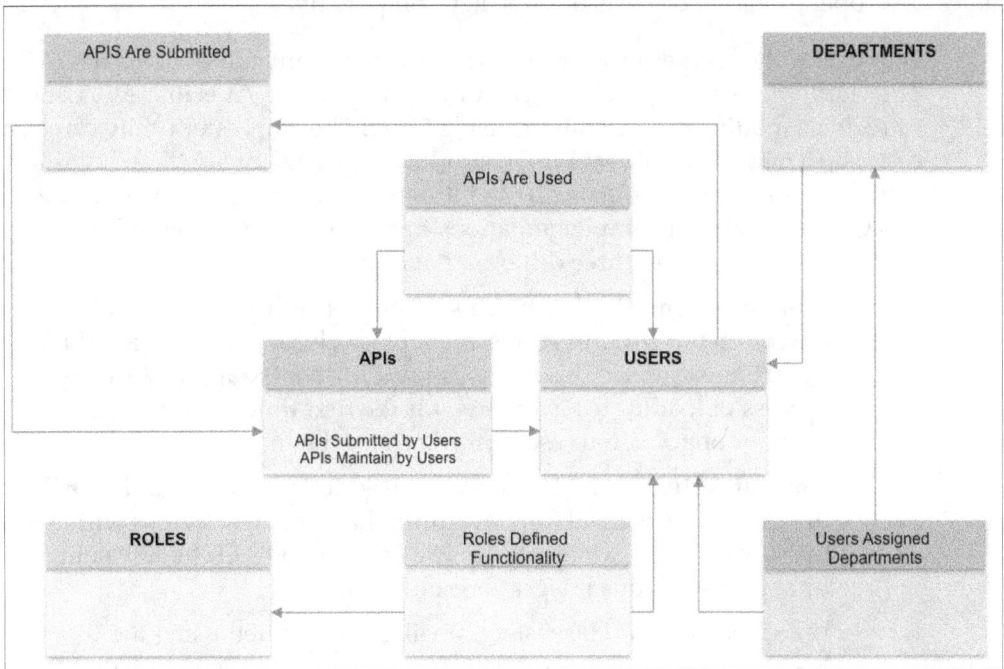

From the diagram it can be concluded that:

- APIs are submitted and edited by users. Therefore even the Harvester and REX API requires a valid user account.
- Departments are created and edited by users. However, departments are only logical groupings in OAC and don't drive any access restrictions or change of behavior in the system. As stated previously, two users with different departments and the same role have access to exactly the same information and have the same permissions.

A user can be assigned to many roles. However, roles cannot be created and/or modified. There are three roles available in OAC: Admin, Curator, and Developer. Each provides different levels of access and permissions.

>  Roles are covered in more detail in the section *OAC roles and user interfaces*.

*Oracle API Catalog Implementation*

## The OAC engine

The OAC engine is at the heart of OAC as it delivers all of the functionality that makes OAC operational. It consists of three key components:

- **Harvester**: The Harvester is one of the most important components of OAC. The Harvester is responsible for creating and updating APIs in OAC. Users can add or modify API definitions using OAC. The Harvester utility can also be used to manually harvest WSDL and WADL URLs into OAC. In addition, it can be configured automatically to introspect existing Oracle SOA Suite and Oracle Service Bus implementations to discover deployed services. The Harvester comes in three different flavors:
    - **Command-line Harvester**: This Harvester utility can be invoked via the command prompt and is available both for Windows and Linux operating systems. This utility is ideal for bootstrapping OAC (the process of loading APIs to OAC for the first time) and may also be used for ongoing harvesting throughout the lifecycle.
    - **Ant Harvester**: An Ant task can be used to import metadata into the OAC. This is ideal for embedding harvesting activities within the software development lifecycle and/or a DevOps ecosystem (that is, continuous integration solution).
    - **WLST Harvester**: Harvesters can also be executed using the **WebLogic Scripting Tool**. This is usually favored by advance administrators who already have several WLST scripts and wish to also include harvesting scripts within their script libraries.

> The Harvester is covered in more detail in the section *SDLC harvesting using the Ant Harvester* of this chapter.

- **REX API**: This is an RPC encoded web service that provides access to several of the OER subsystems. It can be used to extend OAC functionality; for example, adding the creation and/or publication of assets in OAC as part of a broader business process implemented in BPM Suite. It can also be used to integrate OAC with other systems and/or applications (that is, adding runtime metrics into the API description field).

> The REX API is covered in more detail in *The REX API* section of this chapter.

- **OER subsystems**: Although OAC is a product on its own right, it actually uses many of the subsystems of **Oracle Enterprise Repository (OER)**. Note that not all of the functionality of OER is available in OAC. Therefore when using the REX API to interoperate with the OER subsystems it is important to have a good understanding of the constraints imposed on OAC compared to the full OER implementation. *The REX API* section provides a good overview on how to leverage the REX API to access the OER subsystem.

> At this point it is worth highlighting that although OER does overlap with OAC in some capabilities, the main purpose of OER is to address more complex SOA Governance requirements. It is therefore the author's recommendation to implement OAC as a lightweight facility to catalog, document, and discover APIs as it has been recommended in this chapter.
>
> For more complex SOA Governance requirements OER can be implemented with OAC by making use of the import/export utility:
>
>
>
> https://docs.oracle.com/middleware/1213/oac/administer-cat/impexp.htm#CATCG13222
>
> It is also suggested to refer to the book *Oracle SOA Governance 11g Implementation*, Packt Publishing, for details on how to implement OER to address complex SOA Governance requirements, at the following link:
>
> https://www.packtpub.com/application-development/oracle-soa-governance-11g-implementation
>
> Note that although the book makes use of OER *11g*, the recipes and guidelines provided still apply to OER *12c* especially given that only a few changes were introduced in the latest version.

## OAC roles and user interfaces

OAC implements **role-based access control (RBAC)**. Thus, the role a user has been assigned to, determines what actions the user can perform regardless of the user interface being used. The following diagram illustrates the relationship between roles, permissions, and the user interfaces:

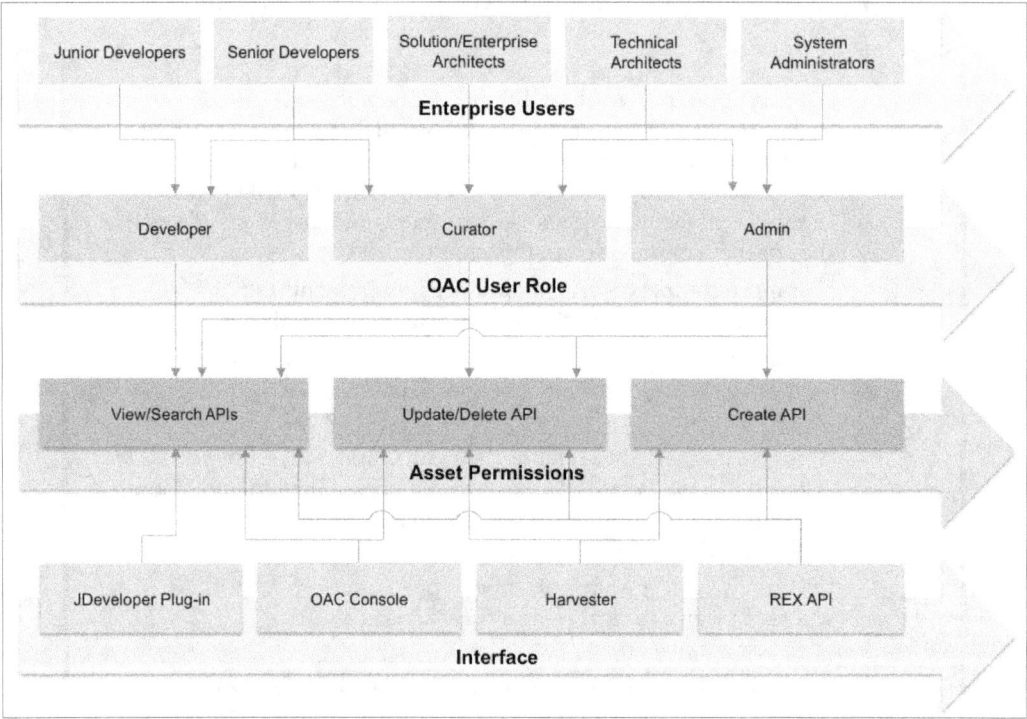

As depicted in the diagram, there are three roles in OAC:

- **Developer**: Developers can search and view published APIs either using the OAC console or through the JDeveloper OER plug-in. In addition developers can add APIs to **My APIs** and also add ratings and remarks. Developers cannot harvest, edit, or delete APIs or access the **Admin** page.

- **Curator**: Curators have the same access permissions as developers but in addition they have access to all APIs regardless of their status (draft or published) and they can also edit and delete APIs. This role is generally assigned to senior developers and/or architects who are responsible for augmenting the API metadata and producing documentation.

>  Curators cannot harvest assets despite what the official documentation states (at least at the time this book was written). Only admin users can harvest assets (unless a new patch that changes this behavior was released after this book was published).

- **Admin**: In addition to the developer and curator roles, an admin role can also access the **Admin** pages and is also able to invoke the Harvester.

There are four ways to access OER functionality:

- **Web console**: This is the main console and has been previously discussed. In subsequent chapters, the OAC web console will be discussed more thoroughly.
- **JDeveloper OER plug-in**: Targeted for API and service developers, this plug-in can be installed in JDeveloper to establish a connection, which allows published APIs to be discovered and consumed. The *Discovering APIs* section covers the use of this plug-in in more detail.
- **Harvester**: As previously discussed, the Harvester comes in three flavors and can be used by the admin users to bootstrap OAC and/or harvest APIs throughout the software development lifecycle or DevOps solutions.
- **REX API**: As previously described, the REX API provides a direct and standard interface to the OER subsystem via an RPC encoded web service. All user roles can make use of the REX API. However, roles are enforced in the same fashion as the web console. For example, a developer can successfully use authentication, search and read related operations. A curator can in addition also invoke edit-related operations. However, if either of them try to use create-related operations, an authorization error will be thrown. Similarly if a developer tries to use an edit-related operation an error will be thrown. Only admin users can make use of all REX operations.

# Implementation use case

As described in the previous chapter (*Chapter 2, Implementation Case Study*), WBCV Telecom has embarked on a digital transformation journey to become more disruptive in the use of their products and services, to be more agile and to deliver a much richer and tailored customer experience across a number of diverse channels. In order to achieve these ambitious goals, the organization's CIO, having already acknowledged the need for a robust API Management solution to enable the digitalization of their business, sponsored an **Enterprise Architecture** (**EA**) initiative aimed at delivering an API Management strategy and subsequent implementation of an API Management solution (refer to the *Recommendations* section of *Chapter 2, Implementation Case Study*, for details the solution recommended).

The EA team supported by 4APPmigos (a niche API Management consultancy) concluded that the Oracle API Management solution would underpin WBCV's API platform (refer to recommendation #2 Technology in the preceding chapter for details on the product comparison made by 4APPmigos and for a detailed description on why Oracle was chosen). As illustrated in the strategic roadmap, the next phase after completion of the API Management strategy was to implement the **Oracle API Catalog** (**OAC**). The rationale behind implementing OAC as a first step was that:

- No one in the organization had an accurate view of all the current services and APIs available across the enterprise estate. Thus, to ensure that no redundancy was introduced in new initiatives, it made sense to determine an accurate inventory of all services and APIs currently available.

> As described in *Chapter 2, Implementation Case Study*, WBCV was already fairly mature in their SOA adoption and many services had been delivered over a number of years. It was important not to throw away this investment; reuse would ultimately save effort and thus costs.

- OAC as a product seemed very simple to implement. Therefore the team reckoned that they could implement it in as few as four weeks. To ensure these timeframes would not be compromised by infrastructure dependencies, the team opted to use cloud-computing resources instead of on-premise servers.

>  Delivering early results (quick wins) would not only boost the sponsor's confidence in the initiation but would also provide enough information to show the business potential and cost benefits that could be realized by simply re-using existing assets.

- As Oracle SOA Suite and Oracle Service Bus underpinned WBCV's SOA platform, OAC Harvester could be used to bootstrap OAC. The Harvester would automatically discover all services deployed on these platforms and then load them into OAC.

>  As WBCV Telecom had a vast amount of services the use of the Harvester alone would save a lot of effort (hence costs) as loading many assets manually can take a long time.

- Once assets had been automatically harvested, they needed to be properly documented and then published. Since documenting assets could be a tedious and time-consuming task, the team decided to reuse any documentation available by simply providing a link to the asset documentation URL from the existing content management system.

>  For those assets that did not have any documentation available, the team decided to produce the required documentation as an ongoing activity since enough contextual information was harvested by default to determine whether an asset for a particular function existed or not. For example, it was still possible to use OAC's search capability to find assets that are related to orders.

# Implementing OAC

In order to implement OAC within the aggressive timelines set, the team produced the following high-level plan:

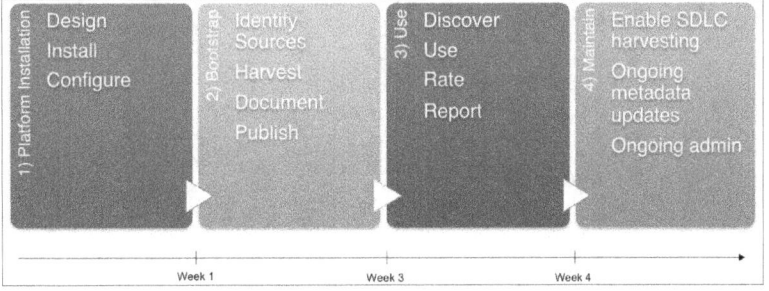

*Oracle API Catalog Implementation*

The subsequent sections of this chapter illustrate how this plan was implemented.

 *Chapter 6, Installation Tips and Techniques,* covers the topology design and installation of OAC along with the other products of the Oracle API Management suite.

## Basic configuration

Following the product installation, the next step was to configure OAC to ensure that assets were adequately harvested and that curators and developers could access the system based on the functions they performed (as indicated in the *OAC roles and user interfaces* section).

Let's look into the steps that were executed in order to configure OAC.

### Logging in to OAC

The following steps were executed to log into OAC:

1. Open a browser and navigate to `http://<OAC server>:<oac port>/oac`.

   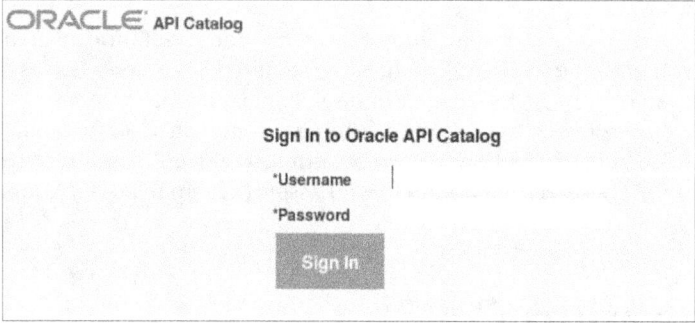

2. Enter the following credentials and then click on **Sign In**.
   - **Username**: `admin`
   - **Password**: `weblogic1`

3. Following first time login, OAC prompted the user to change their password as shown here:

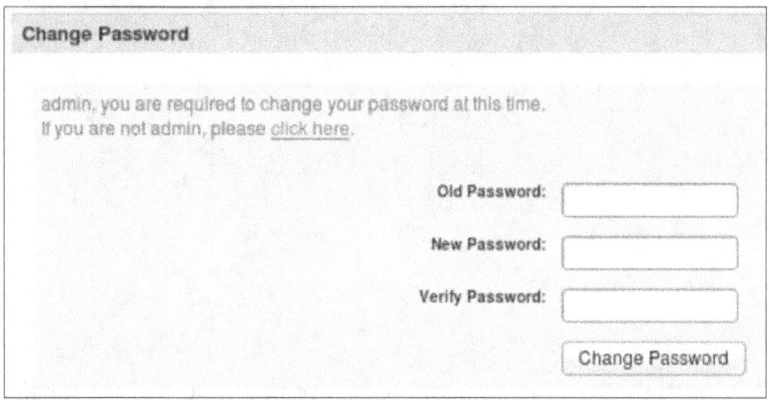

4. Finally, the OAC home page opens.

# Setting up departments

As previously described in *The OAC web console* section, departments in OAC are optional and they don't define any authorization rights in the system. Thus, it doesn't matter what department a user belongs to, the access rights are defined entirely by the user role. Nevertheless, it is good practice to make use of departments as they provide a useful way to logically group different users. This can subsequently prove very useful when conducting user administration tasks.

The following steps were executed to set up departments:

1. Login to OAC as previously indicated.
2. Once the home page opens, click on the **Admin** button located at the top-right hand side of the page.

*Oracle API Catalog Implementation*

3. Once in the **Admin** home page, click on the **Departments** menu option located on the left pane.

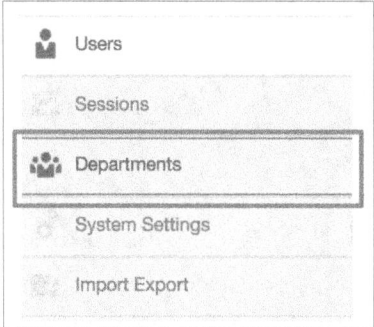

4. The **Departments** home page opens. From here you can see the list of any available departments and click on them to see their description. Click on the Create New icon located on the top-right hand side of the page.

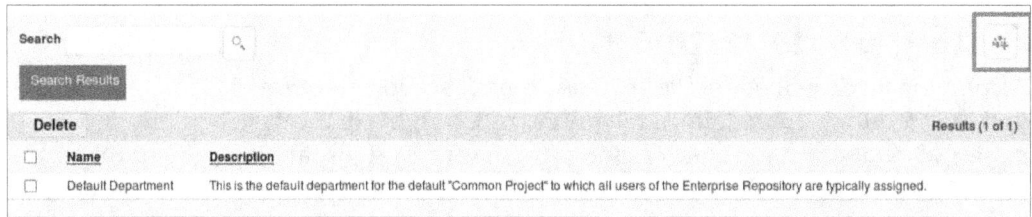

5. Enter the department details as shown here, ensuring that a user-friendly name is provided for the department. Likewise, provide a meaningful description and click on **Save**.

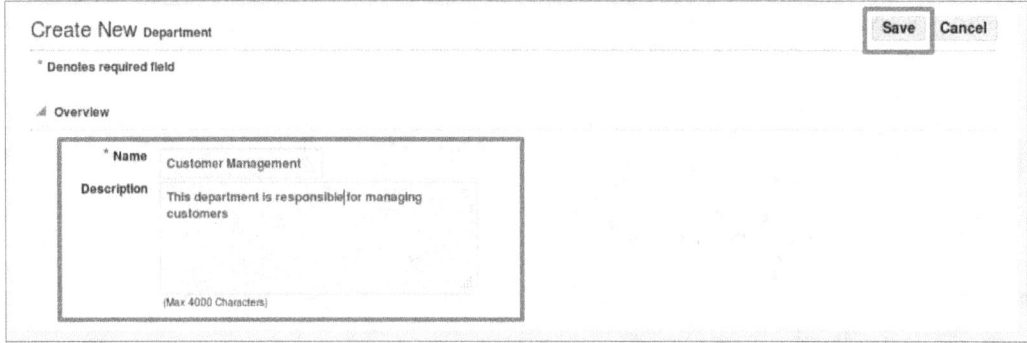

*Chapter 3*

6. Note that a tab opens showing the details of the department. From this tab the user can toggle the view (there are subtabs for each section) and edit or delete a department. It is also possible to click in the home tab to see all departments available.

>  It is also possible to access this tab by clicking on the department's row from the department's home page.

7. Clicking on the Toggle View icon changes the UI as follows:

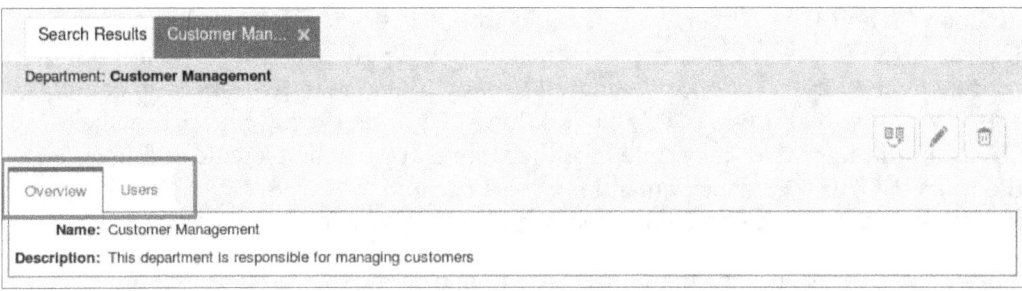

8. Repeat the steps to create as many departments as needed.

| Name | Description |
|---|---|
| Customer Management | This department is responsible for managing customers |
| Default Department | This is the default department for the default "Common Project" to which all users of the Enterprise Repository are typically assigned. |
| Marketing and Offer Management | Marketing and Offer Management department |
| Resource Management | Resource Management Department (HR) |
| Service Management | Service Management Department |
| Supplier/Partner Management | Supplier/Partner Management department |
| Supply Chain Management | Supply Chain Management department |

## Setting up users

Setting up users is one of the most critical activities in OAC. As mentioned earlier, OAC is RBAC based. Therefore, setting up users with the correct roles is key to ensuring the proper functioning of the tool and also to avoiding future authentication and authorization issues, like for example when harvesting or editing assets metadata. When WBCV began this task they had to make a key decision: whether to configure users and roles directly in OAC or to externalize these functions to an LDAP server, such as for example, the organization's MS **Active Directory** (**AD**). Given that any change regarding MS AD was subject to a standard process by the MS AD support team that usually took one to two weeks to complete, WBCV decided that it was overkill to do this integration during the early stages of OAC adoption. Instead, they opted for the simple approach; to create and maintain the users in OAC. Once the demand for users became too large to handle manually, the users would be externalized to the corporate LDAP server.

Another key decision to be made was how to map organization roles to application roles. For this, WBCV architects created a model similar to the one available in the section entitled *OAC roles and user interfaces*. In the model, typical roles such as developers (junior and senior), architects (technical, solution, and enterprise) and system administrators were mapped against application roles. This was simplified by the fact that the same exercise had been previously done for other application roles in other tools across the estate.

>  For further information on how to configure OAC to externalize user authentication and authorization to an LDAP server, please refer to section 7 *Configuring Oracle API Catalog to use External Authentication Tooling* of *Administrator's Guide for OAC*:
>
> https://docs.oracle.com/middleware/1213/oac/administer-cat/extauth.htm#CATCG205

Once the approach was finalized and consensus was reached, the following steps were executed to set up the users:

1. Login to OAC as previously shown.
2. When the home page opens, click on the **Admin** button located at the top-right hand side of the page. Or if already in the admin page, just click on the **Users** menu option located on the left pane.
3. On the user's home page the user can see a list of all users available. Click on the Create New icon located on the top-right hand side of the page to create a new user.

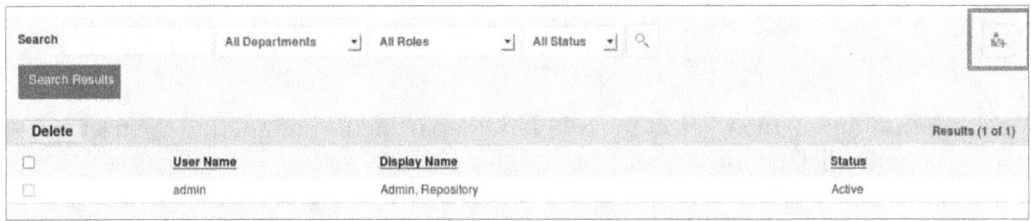

4. When the **Create New** user tab opens, enter the details as follows:
    - **Username**: Try to follow the same convention as your corporate LDAP. This will help if you decide to externalize OAC authentication/authorization in the future.
    - **First Name**: The first name of the user can be inputted here.
    - **Middle Name**: The middle name, if any, can be inputted here.
    - **Last Name**: This is the last name(s).
    - **Email**: Here, the corporate e-mail address can be inputted.
    - **Phone**: Phone number, if available, can be inputted here.

- **Status**: There are four status values available (active, inactive, locked out, and unapproved). Select **Active**.
- **Password**: Enter a simple password and make sure that you select the option **Must change password on next login**. It is also recommended that you leave the option **Password never expires** unselected; it's a good practice to renew passwords regularly.

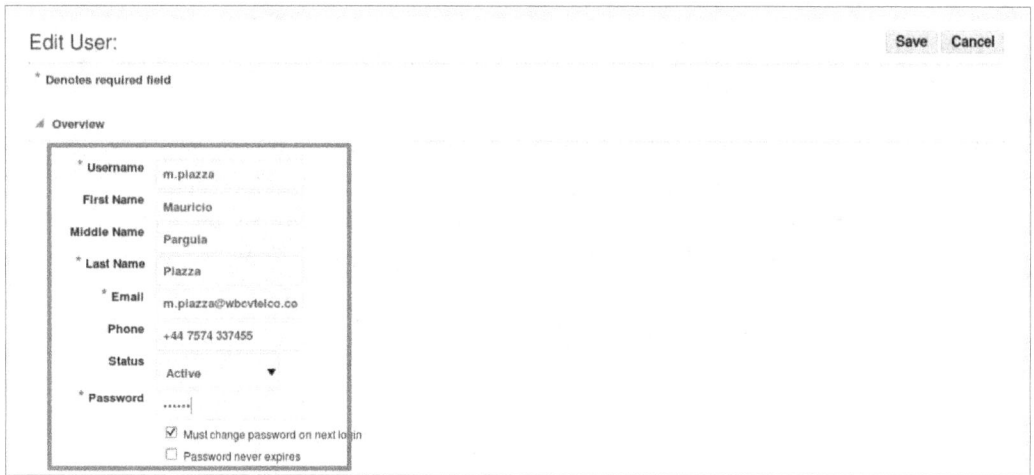

5. Scroll down; then, select the roles and departments assigned to the user. Finally click on **Save**.

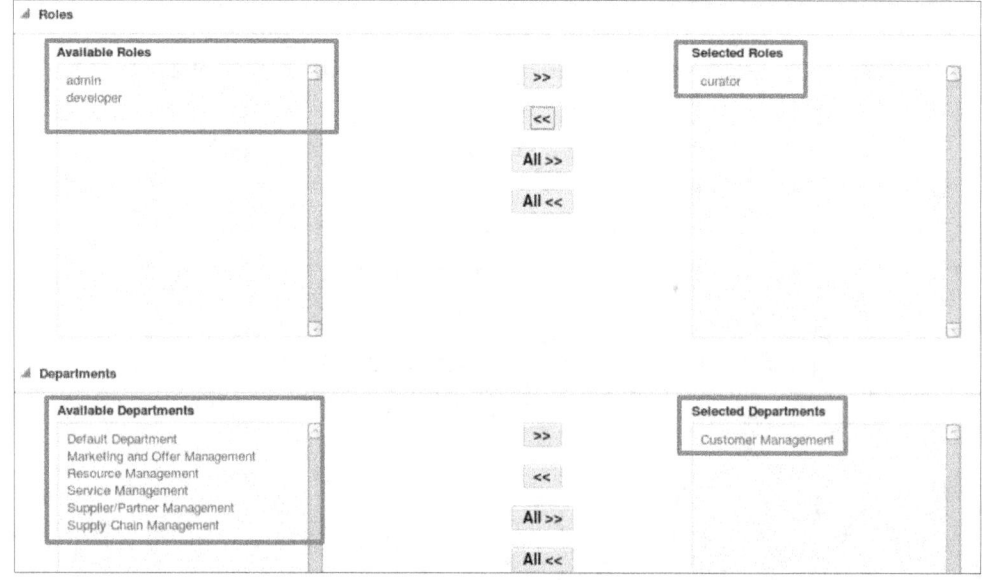

>  Remember that correctly defined roles are critical as they define the access rights a user has in OAC. Departments on the other hand are optional and provide a good mechanism to logically group users.

6. Notice how a new tab is opened showing the details of the newly created user. Similarly to the previous department example, from here it is possible to visualize the user details and to toggle the view and edit and delete the user. Also there is an additional option to copy this user's details to create a new user with similar departments and roles.

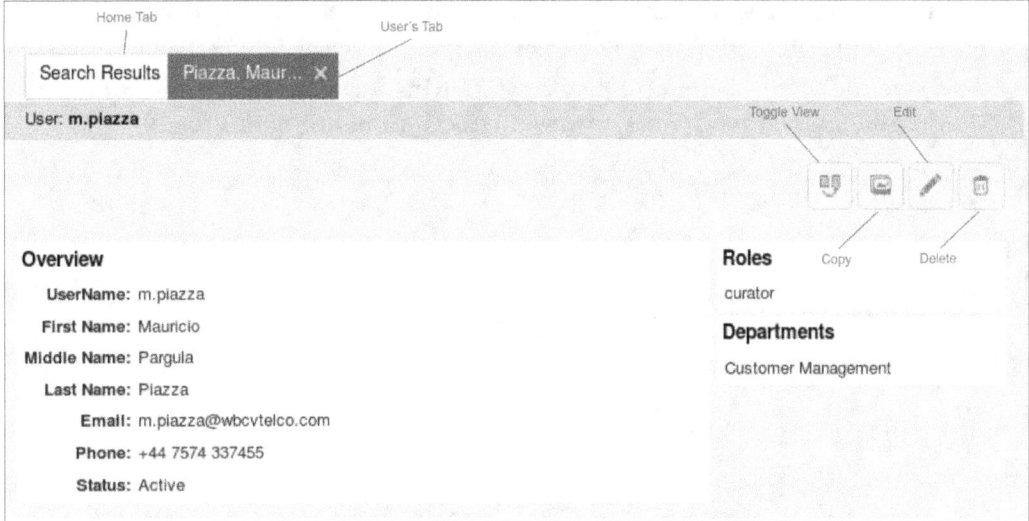

7. Repeat the preceding steps until all initial users are created. Once the user population starts growing, you will need to consider externalizing the users to an existing LDAP server, which is better suited to handle large user populations.

# Changing system settings

As WBCV architects opted not to externalize the user accounts to an LDAP, there were very few changes needed to the initial system settings. There was however one change required.

WBCV architects wanted to have the ability to include rich text information that would allow them to augment the metadata of an asset—for example via the REX API. To achieve this, do the following:

1. Login to OAC as previously indicated.
2. Once the home page opens, click on the **Admin** button located at the top-right hand side of the page. Then click on the **System Settings** menu option located on the left pane.
3. Scroll down until you find the **Server Settings** section. Set the **Asset Editor Enable Embedded HTML in Asset Description** setting to **True**.

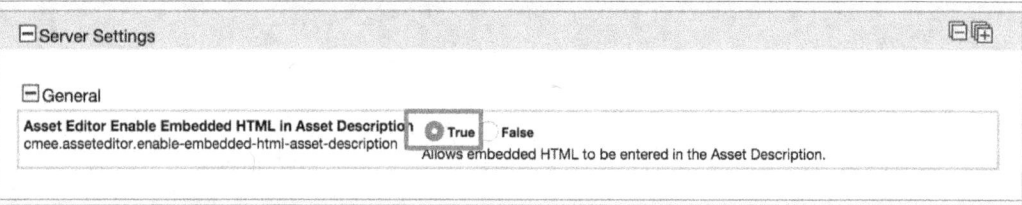

4. Scroll up and click on **Save**.

*Chapter 3*

# Bootstrapping OAC

Bootstrapping is the process of harvesting assets into OAC for the very first time. Once done, you should consider setting up the Harvester for on-going and continuous harvesting.

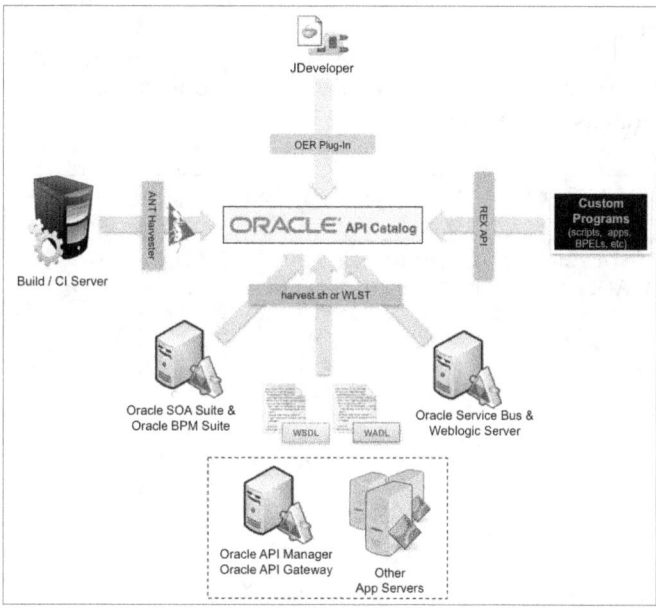

The first step when bootstrapping OAC is the identification of reliable sources to harvest assets. In OAC, this is fairly straightforward as it consists of identifying sources of WSDLs and WADLs.

Unlike OER, where almost every single asset that makes up a service is harvested (that is, WSDLs, BPELs components, Rules components, composite XMLs, XSDs, XSLTs, and so on), OAC is only interested in assets related to an interface. In other words, OAC harvests WSDL and WADL service descriptors. This makes OAC very simple to use and ensures that every user can search, discover, and consume services and APIs very quickly.

Please note that the version of OAC used in this book did not provide support to harvest **RESTful API Modeling Language (RAML)** documents. This feature may be introduced in later versions of the product. Refer to the product documentation for further information at https://docs.oracle.com/middleware/1213/oac/index.html.

[ 77 ]

## Oracle API Catalog Implementation

As mentioned in earlier sections of this chapter (and also in *Chapter 2, Implementation Case Study*), WBCV already had a fairly mature SOA implementation in place, which meant that identifying sources of WSDLs and WADLs was a fairly straightforward process, especially given that WBCV had very few WADLs as a result of just starting out on their API Management journey. In addition, they also needed to identify all sources of service-related documentation that was needed to augment the services and API metadata.

The following table shows a similar inventory to the one created by WBCV architects to identify potential asset sources:

| Source name | Asset(s) type | Environment type | Technology stack | Assets estimate # | Access details |
|---|---|---|---|---|---|
| SOA Platform | WSDLs and WADLs | Development | - Oracle SOA Suite 12.3.1<br>- Oracle Service Bus 12.3.1 | 310 | Owner: System owner<br><br>Accounts: Account details (that is, WebLogic, Oracle for SSH if needed)<br><br>IPs/URLs: Access via HTTP(s) or SSH |
| SOA Platform | WSDLs and WADLs | System Integration Testing | - Oracle SOA Suite 12.3.1<br>- Oracle Service Bus 12.3.1 | 305 | Owner: System owner<br><br>Accounts: Account details (that is, WebLogic, Oracle for SSH if needed)<br><br>IPs/URLs: Access via HTTP(s) or SSH |

| Source name | Asset(s) type | Environment type | Technology stack | Assets estimate # | Access details |
|---|---|---|---|---|---|
| SOA Platform | WSDLs and WADLs | User Acceptance Testing | - Oracle SOA Suite 12.3.1<br>- Oracle Service Bus 12.3.1 | 305 | Owner: System owner<br><br>Accounts: Account details (that is, WebLogic, Oracle for SSH if needed)<br><br>IPs/URLs: Access via HTTP(s) or SSH |
| SOA Platform | WSDLs and WADLs | Performance Testing and Preproduction | - Oracle SOA Suite 12.3.1<br>- Oracle Service Bus 12.3.1 | 300 | Owner: System owner<br><br>Accounts: Account details (that is, WebLogic, Oracle for SSH if needed)<br><br>IPs/URLs: Access via HTTP(s) or SSH |
| SOA Platform | WSDLs and WADLs | Production | - Oracle SOA Suite 12.3.1<br>- Oracle Service Bus 12.3.1 | 300 | Owner: System owner<br><br>Accounts: Account details (that is, WebLogic, Oracle for SSH if needed)<br><br>IPs/URLs: Access via HTTP(s) or SSH |

## Oracle API Catalog Implementation

| Source name | Asset(s) type | Environment type | Technology stack | Assets estimate # | Access details |
|---|---|---|---|---|---|
| Content Management System | Service documentation | Production | WebCenter Portal/Content | 300 | Owner: System owner<br>Accounts: Account details (that is, read-only)<br>IPs/URLs: URL to the document repository so that the different service documentation URL's can be extracted |

> Fortunately, WBCV were already using a WebCenter-based **content management system** (**CMS**) for storing and accessing service documentation. Information related to all services exposed in the SOA platform was already adequately organized in this repository with proper naming conventions and folder taxonomies. This made it very easy for users to find service documentation and opened up the possibility of using the REX API to build a custom script to automate the process of updating the service/API metadata with document references (URLs).
>
> For organizations that don't have a similar solution available for their service documentation, OAC curators and administrators can manually update the asset metadata through the OAC console.
>
> The REX API is covered later in this chapter in *The REX API* section.

Once the sources had been identified, the next step was to define the harvesting strategy. To avoid over-architecting the harvesting strategy, WBCV architects created a similar diagram to the one shown next to cover three main concerns:

- Bootstrapping sources and harvesting method
- SDLC harvesting sources and method
- API metadata editing sources and method

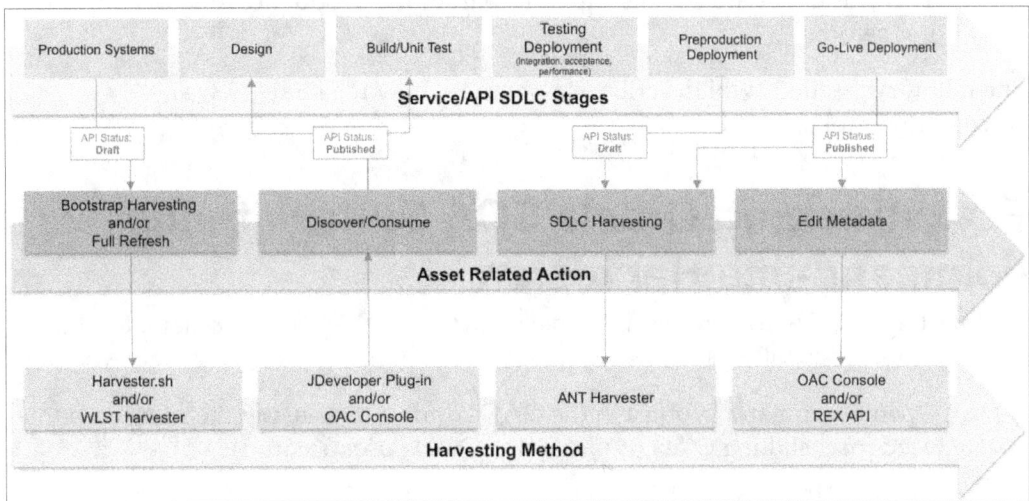

As illustrated in the preceding diagram, while the strategy was simple, it was very effective as it satisfied some of the key requirements around visibility of assets and increased reuse. The key considerations were:

- The SOA production system was initially harvested to bootstrap OAC. Harvesting all available production SOA Suite and OSB domains guaranteed that OAC was bootstrapped with the most up-to-date list of available services and APIs. Since this was a one-off activity, the Harvester command-line utility was used (`harvester.sh`).

- The Harvester command-line utility would also be used to Harvest services and/or APIs that did not reside in the SOA production platform or any other Oracle SOA Suite or Oracle Service Bus platform.

*Oracle API Catalog Implementation*

- Assets would be harvested with a status of the draft (at all stages).
- Assets would be harvested during preproduction deployment. This would help to create a list of services and APIs that needed to be updated with their respective metadata and relevant documentation sources before being published in the production system.
- Assets status values would be updated to be published once the asset metadata was augmented and documentation references were added. This was either after bootstrap or as part of the production deployment—but not before.

The following sections will describe, step by step, how the strategy was successfully implemented.

# Bootstrapping Oracle SOA Suite with the command-line Harvester

To bootstrap OAC with services available in an Oracle SOA Suite domain, use the Harvester utility as follows:

1. Open a command prompt in the OAC admin server using the same account used for installing OAC (typically the Oracle user account).
2. Change directory to `<FMW_HOME>/oer/tools`.

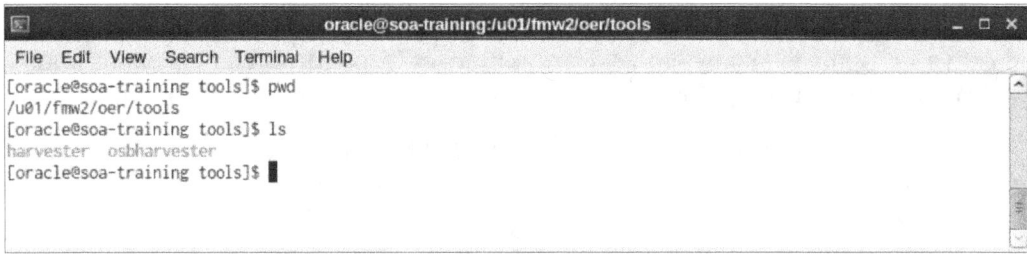

3. Once in this directory there are two folders:
   - `harvester`: This contains the Harvester utility for SOA Suite
   - `osbharvester`: This contains the Harvester utility for OSB

4. Change directory to `./harvester` and then list all files in this directory. Locate `harvester.sh` which is the Harvester utility script and `HarvesterSettings.xml` which contains all SOA Suite and OAC server parameters required by the Harvester utility.

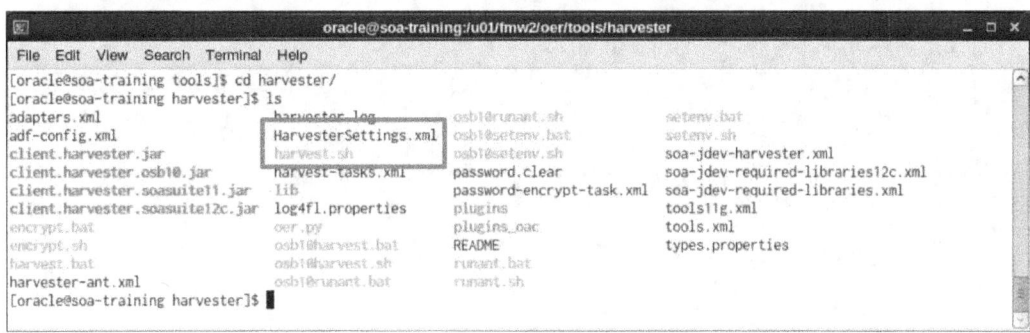

5. Backup `HarvesterSettings.xml` and edit it with a text editor of your choice as follows:
   - `registrationStatus` and `applyRegistrationStatusToExistingAssets`: Since OAC will harvest all assets with the status of draft, these two parameters can be ignored. Note that this might change in future releases of the product.

*Oracle API Catalog Implementation*

- registrationStatus: In this tag include the OAC connection details. The user entered must have OAC admin rights in order to be able to harvest (please note that curators can't harvest). The password can be entered in clear text and then encrypted using the `encrypt.sh` utility. Alternatively, OAC also provides a web utility that can be used to encrypt passwords: `http://<OAC Server>:<port>/oac/diag/encryptstrings.jsp`.

```xml
<?xml version="1.0" encoding="UTF-8"?>
<tns:harvesterSettings xmlns:tns="http://www.oracle.com/oer/integration/harvester" xmlns:xsi="http://www.w3.org/2001/XMLSchema-instance"
xsi:schemaLocation="http://www.oracle.com/oer/integration/harvester Harvester_Settings.xsd ">

    <!--Description to set on created Assets in OER or OAC.-->
    <harvesterDescription/>

    <!--OER Only: Registration status to set on created Assets in OER.
        The Valid Registration states are 1) Unsubmitted 2)Submitted - Pending Review 3)Submitted - Under Review 4)Registered -->
    <registrationStatus>Unsubmitted</registrationStatus>
    <applyRegistrationStatusToExistingAssets>false</applyRegistrationStatusToExistingAssets>

    <!-- OER Only: Categorizations to apply to assets created by the Harvester -->
    <!-- applyCategorization type="" value="" applyCategorizationToExistingAssets="false"/ -->

    <!--Namespace to set on created Assets in OER or OAC. If left empty, this is set based on information from SOA Suite and OSB projects
        when available.  That's generally the best practice, so override this with caution.-->
    <namespace/>

    <!--OER Only: If true, trigger OER events for use by Workflow.  Warning: this can decrease performance.-->
    <triggerEvent>false</triggerEvent>

    <!--  OER Only: Enter in producing project(s).  All assets created from the harvest will be assigned to this OER producing project.  Th
is project must already exist in OER. -->
    <!-- producingProject name="" / -->

    <!--Connection info to OER or OAC -->
    <repository>
        <uri>http://localhost:8111/oac</uri>
        <credentials>
            <user>curator1</user>
            <password>v2_1.yCFfBmPBkrk=</password><!--run encrypt.bat to encrypt this-->
        </credentials>
        <timeout>30000</timeout>
    </repository>
```

6. Scroll down and in the `remoteQuery` tag, enter the Oracle SOA Suite *12c* server details as follows:

    - serverType: Enter SOASuite for *12c* version (for *11g* the value should be set to SOASuite11g).
    - projectName: This refers to any specific SOA Suite project you wish to harvest. Comment out this tag to harvest all projects on the server
    - uri: URL for one of the WLS admin servers for the SOA Suite domain.
    - credentials: Enter credentials for the WebLogic user (or a user with the WLS roles: admin, operator, and monitor) of the SOA Suite domain. Enter the password in clear text and then run the `encrypt.sh` utility or alternatively use the OAC web encryption utility to encrypt passwords: `http://<OAC Server>:<port>/oac/diag/encryptstrings.jsp`.

○ soaPartition: Enter the name of the Oracle SOA partition to harvest or comment out the tag to harvest all partitions in the server.

```xml
<remoteQuery>
    <serverType>SOASuite</serverType>
    <!--<projectName></projectName>-->
    <uri>http://localhost:7111/</uri>
    <credentials>
        <user>weblogic</user>
        <password>v2_1.G+NTr3az8thaGGJBn0vwPg==</password>
    </credentials>
    <soaPartition>WBCV-OrderManagement</soaPartition>
</remoteQuery>
```

7. Save the changes made in `HarvesterSettings.xml` and exit the editor. Then execute `./encrypt.sh HarvesterSettings.xml HarvesterSettings.xml` to encrypt the passwords (only if entered in clear text).

8. Execute the Harvester by executing the command `./harvest.sh`.

```
[oracle@soa-training harvester]$ ./harvest.sh
NOTE: To harvest Oracle Service Bus 10 projects, please use osb10harvest.sh
0    [main] WARN  com.oracle.oer.sync.framework.impl.DefaultPluginManager  - unable to initialize harvester plugin file: /u01/fmw2/oer/tools/harvester/./plugins_oac/soasuite11g.remotereader
37   [main] WARN  com.oracle.oer.sync.framework.impl.DefaultPluginManager  - unable to initialize harvester plugin file: /u01/fmw2/oer/tools/harvester/./plugins_oac/mds.starter
Connecting to: service:jmx:t3://localhost:7111/jndi/weblogic.management.mbeanservers.runtime
984  [main] INFO  com.oracle.oer.sync.framework.MetadataManager  - oracle enterprise_repository_harvester version: v12.1.3.0.0-141011_1907-1631476
1079 [main] WARN  com.oracle.oer.sync.framework.impl.DefaultPluginManager  - unable to initialize harvester plugin file: /u01/fmw2/oac/tools/harvester/./plugins_oac/soasuite11g.remotereader
1097 [main] WARN  com.oracle.oer.sync.framework.impl.DefaultPluginManager  - unable to initialize harvester plugin file: /u01/fmw2/oac/tools/harvester/./plugins_oac/mds.starter
4654 [main] INFO  com.oracle.oer.sync.framework.MetadataManager  - successfully completed the harvest
4655 [main] INFO  com.oracle.oer.sync.plugin.writer.oer.OERWriter  - starting oac shutdown and clean up...
[oracle@soa-training harvester]$
```

> The **warnings (WARN)** that appear after executing the command can be safely ignored as they refer to SOA Suite *11g* classes. These would go away when harvesting SOA Suite *11g* services. However, similar warnings would appear but these would refer to *12c* classes instead.

If the Harvester executed successfully, then the message `successfully completed the harvest` should be visible in the console.

*Oracle API Catalog Implementation*

>
> By adding the -preview true option (./harvester.sh -preview true) it is possible to execute the Harvester in preview mode. This will show you all potential assets that would be harvested without actually committing any submission in OAC.
>
> Also note that the SOA Suite server targeted can be overridden at runtime by adding the option -remote_url <SOA Suite server>.
>
> Please refer to section *5.2.2 Configuring the Harvester for the Command Line* of the *OFM Administrator's Guide for OAC* for further information on all options available when executing the OAC Harvester:
>
> http://docs.oracle.com/middleware/1213/oac/administer-cat/harvest_oac.htm#CATCG443

# Bootstrapping Oracle Service Bus with the command-line Harvester

To bootstrap OAC with proxy and business services available in an Oracle Service Bus domain, use the Harvester utility as follows:

1. The OSB Harvester needs to be executed on the same machine on which the admin server of the OSB domain is running. This can make the process of harvesting OSB domains a bit more complicated specially when harvesting many OSB domains. There are at least three options available to accomplish this:

    - When harvesting many OSB domains, a good option is to network mount (using NFS) the OSB Harvester home on the OAC server (<OAC_FMW_HOME>/oer/tools/osbharvester) into the following path on the OSB admin server (<OSB_FMW_HOME>/osb/tools/harvester). Note that this assumes that the folder structures of all OSB domains are similar; otherwise, it might only work for some domains.

    - When harvesting a single OSB domain, a simpler option is to just copy the entire OSB Harvester home from the OAC server (OAC_FMW_HOME>/oer/tools/osbharvester) into this path in the OSB admin server: <OSB_FMW_HOME>/osb/tools/harvester.

    - If by any chance the OAC admin server and the OSB admin server reside on the same server instance then changes to setenv.sh can be made accordingly so there is no need to copy any files.

>  For all options please make sure that the user and group ownership of the files is consistent with the same user that performed the product installation (typically the Oracle user account).

- Assuming that the previous steps were completed successfully, open a command prompt on the OSB server. This will be used to harvest assets using the Oracle user account or equivalent. Change directory to the OSB Harvester home: `<OSB_FMW_HOME>/oer/tools/osbharvester`

2. Backup `HarvesterSettings.xml` and edit it with a text editor of your choice as follows:
    - `repository`: Enter the details of the OAC server in exactly the same way as was done for the SOA Suite Harvester (see the previous section)

Scroll down and in the tag `remoteQuery` enter the OSB *12c* server details as following:

- `serverType`: Enter `OSB` (same for *11g* or *12c*).
- `projectName`: This refers to any specific OSB project you wish to harvest. Comment out this tag to harvest all projects on the server.
- `uri`: Enter the URL of one of the WLS admin servers for the OSB domain.
- `credentials`: Enter credentials for the WebLogic user (or a user with the WLS role admin) for the OSB domain. Enter the password in clear text and run the `encrypt.sh` utility to encrypt. Alternatively, just use the OAC web encryption utility to encrypt passwords: `http://<OAC Server>:<port>/oac/diag/encryptstrings.jsp`.

```
<remoteQuery>
    <serverType>OSB</serverType>
    <!--<projectName></projectName>-->
    <uri>http://localhost:7111/</uri>
    <credentials>
        <user>weblogic</user>
        <password>v2_1.G+NTr3az8thaGGJBn0vwPg==</password>
    </credentials>
</remoteQuery>
</query>
```

*Oracle API Catalog Implementation*

3. Save the changes made in `HarvesterSettings.xml` and exit the editor. Then execute `./encrypt.sh HarvesterSettings.xml HarvesterSettings.xml` to encrypt the passwords (only if entered in clear text).

4. The last step before harvesting is to modify the file `setenv.sh` to ensure that all environment variables required by the OSB Harvester are configured correctly based on the option chosen in the first step. To do this first backup `setenv.sh` and then edit it using a text editor of your choice as shown here:

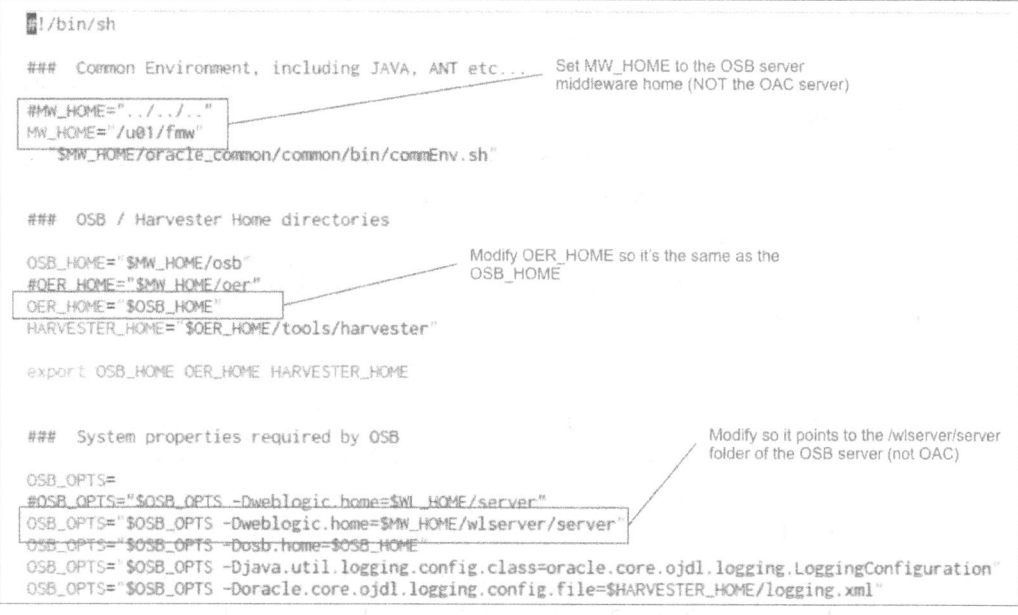

5. To ensure that all environment variables are set correctly, run the following command:

   `./source ./setenv.sh`

*Chapter 3*

6. Run the following command to execute the OSB Harvester:
   `./osb-harvest.sh`.

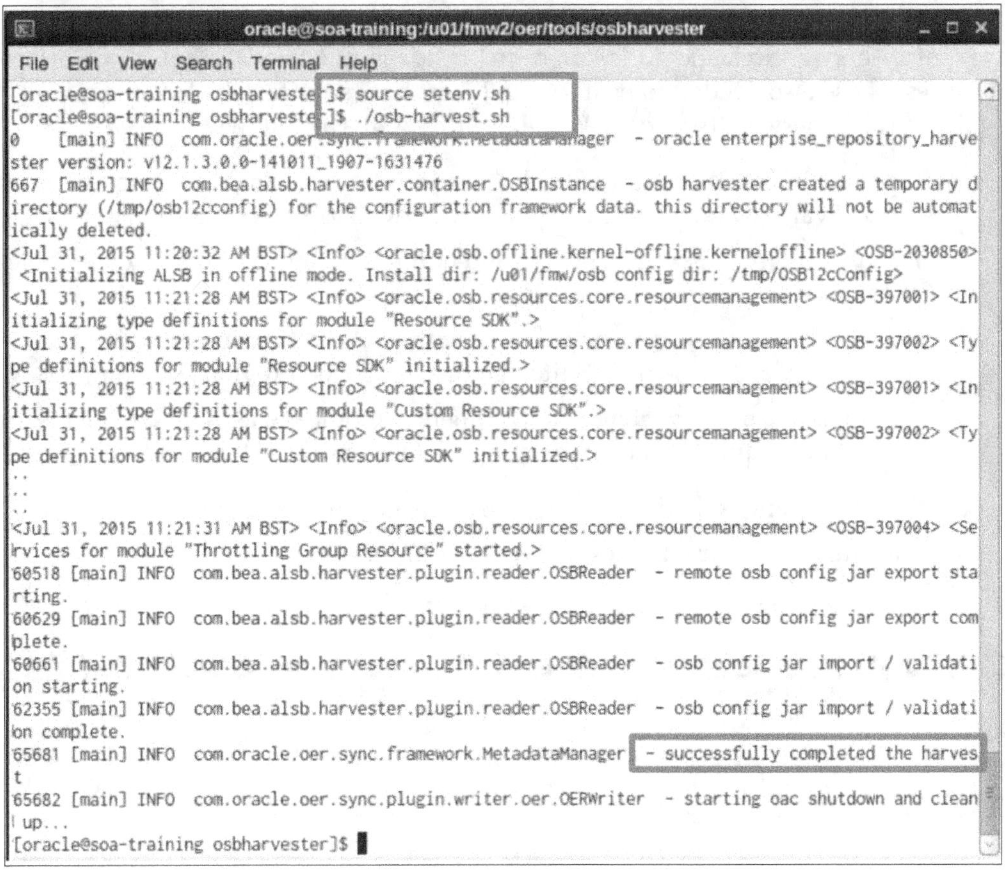

If the OSB Harvester has executed successfully, the message `successfully completed the harvest` should be visible in the console.

> By adding the `-preview true` option (`./osb-harvester.sh -preview true`) it is possible to execute the Harvester in preview mode. This will show you all potential assets that would be harvested without actually committing any submission into OAC.

[ 89 ]

*Oracle API Catalog Implementation*

# Manually bootstrapping WSDLs and WADLs with the command-line Harvester

During the asset sources discovery process, WBCV architects also identified a few relevant ad-hoc services and APIs that didn't reside in Oracle SOA Suite or OSB instances. These also needed to be harvested. For these services, the Harvester was used to directly harvest the service WSDLs and WADLs as follows:

1. Open a command prompt in the OAC admin server using the Oracle account (or equivalent) and change directory to `<FMW_HOME>/oer/tools/harvester`.

2. Backup `HarvesterSettings.xml` and edit it with a text editor of your choice as follows:
    - `repository`: Enter the details of the OAC server in exactly the same way as for the SOA Suite Harvester (see the previous section).
    - `remoteQuery`: Here, you comment out or leave as is. These details are not required when harvesting WSDLs and WADLs.

3. Save the changes made in `HarvesterSettings.xml` and exit.

4. Execute the Harvester by executing this command:

    `./harvest.sh -file <WSDL or WADL URL>`

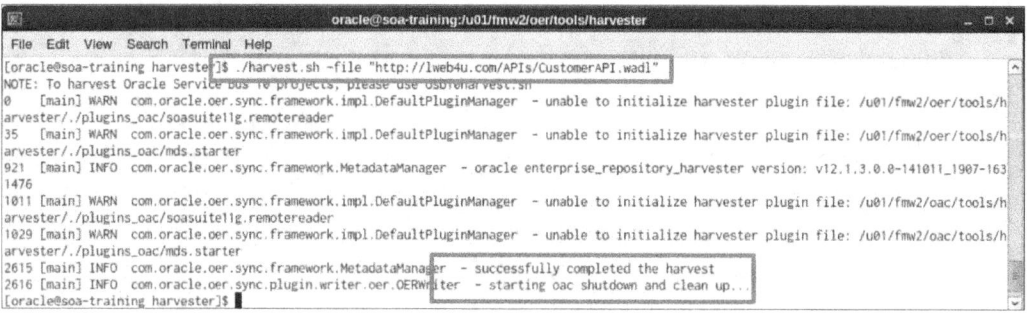

If the Harvester executed successfully the message `successfully completed the harvest` should be visible in the console.

# SDLC harvesting using the Ant Harvester

As described earlier in the bootstrapping strategy, WBCV architects were intending to implement continuous harvesting as part of their release cycle and continuous integration solution. To achieve this, WBCV architects leveraged the Harvester Ant utility to invoke the Ant targets responsible for carrying out a harvesting job. The idea was that during preproduction and production deployments, new services and APIs would also be harvested ensuring that:

- The catalog would not only contain services already *published* in production but also services in *draft* status. This would give curators visibility over assets that required additional metadata before being published.

- Provide curators with the ability to enforce a lightweight policy during production deployment whereby only assets with complete metadata would be published. For the initial releases of the solution the intention was to do this manually. However, the intention was to automate this task later on by implementing a BPM process that would be triggered by the deployment solution prior to conducting any deployment or harvesting activity. This would fire a human workflow process to ensure that there was adequate metadata associated with assets prior to them being deployed. For those assets with the correct metadata, it would also ensure that they could not only be deployed and harvested but also could subsequently be published by a process using the REX API.

The steps which follow in the next section were used by WBCV in order to make use of the Ant Harvester utility. This was used to extend the functionality of their deployment and continuous integration solutions.

 Although these steps will not show how WBCV's deployment and continuous integration solution were customized in detail, enough information has been provided so that this can be accomplished and in different scenarios.

# Using the SOA Suite Ant Harvester

In order to make use of the Ant Harvester utility for SOA Suite harvesting, the following steps were undertaken:

1. Open a command prompt in the OAC admin server using the same account used for installing OAC (typically the Oracle user account).

2. Change directory to `<FMW_HOME>/oer/tools/harvester`.
3. Set the following environmental variables:
    - `BEA_HOME`: Path to the fusion middleware home for OAC
    - `Ant_HOME`: Path to the Ant home

> Apache Ant is open source and can be downloaded from the following URL:
> http://Ant.apache.org

4. Then create a file named `harvest.xml`.

5. Using an editor of your choice, edit `harvest.xml` and add the following Ant tags:
    - `Project`: This is the root tag that defines an Ant project. It should contain two attributes: `file` specifying the name of the Ant project and `default` that defines the Ant target that would be executed by default; in this case the value is set to `Harvest`.
    - `Description`: This tag is used for a brief description of the Ant project.
    - `Taskdef`: This tag is a very important tag as it refers to `havest-task.xml`, which in turns loads all the Harvester libraries to define the Ant Harvester tag `repository.submit`.
    - `Properties`: There are several properties listed that define the target environment details for OAC, SOA Suite, or a SOA Suite project.

○ `Targets`: There are two main Ant targets in this project. `Harvest` can be used to harvest a SOA Suite domain to the specified OAC server. `HarvestFile` can be used to harvest specific SOA Suite projects that are accessible through the file system.

```xml
<?xml version="1.0" encoding="UTF-8"?>
<!-- Ant script for testing Harvester ant tasks -->
<project name="introspector" default="Harvest">
    <description>Ant script for launching Harvester ant tasks from JDeveloper 10</description>

    <!-- Define the task -->
    <taskdef file="harvest-tasks.xml" />

    <!-- OAC settings -->
    <property name="oac.url" value="http://localhost:8111/oac" />
    <property name="oac.username" value="admin" />
    <property name="oac.password" value="v2_1.yCFfBmPBkrk=" />
    <property name="oac.failonerror" value="true" />
    <property name="oac.timeout" value="5000" />
    <property name="oac.debug" value="true" />
    <property name="settings.file" location="HarvesterSettings.xml"/>

    <!-- Harvesting sources settings -->
    <property name="input.file" location="/home/oracle/Desktop/globalweather.wsdl"/>
    <property name="soa.url" value="http://localhost:7111" />
    <property name="soa.username" value="weblogic" />
    <property name="soa.password" value="v2_1.G+NTr3az8thaGGJBn0vwPg==" />
    <property name="soa.partition" value="WBCV-CustomerManagement" />
    <property name="soa.servertype" value="SOASuite" />

    <!-- Harvest SOA Suite -->
    <target name="Harvest" description="execute ANT harvester">
        <echo>Harvesting SOA Suite server: ${soa.url} to OAC server: ${oac.url}</echo>
        <repository.submit repositoryUrl="${oac.url}"
                    repositoryUsername="${oac.username}"
                    repositoryPassword="${oac.password}"
                    timeout="${oac.timeout}"
                    failOnError="${oac.failonerror}"
                    debug="${oac.debug}"
                    >
            <remoteProjects
                    uri="${soa.url}"
                    username="${soa.username}"
                    password="${soa.password}"
                    serverType="${soa.servertype}"
                    soaPartition="${soa.partition}">
                <!-- <projectName>OrderManagementBS_rev1.0</projectName> -->
            </remoteProjects>
        </repository.submit>
    </target>

    <!-- Harvest a File -->
    <target name="HarvestFile" description="Harvest the selected file in JDeveloper">
        <!-- Set "preview" to "true" to enable Preview Mode -->
        <echo>Harvesting file: ${file.path} to OAC server: ${oac.url}</echo>
        <repository.submit repositoryURL="${oac.url}"
                    repositoryUsername="${oac.username}"
                    repositoryPassword="${oac.password}"
                    description="Harvester from ANT"
                    >
            <fileset file="${input.file}"/>
        </repository.submit>
    </target>
</project>
```

- Defines what target to execute when ant harvester is executed
- Ant libraries for the definition of the repository.submit task
- Ant libraries for the definition of the repository.submit task
- Harvesting specific settings
- File based harvester target

*Oracle API Catalog Implementation*

>  Passwords must be encrypted using OAC web encryption utility: `http://<OAC Server>:8111/oac/diag/encryptstrings.jsp`.

6. Save and exit.

7. Backup `HarvesterSettings.xml` and edit with a text editor of your choice. Alternatively you can copy it and rename it differently but you must then ensure that the Ant property `settings.file` is updated in `harvest.xml` to reflect this change.

8. Comment out the tag `remoteQuery` as shown and then save and close.

```xml
<!--
<remoteQuery>
  <serverType>SOASuite</serverType>
  <uri>http://localhost:7111/</uri>
  <credentials>
    <user>weblogic</user>
    <password>v2_1.G+NTr3az8thaGGJBn0vwPg==</password>
  </credentials>
  <soaPartition>WBCV-CustomerManagement</soaPartition>
</remoteQuery> -->
```

9. Execute the Ant Harvester by running the following command:

    `./runAnt.sh -f harvest.xml`

*Chapter 3*

If the Ant Harvester executed successfully, the outputs `successfully completed the harvest` and `BUILD SUCCESSFUL` should appear.

>  For further information on using the Ant Harvester, please refer to section *5.2.3 Invoking the Harvester Using the Repository.Submit Ant Task* of the *OFM Administration Guide for OAC* here:
> `http://docs.oracle.com/middleware/1213/oac/administer-cat/harvest_oac.htm#CATCG433`

## Using the OSB Ant Harvester

In order to make use of the Ant Harvester utility for OSB, the following steps should be undertaken:

1. Open a command prompt while logged in to the Oracle user account (or equivalent) on the OSB server. Change directory to the OSB Harvester home: `<OSB_FMW_HOME>/osb/tools/harvester`.

>  Refer to the section *Bootstrapping Oracle Service Bus with the command-line Harvester* for instructions on how to set up the OSB Harvester.

2. Set the following environmental variables to the values shown here:
   - `BEA_HOME`: Path to the fusion middleware home for OSB
   - `Ant_HOME`: Path to the Ant home

>  Apache Ant is open source and can be downloaded from the following URL:
> `http://Ant.apache.org`

3. Create a file named `osb.harvest.xml`.
4. Using a text editor of your choice, edit `osb.harvest.xml` and add the following Ant tags:
   - `Project`: This is the root tag that defines an Ant project. It should contain two attributes: `file` specifying the name of the Ant project and `default` that defines the Ant target that should be executed by default. In this case it is `HarvestOSBRemote`.

- Description: This is a brief description of the Ant project.
- Properties: There are several properties listed that define the target environment details for OAC, OSB, or an OSB JAR file.
- Targets: There are two main Ant targets in this project. HarvestOSBRemote can be used to harvest an OSB domain to the specified OAC server. HarvestOSBJar can be used to harvest specific OSB JAR files that are accessible through the filesystem.

```xml
<?xml version="1.0" encoding="UTF-8"?>
<!-- Ant script for testing Harvester ant tasks -->
<project name="HarvestOsb" default="HarvestOSBRemote">
    <description>Ant script for launching Harvester ant tasks from JDeveloper 10</description>
    <!-- Global settings -->
    <!-- OAC server seettings -->
    <property name="oac.settings" value="HarvesterSettings.xml" />
    <property name="oac.url" value="http://localhost:8111/oac" />
    <property name="oac.username" value="admin" />
    <property name="oac.password" value="v2_1.yCFfBmPBkrk=" />
    <!-- OSB settings -->
    <property name="osb.file" value="/media/sf_oracle/APIs.jar"/>
    <property name="osb.url" value="http://localhost:7111" />
    <property name="osb.username" value="weblogic" />
    <property name="osb.password" value="v2_1.G+NTr3az8thaGGJBn0vwPg==" />

    <!-- OSB file harvester target -->
    <target name="HarvestOSBJar">
        <ant antfile="osb-harvester-ant.xml" target="harvest.file">
            <!-- OAC server seettings -->
            <property name="harvester.settings" value="${oac.settings}" />
            <!-- <property name="repository.url" value="${oac.url}" />
            <property name="repository.username" value="${oac.username}" />
            <property name="repository.password" value="${oac.password}" />-->
            <!-- OSB file input -->
            <property name="file.name" value="${osb.file}"/>
        </ant>
    </target>

    <!-- OSB remote harvester target -->
    <target name="HarvestOSBRemote">
        <ant antfile="osb-harvester-ant.xml" target="harvest.remote">
            <!-- OAC server seettings -->
            <property name="harvester.settings" value="${oac.settings}" />
            <!--<property name="repository.url" value="${oac.url}" />
            <property name="repository.username" value="${oac.username}" />
            <property name="repository.password" value="${oac.password}" />-->
            <!-- Target OSB server settings -->
            <property name="remote.uri" value="${osb.url}" />
            <property name="remote.username" value="${osb.username}" />
            <property name="remote.password" value="${osb.password}" />
        </ant>
    </target>
```

Annotations:
- Defines what target to execute when ant harvester is executed
- OAC server settings (Note that until a similar bug to Doc Id 1575502.1 is fixed these settings can't be passed via ANT, hence they are commented in the HarvestOSBRemote target below)
- OSB server settings
- OSB file based ANT harvester target
- OSB remote ANT harvester target

[  Passwords must be encrypted using OAC web encryption utility: http://<OAC Server>:8111/oac/diag/encryptstrings.jsp ]

5. Save and exit.

No changes are needed in `HarvesterSettings.xml`.

Execute the Ant OSB Harvester by running the command:

`./runAnt.sh -f osb.harvest.xml`

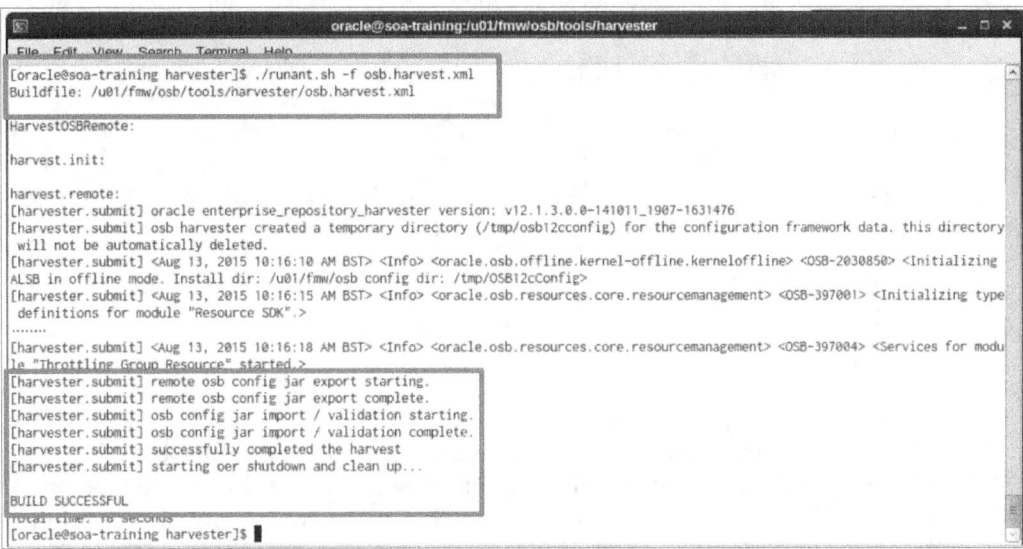

If the Ant Harvester executed successfully the outputs `successfully completed the harvest` and `BUILD SUCCESSFUL` should appear.

# Discovering APIs

Once assets have been harvested into OAC, they can be discovered in several ways. OAC admins and curators can search for drafts and published APIs through the OAC web console. Developers, on the other hand, can only search for published assets in the web console. In addition published APIs can also be discovered using the JDeveloper plug-in.

The following sections describe how WBCV architects and developers can search for and locate relevant APIs.

# Using the OAC console to discover APIs

APIs can be discovered through the OAC console by following these steps:

1. Login to OAC.
2. Once the home page opens, it is possible to search for APIs by entering search criteria into the Search field located on the upper right-hand side of the page and then clicking on the Search button.

>  If no criteria are entered, all APIs available will be returned. Also note that the option to filter based on API status is only available for curators and admins.

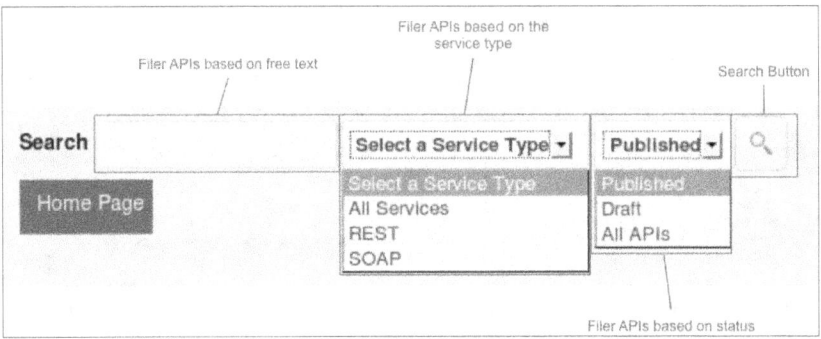

3. Once a search has been executed the search results page displays all APIs that matched the search criteria. From this page it is possible to click on an API to edit it, or to select one or more APIs to perform actions such as export based on the selected format or deletion.

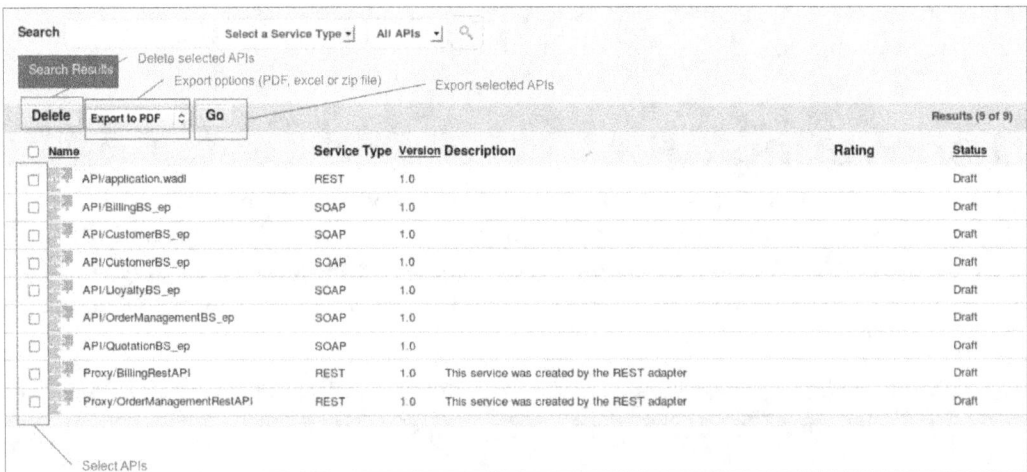

## Chapter 3

When conducting searches as an OAC developer neither the `delete` or `status` columns are available. Also, only published APIs can be searched upon.

The Harvester will default all APIs to version 1.0. This means that if different versions of the same API are harvested, they will all appear with the same defaulted version. However, if you click in one of them you may notice that the namespace reflects the actual version of the API. This can be helpful when setting the APIs to their correct version; either manually or via the REX API. Future version of OAC may solve this issue.

The *Setting up and using the JDeveloper plug-in for OAC* section covers the usage of JDeveloper to discover and use APIs.

# Viewing and editing API metadata

The following steps should be followed to edit APIs:

1. Repeat steps *1* to *3* of the previous section.
2. Click on an API row to view the API details.

*Oracle API Catalog Implementation*

3. Once the API viewer tab opens it will look as follows:

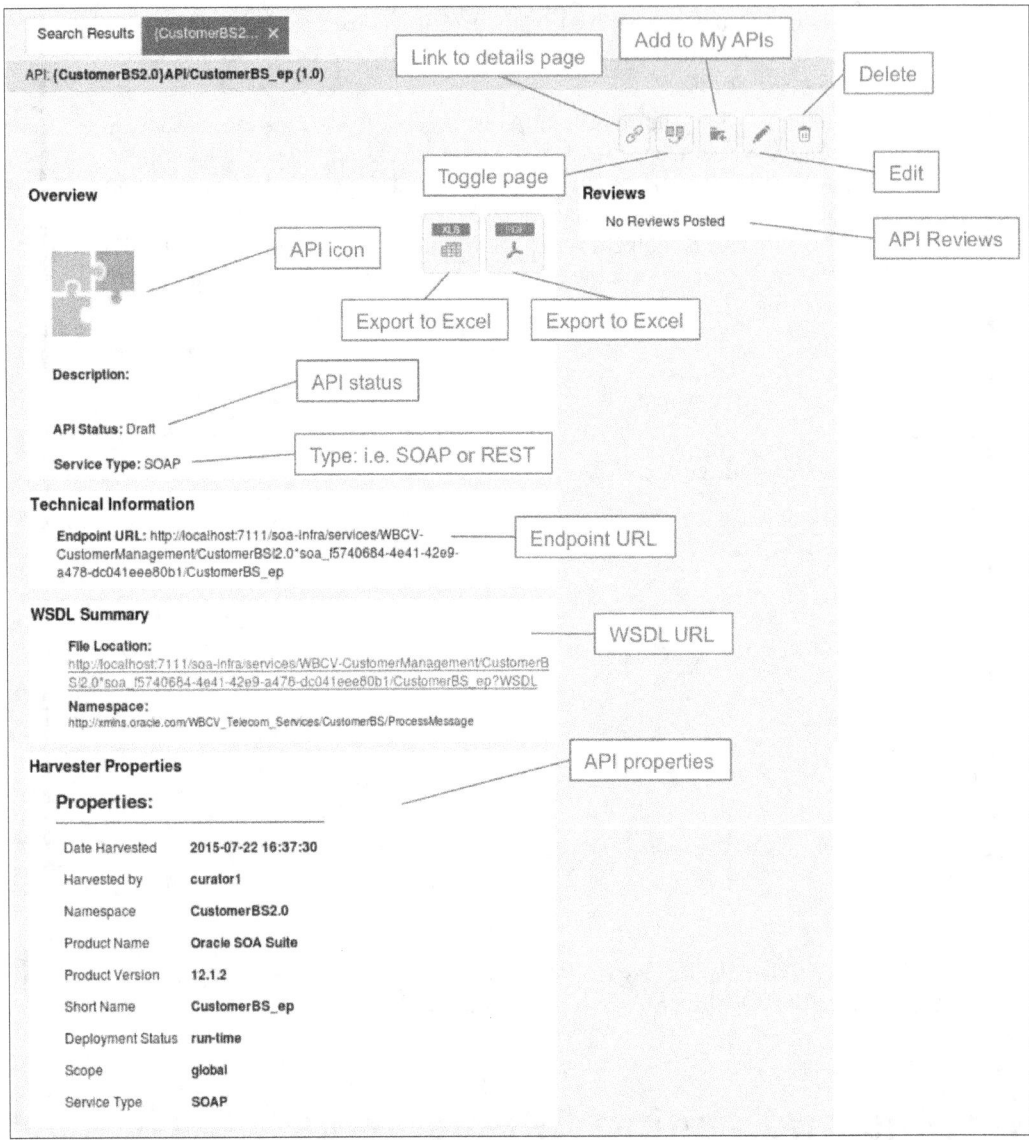

4. Click on the Edit button on the right-hand side of the page to edit the API.
5. Once the API editor page opens, edit the API metadata as indicated:
    - **Name**: This is the name of the API. This usually does not require changing but it could be updated to a more user-friendly name if needed.
    - **Version**: Update the version to be the same as the one suggested in the **Namespace** field as displayed when viewing the asset.
    - **Keywords**: Enter useful keywords that can help find the API.
    - **API Status**: Change the status to **Published** if the API has been harvested from the production system. This can easily be determined by looking at the endpoint URL in the viewer.
    - **Active Status**: Leave set to **Active** unless you wish to retire this API.
    - **Description**: This contains a meaningful description of the functionality of the API.
    - **Documentation URL**: Enter the URL that links to the API documentation. Documentation should describe and provide samples on how to use this API. Undocumented APIs are rarely used so it is important to ensure that documentation is available before publishing an API.

◦ **Icon**: If available, enter an icon that can help promote the API.

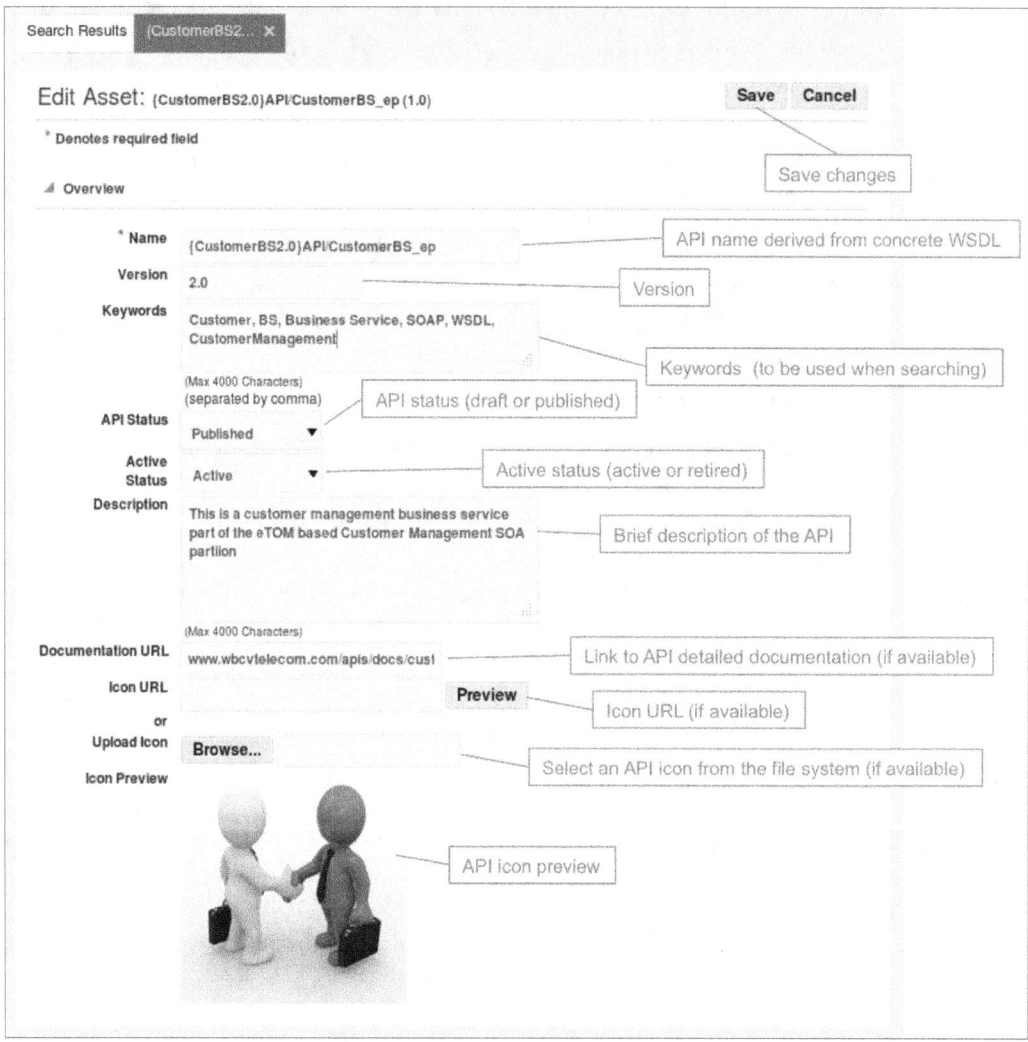

6. Once all metadata details have been entered, click on the **Save** button located at the top-right hand side of the page. This will take you back to the API viewer in the same tab.

7. Once all details have been verified, click on the API Catalog home page.

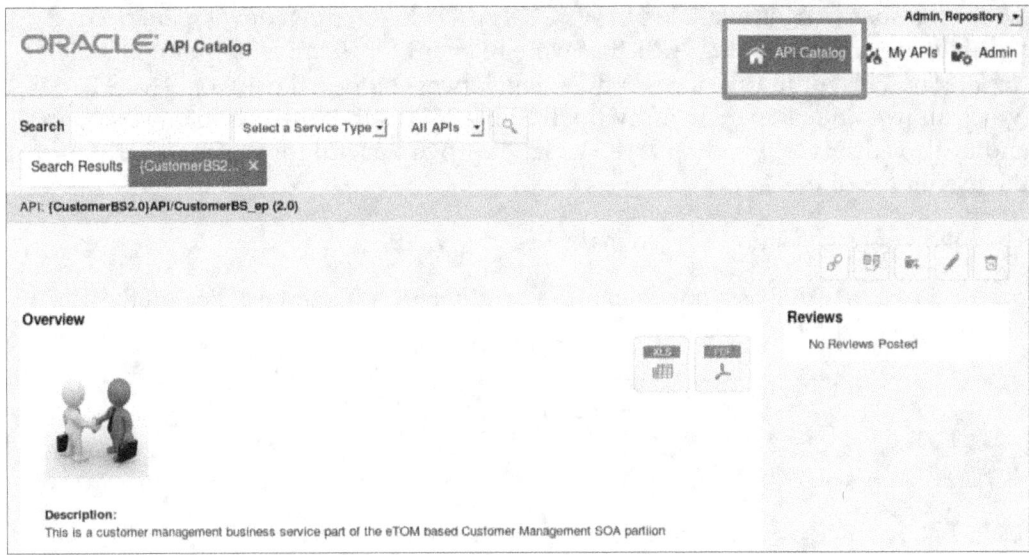

8. Notice how the recently published API now appears in the home page.

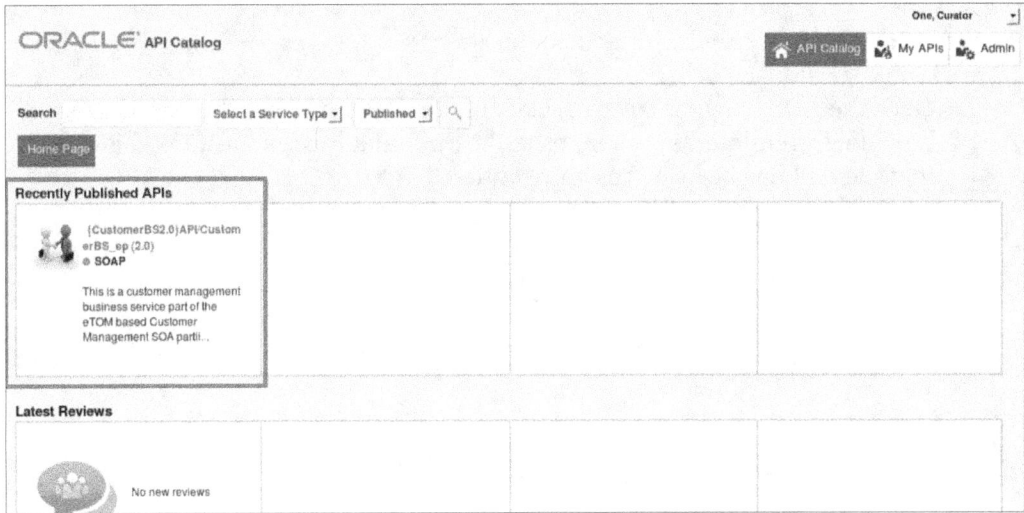

## My APIs and API rating

As the number of APIs available in WBCV's API catalog grew, developers needed the ability to shortlist or tag APIs that were relevant for them: either immediately or for later use. To fulfill this need, WBCV developers could make use of OAC My APIs, which allowed developers to individually collect APIs that they were interested in and to also add *reviews* and *ratings*. The latter proved useful for further insight into the usefulness of the APIs.

The following steps show how to make use of My APIs:

1. Login to OAC as a developer and conduct an API search. Click on the API of choice.

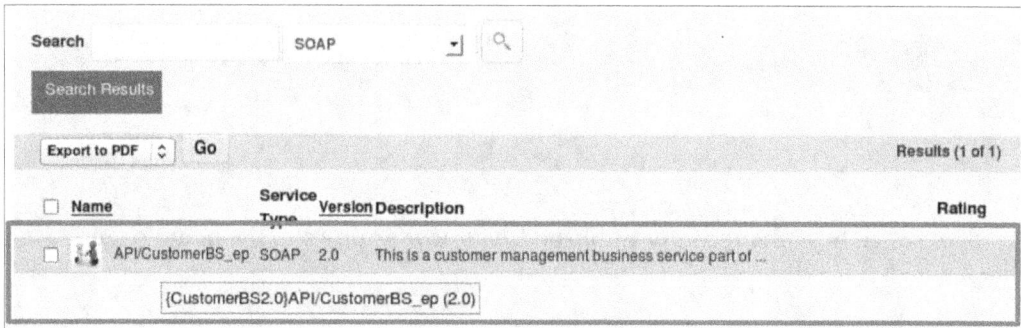

2. Once the API viewer tab opens, click on the Add to My APIs button. Notice how the icon immediate changes to the Submit a Review button. This means that the API has been successfully added.

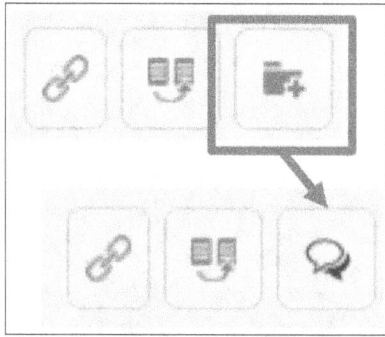

*Chapter 3*

3. Click on the Submit a Review button to enter a review and rate the API.

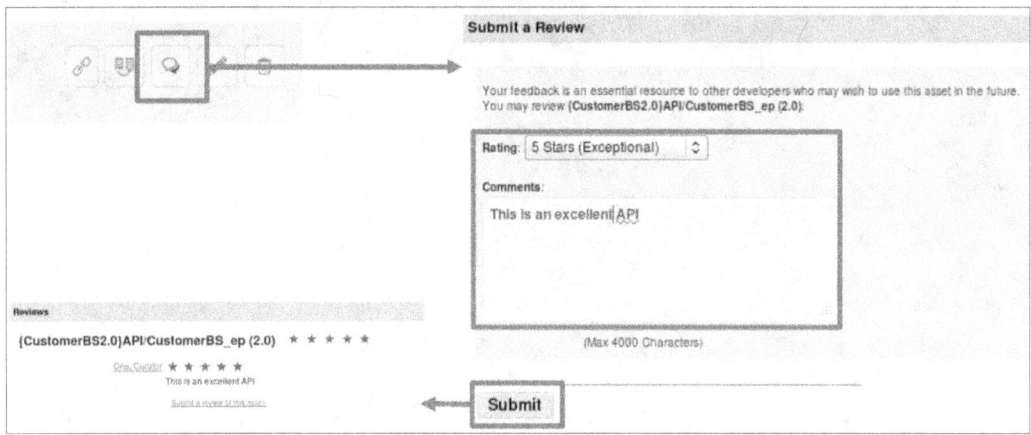

4. Click on the OAC Home button on the top-right hand side of the page. Notice now that the API is listed in the **Latest Reviews** section.

[ 105 ]

5. Click on the **My APIs** button on the top-right hand side of the page to see a full list of the APIs added. From this page it is also possible to add ratings and review and remove APIs from the list.

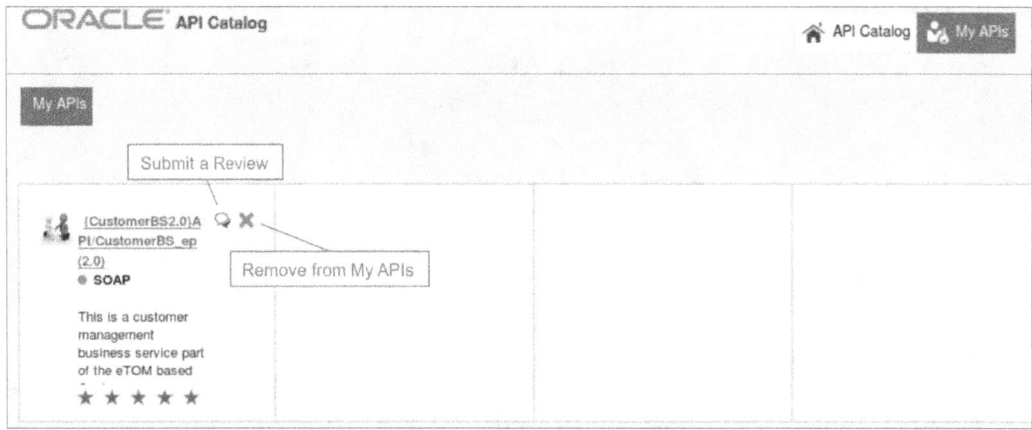

# Setting up and using the JDeveloper plug-in for OAC

As previously described in the *Discovering APIs* section, this plug-in was used by WBCV developers to discover and use APIs directly from JDeveloper. This feature proved very popular with service and API developers because it allowed them to find APIs without having to switch user interfaces and to directly add them into their OSB or SOA Suite projects.

The following sections explain how to install and use the plug-in.

## Installing the OER JDeveloper plug-in

First of all it is important to clarify that there isn't a specific plug-in in JDeveloper for OAC. The plug-in that is used is in fact the **Oracle Enterprise Repository** (**OER**) plug-in. As mentioned in earlier sections, the OER engine empowers the OAC functionality; this is why the OER JDeveloper plug-in is used for OAC as well.

Note that this plug-in does not come with JDeveloper out of the box and therefore needs to be installed as follows:

1. Login to `http://support.oracle.com` and then from the **Patches & Updates** tab search for patch `19721053`.

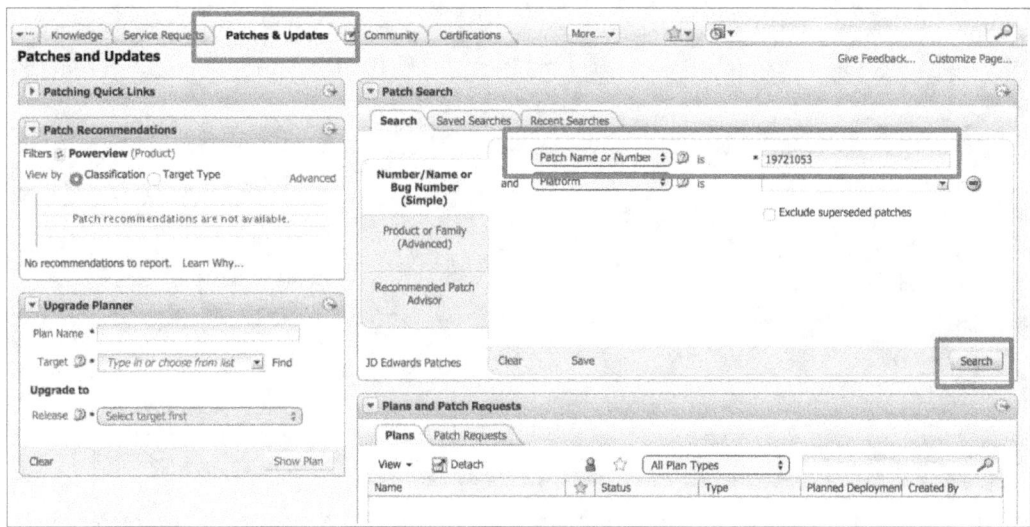

2. On the search results page, make sure that the right patch number was found and then click on the patch name as indicated.

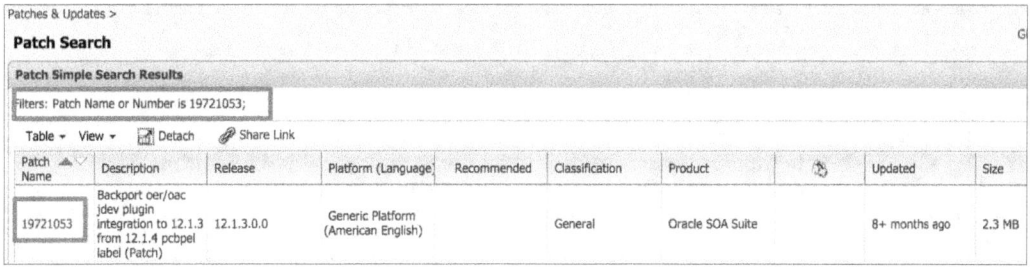

*Oracle API Catalog Implementation*

3. From the patch home page, click on download and when the popup window opens, click on `p19721053_121300_Generic.zip` to download the file.

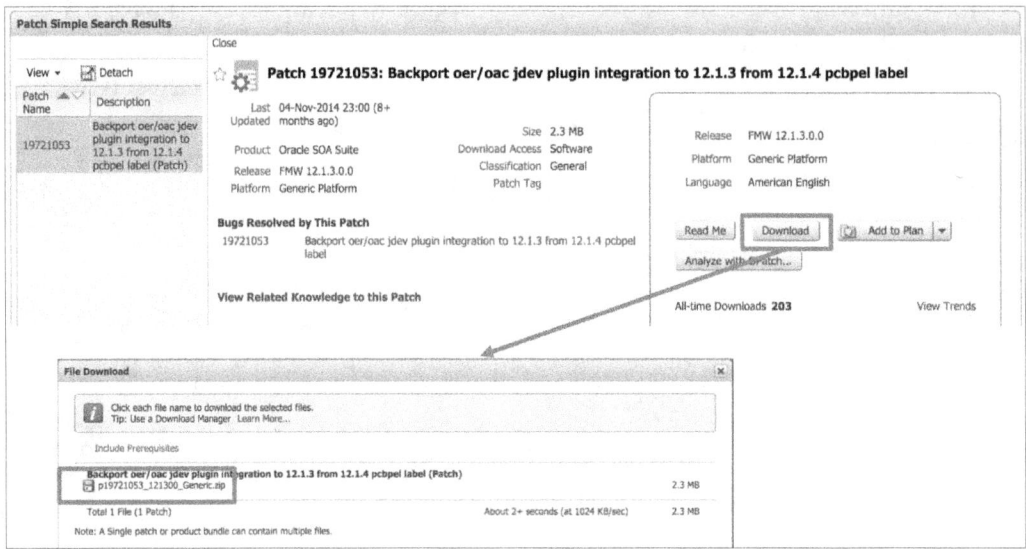

4. Open a command prompt and set the `ORACLE_HOME` environment variable to `<FMW_HOME>/soaquickstart` and then change directory to `<ORACLE_HOME>/OPatch`.

```
Luiss-MacBook-Pro:Downloads luisweir$ export ORACLE_HOME=/Users/luisweir/oracle/ofm1213/soaquickstart;
Luiss-MacBook-Pro:Downloads luisweir$ mv p19721053_121300_Generic.zip $ORACLE_HOME/OPatch/
Luiss-MacBook-Pro:Downloads luisweir$ cd $ORACLE_HOME/OPatch/
Luiss-MacBook-Pro:OPatch luisweir$ unzip -d PATCH_TOP p19721053_121300_Generic.zip
```

 The Oracle home usually is `<FMW_HOME>/soaquickstart`. Note that the fusion middleware home was set when installing JDeveloper *12c* SOA quickstart.

5. Copy the downloaded patch—`p19721053_121300_Generic.zip`—to this folder and unzip it into a folder named `PATCH_TOP`.

6. Change directory to `PATCH_TOP/19721053` and execute this command:

   `../../opatch apply`

```
Luiss-MacBook-Pro:19721053 luisweir$ ../../opatch apply
Oracle Interim Patch Installer version 13.2.0.0.0
Copyright (c) 2014, Oracle Corporation.  All rights reserved.


Oracle Home       : /Users/luisweir/oracle/ofm1213/soaquickstart
Central Inventory : /Users/luisweir/oracle/oraInventory
   from          : /Users/luisweir/oracle/ofm1213/soaquickstart/oraInst.loc
OPatch version    : 13.2.0.0.0
OUI version       : 13.2.0.0.0
Log file location : /Users/luisweir/oracle/ofm1213/soaquickstart/cfgtoollogs/opatch/19721053_Jul_27_2015_15_36_25/apply2015-07-27_15-36-18PM_1.log

OPatch detects the Middleware Home as "/Users/luisweir/oracle/ofm1213/soaquickstart"

Jul 27, 2015 3:36:25 PM oracle.sysman.oii.oiii.OiiiInstallAreaControl initAreaControl
INFO: Install area Control created with access level 0
Applying interim patch '19721053' to OH '/Users/luisweir/oracle/ofm1213/soaquickstart'
Verifying environment and performing prerequisite checks...
All checks passed.
Please shutdown Oracle instances running out of this ORACLE_HOME on the local system.
(Oracle Home = '/Users/luisweir/oracle/ofm1213/soaquickstart')

Is the local system ready for patching? [y|n]
y
User Responded with: Y
Backing up files...
Patching component oracle.soacommon.plugins, 12.1.3.0.0...

Patching component oracle.soacommon.plugins, 12.1.3.0.0...

Verifying the update...
Patch 19721053 successfully applied
Log file location: /Users/luisweir/oracle/ofm1213/soaquickstart/cfgtoollogs/opatch/19721053_Jul_27_2015_15_36_25/apply2015-07-27_15-36-18PM_1.log

OPatch succeeded.
```

7. When prompted enter `Y` and hit *Enter*.

# Oracle API Catalog Implementation

8. If the patch was successfully applied the output `OPatch succeeded` is displayed. Alternatively execute the command `../../opatch inventory` and verify that the patch is listed.

```
Luiss-MacBook-Pro:19721053 luisweir$ ../../opatch lsinventory
Oracle Interim Patch Installer version 13.2.0.0.0
Copyright (c) 2014, Oracle Corporation.  All rights reserved.


Oracle Home       : /Users/luisweir/oracle/ofm1213/soaquickstart
Central Inventory : /Users/luisweir/oracle/oraInventory
   from          : /Users/luisweir/oracle/ofm1213/soaquickstart/oraInst.loc
OPatch version    : 13.2.0.0.0
OUI version       : 13.2.0.0.0
Log file location : /Users/luisweir/oracle/ofm1213/soaquickstart/cfgtoollogs/opatch/opatch2015-07-27_15-41-42PM_1.log

OPatch detects the Middleware Home as "/Users/luisweir/oracle/ofm1213/soaquickstart"

Jul 27, 2015 3:41:49 PM oracle.sysman.oii.oiii.OiiiInstallAreaControl initAreaControl
INFO: Install area Control created with access level 0
Lsinventory Output file location : /Users/luisweir/oracle/ofm1213/soaquickstart/cfgtoollogs/opatch/lsinv/lsinventory2015-07-27_15-41-42PM.txt

--------------------------------------------------------------------------------
Interim patches (1) :

Patch  19721053     : applied on Mon Jul 27 15:37:23 BST 2015
Unique Patch ID:  18120653
Patch description:  "One-off"
   Created on 29 Oct 2014, 09:45:19 hrs PST8PDT
   Bugs fixed:
     19721053
```

## Using the OER JDeveloper plug-in with OAC

Once the plug-in is installed, it can be used within JDeveloper to find APIs published in OAC and to consume them directly. The example here shows how to consume a REST API using OSB *12c*:

1. Open JDeveloper *12c* and create a new OSB project.

2. Go to **File | New** and select the option **From Gallery**.

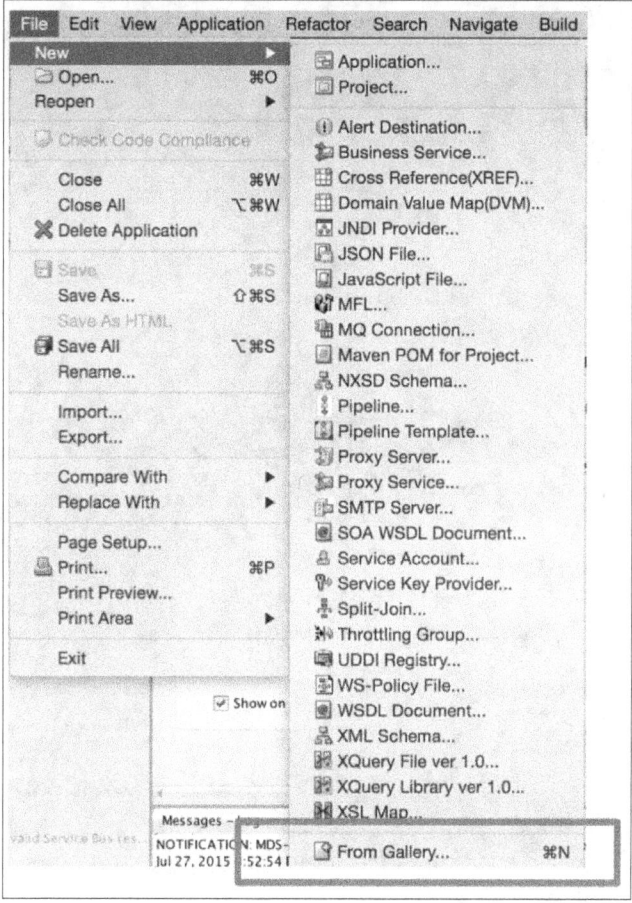

*Oracle API Catalog Implementation*

3. When the **New Gallery** window opens, select the category **Connections** and on the right-hand side scroll down until you find **Oracle Enterprise Repository Connections**. Select it and then click **OK**.

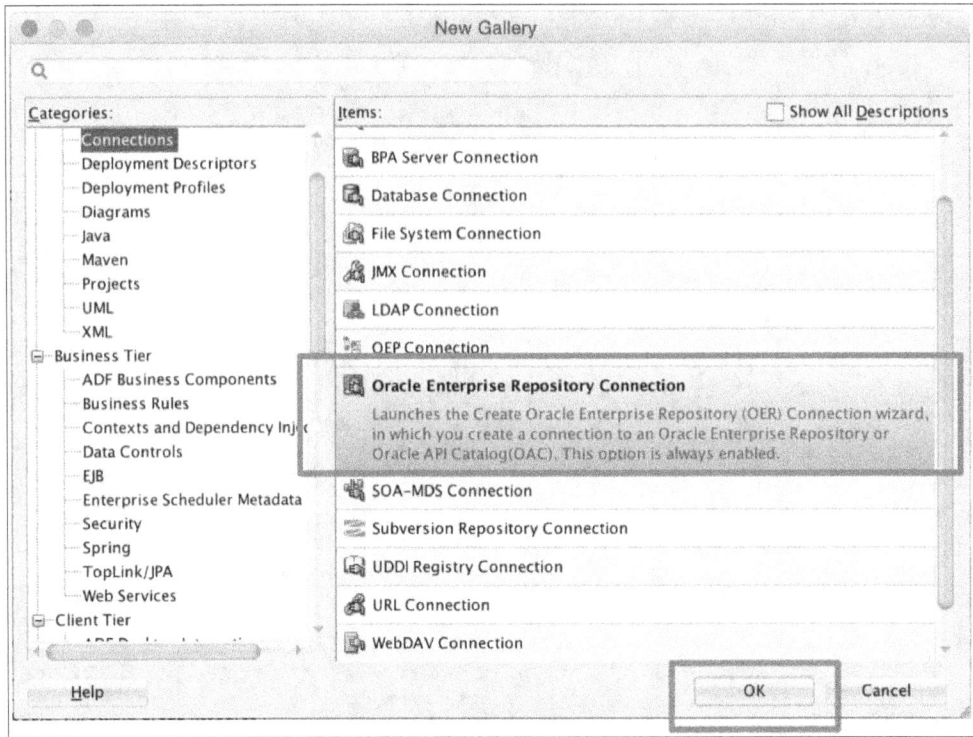

4. Select the option **Oracle API Catalog (OAC)** and then enter the OAC server connection details to connect to. Click on **Test Connection** and if successful click **OK**.

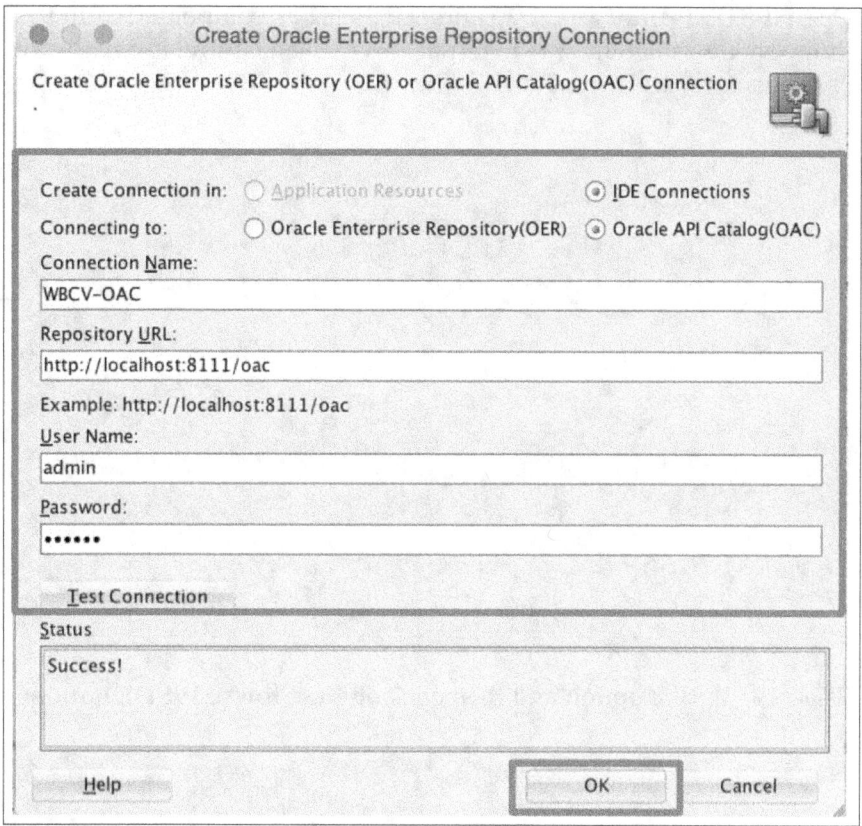

5. On the JDeveloper Resources tab (on the right-hand side pane), under **IDE-Connections**, check that the new OAC connection is now available. Expand it and ensure that it is possible to browse through the list of published APIs.

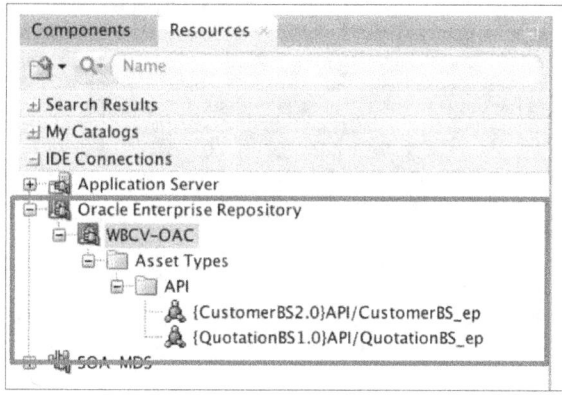

*Oracle API Catalog Implementation*

6. Open the OSB editor and drag and drop a HTTP component from the Components pallet into the External Services lane. Provide a name to the OSB business service and click on **Next**.

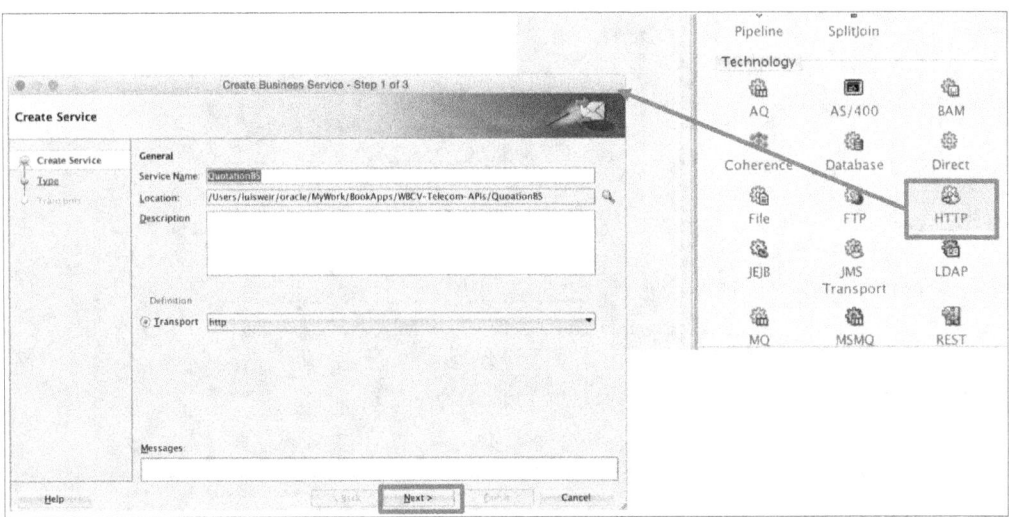

7. Select the **WSDL** option and then click on the **Browse WSDL** button.

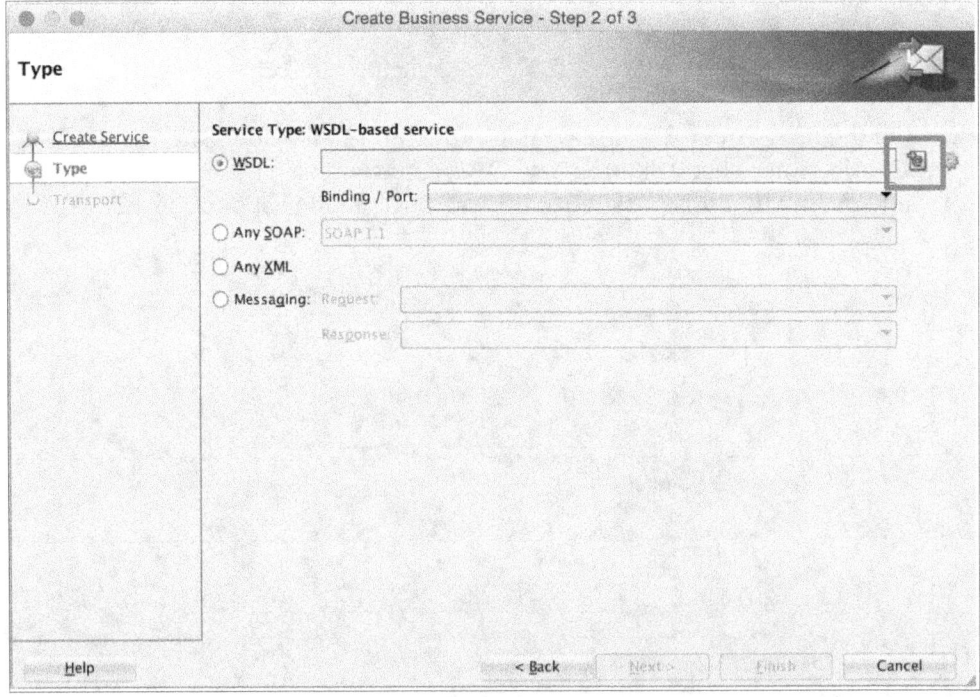

[ 114 ]

8. On the WSDL browser, select **Oracle Enterprise Repository** as the source. Expand the **Asset Types** menu tree and select an API. Then click **OK**.

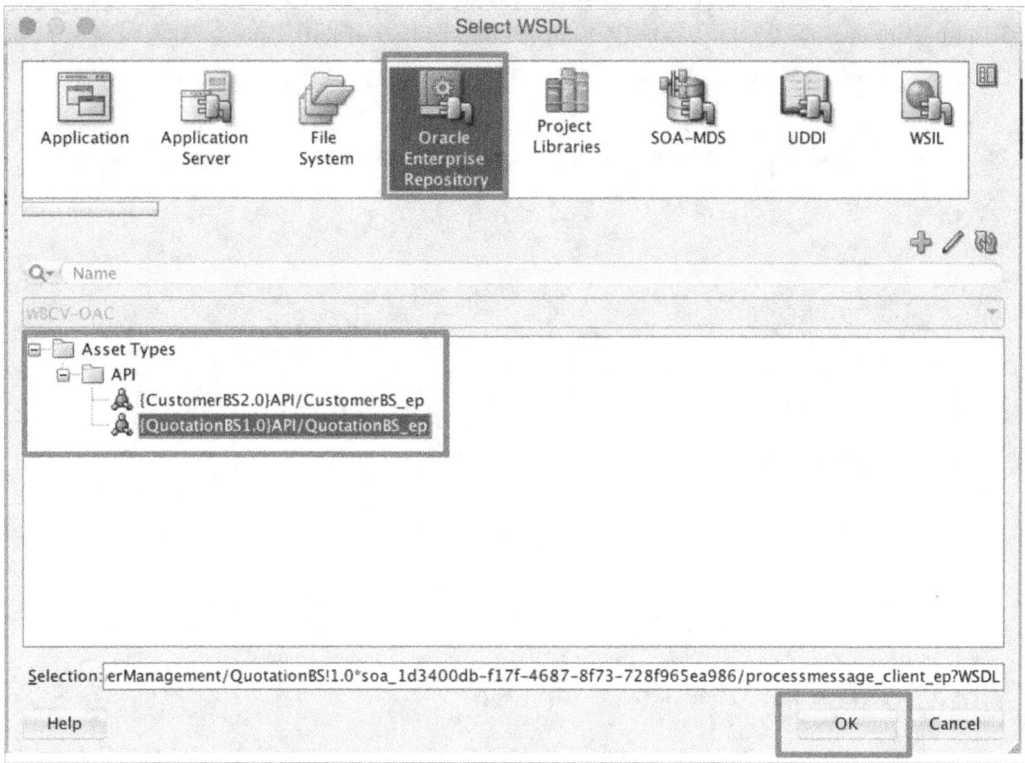

> At this point there is a known bug that might affect you.
>
> ```
> Error description: SEVERE: oracle.jdeveloper.oer.
> RepositoryException: Error [9,024]: User is not
> authorized to view projects.
> ```
>
>
>
> The error is related to access rights to OAC via this interface. To get around this issue, request your OAC administrator to grant you the OAC admin role only for a short period and repeat these steps. Once you have completed all these steps, the admin role can be revoked.
>
> This is a known bug and will be fixed in a subsequent patch (note that the patch might have already been released by the time this book is published).

*Oracle API Catalog Implementation*

9. Select the resources to import as indicated and click on **Finish**.

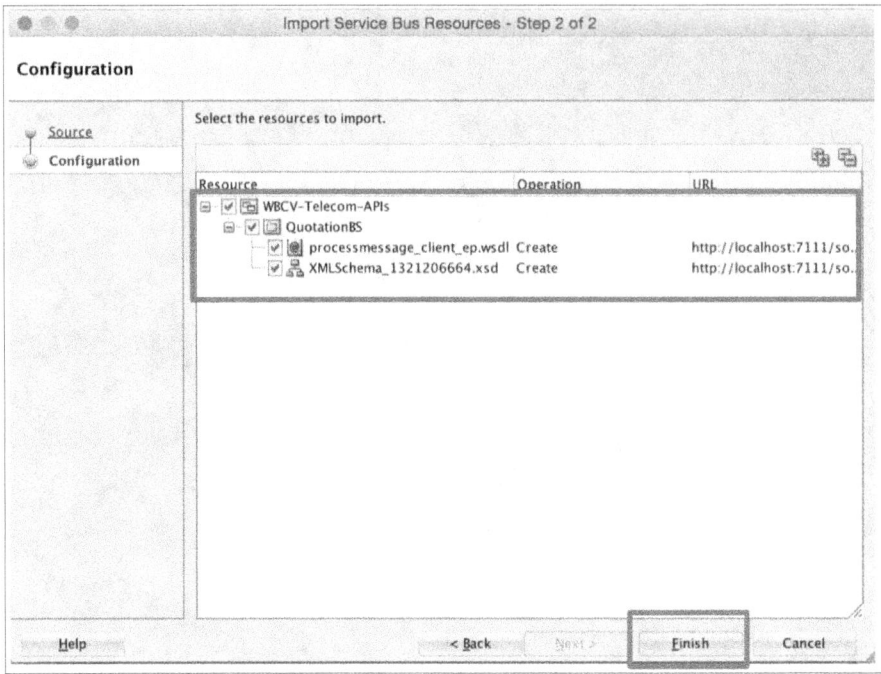

10. Once the window closes click on **Next**.

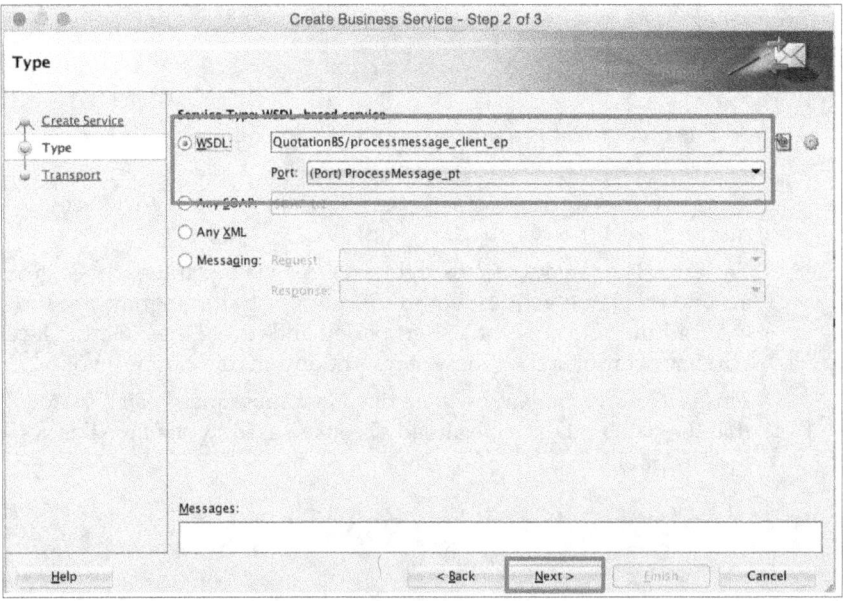

11. Click on **Finish**.

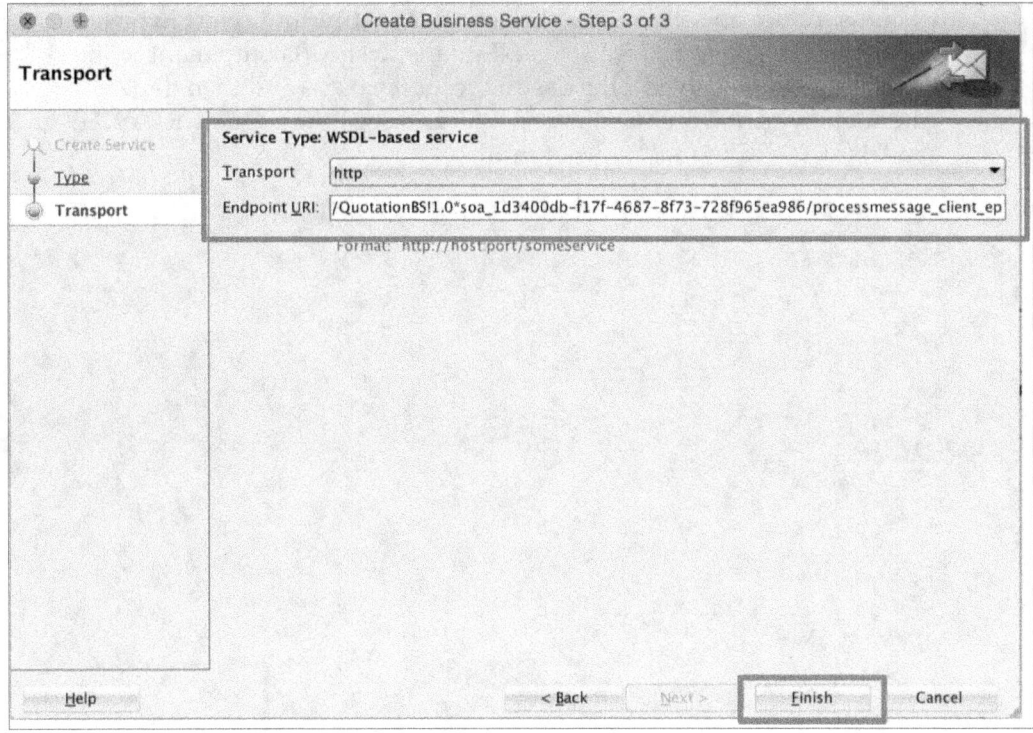

Oracle API Catalog Implementation

12. Next, drag and drop a **Pipeline** component and assign a WSDL (in this example the same WSDL imported was used). Connect the **Pipeline** to the business service and then right-click on the **Pipeline** and select **Expose as Rest** to autogenerate a REST API. Edit the Rest API component in the Proxy Services lane to add the desired resource paths and then deploy. After deployment, you may harvest OSB and see how the new REST API is available in OAC with a status of draft.

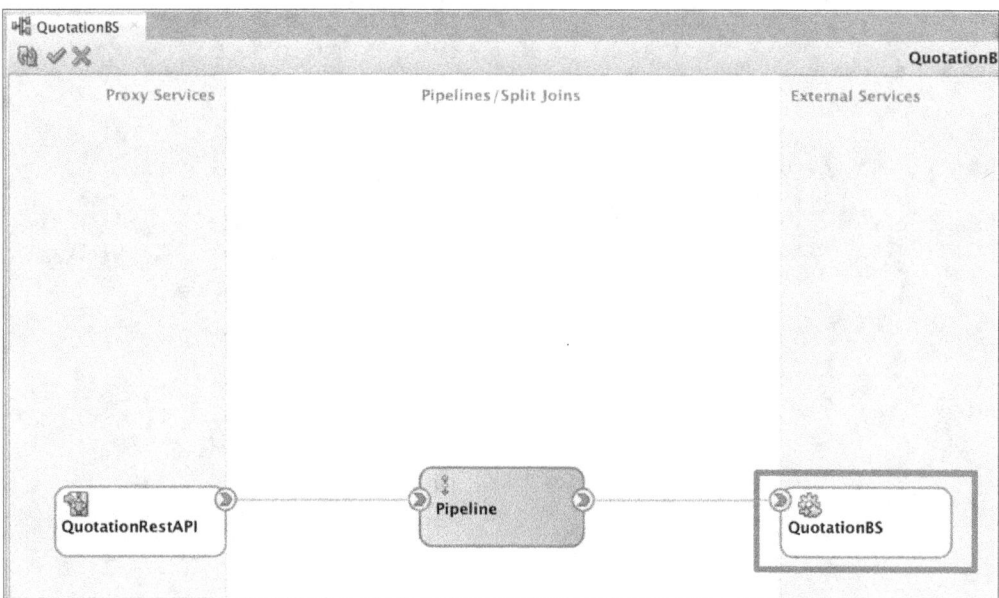

# Exporting and importing configuration and assets

The Import/Export utility can be very useful when creating regular backups of OAC and to restore OAC to a previous state if required. The utility can also be helpful when moving assets between OAC catalogs or between OAC and OER.

> Refer to section *4 Import Export Tool* of the *OFM Administration Guide* for further info in export/import combinations supported here:
>
> http://docs.oracle.com/middleware/1213/oac/administer-cat/impexp.htm#CATCG13220
>
> APIs can also be exported from the API search result page as described in the section *Using the OAC console to discover APIs*.

# Exporting assets using the Import/Export utility

The following steps describe how to do a full export of all OAC assets:

1. Login to OAC as an admin user and navigate to the **Admin** page. From there, click on the **Import Export** option on the left pane. Then on the right hand-side of the page, click on the Launch Import/Export client button. Once utility opens, in the **Select Target File** enter the name of the file to export (with the .zip extension) and click on **Next**.

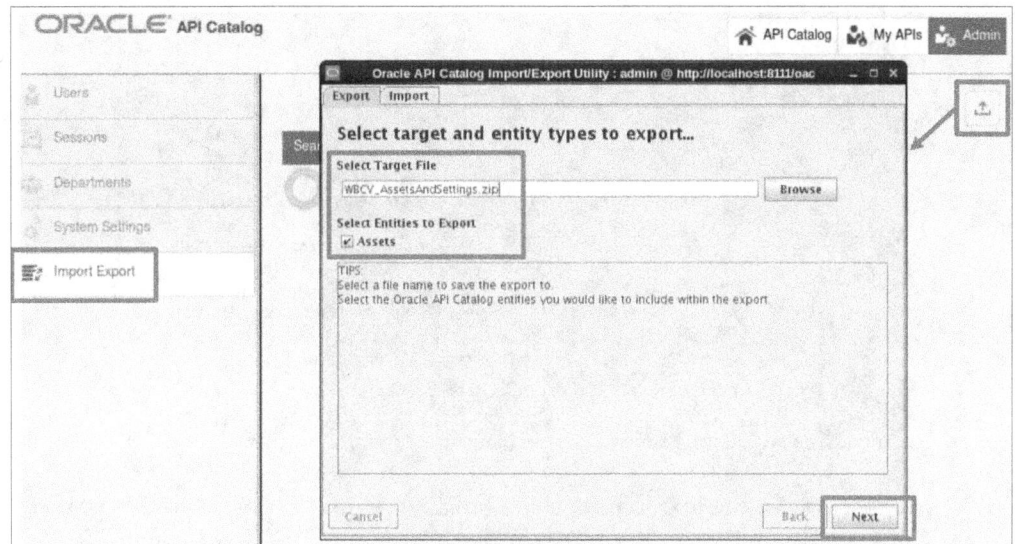

 For this to work properly Java Web Start has to be enabled to run in your browser. Refer to http://docs.oracle.com/middleware/1213/oac/administer-cat/basic.htm#CATCG13804 for further instructions on how to do this.

2. Click on **Search**. Once all assets available are displayed click on **All >>** to select all assets. Then click on **Next**.

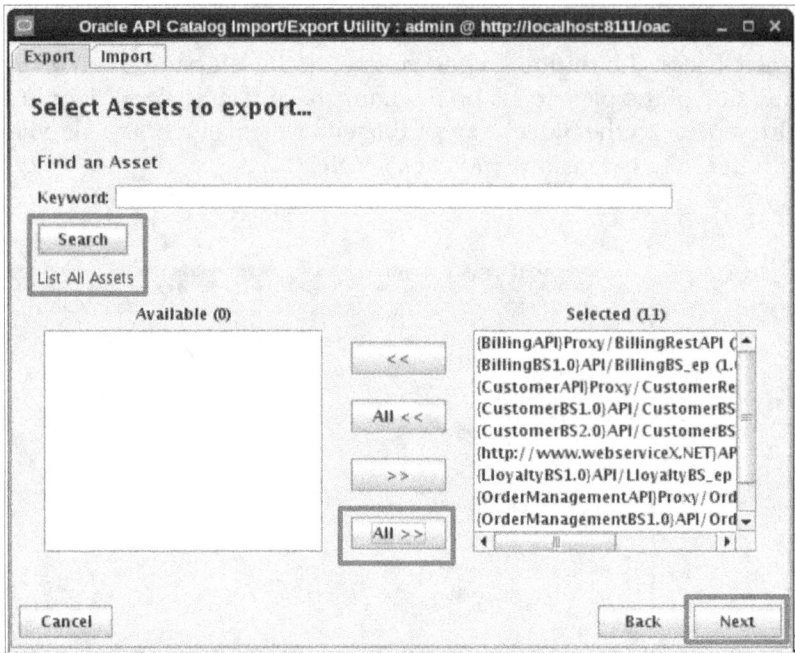

3. Make a note of the text in data stored in as the file is exported to this path. Click on **Finish**.

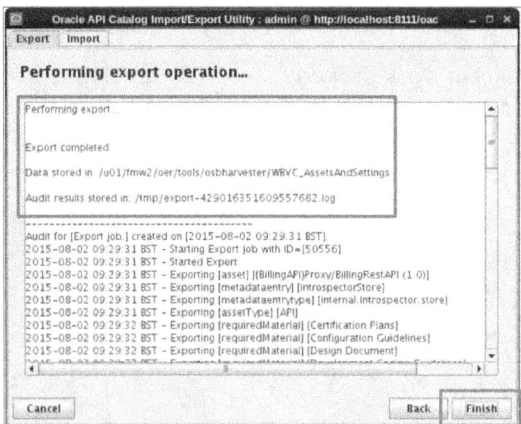

## Importing assets using the Import/Export utility

The following steps describe how to do import assets into OAC:

1. Open the Import/Export utility as explained previously.
2. Click on the **Import** tab, click on the **Browse** button to select a file to import and then click on **Next**.

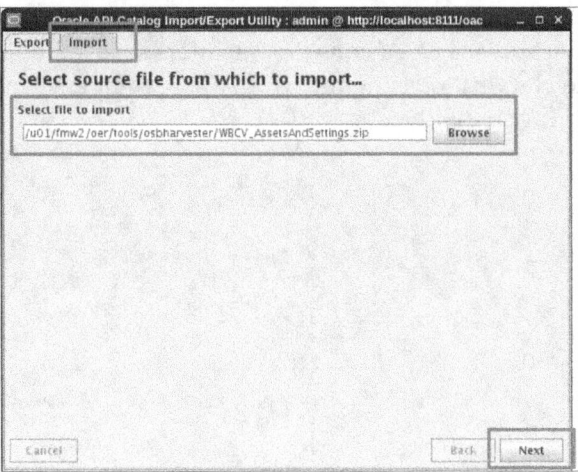

3. Ensure that the operation gets completed successfully and click on **Finish**.

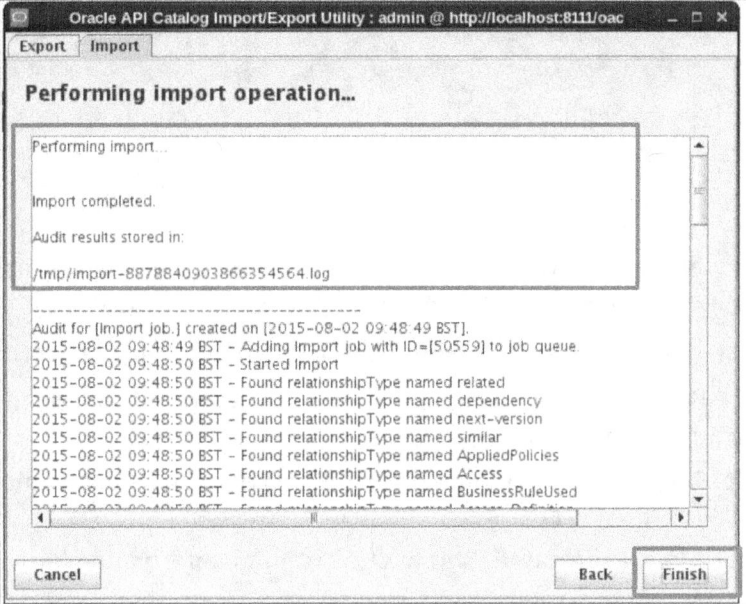

# The REX API

OAC is a fairly simple product offering just enough functionality to locate and consume services and APIs. However, there may be a need within an organization to extend its functionality to meet business requirements. So, how do we extend the capabilities of OAC?

The **Repository Extensibility Framework (REX)** is an RPC/Encoded SOAP API that essentially exposes all subsystems of OAC as web services. This is the same subsystem that underpins the OAC console, the interface used by the JDeveloper plug-in and also the Harvester. Using the REX API developers can extend OAC beyond its standard functionality.

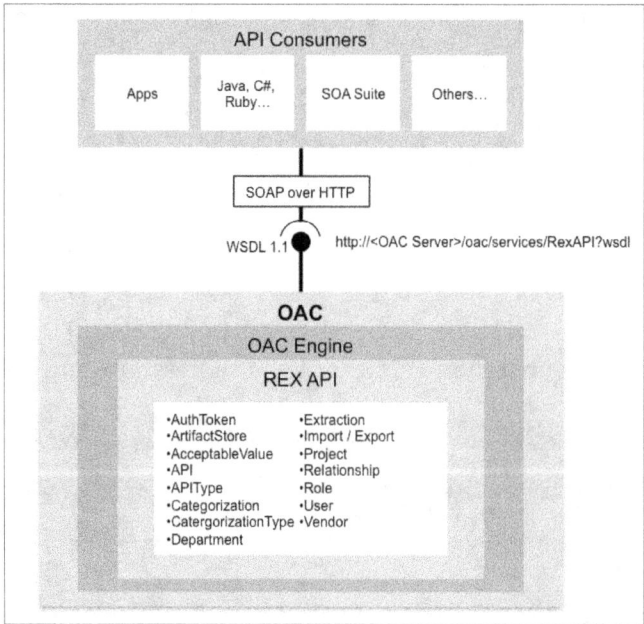

There are several use cases where extending OAC makes sense. In the case of WBCV, the following use cases were considered, some of which were actually implemented:

- Automatic harvesting of documentation (when bootstrapping OAC)
- Integration of OAC with a deployment framework and continuous integration solution; using the Ant Harvester and the REX API
- BPMN 2.0 process for automatic verification of metadata and automatic publishing of APIs after deployment to production
- Oracle API Manager (OAPIM) to OAC runtime information harvesting

Before considering implementing these or any other use case, it is critical to fully understand the REX API. The following example will explain how to make use of the REX API to support a simple scenario.

## Using the REX API to find and update an API

In the following example, we will make use of the REX API to achieve the following functionality:

- Invoke the `authTokenCreate` operation to obtain an authentication token. This is needed to perform any subsequent invocations
- Search APIs by invoking the `assetQuerySummary` operation and using similar criteria to that available in the OAC console home page
- Read the metadata of an API by invoking the `assetRead` operation
- And finally, update an API metadata by invoking the `assetUpdate` operation

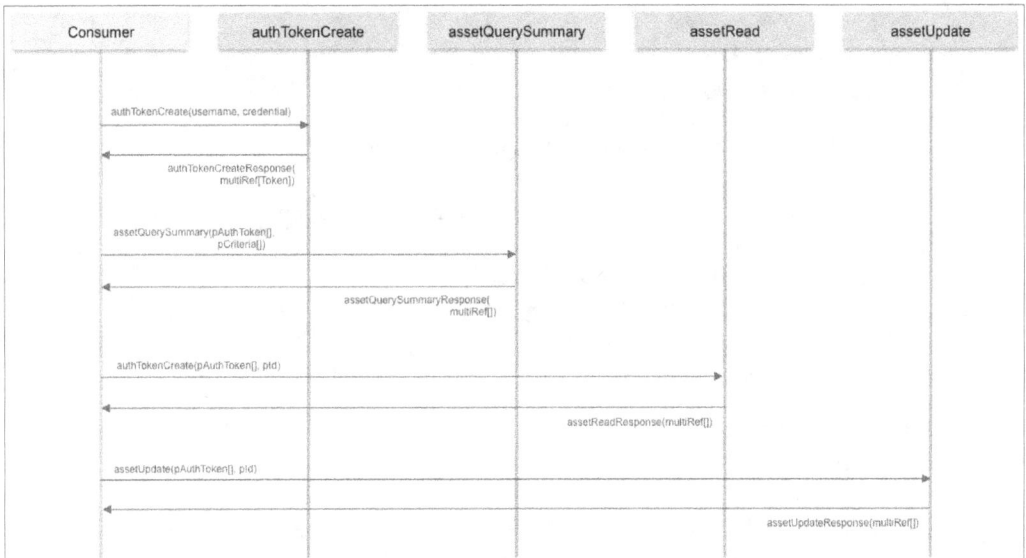

> Further details on using the REX API are available in section 5 *Using the Repository Extensibility Framework* of the *OFM Developer's Guide for OAC* here:
>
> https://docs.oracle.com/middleware/1213/oac/develop-cat/overview.htm#CATIN319

*Oracle API Catalog Implementation*

The following steps describe how to invoke the REX API in order to accomplish this use case:

1. Ensure that you obtain the REX API WSDL from the following URL:

    `http://<OAC Server>/oac/services/RexAPI?wsdl`

2. Using your language of choice (for example, Java) or simply using a web service client utility like SOAPUI, implement the following invocations.

3. Invoke the `authTokenCreate` operation with a similar payload as shown next. Enter the OAC's admin or curator credentials in the tags `username` and `credential`.

    ```
    <soapenv:Envelope
    xmlns:xsi="http://www.w3.org/2001/XMLSchema-instance"
    xmlns:xsd="http://www.w3.org/2001/XMLSchema"
    xmlns:soapenv="http://schemas.xmlsoap.org/soap/envelope/"
    xmlns:v300="http://service.openapi.registry.flashline.com/v300">
        <soapenv:Header/>
        <soapenv:Body>
            <v300:authTokenCreate
            soapenv:encodingStyle=
            "http://schemas.xmlsoap.org/soap/encoding/">
                <!-- OAC admin user credentails -->
                <userName xsi:type="xsd:string">admin</userName>
                <credential
                xsi:type="xsd:string">oracle</credential>
            </v300:authTokenCreate>
        </soapenv:Body>
    </soapenv:Envelope>
    ```

4. From the `authTokenCreateResponse` message take note of the token provided in the tag `token`.

    ```
    <soapenv:Envelope
    xmlns:soapenv="http://schemas.xmlsoap.org/soap/envelope/"
    xmlns:xsd="http://www.w3.org/2001/XMLSchema"
    xmlns:xsi="http://www.w3.org/2001/XMLSchema-instance">
        <soapenv:Body>
            <ns1:authTokenCreateResponse
            soapenv:encodingStyle="http://schemas.xmlsoap.org/
            soap/encoding/" xmlns:ns1="http://
            service.openapi.registry.flashline.com/v300">
                <authTokenCreateReturn href="#id0"/>
            </ns1:authTokenCreateResponse>
    ```

```xml
      <multiRef id="id0" soapenc:root="0"
      soapenv:encodingStyle="http://schemas.xmlsoap.org/
      soap/encoding/" xsi:type="ns2:AuthToken"
      xmlns:soapenc="http://schemas.xmlsoap.org/soap/
      encoding/" xmlns:ns2="http://entity.openapi.
      registry.flashline.com">
         <applicationToken xsi:type="xsd:string"
         xsi:nil="true"/>
         <token xsi:type="xsd:string">
         -5858423-14ed3a382db--7bca</token>
      </multiRef>
   </soapenv:Body>
</soapenv:Envelope>
```

5. Invoke the `assetQuerySummary` operation as described in the following example. Ensure that the token is entered in the `pAuthToken.token` tag. Enter each search criteria as a `searchTerms.searchTerm` tag.

```xml
<soapenv:Envelope
xmlns:xsi="http://www.w3.org/2001/XMLSchema-instance"
xmlns:xsd="http://www.w3.org/2001/XMLSchema"
xmlns:soapenv="http://schemas.xmlsoap.org/soap/envelope/"
xmlns:v300="http://service.openapi.registry.flashline.com/
v300" xmlns:soapenc="http://schemas.xmlsoap.org/soap/
encoding/">
   <soapenv:Header/>
   <soapenv:Body>
      <v300:assetQuerySummary
      soapenv:encodingStyle="http://schemas.xmlsoap.org/
      soap/encoding/">
         <!-- Authentication token received form invoking
         authTokenCreate -->
         <pAuthtoken xsi:type="ent:AuthToken"
         xmlns:ent="http://entity.openapi.registry.
         flashline.com">
            <applicationToken xsi:type="xsd:string"/>
            <token xsi:type="xsd:string">
            -5858423-14ed3a382db--7bca</token>
         </pAuthtoken>
         <!-- Search criteria -->
         <pCriteria xsi:type="quer:AssetCriteria"
         xmlns:quer="http://query.openapi.registry.
         flashline.com">
            <searchTerms xsi:type="v300:ArrayOf_tns3_
            SearchTerm" soapenc:arrayType="quer:
            SearchTerm[]">
```

# Oracle API Catalog Implementation

```xml
            <!-- Search based on name of API. Comment tag
            for no filter -->
            <searchTerm>
              <key xsi:type="xsd:string">name</key>
              <operator xsi:type="xsd:string">LIKE</operator>
              <value xsi:type="xsd:string">Customer</value>
                </searchTerm>
                <!-- true for retrieving only Published
                APIs, false for Draft APIs, comment tag
                for no filter -->
                <searchTerm>
            <key xsi:type="xsd:string">registered</key>
            <operator xsi:type="xsd:string">eq</operator>
            <value xsi:type="xsd:string">false</value>
                </searchTerm>
                <!-- SOAP or REST. Comment tag for
                no filter -->
                <searchTerm>
              <key xsi:type="xsd:string">/asset/
            custom-data/service-type</key>
              <operator xsi:type="xsd:string">eq</operator>
              <value xsi:type="xsd:string">SOAP</value>
                </searchTerm>
              </searchTerms>
            </pCriteria>
        </v300:assetQuerySummary>
    </soapenv:Body>
</soapenv:Envelope>
```

6. From `assetQuerySummaryResponse`, each API found will be contained in a tag called `multiRef`. By looking at the `multiRef.longName` and `multiRef.name` fields decide which API to use and take note of their `multiRef.ID`. Again ensure that the token is entered in the `pAuthToken.token` tag.

```xml
<soapenv:Envelope
xmlns:soapenv="http://schemas.xmlsoap.org/soap/envelope/"
xmlns:xsd="http://www.w3.org/2001/XMLSchema"
xmlns:xsi="http://www.w3.org/2001/XMLSchema-instance">
    <soapenv:Body>
        <ns1:assetQuerySummaryResponse
        soapenv:encodingStyle="http://schemas.xmlsoap.org/
        soap/encoding/" xmlns:ns1="http://service.openapi.
        registry.flashline.com/v300">
```

```
            <assetQuerySummaryReturn
            soapenc:arrayType="ns2:AssetSummary[1]"
            xsi:type="soapenc:Array"
            xmlns:ns2="http://entity.openapi.registry.
            flashline.com" xmlns:soapenc="http://
            schemas.xmlsoap.org/soap/encoding/">
                <assetQuerySummaryReturn href="#id0"/>
            </assetQuerySummaryReturn>
       </ns1:assetQuerySummaryResponse>
       <multiRef id="id0" soapenc:root="0"
       soapenv:encodingStyle="http://
       schemas.xmlsoap.org/soap/encoding/"
       xsi:type="ns3:AssetSummary" xmlns:soapenc="http://
       schemas.xmlsoap.org/soap/encoding/"
       xmlns:ns3="http://entity.openapi.registry
       .flashline.com">
            <ID xsi:type="xsd:long">50561</ID>
            <UUID xsi:type="xsd:string">
            c065ab34-3085-11e5-8356-4709e78df78c</UUID>
            <longName xsi:type="xsd:string">{
            CustomerBS1.0}API/CustomerBS_ep (1.0)</longName>
            <name xsi:type="xsd:string">{
            CustomerBS1.0}API/CustomerBS_ep</name>
            <typeID xsi:type="xsd:long">100</typeID>
            <version xsi:type="xsd:string">1.0</version>
       </multiRef>
   </soapenv:Body>
</soapenv:Envelope>
```

> Before updating an API you must obtain all the API metadata details. This is because the REX API expects all values to be passed during an update otherwise it will update these values with empty content.

7. In the `pId` tag enter the `multiRef.ID` instance obtained in the previous call. Also ensure that the token is entered in the `pAuthToken.token` tag:

```
<soapenv:Envelope
xmlns:xsi="http://www.w3.org/2001/XMLSchema-instance"
xmlns:xsd="http://www.w3.org/2001/XMLSchema"
xmlns:soapenv="http://schemas.xmlsoap.org/soap/envelope/"
xmlns:v300="http://service.openapi.registry.flashline.com/
v300">
    <soapenv:Header/>
```

## Oracle API Catalog Implementation

```
        <soapenv:Body>
           <v300:assetRead soapenv:encodingStyle=
           "http://schemas.xmlsoap.org/soap/encoding/">
              <!-- Authentication token received when invoking
              authTokenCreate -->
              <pAuthtoken xsi:type="ent:AuthToken"
              xmlns:ent="http://entity.openapi.registry.
              flashline.com">
                 <applicationT<multiRef id="id0" oken
                 xsi:type="xsd:string"/>
                 <token xsi:type="xsd:string">
                 -5858423-14ed3a382db--7bca</token>
              </pAuthtoken>
              <!-- Asset id received when invoking
              assetQuerySummary -->
              <pId xsi:type="xsd:long">50560</pId>
           </v300:assetRead>
        </soapenv:Body>
     </soapenv:Envelope>
```

8. In `assetReadResponse`, all asset details will be embedded in `multiRef` tags. The tag `multiRef id="id0"` contains the main API details that we are interested in. From this tag, make a note of the following tags as they will be needed when updating the asset: `customData`, `description`, `displayName`, `files`, `keywords`, `longName`, `name`, `typeID`, `updatedDate`, and `version`:

```
<soapenv:Envelope
xmlns:soapenv="http://schemas.xmlsoap.org/soap/envelope/"
xmlns:xsd="http://www.w3.org/2001/XMLSchema"
xmlns:xsi="http://www.w3.org/2001/XMLSchema-instance">
   <soapenv:Body>
      <ns1:assetReadResponse
      soapenv:encodingStyle="http://schemas.xmlsoap.org/
      soap/encoding/" xmlns:ns1="http://service.openapi.
      registry.flashline.com/v300">
         <assetReadReturn href="#id0"/>
      </ns1:assetReadResponse>
      <multiRef id="id0" soapenc:root="0"
      soapenv:encodingStyle="http://schemas.xmlsoap.org
      /soap/encoding/" xsi:type="ns2:Asset"
      xmlns:soapenc="http://schemas.xmlsoap.org/soap/
      encoding/" xmlns:ns2="http://entity.openapi.registry.
      flashline.com">
```

```xml
<ID xsi:type="xsd:long">50560</ID>
<SFIDInfos soapenc:arrayType="ns2:SFIDInfo[0]" xsi:type="soapenc:Array"/>
<UUID xsi:type="xsd:string">24796224-3828-11e5-b011-bb67ff3c9169</UUID>
<acceptedByEmail xsi:type="xsd:string">admin@example.com</acceptedByEmail>
<acceptedByID xsi:type="xsd:long">99</acceptedByID>
<acceptedByName xsi:type="xsd:string">Admin, Repository</acceptedByName>
<acceptedDate xsi:type="xsd:dateTime">2015-08-02T08:54:46.000Z</acceptedDate>
<activeStatus xsi:type="xsd:int">0</activeStatus>
<activeStatusBaseName xsi:type="xsd:string">Active</activeStatusBaseName>
<appliedComplianceTemplateProjectsIDs soapenc:arrayType="xsd:long[0]" xsi:type="soapenc:Array"/>
<artifactSFID xsi:type="ns2:SFIDInfo" xsi:nil="true"/>
<assigned xsi:type="xsd:boolean">false</assigned>
<assignedDate xsi:type="xsd:dateTime" xsi:nil="true"/>
<assignedToID xsi:type="xsd:long">0</assignedToID>
<assignedUsers soapenc:arrayType="ns2:AssignedUser[0]" xsi:type="soapenc:Array"/>
<categorizationTypes soapenc:arrayType="ns2:CategorizationType[11]" xsi:type="soapenc:Array">
   <categorizationTypes href="#id1"/>
   ......
   <categorizationTypes href="#id11"/>
</categorizationTypes>
<categorizations soapenc:arrayType="ns2:Categorization[0]" xsi:type="soapenc:Array"/>
<contacts soapenc:arrayType="ns2:Contact[0]" xsi:type="soapenc:Array"/>
<createdByEmail xsi:type="xsd:string">admin@example.com</createdByEmail>
<createdByID xsi:type="xsd:long">99</createdByID>
<createdByName xsi:type="xsd:string">Admin, Repository</createdByName>
<createdDate xsi:type="xsd:dateTime">2015-08-02T08:54:46.000Z</createdDate>
```

```xml
            <customAccessSettings soapenc:arrayType=
            "xsd:string[0]" xsi:type="soapenc:Array"/>
            <customData xsi:type="xsd:string">
<![CDATA[<custom-data>
 <uddi>
  <service-key>uddi:bea.com:servicebus:
  CustomerAPI:CustomerRestAPI</service-key>
 </uddi>
 <endpoint-uri>http://localhost:
 7111/CustomerAPI/CustomerRestAPI</endpoint-uri>
 <service-type>REST</service-type>
 <wadl-url>http://localhost:7111/sbresource?
 PROXY/CustomerAPI/CustomerRestAPI</wadl-url>
 <documentation>
  <document>
   <document-url>http://wbcvtelecom.com/sharepoint/
   APIs/CustomerAPI</document-url>
   <document-approved>true</document-approved>
  </document>
 </documentation>
</custom-data>]]>
            </customData>
            <deleted xsi:type="xsd:boolean">false</deleted>
            <description xsi:type="xsd:string">Customer
            management business service</description>
            <displayName xsi:type="xsd:string">{
            CustomerAPI}Proxy/CustomerRestAPI
            (1.0)</displayName>
            <extractable xsi:type="xsd:boolean">
            true</extractable>
            <files soapenc:arrayType="ns2:FileInfo[1]"
            xsi:type="soapenc:Array">
                <files href="#id12"/>
            </files>
            <fullAsset xsi:type="xsd:boolean">true</fullAsset>
            <inactive xsi:type="xsd:boolean">false</inactive>
            <keywords soapenc:arrayType="xsd:string[1]"
            xsi:type="soapenc:Array">
                <keywords xsi:type="xsd:string">Customer API
                REST WADL</keywords>
            </keywords>
            <loadedDate xsi:type="xsd:dateTime">
            2015-08-13T12:55:27.000Z</loadedDate>
```

```xml
<longName xsi:type="xsd:string">{
CustomerAPI}Proxy/CustomerRestAPI (1.0)</longName>
<name xsi:type="xsd:string">{
CustomerAPI}Proxy/CustomerRestAPI</name>
<notificationEmail xsi:type="xsd:string"/>
<notifyUpdatedRelationships xsi:type=
"xsd:boolean">false</notifyUpdatedRelationships>
<policyAssertionResults soapenc:arrayType=
"ns2:PolicyAssertionResult[0]"
xsi:type="soapenc:Array"/>
<policyAssertions soapenc:arrayType=
"ns2:PolicyAssertion[0]"
xsi:type="soapenc:Array"/>
<producingProjectsIDs soapenc:arrayType="xsd:
long[0]" xsi:type="soapenc:Array"/>
<quickSubmit xsi:type="xsd:boolean">false
</quickSubmit>
<registeredByEmail xsi:type="xsd:string">
admin@example.com</registeredByEmail>
<registeredByID xsi:type="xsd:long">
99</registeredByID>
<registeredByName xsi:type="xsd:string">Admin,
Repository</registeredByName>
<registeredDate xsi:type="xsd:dateTime">
2015-08-02T13:22:31.000Z</registeredDate>
<registrationStatus xsi:type="xsd:int"
>100</registrationStatus>
<registrationStatusBaseName xsi:type="xsd:string">
Registered</registrationStatusBaseName>
<registrationStatusRegistered xsi:type="xsd:
boolean">true</registrationStatusRegistered>
<registrationStatusRejected xsi:type="xsd:
boolean">false</registrationStatusRejected>
<registrationStatusSubmittedPendingReview
xsi:type="xsd:boolean">false</
registrationStatusSubmittedPendingReview>
<registrationStatusSubmittedUnderReview
xsi:type="xsd:boolean">false</
registrationStatusSubmittedUnderReview>
<registrationStatusUnsubmitted
xsi:type="xsd:boolean">false</
registrationStatusUnsubmitted>
<relationshipTypes soapenc:arrayType=
"ns2:RelationshipType[27]"
xsi:type="soapenc:Array">
```

*Oracle API Catalog Implementation*

```xml
            <relationshipTypes href="#id13"/>
...
            <relationshipTypes href="#id39"/>
</relationshipTypes>
<retired xsi:type="xsd:boolean">false</retired>
<submissionFiles soapenc:arrayType=
"ns2:SubmissionFileInfo[1]"
xsi:type="soapenc:Array">
            <submissionFiles href="#id40"/>
</submissionFiles>
<submittedByEmail xsi:type="xsd:string">
admin@example.com</submittedByEmail>
<submittedByID xsi:type="xsd:long">99
</submittedByID>
<submittedByName xsi:type="xsd:string">
Admin, Repository</submittedByName>
<submittedDate xsi:type="xsd:dateTime">
2015-08-02T08:54:46.000Z</submittedDate>
<subscribers soapenc:arrayType=
"ns2:RegistryUser[0]" xsi:type="soapenc:Array"/>
<typeID xsi:type="xsd:long">100</typeID>
<typeIcon xsi:type="xsd:string">../../
images/tree/enterprise/assets/component.gif
</typeIcon>
<typeName xsi:type="xsd:string">API</typeName>
<uniqueElement xsi:type="ns2:UniqueElement"
xsi:nil="true"/>
<updatedDate xsi:type="xsd:dateTime">
2015-08-13T12:55:27.000Z</updatedDate>
<vendorID xsi:type="xsd:long">0</vendorID>
<vendorName xsi:type="xsd:string"/>
<version xsi:type="xsd:string">1.0</version>
<visible xsi:type="xsd:boolean">true</visible>
</multiRef>
<multiRef id="id7" soapenc:root="0"
soapenv:encodingStyle="http://schemas.xmlsoap.org/
soap/encoding/" xsi:type="ns3:CategorizationType"
xmlns:ns3="http://entity.openapi.registry.
flashline.com" xmlns:soapenc="http://schemas.
xmlsoap.org/soap/encoding/">
     <ID xsi:type="xsd:long">112</ID>
     <assetAssignable xsi:type="xsd:boolean">true
</assetAssignable>
     <displayName xsi:type="xsd:string">
AssetLifecycleStage</displayName>
```

```xml
      <displayPlural xsi:type="xsd:string">Asset
      Lifecycle Stages</displayPlural>
      <displaySingular xsi:type="xsd:string">
      Asset Lifecycle Stage</displaySingular>
      <exclusiveAssign xsi:type="xsd:boolean">true
      </exclusiveAssign>
      <externalIDs soapenc:arrayType=
      "xsd:string[0]" xsi:type="soapenc:Array"/>
      <name xsi:type="xsd:string">AssetLifecycleStage
      </name>
      <projectAssignable xsi:type="xsd:boolean">false
      </projectAssignable>
      <updatedDate xsi:type="xsd:dateTime"
      xsi:nil="true"/>
    </multiRef>
    <multiRef id="id..
   ...
    </multiRef>
  </soapenv:Body>
</soapenv:Envelope>
```

9. Construct an `assetUpdate` invocation with the details previously obtained. At this point it is also possible to override the existing values with new ones. In this example, we will update the tag description with HTML text providing useful API runtime information; by default this is not currently an option that is available. The field `updateDate` will also be updated to ensure that we have a record of when the update took place.

```xml
<soapenv:Envelope
xmlns:xsi="http://www.w3.org/2001/XMLSchema-instance"
xmlns:xsd="http://www.w3.org/2001/XMLSchema"
xmlns:soapenv="http://schemas.xmlsoap.org/soap/envelope/"
xmlns:v300="http://service.openapi.registry.flashline.com/
v300" xmlns:soapenc="http://schemas.xmlsoap.org/soap
/encoding/">
  <soapenv:Header/>
  <soapenv:Body>
    <v300:assetUpdate soapenv:encodingStyle="http://
    schemas.xmlsoap.org/soap/encoding/">
      <!-- Authentication token received
      when invoking authTokenCreate -->
      <pAuthtoken xsi:type="ent:AuthToken" xmlns:
      ent="http://entity.openapi.registry.
      flashline.com">
        <applicationToken xsi:type="xsd:string"/>
```

```xml
            <token xsi:type="xsd:string">
            -5858423-14ed3a382db--7c8e</token>
        </pAuthtoken>
        <pAsset xsi:type="ent:Asset" xmlns:ent=
        "http://entity.openapi.registry.flashline.com">
            <!-- Asset id received when invoking
            assetQuerySummary -->
            <ID xsi:type="xsd:long">50560</ID>
            <!-- CustomData as received when invoking
            assetQuerySummary or updated one -->
            <customData xsi:type="xsd:string">
                <![CDATA[<custom-data>
        <uddi>
        <service-key>uddi:bea.com:servicebus:
        CustomerAPI:CustomerRestAPI</service-key>
        </uddi>
        <endpoint-uri>http://localhost:7111/CustomerAPI/
        CustomerRestAPI</endpoint-uri>
        <service-type>REST</service-type>
        <wadl-url>http://localhost:7111/sbresource?PROXY
        /CustomerAPI/CustomerRestAPI</wadl-url>
        <documentation>
        <document>
            <document-url>http://wbcvtelecom.com/
            sharepoint/APIs/CustomerAPI</document-url>
            <document-approved>true</document-approved>
        </document>
        </documentation>
        </custom-data>]]>
        </customData>
        <!-- Description as received when invoking
        assetQuerySummary or updated one -->
            <description xsi:type="xsd:string">
            <![CDATA[
        <p><strong>This asset was edited using the REX
        API</strong></p>
        <span style='font-size:12';
        class='bold'>Runtime Metadata</span>
<p>Managed by API Manager? <strong>Yes</strong></p>
        <p>Number of successful calls: <strong>1566</strong></p>
        <p>Number of failed calls:
        <strong>40</strong></p>
        ]]>
        </description>
```

```xml
            <!-- DisplayName as received when invoking
            assetQuerySummary or updated one -->
            <displayName xsi:type="xsd:string">{
            CustomerAPI}Proxy/CustomerRestAPI
            (1.0)</displayName>
            <!-- FileInfo as received when invoking
            assetQuerySummary -->
            <files soapenc:arrayType=
            "ns2:FileInfo[1]" xsi:type="soapenc:Array">
                <FileInfo>
        <ID xsi:type="xsd:long">50102</ID>
<URI xsi:type="xsd:string">rep://UPLOAD/50560
/icon/LWPic.jpg</URI>
        <description xsi:type="xsd:string"/>
        <displayName xsi:type="xsd:string">icon</displayName>
        <downloadURI xsi:type="xsd:string">http://
        soa-training.oracle.com:8111/oac/custom/upload
        /50560/icon/LWPic.jpg</downloadURI>
        <fileStorage xsi:type="xsd:string"/>
        <fileType xsi:type="ns30:FileType" xsi:nil="true"/>
        <fileTypeID xsi:type="xsd:string"/>
        <name xsi:type="xsd:string">icon</name>
        <relativeUri xsi:type="xsd:string"/>
        <securitySettings soapenc:arrayType="xsd:string[0]"
        xsi:type="soapenc:Array"/>
        <updatedDate xsi:type="xsd:dateTime" xsi:nil="true"/>
                </FileInfo>
            </files>
            <!-- Keywords as received when invoking
            assetQuerySummary or updated one-->
            <keywords soapenc:arrayType="xsd:string[1]"
            xsi:type="soapenc:Array">
                <keywords xsi:type="xsd:string">
                Customer API REST WADL</keywords>
            </keywords>
            <!-- LongName as received when invoking
            assetQuerySummary or updated one-->
            <longName xsi:type="xsd:string">{
            CustomerAPI}Proxy/CustomerRestAPI
            (1.0)</longName>
            <!-- Name as received when invoking
            assetQuerySummary or updated one-->
            <name xsi:type="xsd:string">{
            CustomerAPI}Proxy/CustomerRestAPI</name>
```

## Oracle API Catalog Implementation

```xml
                <!-- TypeID as received when invoking
                assetQuerySummary or updated one-->
                <typeID xsi:type="xsd:long">100</typeID>
                <!-- New updated time when service
                invocation takes place -->
                <updatedDate xsi:type="xsd:dateTime">
                2015-08-02T13:35:36.000Z</updatedDate>
                <!-- Version as received when invoking
                assetQuerySummary or updated one-->
                <version xsi:type="xsd:string">1.0</version>
            </pAsset>
        </v300:assetUpdate>
    </soapenv:Body>
</soapenv:Envelope>
```

10. The `assetUpdateResponse` will include the entire API metadata again. Verify that all updates took place successfully.

```xml
<soapenv:Envelope
xmlns:soapenv="http://schemas.xmlsoap.org/soap/envelope/"
xmlns:xsd="http://www.w3.org/2001/XMLSchema"
xmlns:xsi="http://www.w3.org/2001/XMLSchema-instance">
    <soapenv:Body>
        <ns1:assetUpdateResponse
        soapenv:encodingStyle="http://schemas.xmlsoap.org/
        soap/encoding/" xmlns:ns1="http://service.openapi.
        registry.flashline.com/v300">
            <assetUpdateReturn href="#id0"/>
        </ns1:assetUpdateResponse>
        <multiRef id="id0" soapenc:root="0"
        soapenv:encodingStyle="http://schemas.
        xmlsoap.org/soap/encoding/" xsi:type="ns2:Asset"
        xmlns:soapenc="http://schemas.xmlsoap.org/soap/
        encoding/" xmlns:ns2="http://entity.openapi.registry.
        flashline.com">
            <ID xsi:type="xsd:long">50560</ID>
            <SFIDInfos soapenc:arrayType="ns2:SFIDInfo[0]"
            xsi:type="soapenc:Array"/>
            <UUID xsi:type="xsd:string">
            24796224-3828-11e5-b011-bb67ff3c9169</UUID>
...
    </multiRef>
        <multiRef id="id..
...
        </multiRef>
    </soapenv:Body>
```

# Summary

The chapter started by providing a full architectural overview of the OAC. It explained the different layers that build up the product architecture and how these relate to one another. It further described the OAC user interface, the roles supported by the product and concepts such as organizational roles, application roles, and departments.

The chapter continued by detailing a realistic use case based on WBCV's API Management implementation journey. It explained the challenges faced by WBCV, such as lack of API visibility which led to little or no service reuse, and described how OAC was implemented in order to resolve these issues.

In subsequent sections we described how to bootstrap OAC by firstly identifying key sources of available APIs and then how to capture these to create an inventory of API sources. We described how to use the Harvester command line utility to harvest services from Oracle SOA Suite *12c* and *Oracle Service Bus* (*OSB*) *12c* and also how to implement the Ant Harvester as part of continuous harvesting during the software development lifecycle process.

We further explained in detail how to use the OAC user interface to search and edit APIs, administer OAC, and also how to add APIs to My APIs page. We saw how to set up the JDeveloper *12c* OER plug-in and how developers can use it to discover and consume APIs directly from the JDeveloper.

In the final sections, the Import/Export utility was used to export and import asset data and we explained when and how to extend OAC by making use of the REX API. To this end, a few samples were provided on how to consume different operations in order to authenticate, search, read, and update an API.

# 4
# Oracle API Manager Implementation Overview

This chapter will introduce **Oracle API Manager**, which is a key product in Oracle's API Management solution. This product is brand new (released in Q1 2015) and was first released as part of the *12c* stack. The concerns addressed by this product, such as the API portal, community management and API keys management are fundamental to an organization's API strategy.

The following sections will detail the product's capabilities and explain how it is intended to fit into established Service Oriented Architecture. We will extend the use case presented in previous chapters to demonstrate API Manager's functionality.

After reading this chapter, the reader should be able to:

- Understand the product's architecture and its capabilities
- Explain Oracle API Manager's role and relevance for an organization's API strategy including how it can be implemented to address real life requirements
- Manage APIs through their lifecycle using Oracle API Manager and understand the different participants and activities involved in the process
- Put into practice the different features of the product such as promoting OSB proxy services as APIs, developer onboarding through the portal, API key generation, and runtime monitoring

## Understanding API Management

As a likely result of implementing an **ASG** strategy, applications will increasingly be encouraged and even required to both consume and expose **APIs**. These APIs can be developed by internal or external entities, usually providing access to **enterprise information systems** in the organization's backend.

In this regard, it is also normal that the quantity of available APIs increases year on year. This growth rate will hardly be deterministic, as both strategic projects and tactical operations may cause API production to spike across particular time periods.

The following graph depicts a clear example of how an opportunistic organization can go from having just a few published APIs to over a hundred of them as a result of controlled strategic initiatives as well as tactical responses to unpredictable market conditions and emerging business requirements.

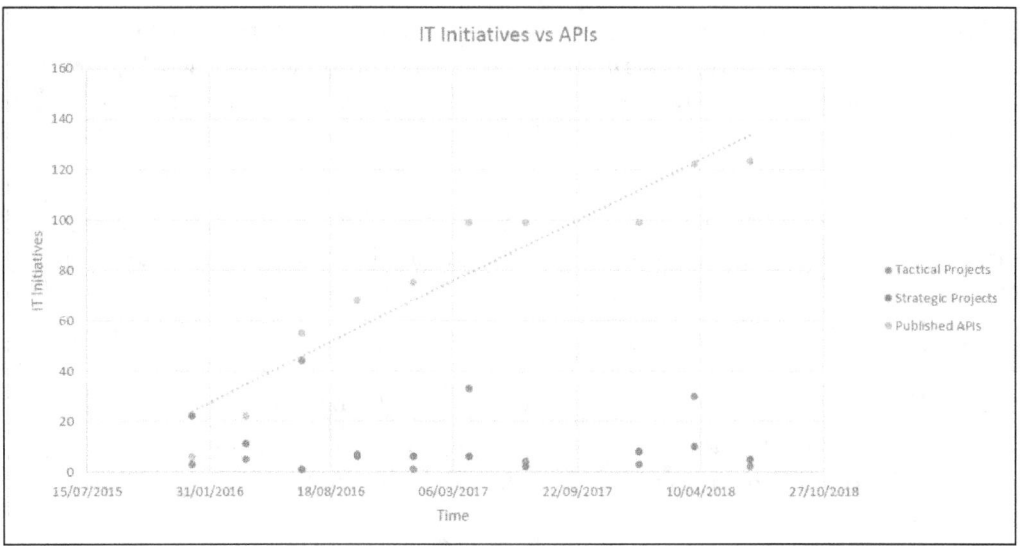

This, in addition to the increasing business need to become digital, implies that even more APIs are created in support of a business multi-channel strategy (mobile applications, cloud integration, IoT, and many others).

As the trend continues, the manageability and visibility of these APIs becomes paramount to the organization, and the need for API Management becomes obvious.

Let's take a look at the following paragraph, which can be considered as a standard definition for the latter:

> API Management is the process of publishing, promoting, and overseeing APIs in a secure, scalable environment. It also facilitates community management and includes the creation of end user support resources that define and document the API.

As stated in *Chapter 1, Application Services Governance*, API Management and SOA Governance converge into what Gartner refers to as ASG. In this regard, Oracle API Manager aims to combine the best of both worlds and deliver a cohesive and comprehensive solution built on top of a strong SOA foundation but also addresses the main API Management requirements.

For practical purposes, API Management is the discipline that governs APIs throughout the following lifecycle stages:

- API creation and publishing
- API promotion and/or deprecation
- API availability and subscription management
- API documentation
- API usage and performance monitoring

We must never lose sight of the key API Management tenets, which, as described in *Chapter 1, Application Services Governance*, typically are:

- Information asset and business functionality externalization
- Collaboration and community management fostering
- API monetization
- Continuous delivery
- Global deployment model adoption

> It is important for the reader to gain a good understanding of these concepts as they will be constantly referenced in subsequent sections.

# Oracle API Manager overview

## Introduction

Oracle API Manager facilitates and streamlines the API Management lifecycle by providing the following capabilities:

- Allows users to easily manage OSB proxy services as APIs
- Generation and management of API keys
- API metadata management
- API publishing, retirement, and deprecation
- API discovery
- API subscription management
- API runtime monitoring and analytics

>  API Manager is not a development tool, an IDE, or a runtime platform in itself. In short, it is a runtime-governance tool that delivers API lifecycle management capabilities.

The following diagram shows how Oracle API Manager fits in the service/integration strategy and platform:

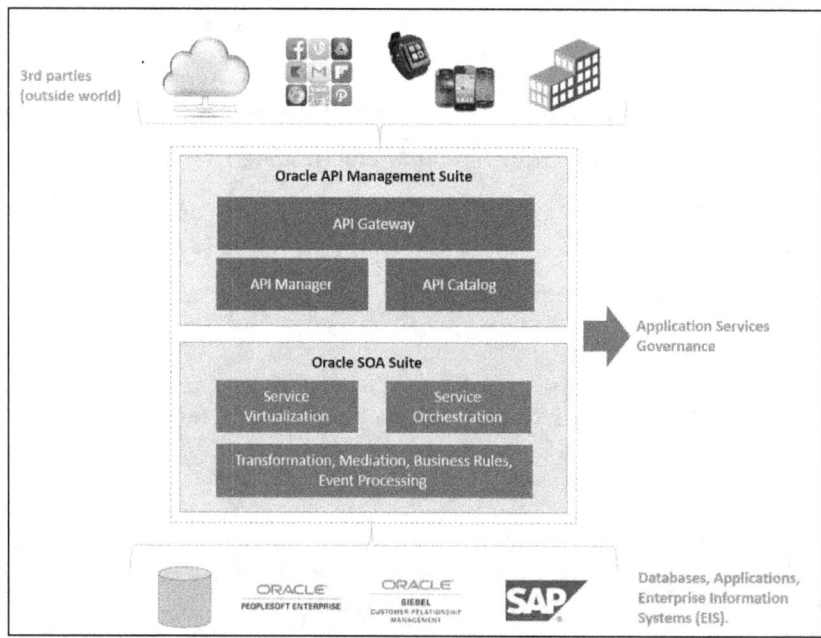

The diagram shows the different elements of a common service platform. These are service orchestration, business rules, processes, virtualization, routing, transformation, and mediation. All these elements form the foundations on which APIs are built.

The APIs are built on top of a defined service strategy, which in Oracle terms is usually deployed in Oracle Service Bus. Oracle API Manager leverages the following capabilities of OSB:

- Routing and transformation
- Throttling
- Operations pipelines
- Adapters
- Services endpoints
- Deployment
- Transaction monitoring

**Oracle API Manager (OAPIM)** is used to publish a set of APIs to consumers, thereby leveraging the existing service strategy by exposing APIs that are already created and deployed into an organization's service layer. This explains the relevance of Oracle Service Bus: not only in terms of the runtime execution of Oracle API Manager, but also because OSB is the tool of choice for efficiently exposing services to consumers.

OAPIM is the focal point for external developers and consumers wishing to discover and invoke APIs. It connects to the internal services platform (Oracle Service Bus) as well as to external elements of the architecture, such as the API Gateway, and allows the APIs to be published and secured.

Internal API curators create the APIs and register them in API Manager. Interested consumers and external developers use API Manager to discover and invoke this functionality. OAPIM provides the capability to register APIs and applications and to define which APIs can be used by which consumer, thus providing a rich security layer.

> *Chapter 6, Installation Tips and Techniques*, describes how to install the different components of the Oracle API strategy. It also includes a block diagram that explains where and how all these components should be deployed.

*Oracle API Manager Implementation Overview*

## Architecture and functional overview

OAPIM's internal architecture is illustrated by the following diagram:

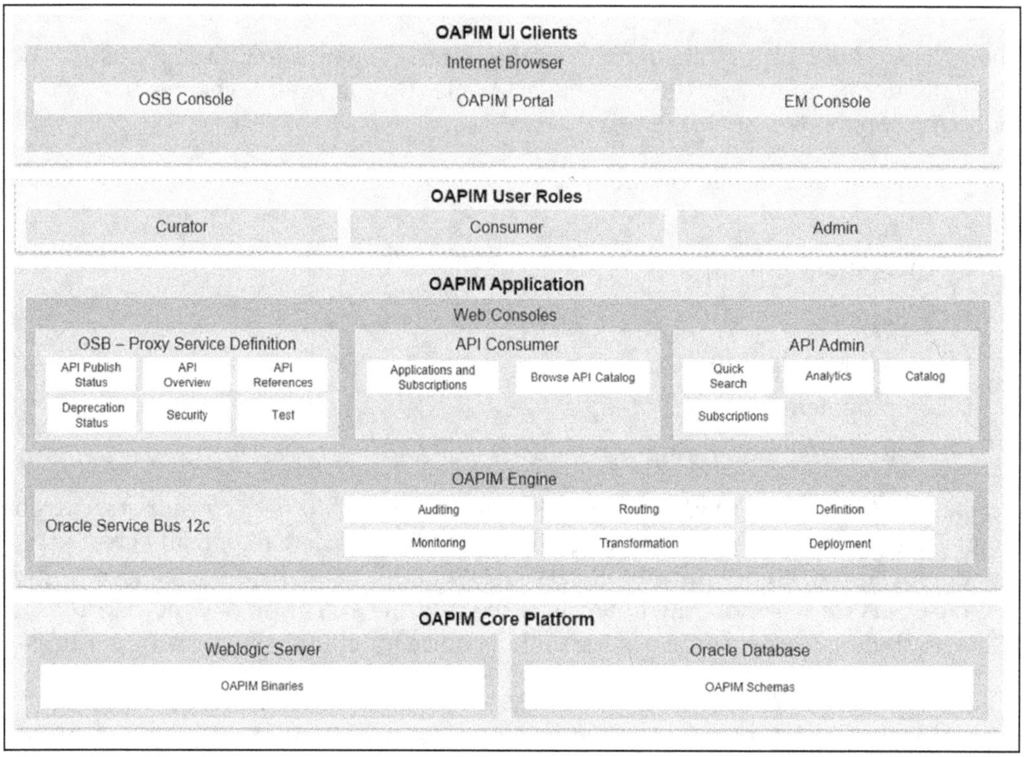

As depicted by the preceding diagram, OAPIM must be installed on top of an **Oracle Service Bus** (**OSB**) *12c* domain, and therefore requires an installation of Oracle Service Bus (a domain with just OAPIM is not technically possible).

If an OSB implementation is already present in the organization, it is strongly suggested that a new OSB domain is created in order to host OAPIM and federate existing domains, rather than to extend any one of these for API Management purposes. An example of this kind of scenario is shown in the following diagram:

*Chapter 4*

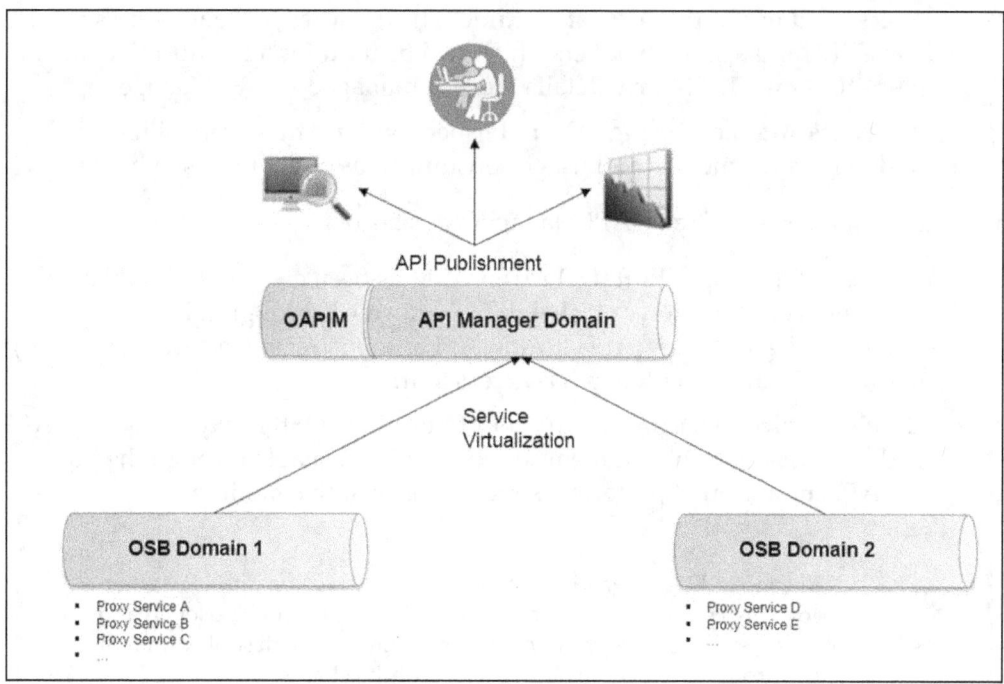

In an environment such as the one described, internal OSB Developers are usually tasked with the design and deployment of services which, in order to be promoted as APIs, first need to be virtualized in the **Master OSB** (OAPIM Domain). Once the latter is done, the available proxy services can be managed and published as APIs by an API curator.

# Oracle API Manager capabilities and components

API Manager *12c* provides the following features/capabilities:

- **API creation**: API Manager will take OSB proxies and use them to create an API.
- **Documentation of the API**: With the ability to incorporate metadata into the APIs, it is possible to document APIs and classify them. This is a task performed by the API curator. The API metadata, together with the API contract, is then published via the API Manager portal.
- **Search and Discovery**: API consumers and third-party developers will access the API Manager to search for and discover APIs.

- **Access and use of the APIs at runtime**: Third parties will gain access to APIs via a URL and a security token which will be used for authentication and identification. Third-party details are also managed in API Manager.
- **Analytics and monitoring**: API publishers will use these capabilities to understand the metrics and usage consumptions of the published APIs.

From a user perspective, Oracle API Manager consists of:

- **Oracle API Manager Portal**: Once an API has been created and published, any other configuration or task will be performed through this interface. All of the application roles (API curator, API administrator, and API consumer) discussed in the next section has access to it.
- **Oracle Service Bus Console**: In order to promote OSB Proxy Services to APIs and subsequently publish them so they can be available through the portal, the API curator must perform a series of tasks in this module.

> OFM control *12c* (Enterprise Manager) may also come into play when performing certain administrative tasks like, for example, user creation, role provisioning, and group mappings. This will be described in more detail through the case study at the end of the chapter.

## Oracle API Manager roles

Oracle API Manage *12c* supports the following application roles:

- **API curator**: He/she is responsible for publishing the APIs into the API Manager portal and is also responsible for documenting and maintaining the metadata associated with these APIs. Their main responsibility is to maintain the API metadata in the portal. This role is equivalent to the OAC curator.
- **API administrator**: He/she is a system administrator with full access to the system. He/she has the ability to change system settings and also access information such as runtime metrics, analytics, and subscription information. This role is equivalent to the OAC admin.

- **API consumer**: API consumers are third-party or internal developers using the API Management portal in order to discover and consume APIs.

 An API developer role may also be defined, in order to grant OSB Console access to internal developers tasked with API creation-related activities.

The following diagram puts into context the aforementioned roles by mapping them to their associated functions within the product, as well as to the enterprise users who will be tasked with such activities:

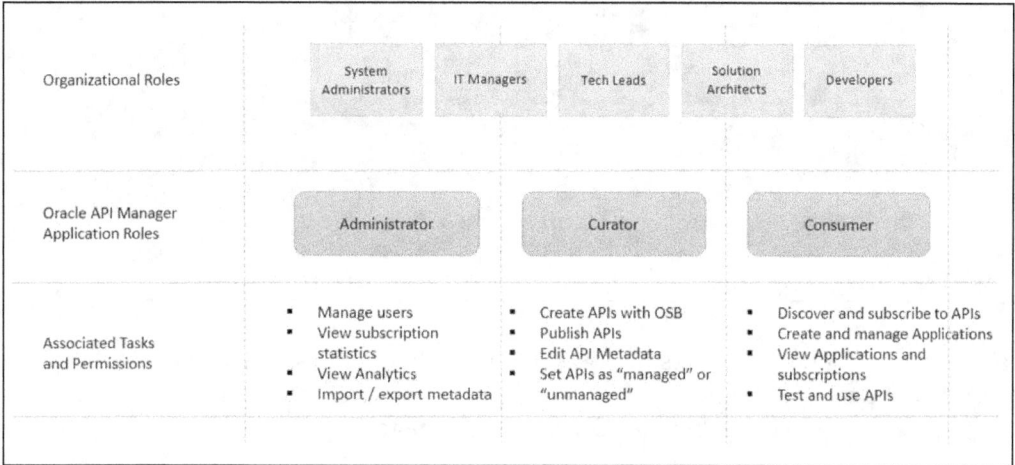

Regarding the OSB Console, which in most cases will end up being a starting point for API creation, among the roles previously described, only the API curator and API developer will have access to it.

As the case study example will clearly detail, the curator will have read-only access to service development, configuration and lifecycle functions, but will be able to perform API-related activities such as publishing SOAP/REST proxy services as APIs and optionally marking them as managed.

Overall, and taking into account most of the elements discussed so far in this overview, the general steps APIs will usually undergo when promoting and managing them through Oracle API Manager. This is shown in the following diagram:

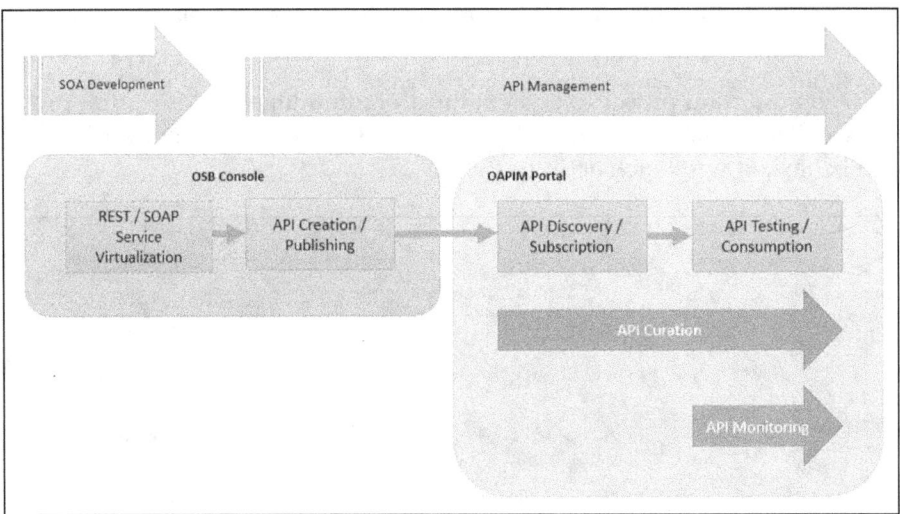

In the preceding diagram, it is important to note the seamless convergence of the SOA development process, in this case supported by Oracle OSB, with the API Management lifecycle enabled by Oracle API Manager.

> For additional information about Oracle API Manager (documentation, downloads, samples, and so on), go to the official site right here:
> https://docs.oracle.com/middleware/1213/apimgr/index.html

# API Manager case study background

WBVC has started an initiative to become a **Mobile Virtual Network Enabler** (**MVNE**). This new business model requires them to expose functionality to **Mobile Virtual Network Operators** (**MVNOs**) to allow them to activate SIM offerings, provide SIM changes, portability and recharge (among many other services).

WBVC have identified a list of candidate internal services to be exposed as APIs in support of this new offering. However, they face a number of technical challenges when publishing the APIs since the underlying services were not originally designed to be open to third parties.

WBVC have identified that they need to make the following changes to support this new business model:

- Provide business offerings by publishing a set of APIs to selected third parties. Services will be exposed as RESTFUL APIs. This represents a technical challenge and a management challenge, both in terms of deciding which APIs to publish, and how to manage the security and lifecycle of those APIs. These exposed services will be used by the MVNOs to offer mobile services (voice and data) to their clients.
- All APIs must be carefully managed. Policies need to be applied to each exposed API and each must be managed to provide seamless access to the different MVNOs that will consume them.
- The current SOA platform (Oracle SOA Suite), and in particular Oracle Service Bus, will be used as the technology platform for the exposed APIs. These will be integrated with the API Management components.
- A simple process is required to curate and manage the APIs. Both the developers and MVNOs will have access to the APIs, so the constant update and upgrade of APIs will be a challenge that needs to be resolved

Oracle API Manager has been chosen by WBVC to overcome these challenges due to its rich functionality and full lifecycle support. It will be utilized to publish APIs and provide a portal through which the MVNOs and third parties will gain access to them. It also provides excellent runtime and design time tooling, allowing the internal development team to easily create, document, publish, and secure APIs.

# Performing administrative tasks prior to the use of Oracle API Manager

WBCV already has a mature SOA infrastructure and governance framework in place. Numerous internal services have been defined, created, and rolled out across the enterprise using the Oracle SOA Suite stack. Most of the business operations take place within the SOA platform. Current service implementations include functionality to support:

- Subscribers
- Activation
- Plan creation
- Portability
- Logistics

*Oracle API Manager Implementation Overview*

These services are exposed to consumers using the Oracle Service Bus. WBCV has full control of all service implementations in terms of monitoring, versioning, activation and deactivation, fault handling, and service metrics.

As previously discussed, some of these services need to be exposed to the MVNOs. WBCV has already conducted numerous capacity planning exercises and proven that the current architecture is scalable enough to support access by MVNOs. Further analysis has also shown that services require very few modifications in order to support the inclusion of external mobile network operators.

As described earlier, Oracle API Manager is a piece of software that runs on top of Oracle Service Bus. Since WBCV already has OSB in place, it is a straightforward process to start publishing their APIs.

The first API that WBCV chose to externalize to their MVNOs was the Subscriber API. This API will offer many operations but the most relevant ones are:

- `getSubscriberBalance`
- `getSubscriberInfo`
- `simChange`

The first step for WBCV was to create an organization structure to manage, publish, and curate the APIs. External users were created to provide third-party developers access to APIs via the API portal. The API portal provides access to these external users to allow them to review the API documentation, to download API definitions, and gain access to the API keys.

Users are managed and handled using WebLogic security providers. WBCV had previously decided to use the Oracle Unified Directory as their LDAP platform. WBCV administrators use **Oracle Fusion Middleware (OFM)** control to provision access to users and to assign API Manager roles. This section demonstrates how this was achieved.

> For more information on OFM control, please navigate to `http://docs.oracle.com/middleware/1212/cross/emtasks.htm`.

*Chapter 4*

1. To access the OFM control, open a browser and go to the following URL: `http://<IPhttp://<IP ADDRESS>:<PORT>/em`.

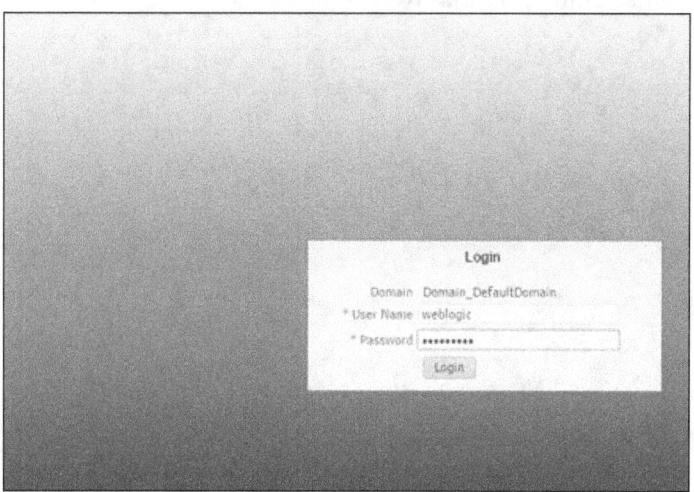

2. In order to be able to perform the desired administrative tasks, login must be done with a user who has been granted administrative privileges. For the purpose of this example, `weblogic` is used.

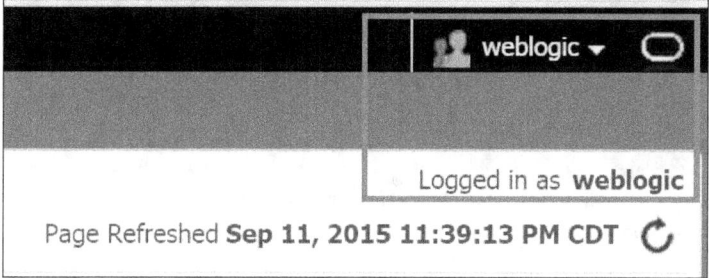

*Oracle API Manager Implementation Overview*

3. Go to the API Manager domain in OFM controls and right-click on the domain name to access the **Security** option and the **Application Roles** sub-option, as illustrated here:

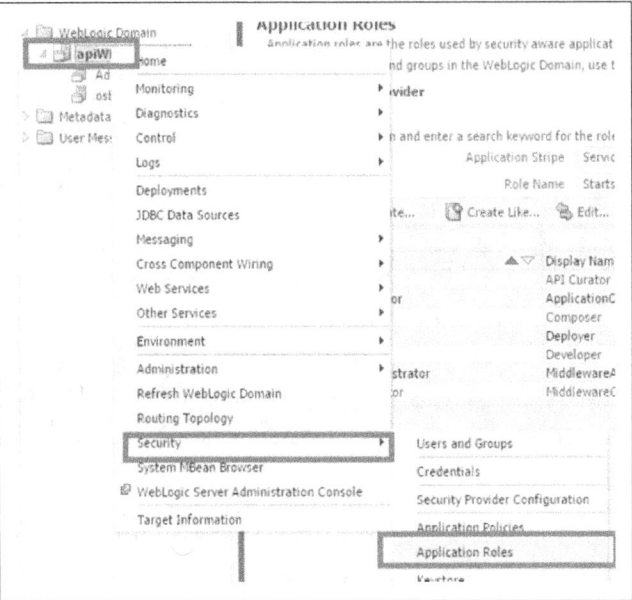

4. Selecting **Application Roles** will open the application roles page on the right-hand side of the OFM control console, as follows:

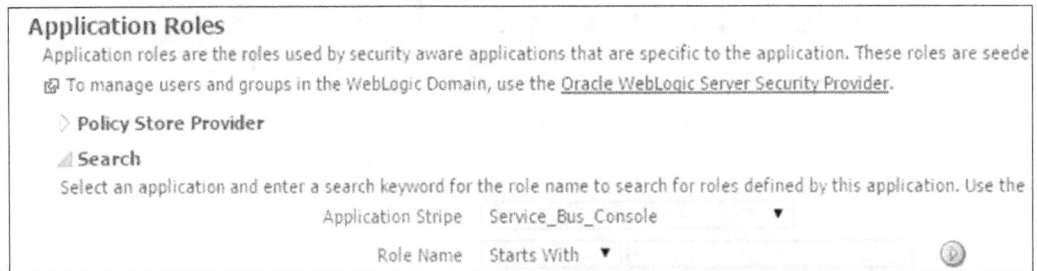

This will have two options as follows:

- **Application Stripe**: This is the name of the application where roles are going to be managed. Examples are API Manager and Service Bus Console.
- **Role Name**: This is the role to be managed.

5. Bear in mind that API Manager is built on top of Oracle Service Bus, so some of the roles are related to OSB. When configuring user access for API Manager, the administrator is required to assign OSB roles. If we choose API Manager as the application stripe, the following will be displayed:

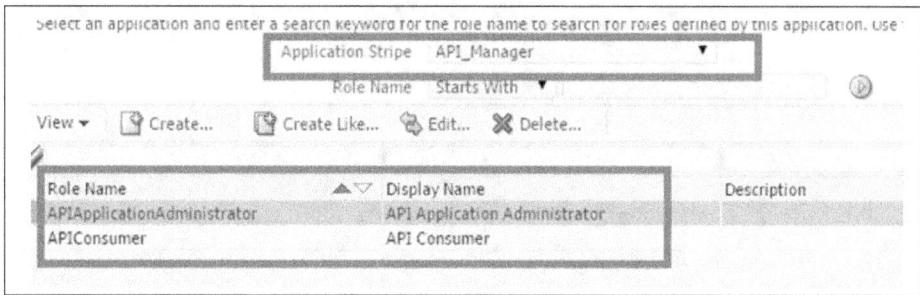

6. There are two important roles: `APIConsumer` and `APIApplicationAdministrator`. We have described these in previous paragraphs. The API Curator role can be found in the Oracle Service Bus console application. To find it, change the **Application Stripe** drop-down menu to **Service_Bus_Console**:

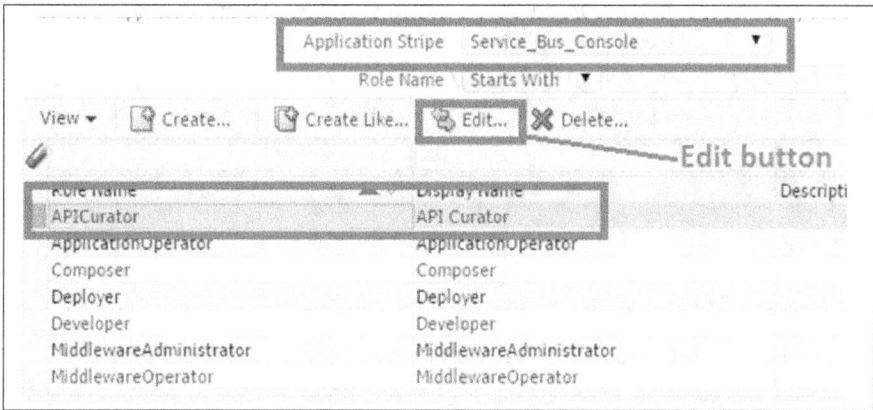

*Oracle API Manager Implementation Overview*

7. To assign users/groups to these roles, just click on the **Edit** button (see the previous screenshot) and the following page will be displayed:

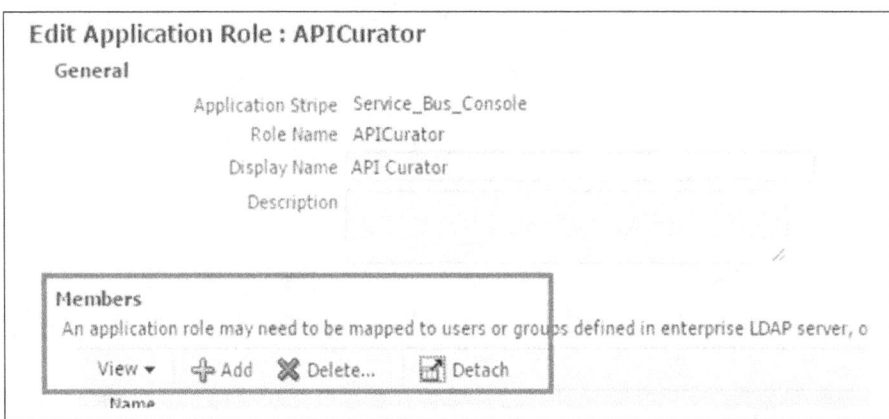

8. By using the **Add** and **Delete** options, it is possible to assign or revoke users/group access to the particular role.

> For more information on how users are created and managed, please refer to the Oracle documentation at the following site:
> ```
> https://docs.oracle.com/middleware/1213/apimgr/using-
> apimgr/GUID-0CA2641A-BA29-43D2-8F8E-E43EA4048F17.
> htm#OSBAM406
> ```

*Chapter 4*

# Publishing APIs from the OSB Console as an API curator

The next step is to expose existing proxy services as APIs. WBCV made use of the Service Bus Console to publish/manage its APIs, as follows:

1. Open up the OSB console using the following URL:

   `http://machine:port/sbconsole`

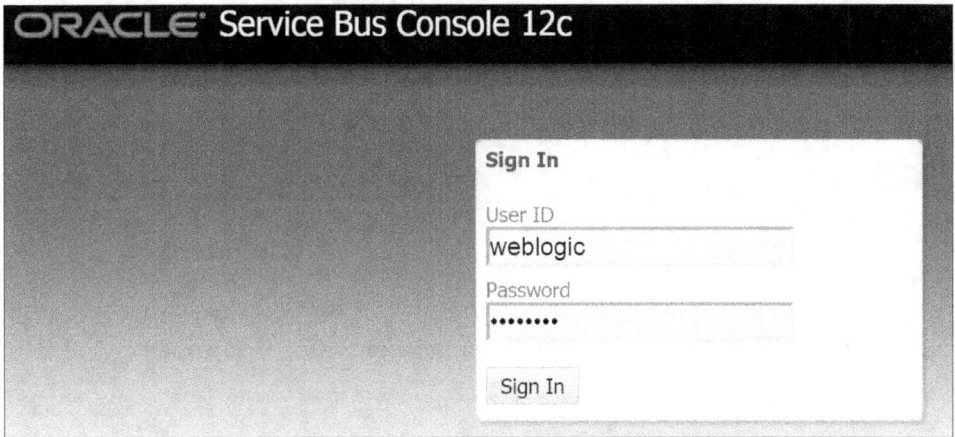

2. Log in to an account that has been granted the API Curator role.
3. After gaining access to the console, the user can browse candidate services to be published. On the left-hand side of the window, click on the OSB proxy service that will be published as an API, in this case `SubscriberAPI`.

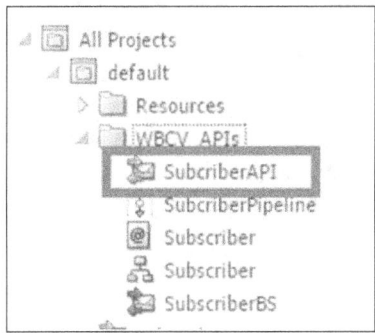

[ 155 ]

## Oracle API Manager Implementation Overview

4. When OSB is patched with the OAPIM installer notice, an additional tab called **API** is added to the **Proxy Service Definition**.

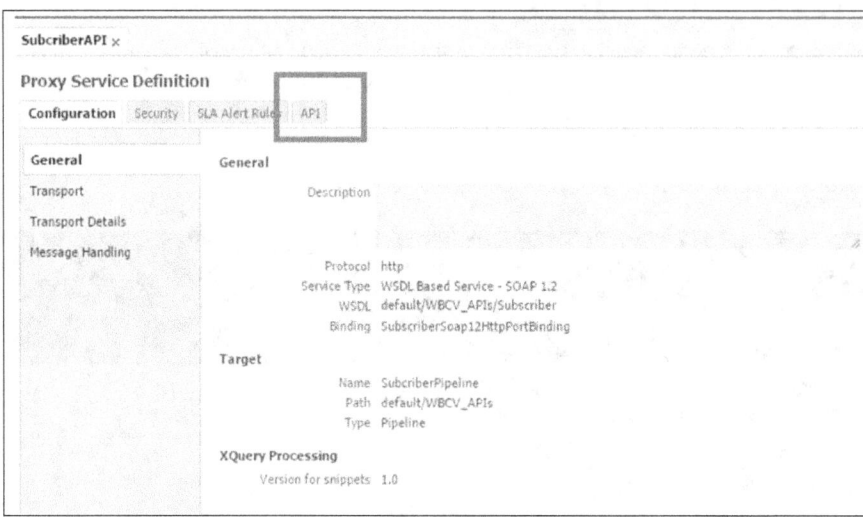

5. Click on the **API** tab, and the following information will appear:

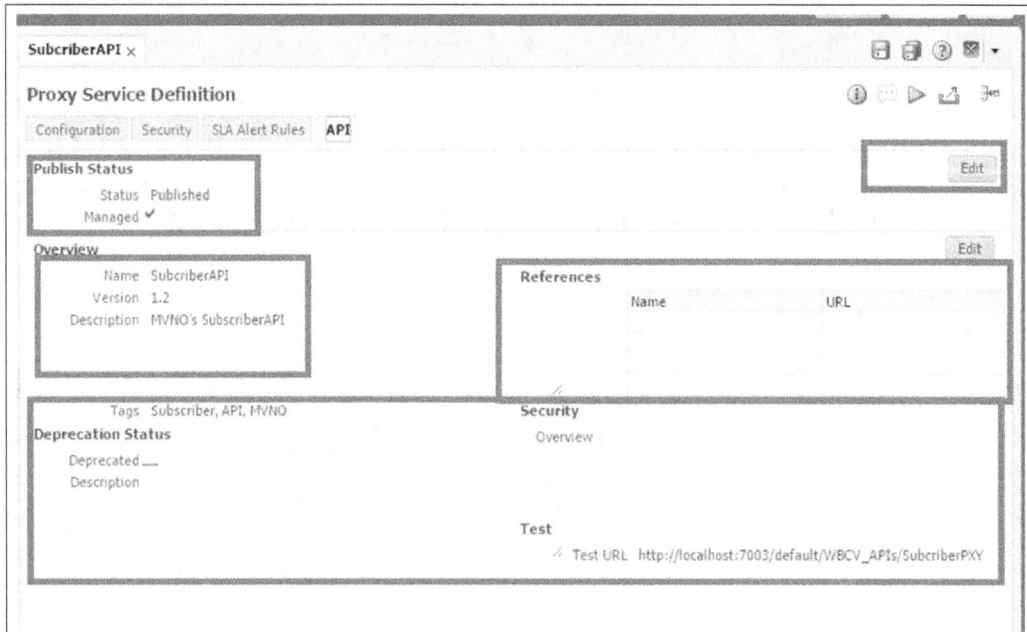

6. There are different sections on the **API** tab, which are described as follows:

    ◦ **Publish Status**: This will identify if this particular API is published. If that is the case, then the API will be accessible to users on the API portal. The possible options are: **Published**, **Private**, and **Draft**. **Managed** means that the API will be published and an API key is required for third parties to consume the API. However, if this option is unchecked, then an API key will not be required.

    ◦ **Overview**: This section shows the name of the published API, its current version, description, and associated tags; these are very important elements because tags will be searchable within the API portal. These fields are editable by the API administrator only.

    ◦ **References**: Any type of documentation associated with the API can be registered here.

    ◦ **Deprecation Status**: If checked, the API portal will publish this API as deprecated. A brief description can be added to explain why the API is deprecated

    ◦ **Security**: This is a text field to document the security aspects of the API

    ◦ **Test**: This is the test URL for this particular API.

7. All these sections are editable if the **Edit** button is clicked. For example, for the **Publish Status** section, the user can change the **Published Status**, as illustrated:

8. Equally, the **Overview** section can be modified, as shown here:

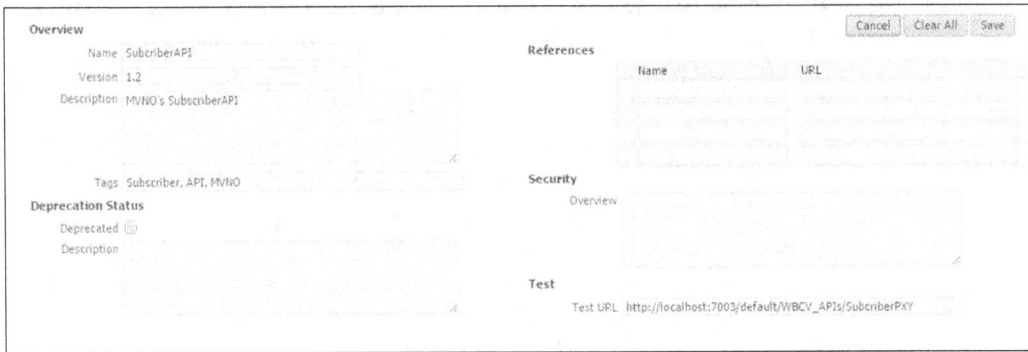

9. As an example addition on the same page, add the following in the **References** section:

    ○ **Name:** Documentation

    **URL:** `http://localhost:7003/default/WBCV_APIs/documentation`

    ○ **Name:** Samples

    **URL:** `http://localhost:7003/default/WBCV_APIs/samples`

    The API definition will now look like this:

    | References | | |
    |---|---|---|
    | | Name | URL |
    | | Documentation | http://localhost:7003/default/WBCV_APIs/docu... |
    | | Samples | http://localhost:7003/default/WBCV_APIs/sam... |

10. When a change is made to any of the fields and saved, it is immediately published to the API portal. Since this API has the **Published** option checked, it is already available via the API portal.

# Accessing the Oracle API portal as an administrator

To access the OAPIM portal as an admin, the following steps were followed:

1. Open a new browser window and enter the following URL:

   `http://machine:port/apimanager`

2. The following authentication page appears:

3. Sign in as an administrator.

>  An administrator is a WebLogic user that has been assigned the Administrator role as described in previous sections.

4. Once authenticated, the following window appears:

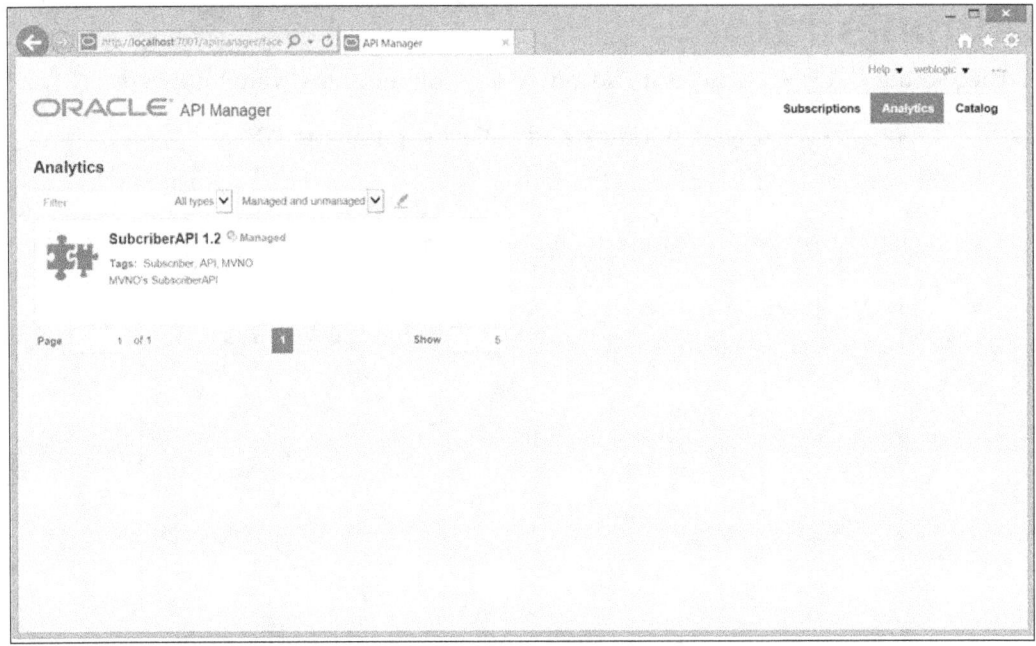

5. Here the administrator can filter the APIs using the following options:

Note that filtering can be done by name, type (SOAP, REST) and whether the API is managed or unmanaged.

*Chapter 4*

6. In the top-right corner, the API administrator also has the following options:

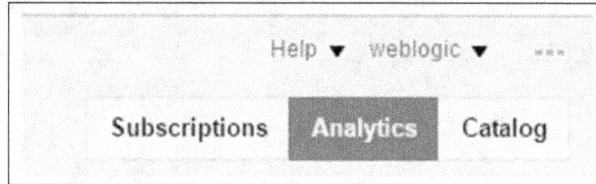

7. By clicking on **Catalog**, the following screen appears:

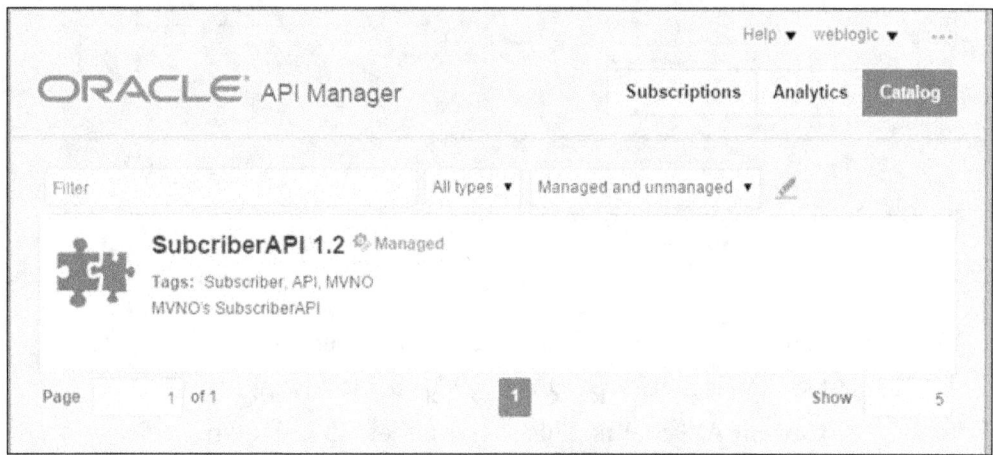

8. This page will basically list all available OAPIM APIs. Placing the cursor over an individual API will cause an option to appear in the top right corner of the API as follows:

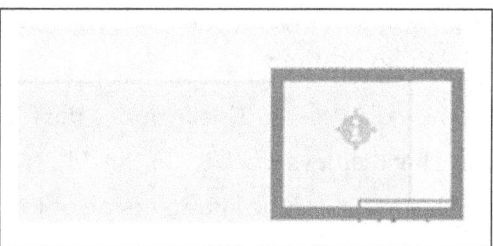

*Oracle API Manager Implementation Overview*

9. Clicking on the icon will display the API details page. In this page, runtime statistics and other API metadata is displayed.

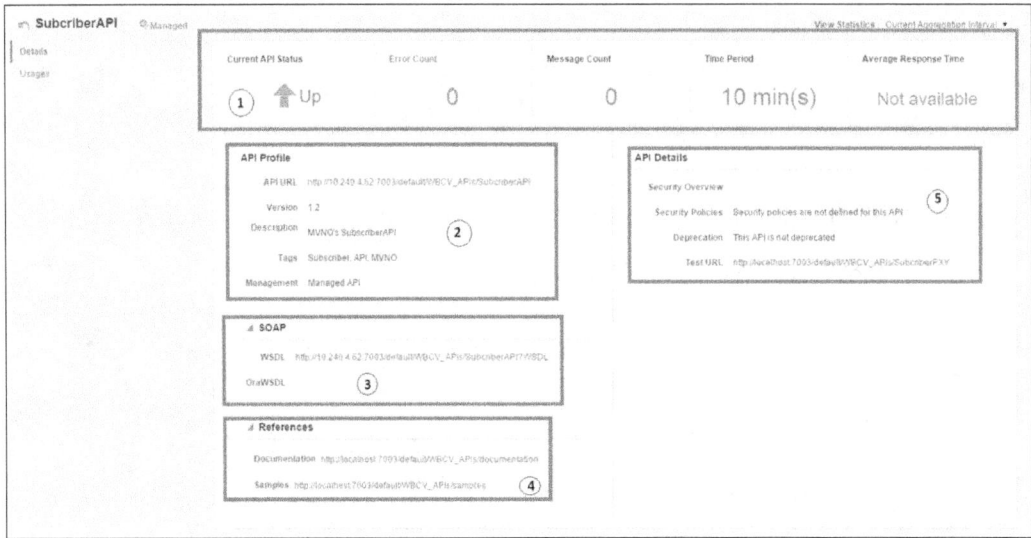

10. There are five sections, which show all the API details.

    The first section is **Statistics**. This includes the following:
    - **Current API Status**: This shows either **Up** or **Down**
    - **Error Count**: This count shows the numbers of errors the API has reported while being consumed
    - **Message Count**: The number of times the API has been invoked
    - **Time Period**: This shows how long the API has been available
    - **Average Response Time**: This reports the average response time across all API invocations

    The second section is **API Profile**. This includes the following:
    - **API URL**: This displays the URL of the API
    - **Version**: This indicates the latest version of this API
    - **Description**: The description entered within the API definition section that was described previously

*Chapter 4*

- ° **Tags**: This displays the tags that were defined in the API definition creation
- ° **Management**: This indicates whether this API is managed or not

The third section is **SOAP** or **REST** section. This shows the service descriptor URL. Depending on whether the API is SOAP or REST-based, this section will show the WSDL or WADL URL.

Then, we have the **References** section. This displays all references included in the API definition. The two that were included in the previous section (**Documentation** and **Samples**) are displayed here.

The last section is **API Details**. This displays the test URL, security definitions, and whether the API is deprecated

11. The analytics displayed will depend on the value in **View Statistics**. This can be filtered as follows:

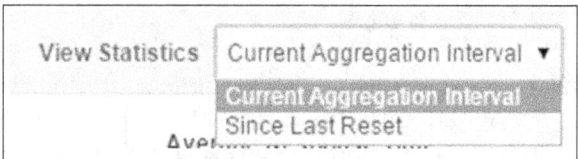

12. **Current Aggregation Interval** will display analytics for the current aggregation level. This is configured for this API within Oracle Service Bus.

For more information on how to configure an aggregation interval for a Service/API within Oracle Service Bus, please refer to the following documentation:
`http://docs.oracle.com/middleware/1213/osb/administer/GUID-7535D97D-6EBD-4969-8A6D-C736B44C5555.htm#OSBAG2088`

13. The other option is **Since Last Reset**, which displays statistics since the server was last rebooted or the API was last stopped.

14. Now open the **Subscriptions** page by clicking on the **Subscription** button located on the upper-right hand side of the screen.

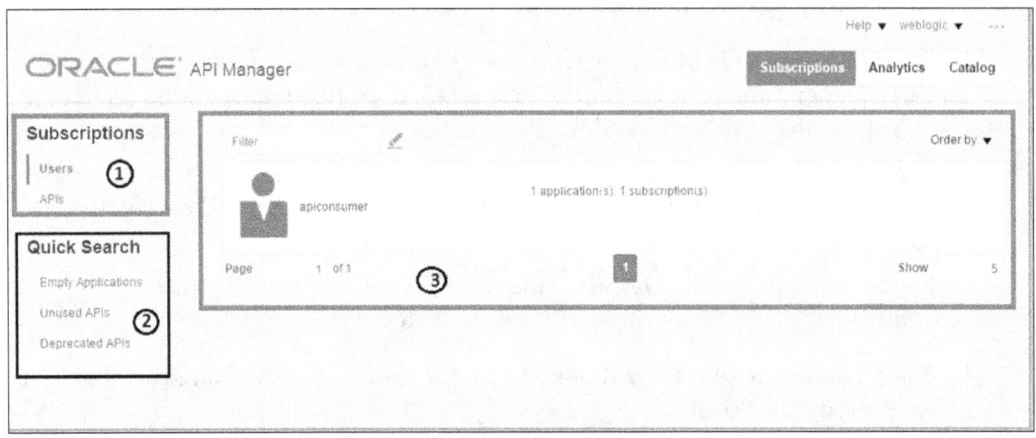

15. This page contains three main sections.

    The first section is **Subscriptions**. This lists subscriptions by **Users** or **APIs**. The **Users** option will display the APIs that particular users are subscribed to. For example, in this screenshot, we can see `apiconsumer` as a user; this user is subscribed to one API. The other option is **APIs**, which will show APIs that users have already subscribed to.

    Then, we have the **Quick Search** section. This section has three options:
    - **Empty Applications**: Those consumer applications that have no API subscriptions will be listed here
    - **Unused APIs**: This stands for those APIs that no one is using
    - **Deprecated APIs**: Those APIs that have a deprecated status

    In the middle of the page (marked with number 3), all users will be listed together with information on how many applications and subscriptions each user has. In the current example there is one application and one subscription.

16. Positioning the cursor on a user will display a **Details** button in the right-hand top corner, as follows:

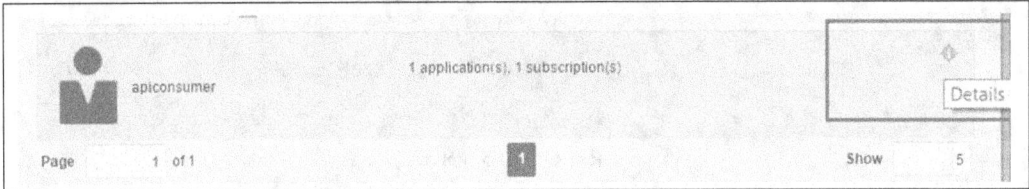

17. Clicking on the Details icon will result in the following information being displayed:

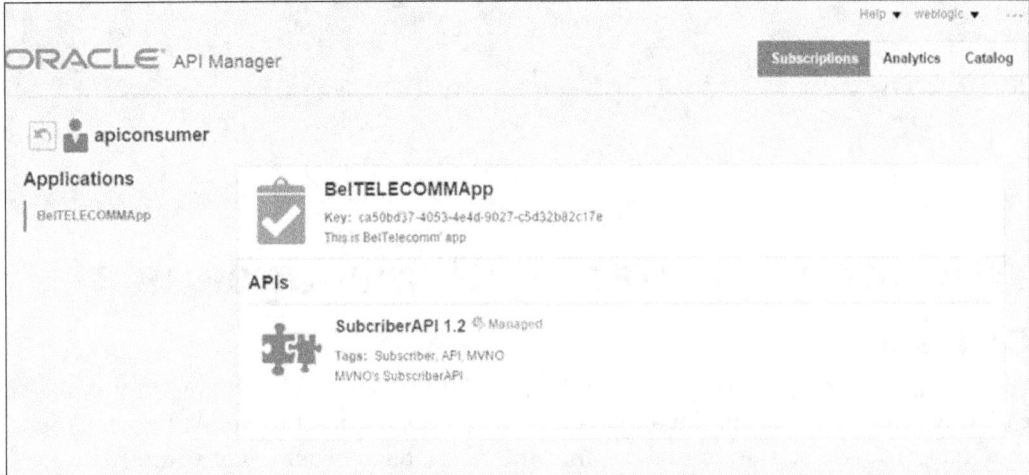

This user details page will show the APIs and applications that a user is consuming.

18. Now open the **Analytics** page by clicking on the **Analytics** button located on the upper-right hand side of the screen.

*Oracle API Manager Implementation Overview*

19. To view analytics for an API, click on the **Details** button. A graph will appear showing the error and message counts in the right-hand side of the screen.

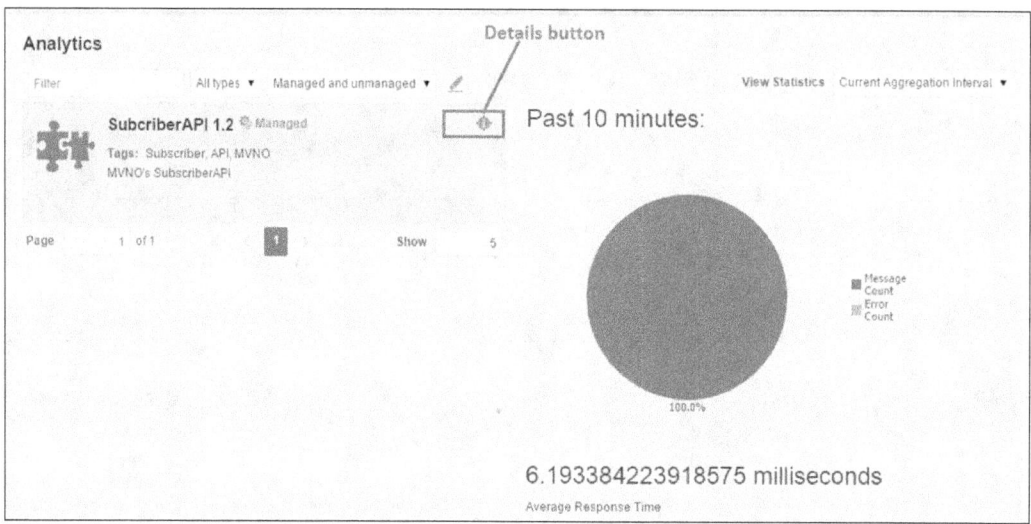

# Working with Oracle API Manager as a consumer

WBCV has already started to work with an MVNO telecommunications company called BelTelecomm. Their developers have been provisioned in the API portal and they have already started to make some subscriptions in order to consume APIs. Let's take a look at API Manager from the perspective of an API consumer (in this case BelTelecomm).

1. Log in to the OAPIM portal as an API Consumer by using the same URL: http://machine:port/apimanager.

*Chapter 4*

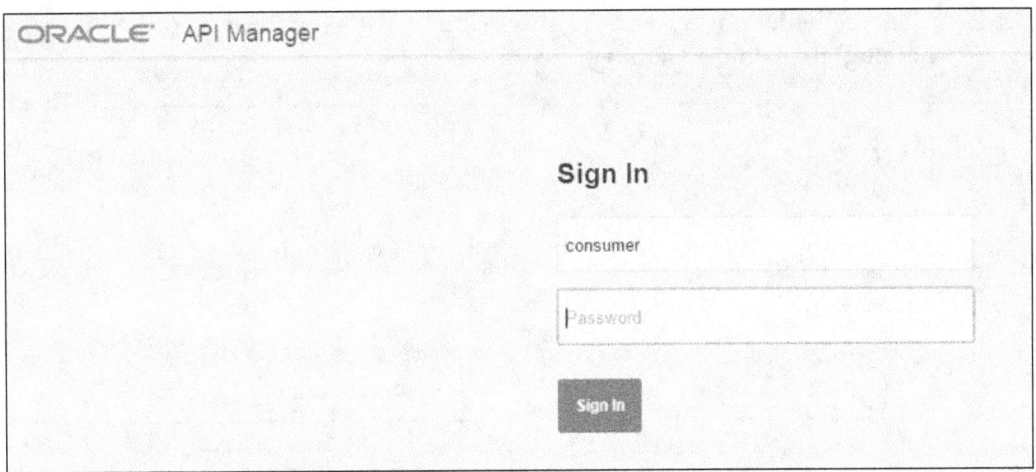

Notice how the OAPIM home page looks for API consumers. From this page, users can either go to the **Applications and Subscriptions** page to create and manage applications, and/or discover available APIs by browsing the API catalog.

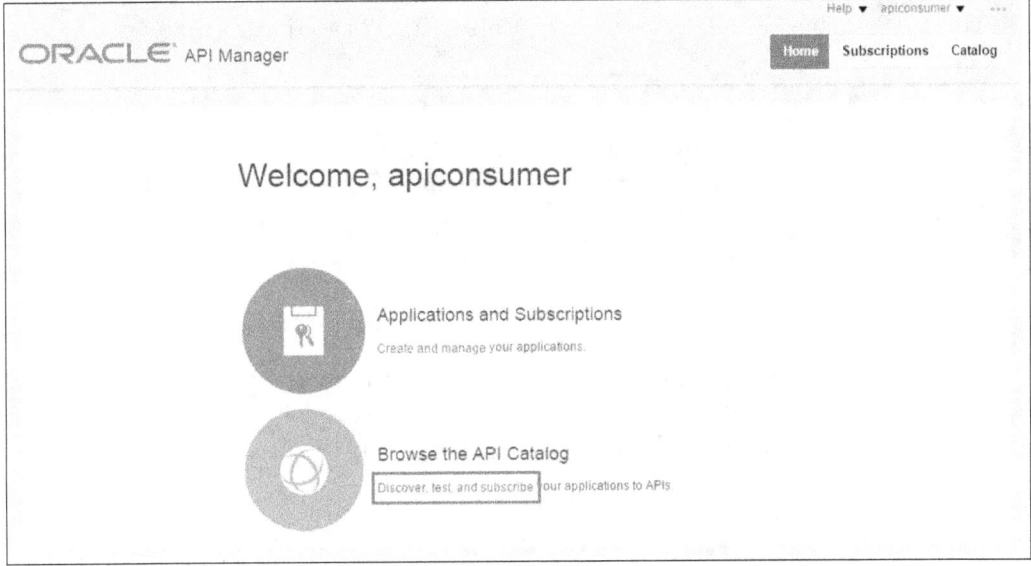

 An application is basically the consumer of the APIs published in the OAPIM catalog.

# Oracle API Manager Implementation Overview

2. Click on the **Discover, test and subscribe** links (below **Browse the API Catalog**) to open the **Catalog** page:

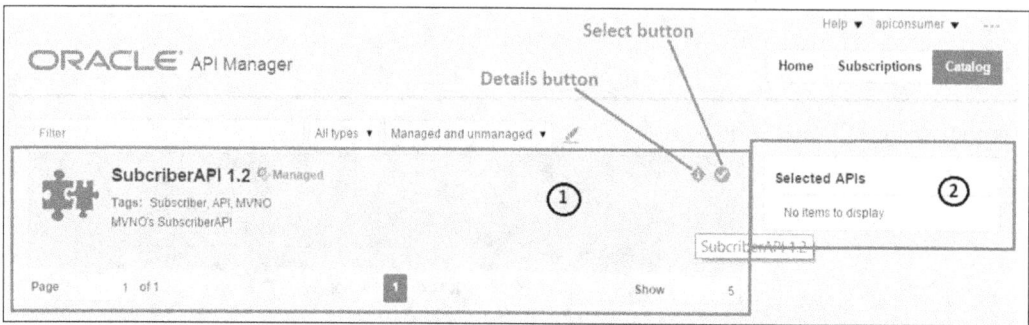

The first section shows a list of all available APIs published by WBCV.

The second section displays the APIs subscribed to by this user.

3. BelTelecomm is now going to consume the SubscriberAPI. Subscription to this service requires the following steps:

    1. Click on the **Select** button (refer to the previous diagram).
    2. The API will appear in the **Selected APIs** section, as follows:

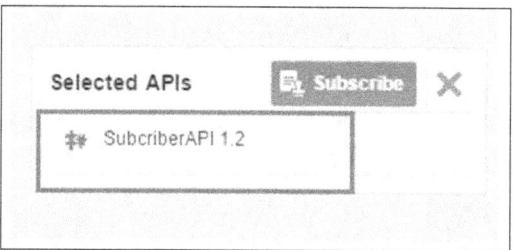

    3. Ideally, by clicking on the **Subscribe** button, the subscription should be completed. However, in order to do so, an application is required to see which subscription it is associated with.

4. To create an application, go back to the home page and click on the **Create and manage applications** link under **Applications and Subscriptions**.

5. Once clicked, the **Subscription** page appears, as follows:

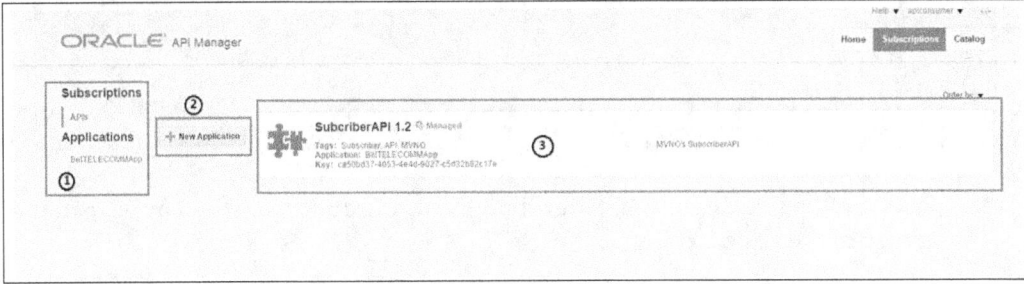

6. There are three main sections to this page and they are as follows:
    - On the left-hand side is the list of API subscriptions and applications available for the user.
    - Next is a button to create new applications.
    - In the right-hand side of the page is the Details section. If you click on an available subscription or available application, this section will be updated to display the details of the selected item.

7. Click on **New Application** to create a new applicator for the user and enter the details as follows:

    **Name**: `BelMobileApp`. This is the name of the application.

## Oracle API Manager Implementation Overview

**Description**: This mobile application will provide important information for our Subscribers.

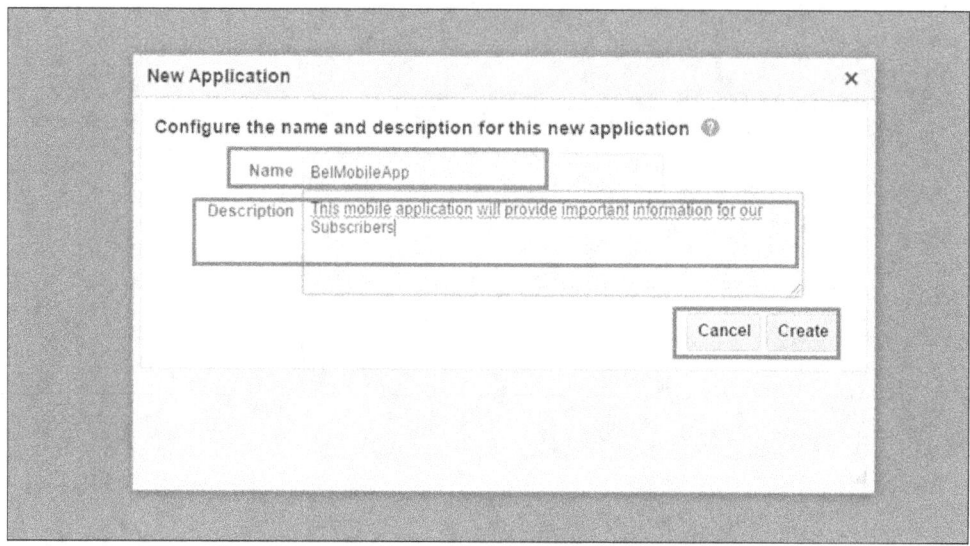

8. Click on the **Create** button. After that, the application page will appear in the center of the page.

9. From here it is also possible to directly subscribe to APIs by clicking on the **Add API** button located on the lower right-hand side of the application details section.

*Chapter 4*

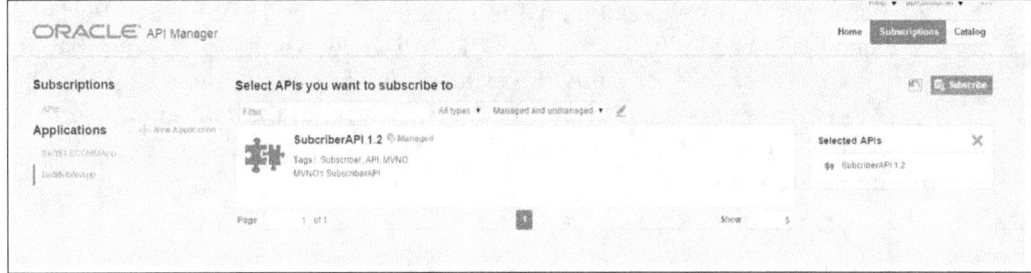

10. Click on the green **Subscribe** button on the right.

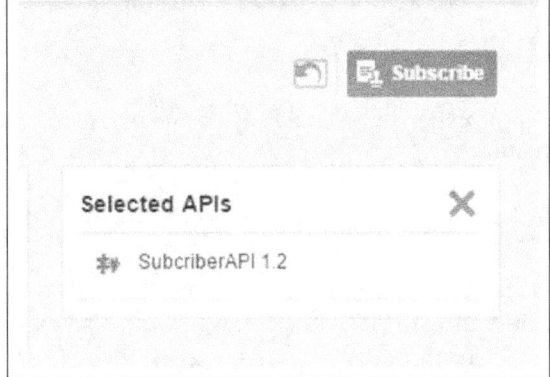

11. Once clicked, the API will be shown within the **APIs** subsection of the **Application** section, indicating that the user has subscribed to this API.

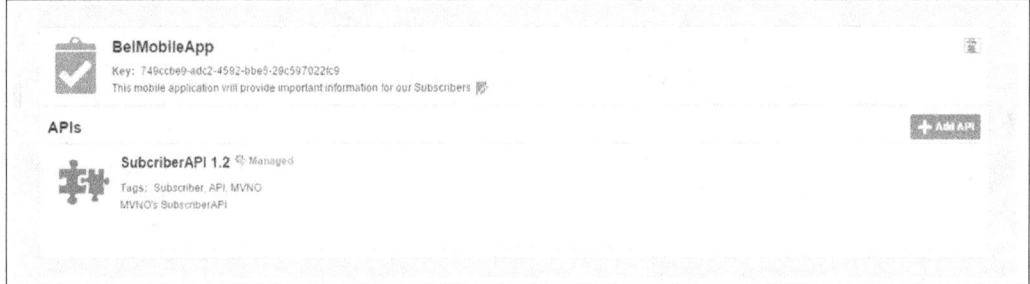

12. BelTelecomm has now created an application and subscribed to an API. The next step was to actually make use of the API. However, before doing that, it is critical to take notice of the **API Key** attribute. For every invocation made, this API key has to be included in the HTTP header of the call, so that API Manager can identify which application is actually making the API invocation

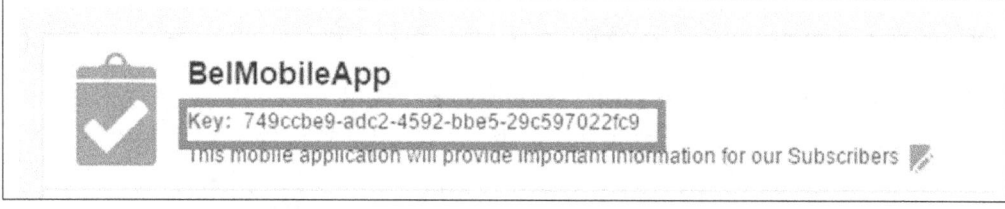

 For more information on what API Keys are, please refer to the following documentation:
`https://en.wikipedia.org/wiki/Application_programming_interface_key`

13. As mentioned, for BelTelecomm to consume this API they must provide the key value in the request HTTP header; without this key, it is not possible to consume the API. To demonstrate this, we will use SOAPUI to test the API.

 SOAPUI can be downloaded from the following URL:
`http://www.soapui.org/downloads/latest-release.html`

14. Open the details page of the SubscriberAPI and take note of the WSDL available in the **API Profile** section.

Chapter 4

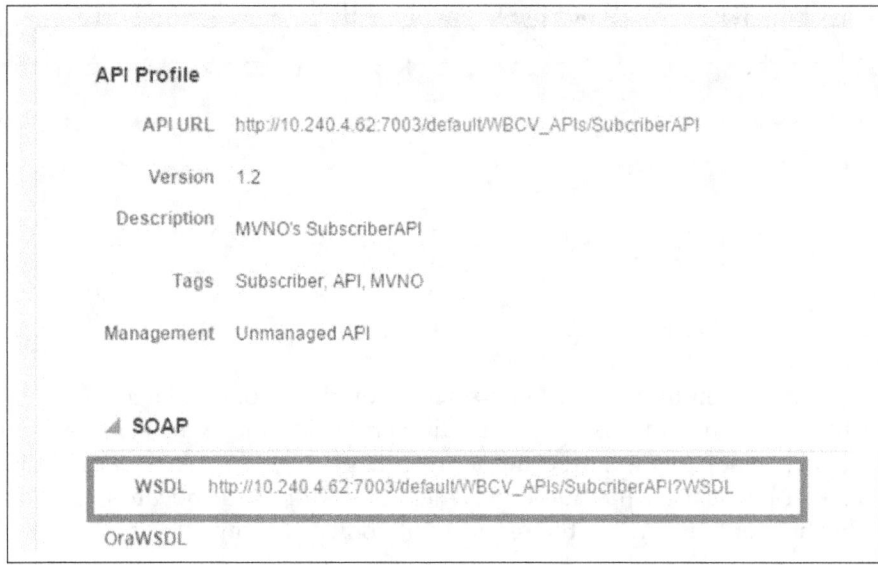

15. Open SOAPUI and create a new project using this WSDL. It should look as follows:

16. Let's suppose BelTelecomm wants to use the operation `simChange`. The request may look like this:

```
<soap:Envelope xmlns:soap="http://ww
    <soap:Header/>
    <soap:Body>
        <wbcv:simChange>
            <!--Optional:-->
            <arg0>?</arg0>
            <!--Optional:-->
            <arg1>?</arg1>
        </wbcv:simChange>
    </soap:Body>
</soap:Envelope>
```

## Oracle API Manager Implementation Overview

17. Invoking the API without the key will result in the following error.

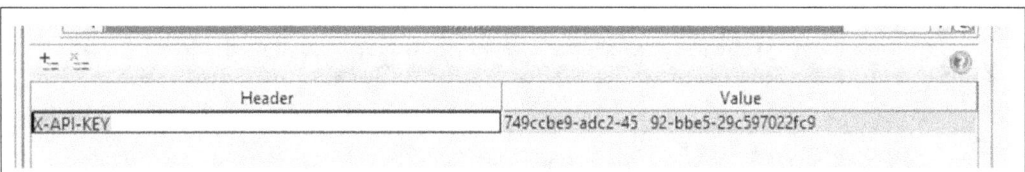

18. As can be seen in the preceding screenshot, the error is related to authorization, and this is because this service is a managed service and the key was not provided. In order to include the key, the `X-API-KEY` HTTP header needs to be included with the API key of the application. By adding this header to SOAPUI, the request will look as follows:

| Header | Value |
| --- | --- |
| X-API-KEY | 749ccbe9-adc2-45 92-bbe5-29c597022fc9 |

19. By calling the service again, but this time with the `X-API-KEY` header, the response should be successful:

```xml
<S:Envelope xmlns:S="http://www.w3.org/2003/05/soap-envelope">
    <S:Body>
        <ns0:simChangeResponse xmlns:ns0="http://wbcv.com/">
            <return>true</return>
        </ns0:simChangeResponse>
    </S:Body>
</S:Envelope>
```

20. This clearly illustrates the fact that since this API is managed, a key is required to consume it. If WBCV decide to not make it a managed API, then the key will not be required. Note that, as mentioned earlier, the managed option is found in the **API** tab within the Service Bus console, as follows:

*Chapter 4*

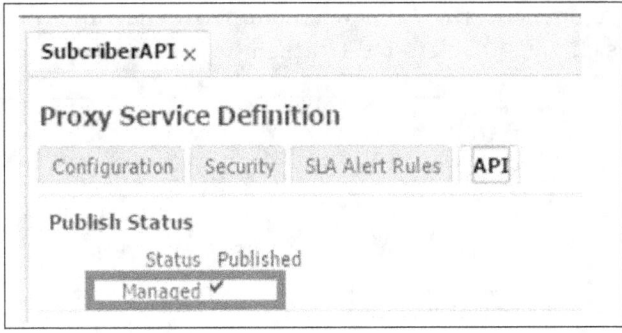

21. If this is changed to non-managed, the key will not be required. To illustrate this, let's update it to a non-managed API by unchecking, as follows:

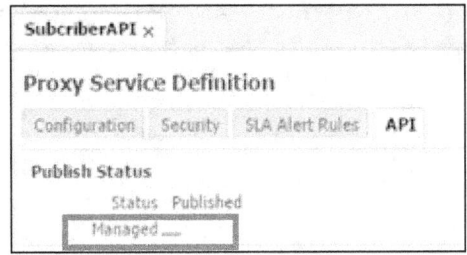

22. Now an invocation without the API key should also be successful.

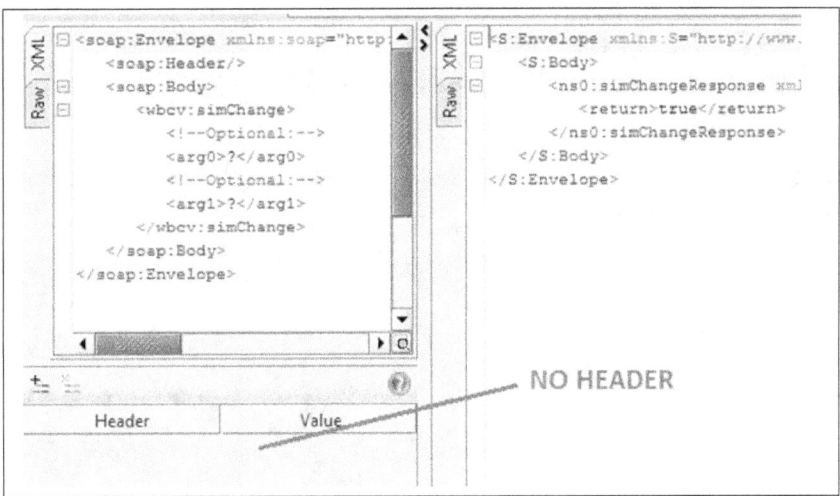

23. As can be seen in the preceding screenshot, the call was successful without any key being passed.

*Oracle API Manager Implementation Overview*

24. Another scenario to consider is what happens when an API is in the **Draft** status or is changed back to the **Draft** status.

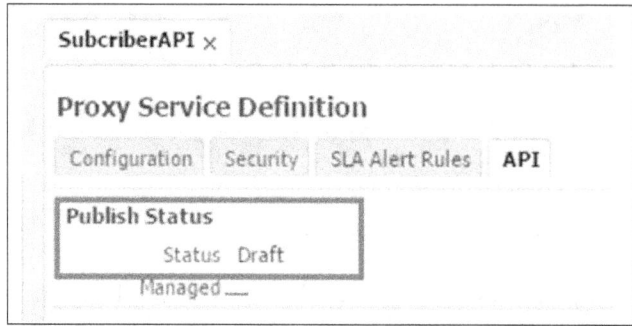

25. When this happens, an API consumer will no longer be able to view the API from the API portal as demonstrated here:

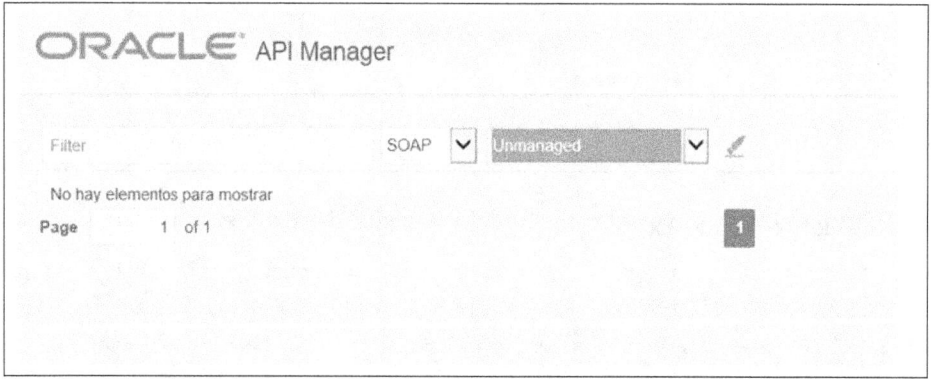

26. By simply publishing this API, the API will once again appear in the API portal from the **OSB API** tab:

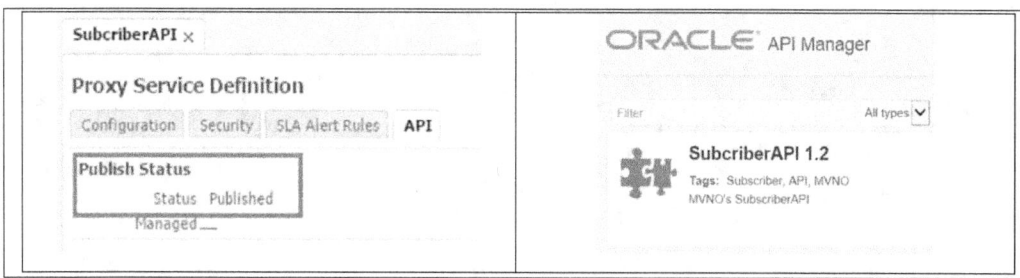

*Chapter 4*

# Using API Manager to work with JSON/REST-based APIs

In order to optimize the available services for mobile use, WBCV decided to implement a REST/JSON interface on its OSB proxy services. To do this, they made use of the REST adapter available in Oracle Service Bus *12c* and JDeveloper *12c*. Following are the steps they undertook to manage recently created REST APIs:

> For details on creating REST APIs using Oracle Service Bus *12c*, refer to the following documentation:
> https://docs.oracle.com/middleware/1213/osb/develop/GUID-C346DF7D-041D-4E10-BE1C-451F50719106.htm#OSBDV89235

1. By opening an OSB *12c* project, a pipeline can be REST-enabled by simply right-clicking on it. Once this is done, it should look as follows:

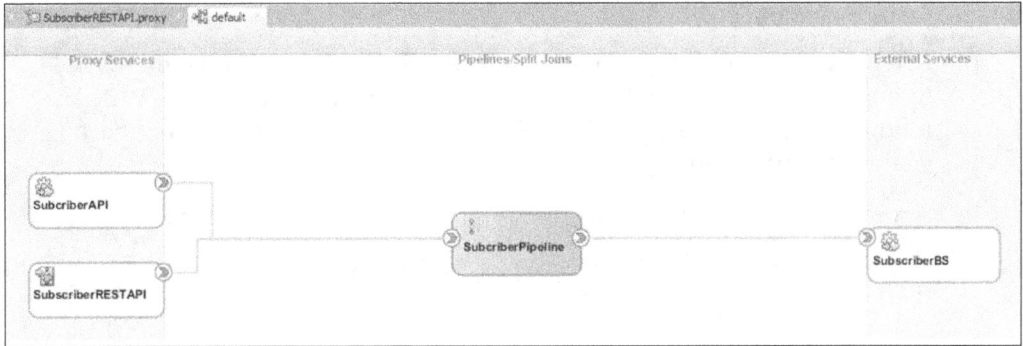

2. In the Project **Navigator** window, the REST API is shown as follows:

[ 177 ]

## Oracle API Manager Implementation Overview

3. Just as with the Subscriber soap based API, it is possible to select the **API** tab and configure the API as follows:

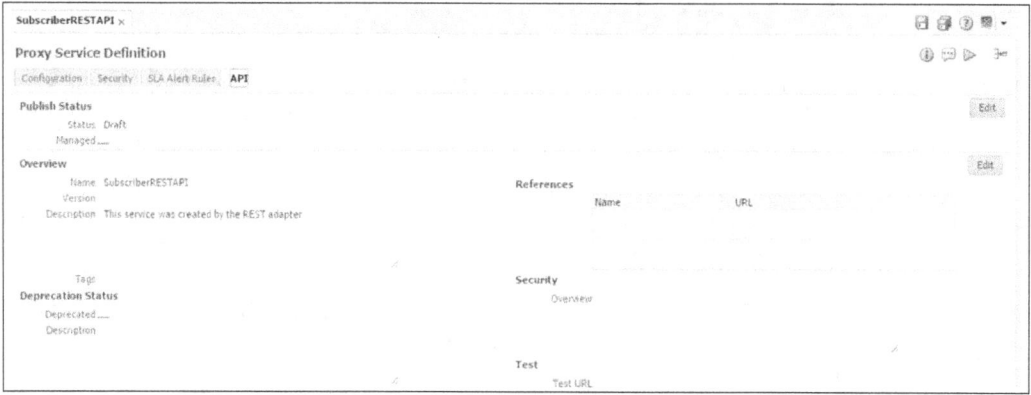

4. As seen in the preceding diagram, there is nothing configured after creating the REST API. Also this API is not published and is in **Draft** mode. From this page it is possible to change the status of the API to publish and also add further metadata.

5. After WBCV publishes and deploys this API then an API consumer is able to find it in the API portal. The steps to publish it are the same as WBCV followed to publish the previous SOAP-based API. The screenshot here shows the published API:

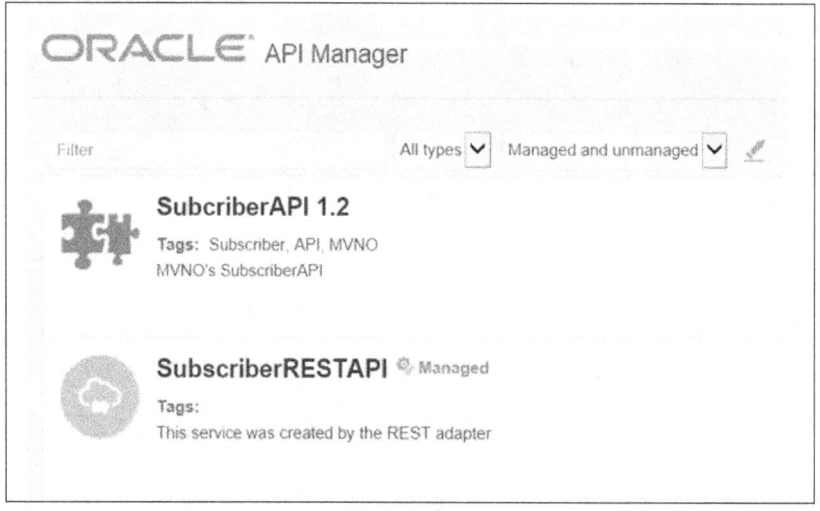

6. Notice that there are two different colors and images to differentiate the SOAP and REST APIs: blue for SOAP and green for REST. The details page of this new API appears like this:

7. Follow similar steps, as shown in the previous section, to subscribe to this API. For example, if this API is added to the previously created application (BelMobileApp) it is possible to also consume this API using the same API key generated for the application.

# Summary

This chapter started by defining the concept of API Management and its importance within an ASG strategy. It went on to describe the fundamental capabilities of Oracle API Manager and its importance with respect to the management of the API lifecycle.

The different application roles and components which are part of the product were also explained, as well as the OAPIM product architecture.

In order to illustrate Oracle API Manager's functionality, a use case was presented portraying the current situation of WBVC, a leading Telco provider on the verge of evolving its interactions with its consumers and partners. Particularly, due to their new **Mobile Virtual Network Enablers** (**MVNE**) offering, they needed to publish a set of APIs for **Mobile Virtual Network Operators** (**MVNO**) to consume.

With the help of the use case, the chapter further describes the key components of Oracle API Manager and how they fit into the WBCV API Architecture.

This chapter also demonstrates the steps which have to be followed in order to publish an API and how to protect it with an API key. It also describes the steps a consumer needs to take to discover and subsequently subscribe to an API.

Finally, the chapter explains the relationship between Oracle API Manager and Oracle Service Bus, and how the Service Bus console is used to curate the APIs and how APIs can be edited and published also using JDeveloper *12c*.

# 5
# Oracle API Gateway Implementation Overview

This chapter will introduce **Oracle API Gateway** (**OAG**), providing an in-depth look at its architecture and capabilities and how OAG fits into an existing and established **Service Oriented Architecture** (**SOA**). The chapter details OAG's functionality, providing detailed examples of how to use the product to expose APIs to external consumers. Finally, a detailed OAG use case will be presented to fully show and describe how the product can be used in a real world setting.

It is important to note that this chapter is not meant to be a full tutorial for OAG. Readers are strongly encouraged to seek alternative sources for more detailed information on the product and the diverse scenarios in which it can be used.

After reading this chapter, the reader should be able to:

- List and describe OAG's main components and capabilities
- Define a typical architecture for OAG
- Understand the sample use case for OAG and its implementation steps
- Justify the use of OAG and identify where it fits into an existing SOA architecture

## OAG overview

OAG provides a standards-based, policy-driven, standalone solution for exposing and securing enterprise APIs, and for managing them and their consumers in a scalable and highly available environment. OAG provides a runtime execution environment for APIs, providing key capabilities such as authentication and authorization, virtualization, and multi-protocol exchange.

When APIs are exposed to multiple consumers outside of an organization's trust boundary, organizations can be left vulnerable to external threats such as denial of service attacks, XML bombs, brute-force attacks, to name but a few. OAG provides a standard-based and policy-driven way to secure these exposed APIs. This goes further than just promoting the usage of a secure channel; it provides several layers of standards-based tools for authentication, authorization, confidentiality, and integrity, protecting all externally exposed APIs.

## OAG features

OAG is used to secure and manage APIs throughout their lifecycle. This is an essential requirement when exposing APIs to publicly accessible or unsecure networks. Equally, when exposing functionality to third parties in a commercial environment, it is important for organizations to have a toolset that allows them to measure, audit, and monitor a consumer's activity and usage level, which facilitates the creation of new business models in which consumers are charged on a per usage basis. Oracle OAG provides all these essential capabilities.

> OAG is not meant to provide full API Management capabilities. Full API lifecycle management of APIs is done via Oracle API Manager, which is covered in the following chapter.

The following table shows the key features offered by OAG for managing the lifecycle of protected APIs:

| Quality of Service | • QoS monitoring, alerting, and enforcement<br>• Real-time and offline performance monitoring<br>• Client-based policies |
|---|---|
| **Dynamic Transformation and Routing** | • Routing based on client and device identity, message type, network, condition and geography<br>• Content and context-based routing<br>• Protocol bridging (e.g. REST to SOAP)<br>• Data Transformation<br><br>> The last three characteristics of this use case overlap with Oracle Service Bus's 12c functionality. The best practice from an architectural point of view is to handle them through OSB. |

| | |
|---|---|
| **Monitoring and Reporting** | • Auditing and logging<br>• Real time monitoring and alerting<br>• Analytics and usage statistics<br><br>[  This last capability overlaps with and should be handled preferably by Oracle API Manager 12c ] |

[  API Management capabilities provided by Oracle API Manager will be covered in *Chapter 4, Oracle API Manager Implementation Overview*, of this book. As stated earlier, Oracle API Manager represents the cornerstone of API Management within Oracle's strategy. ]

# API security with OAG

Several layers of security are usually imposed between API consumers and providers to fully protect organizations from outside threats and attacks. The first security layer, or **perimeter security**, is referred to as the **demilitarized zone** or more simply as the **DMZ**. The second security layer, or green zone, is located behind the inner firewall of the DMZ. In some cases, the green zone may include several security sub-layers designed to further filter access to internal components and/or services. Finally, agents may be co-located within the core application logic to provide protection at the application layer. This is the last security layer, or last-mile security.

OAG is commonly deployed in the DMZ form as an organization's first line of defense from a software perspective.

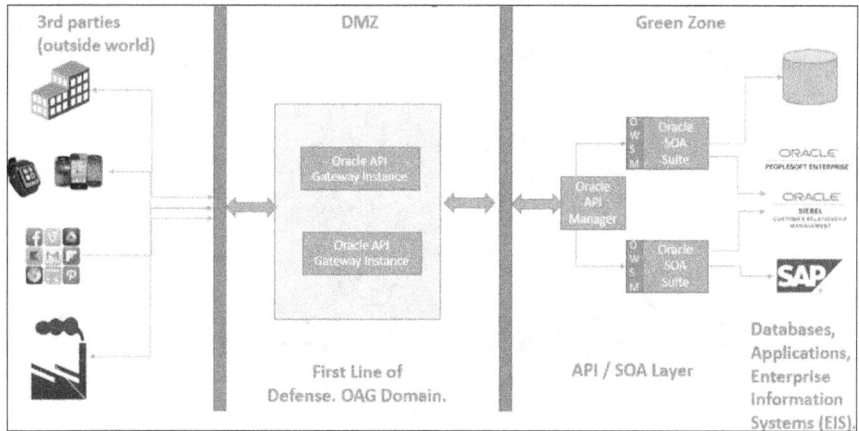

*Oracle API Gateway Implementation Overview*

OAG enables enterprises to leverage their existing **Identity and Access Management** investments by extending authentication, authorization, and risk policies to mobile, cloud, and enterprise solutions that involve publishing APIs for consumption. OAG is designed to protect APIs without the need to alter the underlying backend applications, thereby providing a non-obtrusive way of securing applications.

The following table describes OAG's key security-related capabilities:

| Threat Protection | <ul><li>Payload inspection</li><li>Parameter, data structure, and schema validation</li><li>SQL Injection, **cross-site scripting** (**XSS**) and **denial-of-service** (**DoS**) attack protection</li></ul> |
|---|---|
| Identity and Access Control | <ul><li>Identity token conversion</li><li>Support for authentication: HTTP basic, SSL, Kerberos, SAML, X.509 certificates, LDAP, OAuth, API Key, and so on</li><li>Unified Access enforcement through native integration with the following: Oracle Access Manager, Oracle Entitlements Server, Oracle Directory Services, CA SiteMinder, RSA Access Manager, Microsoft Active Directory, and IBM Tivoli.</li></ul> |
| Data Security | <ul><li>Redaction and encryption of sensitive data</li></ul> |

# OAG architecture overview

The OAG architecture consists of different components that deliver all of the capabilities described earlier. The following diagram provides a comprehensive view of the product's architecture:

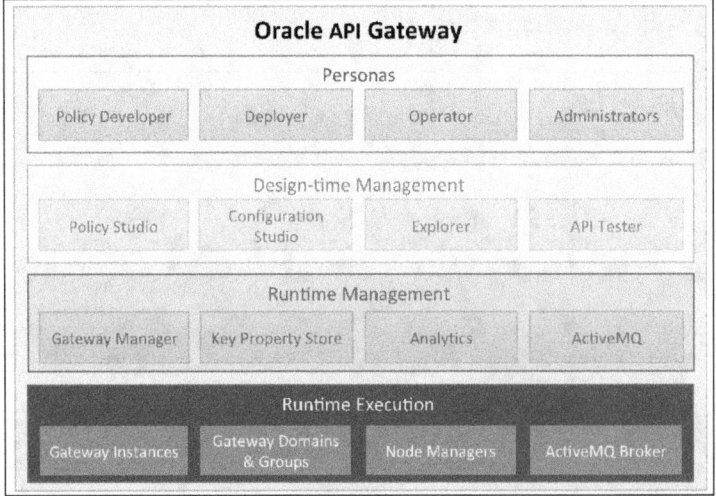

The elements presented in the preceding diagram are described as follows:

- **Personas**:
    - **Policy developer**: Virtualize APIs and develop security policies based on defined policy definitions. This may involve extending current policies or developing new ones as appropriate.
    - **Deployer**: Promote policies and configurations in different environments.
    - **Operator**: Uses the analytical and monitoring capabilities of the Gateway to monitor the API Gateway
    - **Gateway administrator**: Administer and troubleshoot the OAG platform ensuring that it is always up and running. They are also in charge of stopping, starting, and maintaining the Gateway
    - **Key property store administrator**: Create specific key values that will be used by the policies. This user has the ability to modify these properties at runtime, providing agility and real-time modifications for the APIs

- **Design-time management**:
    - **Policy studio**: This is both a development and configuration tool, in which engineers are able to establish and define policies for specific APIs. It is normally deployed on a separate client machine, in order to allow remote administration of policies

> Typically, the machines where OAG's service components are deployed will be subject to a *hardening* process. This means that installed components, applications, operating system tasks, capabilities and protocols will be reduced to a minimum for security reasons. In this regard, it wouldn't make a lot of sense to have the OAG Policy Studio deployed on the same infrastructure as the runtime components.

    - **Configuration studio**: This is the graphical tool used by the Gateway administrator.
    - **Explorer**: This tool enables users to test APIs. It can be used to generate sample/test messages to validate APIs deployed to OAG. This is a very important tool for testing and validation purposes.
    - **API Tester**: This team is responsible for extensively testing APIs prior to release, both from a functional and security point perspective.

*Oracle API Gateway Implementation Overview*

- **Runtime management**:
    - **Gateway Manager**: A centralized web-based application which allows administrators to manage OAG's global settings.
    - **Key Property Store**: This tool is used to store parameters that may be passed into policies at runtime. It allows the user to modify, delete, or create specific properties to be applied in conjunction with the policies.
    - **API Gateway Analytics**: Provides a centralized user interface to visualize metrics generated by the APIs virtualized within OAG. This component should be installed separately from OAG's runtime.
    - **Apache ActiveMQ**: A robust messaging platform, which supports JMS communications and a variety of integration patterns, including a number of cross-language clients and protocols. This enables the API Gateway to integrate external-facing REST APIs and SOAP Web services with backend systems and applications, using reliable, asynchronous messaging.

- **Runtime execution**:
    - **Gateway instances**: An API Gateway instance exposes APIs and policies to consumers.
    - **Gateway domains**: Provides a way to group and manage a set of gateway instances and gateway groups as a single unit. Usually, APIs are logically organized by taxonomy, business domain, environment (Test, Production) or the type of consumers that will be using them.
    - **Node managers**: Manages Gateway instances for a domain.
    - **ActiveMQ brokers**: The API Gateway installation includes the ActiveMQ Java JMS client library, which applications can use to send and receive messages to and from the queues and topics hosted on the embedded ActiveMQ broker. In addition, ActiveMQ clients that use the OpenWire protocol (ActiveMQ default transport protocol) can interact with the embedded broker.

> For further information on this topic, please refer to the Oracle API Gateway Concepts Guide documentation available at the following URL:
>
> http://docs.oracle.com/cd/E55956_01/doc.11123/concepts_guide/index.html

As mentioned earlier, OAG is typically deployed in the **Demilitarized Zone**, becoming not only the organization's first line of defense, but also allowing it to streamline the process of exposing and protecting specific APIs. The following diagram explains where Oracle API Gateway fits and how it relates with the rest of the components of a common **Oracle Fusion Middleware** deployment.

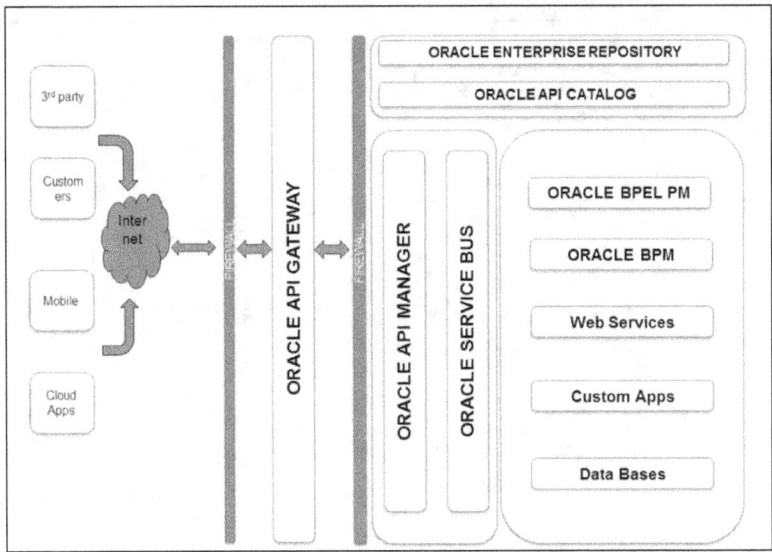

OAG's underlying architecture is primarily based on **service gateway** technology.

> A service gateway is a type of software program commonly found in the request processing logic of a SOA platform. Its primary role is to perform some form of automated processing prior to the transmission and receipt of messages.
>
> Service gateways usually address cross-cutting concerns, providing generic functionality to decouple these responsibilities from core API logic.
>
> A gateway program usually exists as a lightweight, standalone application with a fairly small memory footprint.

*Oracle API Gateway Implementation Overview*

This kind of deployment model allows for the interception of requests before they reach the SOA infrastructure. It is non-obtrusive, requiring no code changes by the development team. OAG can provide both passive (which doesn't modify message content) and active functionalities as demonstrated here:

| Passive | Active |
| --- | --- |
| Payload inspection | Data encryption |
| Parameter/schema validation | Data format transformation |
| Monitoring and alerting | Protocol bridging |
| Auditing and logging | |

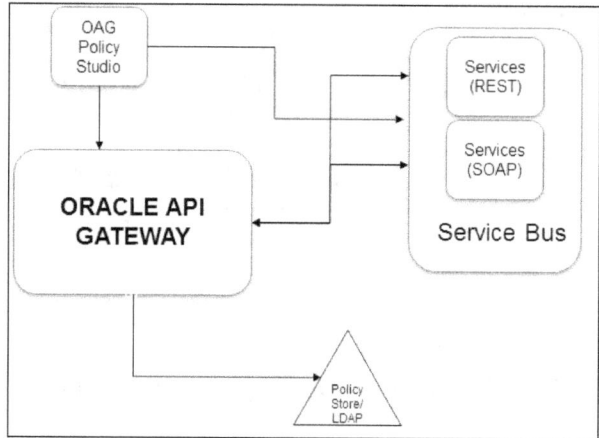

Typically, the first step after capturing a request within OAG is to create a session in which to authenticate the API consumer. Once the authentication process is successfully completed, OAG evaluates the message contents in order to identify and subsequently apply specified security policies. Policies can be linked together to form a chain of defense. Once the execution of this policy chain has successfully completed, OAG will then proceed to:

- Route the request to an endpoint or make a transport/protocol translation
- Translate a JSON/Rest call to an HTTP/SOAP call, if required

# Implementing use cases

As described in *Chapter 2, Implementation Case Study*, WBCV Telecom already has a fairly mature SOA implementation in place and is looking to externalize many of its SOAP/WSDL based business services as APIs. By externalizing these services, the **Chief Technology Officer (CTO)** hopes to unlock business functionality and data assets that were previously only available internally. These can potentially be leveraged by mobile developers, web developers, and business partners wishing to build and/or enhance solutions in order to offer a much richer and seamless user experience while also offering greater functionality.

Naturally, security is a top priority for the organization's CTO and the architecture team. The CTO is very aware that, by externalizing more business functionality and data through APIs, the organization is also exposing itself to a number of external threats such as the ones listed by the **Open Web Application Security Project (OWASP)**.

Refer to:

OWASP top 10 projects: `https://www.owasp.org/index.php/Top10#OWASP_Top_10_for_2013`

OWASP top 10 mobile risks: `https://www.owasp.org/index.php/OWASP_Mobile_Security_Project#tab=Top_10_Mobile_Risks`

The CTO and WBCV architects fully understood that the potential security threats imposed a huge risk on the organization and that, without a robust strategy in place, such a risk would place the entire open API strategy in jeopardy. Equally, the organization's rather cautious **Chief Security Officer (CSO)**, concerned with all the recent Internet-based attacks unleashed upon several big corporations, decided to hire an external consultancy to perform extensive penetration / vulnerability tests to highlight potential threats and weaknesses. Upon receiving a detailed report showing the results of the testing, the CSO, utterly alarmed, presented the following findings to the board of directors and requested that a robust security solution be put in place before APIs could be made externally available.

## Oracle API Gateway Implementation Overview

The report findings are discussed here:

- As depicted in the diagram, the current infrastructure relies heavily on a **Demilitarized Zone** and web (HTTP) proxy

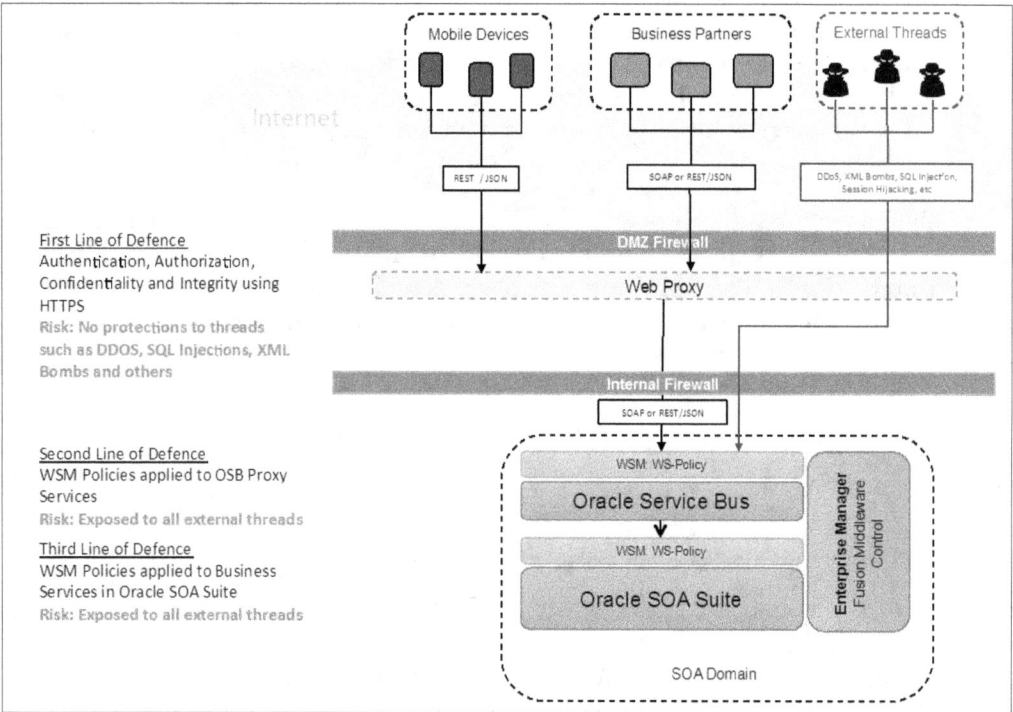

- The current infrastructure would leave APIs highly vulnerable to denial-of-service, SQL injection, and cross-site scripting attacks (which may come from one or more of the newly enabled channels) as the existing web proxy only provides very basic security based on HTTPS

- Since the existing SOAP/WSDL based services were originally designed for WBCV's internal use only, their security mechanisms are fairly weak (HTTP basic authentication and SSL in some cases). This characteristic renders them prime targets for insufficient authorization attacks, message tampering, malicious intermediaries, and payload eavesdropping.

- The current DMZ infrastructure lacks the ability to detect anomalies. This means that any message reaching a service endpoint in the DMZ will be routed to the internal SOA infrastructure therefore leaving it vulnerable to external attacks. The operations team also lacked the ability to monitor and trace and audit incoming and/or outgoing messages.

Fortunately (as described in *Chapter 2, Implementation Case Study*) the team responsible for proposing the API strategy had already considered these security challenges. To address the concerns, the API strategy team recommended the implementation of an API gateway capable of:

- Protecting APIs against external security threats, such as those listed by OWASP
- Provide rich functionality so that all the security requirements imposed by the network security team , specifically those around authentication, authorization, availability, integrity, and confidentiality, could be satisfied
- Provide protocol conversion capabilities such as REST/JSON to SOAP and vice-versa
- Throttling capabilities to prevent **distributed denial of service (DDoS)** attacks
- Issuing public and private keys to provide confidentiality and integrity in message interchange
- Provide support for major standards such as WS-Security and OAuth 2.0
- The gateway should not become a bottleneck to high volume transactions and thus be lightweight and scalable

Based on the recommendations made available in the API strategy and, also after a careful product evaluation, the CTO's architecture team decided to adopt Oracle API Gateway and defined the following high-level architecture:

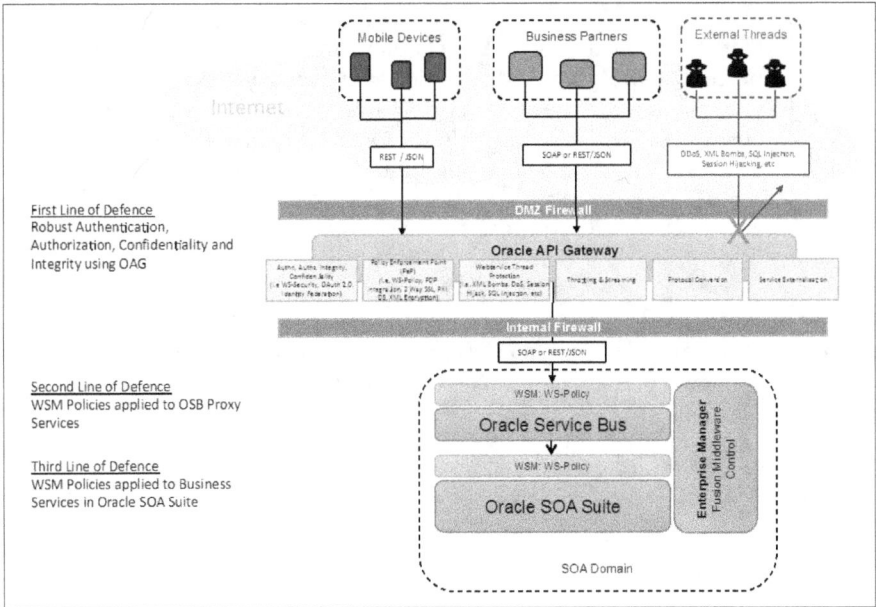

# Implementing OAG

The first step when opening up functionality to partners via APIs was to identify which business services were to be externalized. Once done, subsequent steps were required to apply suitable **Web Service Manager (WSM)** policies and API Gateway policies to satisfy first-line and second-line defense security requirements. This was achieved as follows:

- Identify which business services are the candidates to be exposed as an API
- Work jointly with the security team to define a set of policies to be applied to these APIs, both first line and second line of defense:
    - Authentication: where to authenticate the external users?
    - Authorization: once they are authenticated, authorize users to determine access rights to an API?
    - Service-level agreements: define whether the services should be highly available and define any time restrictions on usage?
    - Specify if the identity of the consumer needs to be propagated throughout the chain of execution?
- Identify suitable integrity and configuration mechanisms, such as implementing SSL certificates with two-way authentication in REST APIs
- Configure OAG for maximum API protection from attacks such as DoS, XSS, SQL Injection, among others

Note that the purpose of this chapter is not to elaborate on the process of applying WSM policies to OSB proxy services. For this, you may refer to the section on *Securing Oracle Service Bus with Oracle Web Services Manager* in the Oracle document: *Developing Services with Oracle Service Bus* at `https://docs.oracle.com/middleware/1213/osb/develop/GUID-1CE01E95-8B9B-4369-AAC9-28F4C5B6EF63.htm#OSBDV1681`.

The steps for installing OAG as well as other hardening recommendations are covered in *Chapter 6, Installation Tips and Techniques*.

*Chapter 5*

## Service discovery

This process was used to identify the candidate business services for externalization and to determine their URLs. Given that **Oracle API Catalog** was already implemented in the organization, the discovery process was fairly straightforward and painless.

>  Please refer to *Chapter 3, Oracle API Catalog Implementation*, and *Chapter 4, Oracle API Manager Implementation Overview*, for further information on how to implement Oracle API Catalog for discovering APIs.

## API registration in OAG

Assuming that all business services have already been secured with WSM policies, the next step is to register the service WSDL and the relevant operations in OAG.

The high level steps are the following:

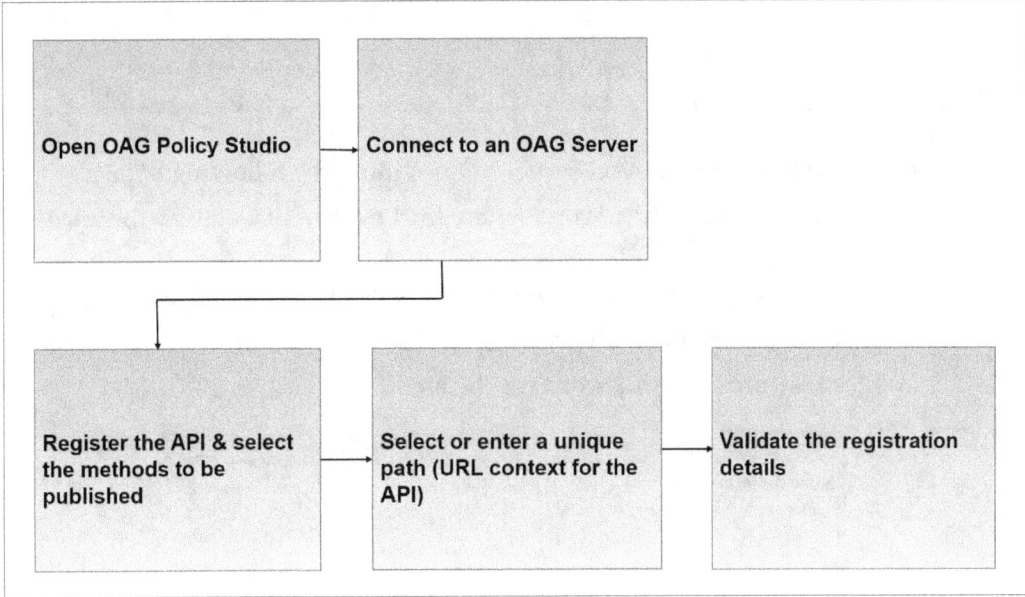

## Oracle API Gateway Implementation Overview

To achieve this, the following steps were executed:

1. Open OAG Policy Studio.

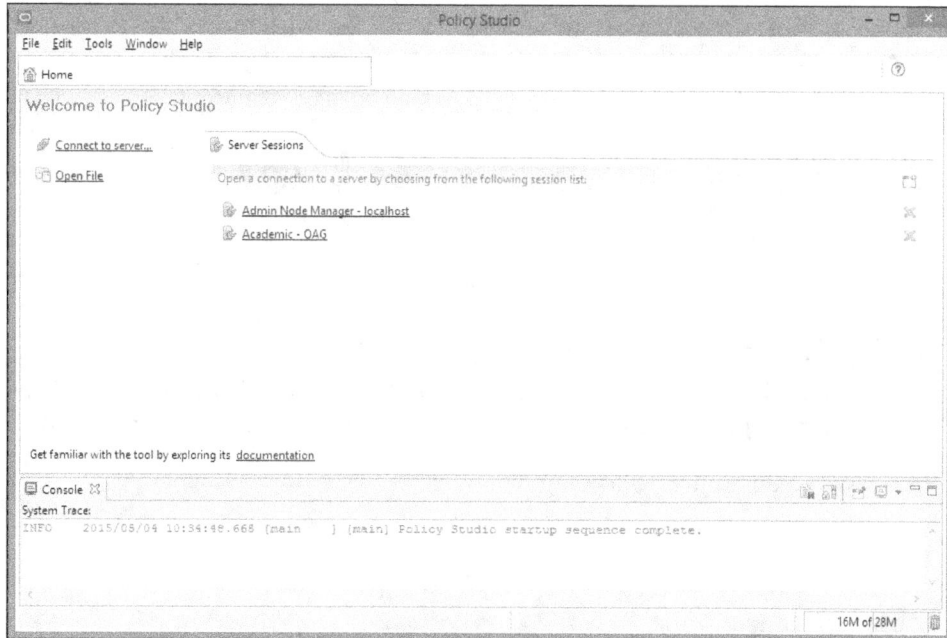

2. Connect to the relevant OAG Server by providing the following details:
   - **Host**: Name or IP address where the Oracle API Gateway instance is running
   - **Port**: TCP port number for the Oracle API Gateway instance
   - **User**: Username with privileges for policy creation
   - **Password**: The password for the user

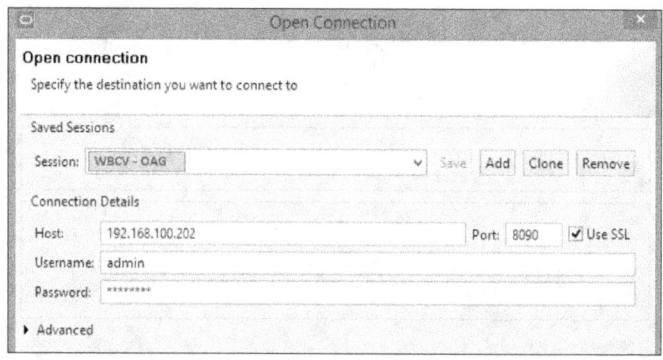

*Chapter 5*

3. Expand the **Business Services** navigation bar on the left menu of the screen.

4. On the right-hand window, click on **Register Web Service**.

When the window **Import WSDL** opens there will be an option to load a WSDL either from **WSDL File**, **WSDL URL**, or **WSDL from UDDI**. Choose **WSDL URL**.

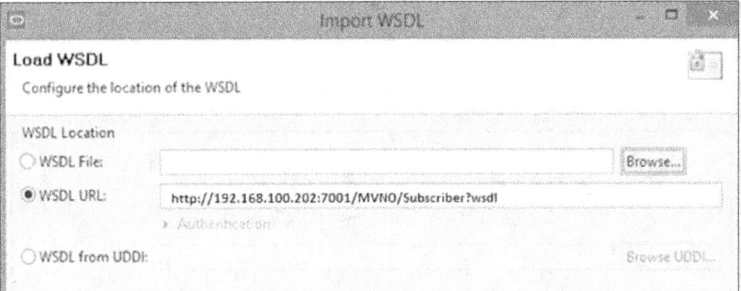

 You may recall that this service URL was previously discovered using the Oracle API Catalog during the service discovery phase.

*Oracle API Gateway Implementation Overview*

5. Select the relevant operations that will be externalized and then click on **Next**.

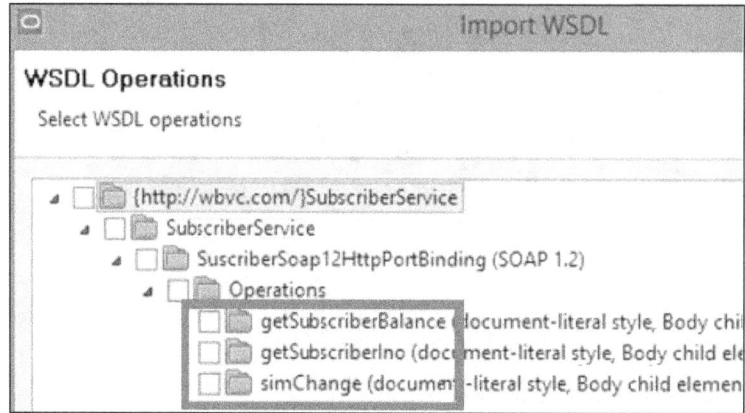

6. The following screen asks if WS-Policy should be implemented to enforce security. However, because the business service will not be directly exposed (a wrapper REST API interface will be created) then this option does not apply, so just click on **Next**.

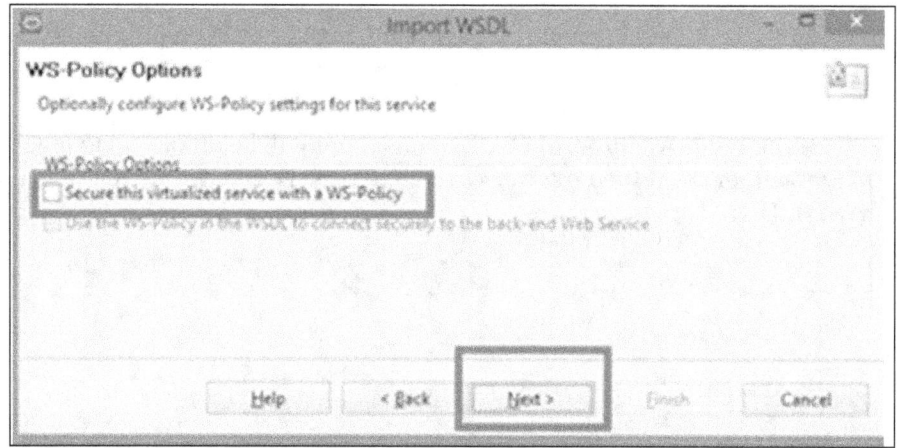

WS-Policy Options checkboxes

7. Select or enter a unique path, then click on **Finish**. A unique path is the URL context where the API will be receiving the requests. In this example, it will only respond to OAG internal requests and not to external ones. This is because the concrete external API that will be exposed is JSON/REST, and the HTTP/SOAP based one is just going to be used for the internal conversion.

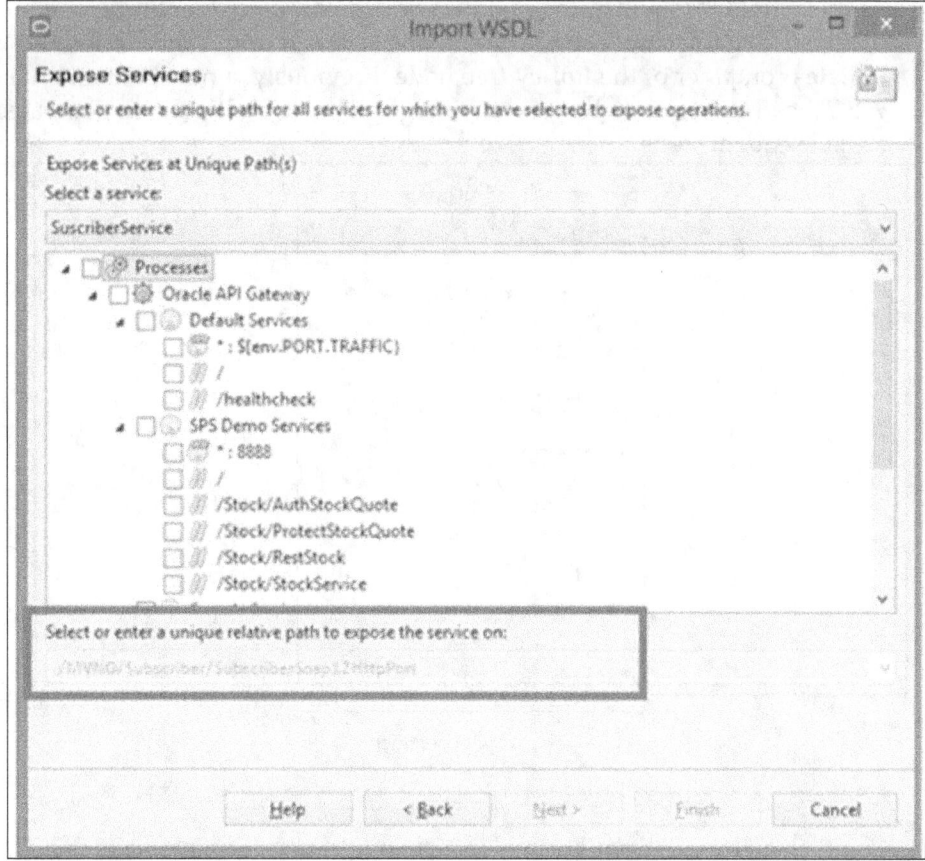

8. In the **Summary** screen, verify that all details are correct and then click **OK**.

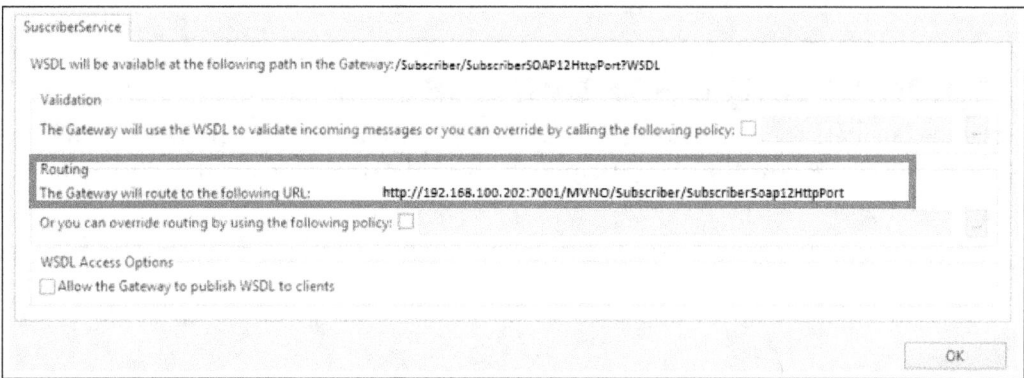

9. At this point OAG will autogenerate a new policy container and a new policy, both named after the service being exposed under the **Generated Policies** container of the **Policy** tree node. Previously, a new container named WBCV had been manually created to logically group all policies generated in the subsequent steps.

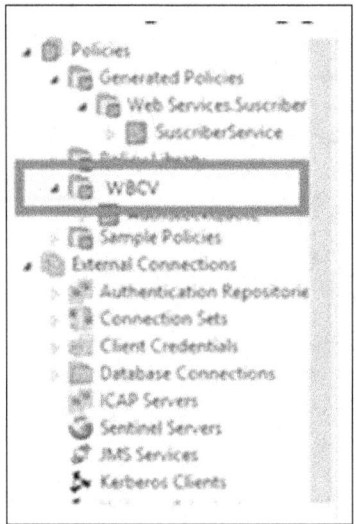

The WBCV container

 Policy containers are used to logically group policies together. This is very useful especially as the number of policies grow. Policy containers can be generated by right-clicking on the **Policies** tree node itself or on another container.

## Implementing OAG policies

Since the business service was registered in OAG for internal use only, the following steps will describe how the services are secured and exposed as REST APIs using OAG policies.

# Creating a policy to handle authentication and authorization using LDAP and OAuth

In order to make sure that only authorized users can consume APIs, WBCV created an OAG policy which links to an LDAP server. For this implementation, WBCV decided to install and configure a new LDAP server using **Oracle Unified Directory** rather than reuse the internal MS Active Directory implementation.

 OAG supports integration with any LDAP v3 compliant server. This chapter just provides a flavor of how to authenticate and authorize using an external LDAP, which has been provisioned exclusively for the management of external users.

The high level steps for this section are shown in the following diagram:

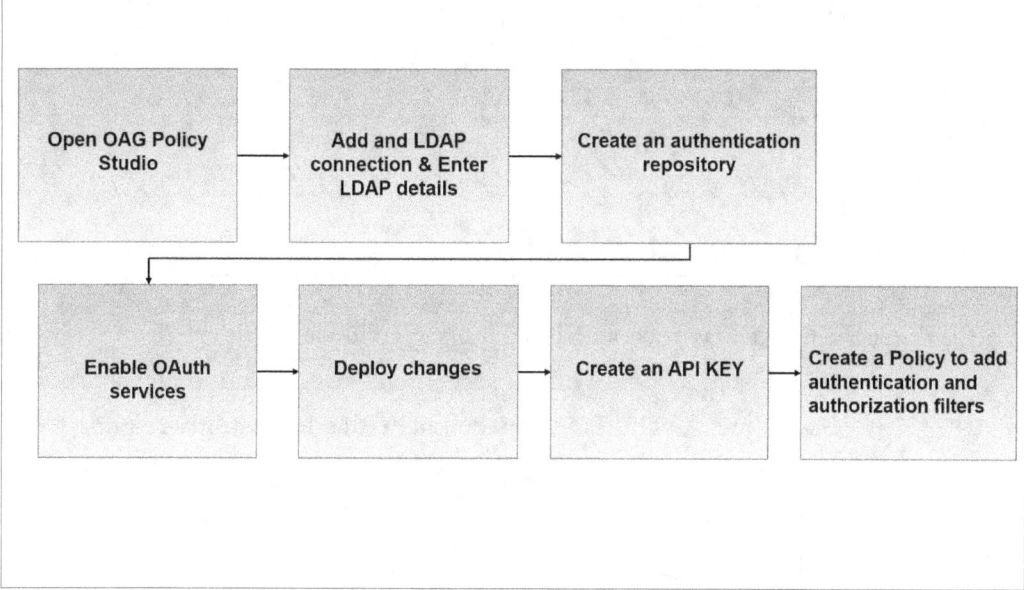

*Oracle API Gateway Implementation Overview*

The detailed steps are the following:

1. Open OAG Policy Studio and connect to the relevant OAG server, as described in steps 1 and 2 of the previous section.
2. At the left-hand side of the Policy Studio, navigate to the LDAP Connections section under the **External Connections** node, click on it and then, in the right-hand side of the window, click on **Add a LDAP Connection**.

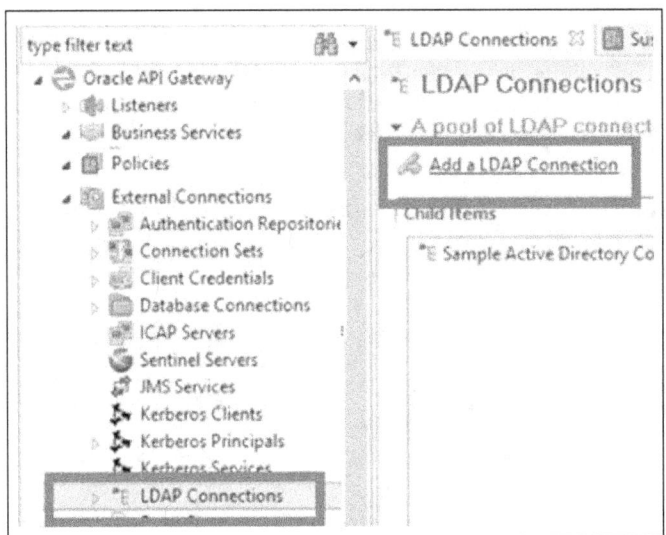

3. Enter the LDAP server connection details as follows:
    - **URL**: The URL of the LDAP server to be used to authenticate users.
    - **Username**: A valid LDAP username with administrative rights.
    - **Password**: The password for the LDAP user.
    - **SSL**: Check this option if the communication to the LDAP server is over SSL.
    - **Type**: Denotes the type of authentication to be used. If the authentication is simple then user and password is used. However, there are further options, such as **Digest-MD5**, **External**, or even **None** (denoting an anonymous connection).
    - **Realm**: Used with Digest-MD5 authentication. This is required when a hash for the password is provided or to identify the required realm in a multiple realm setup.

Chapter 5

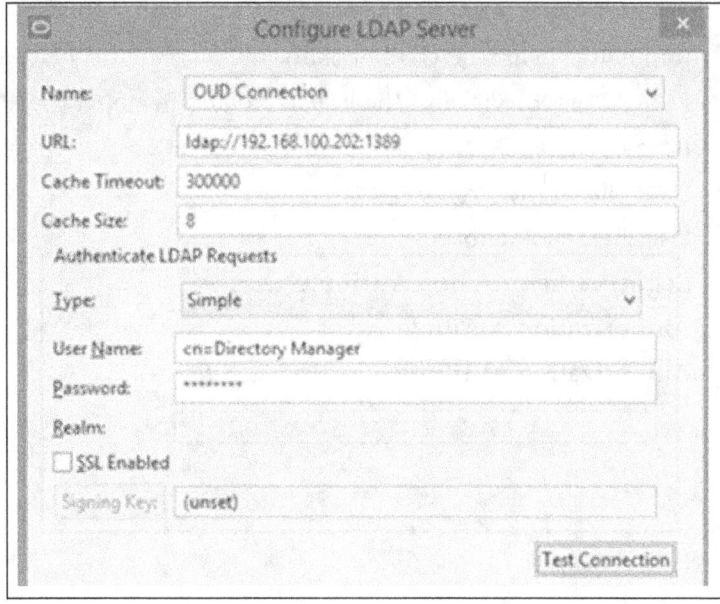

4. Leave the default values for the rest of the fields.
5. To verify the connection, click on **Test Connection**. If all details are correct, a message should be received saying **The connection was successful**.
6. Create a new LDAP Authentication Repository. In order to do this, on the left hand side of the Policy Studio, go to the **LDAP Repositories** section: click on it and then, in the right hand side of the window, click on **Add new Repository**.

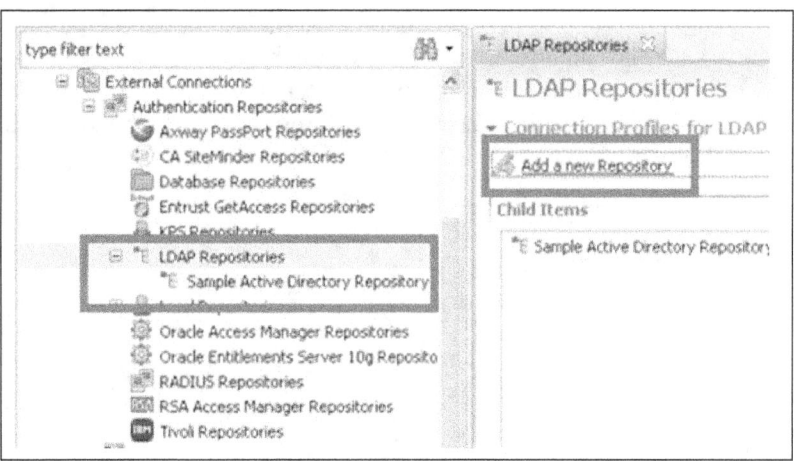

7. Enter the repository information as follows:
    - **Repository Name**: OUD Repository
    - **LDAP Directory**: Select the LDAP created in step 3
    - **Base Criteria**: `ou=People,dc=example,dc=com`
    - **User Class**: `inetOrgPerson`
    - **User Search Attribute**: `uid`
    - **Login Authentitcation Attribute**: `uid`
    - **Authorization Attribute**: `uid`
    - **Authorization Attribute Format**: `User Name`

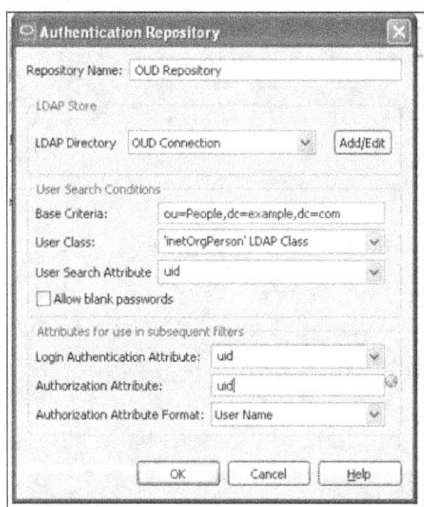

8. The next step is to enable **OAuth Services**. This step is executed once for every OAuth integration. Navigate to the left-hand side of the **Policy Studio** window, go to **Listeners | Oracle API Gateway | OAuth 2.0 Services** and then **click Ports**:

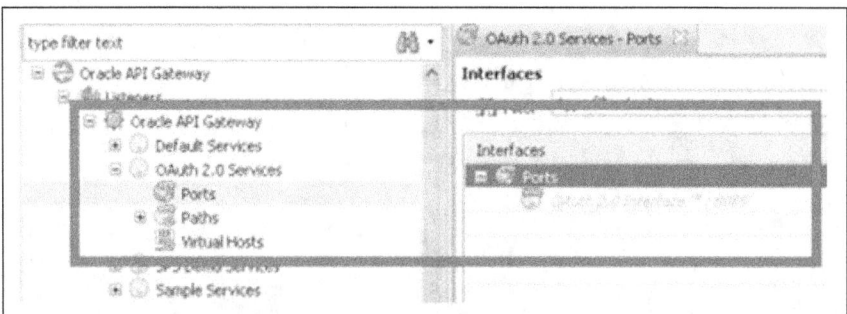

9. Double-click on **OAuth 2.0 Interface** and enable the interface. Hit the **OK** button:

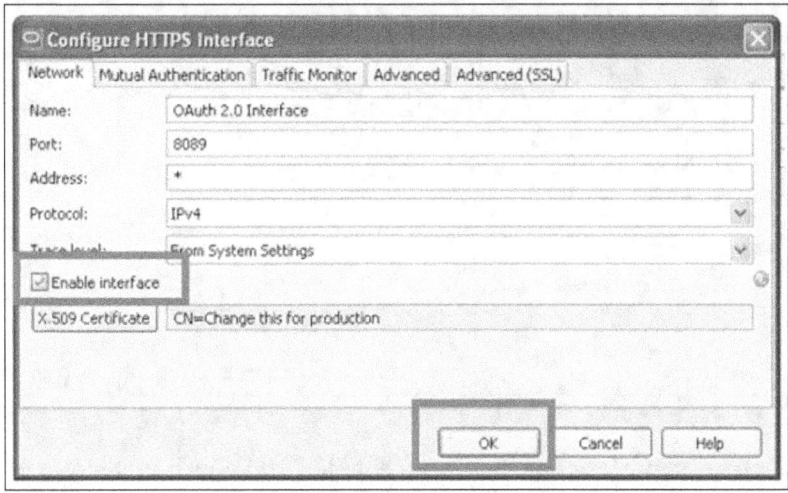

10. Now create a local user to access the OAuth interface. Follow these steps to do this:

   1. Go to the left-hand side of the **Policy Studio** window, expand **Users** and **Groups** and then click on **Users**.

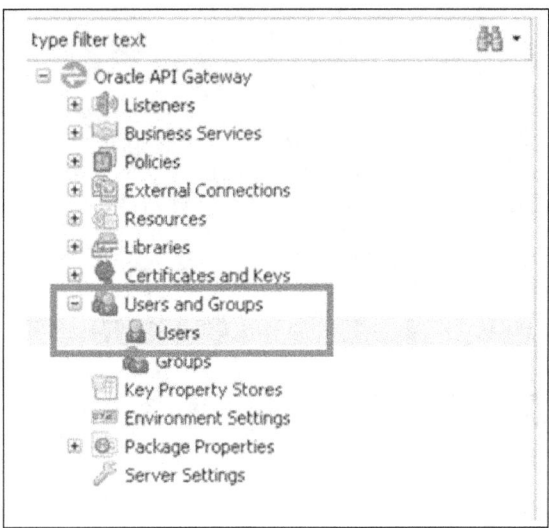

## Oracle API Gateway Implementation Overview

2. Click on **Add**, and fill the information:
   - **Username**: oauthusr
   - **Password**: A password

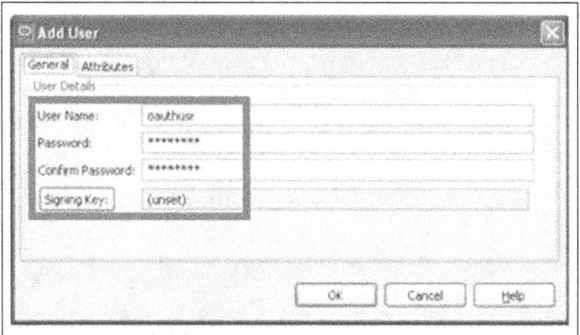

11. The OAuth interface has now been enabled and a user created to use it. The next step is to deploy the changes to the OAG instance. Click on **Sync button**:

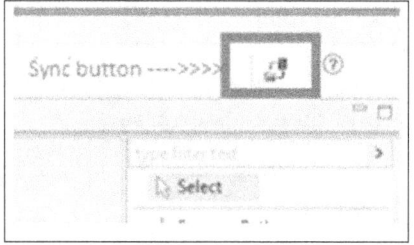

12. Once the **Deploy** window opens, select the required OAG gateway group from the **Group** dropdown and then select the specific gateway instances onto which you wish to deploy the policies. Then click on **Deploy**.

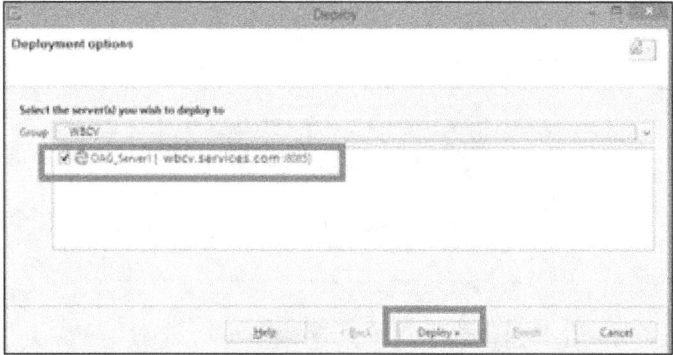

The Deploy window

*Chapter 5*

13. After deploying the changes, go to the **OAuth Console** using the URL `https://<APIGATEWAYHOST>:8089` and enter the newly created user credentials:

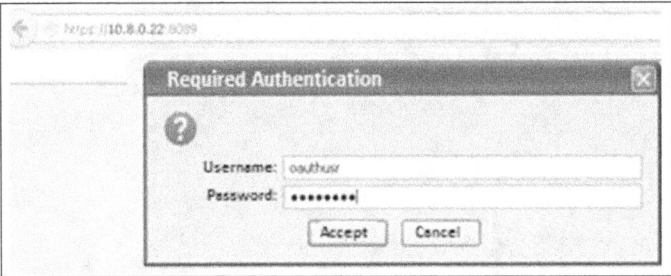

14. The following landing page appears

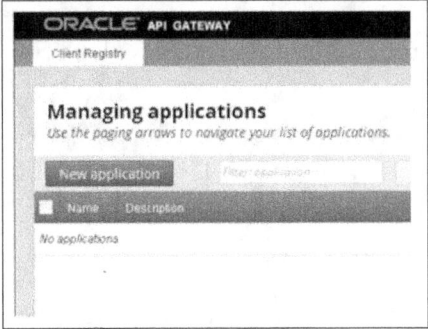

15. Under the **Create new application** section, click on **Create** and fill the information.

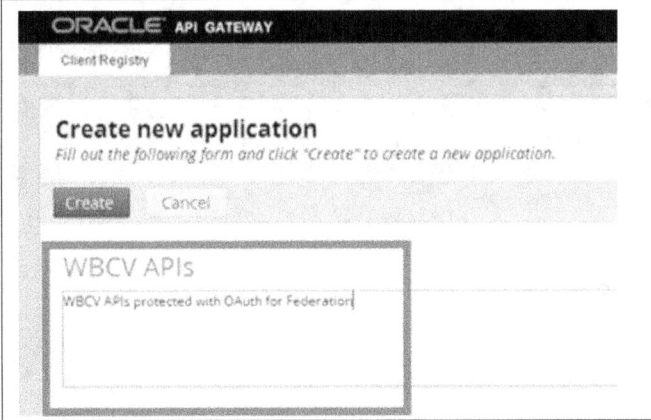

[ 205 ]

16. In the next window, click on **New API Key** to generate the **API Key**:

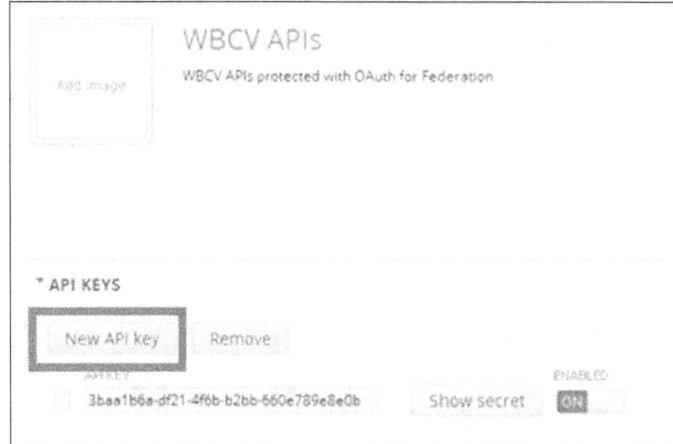

17. Now, create a **ClientID**. In this case, this will be confidential.

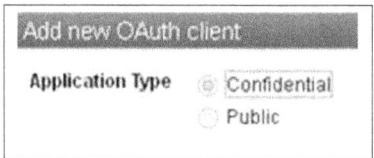

18. The next step is to create a new policy and then add authentication and authorization filters to it. To do this, go to the left hand side of the **Policy Studio**, expand the **Policies** tree node and then right-click on the newly created WBCV container and then click on **Create a new policy**.

>  OAuth is an open standard for authorization. OAuth provides client applications with secure delegated access to server resources on behalf of a resource owner. It specifies a process for resource owners to authorize third-party access to their server resources without sharing their credentials. For further information please refer to http://en.wikipedia.org/wiki/OAuth.

19. The policy creation window will come up:

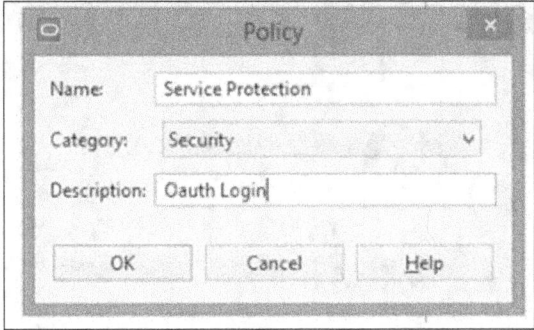

- **Name**: The name of this policy. In this case, `Service Protection`.
- **Category**: `Security`.
- **Description**: A meaningful description.

20. Click on the **OK** button and the window will close.
21. Navigate to the **Filters** menu on the right-hand side of **Policy Studio**, search for filters relevant to OAuth by typing this word into the **Search** field.

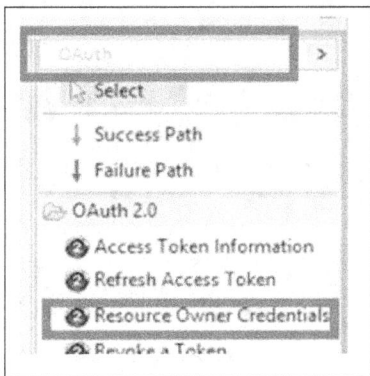

Oracle API Gateway Implementation Overview

22. Drag and drop the **Resource Owner Credentials** filter onto the canvas.

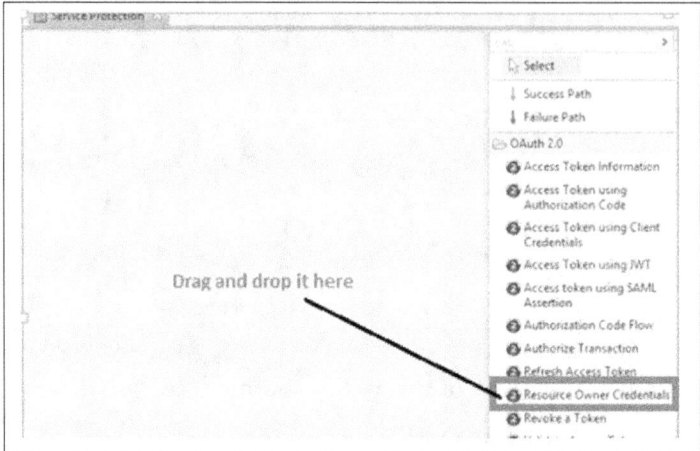

23. The **Configure a new Resource Owner Credentials** window will appear. There are three tabs: **Application Validation, Access Token,** and **Monitoring**. Specific details apply for each category. Under the **Application Validation** tab, in the **Authentication credentials using this repository** field, select the LDAP connection **OUD Repository** (this is the one created in earlier steps).

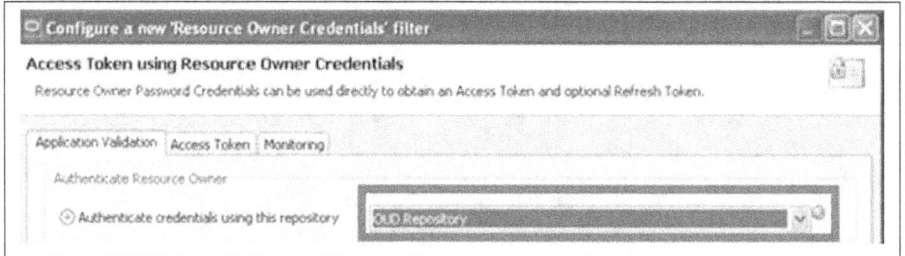

24. Move the **Access Token** tab and click the dialog button next to the **Access Token will be stored here** field.

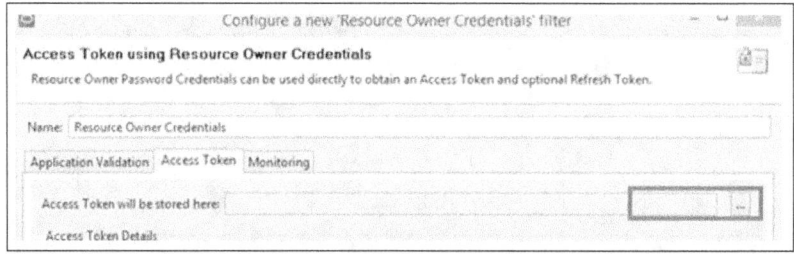

25. Once the **Access Token** window opens, choose **OAuth Access Token Store** and click the **OK** button.

26. Once the dialog window closes, complete the **Access Token** tab by including an expiry time frame for the token in the **Access Token Expiry** field, the length for the token in the **Access Token Length** field, and also, if desired, a **Refresh Token Expiry** time frame.

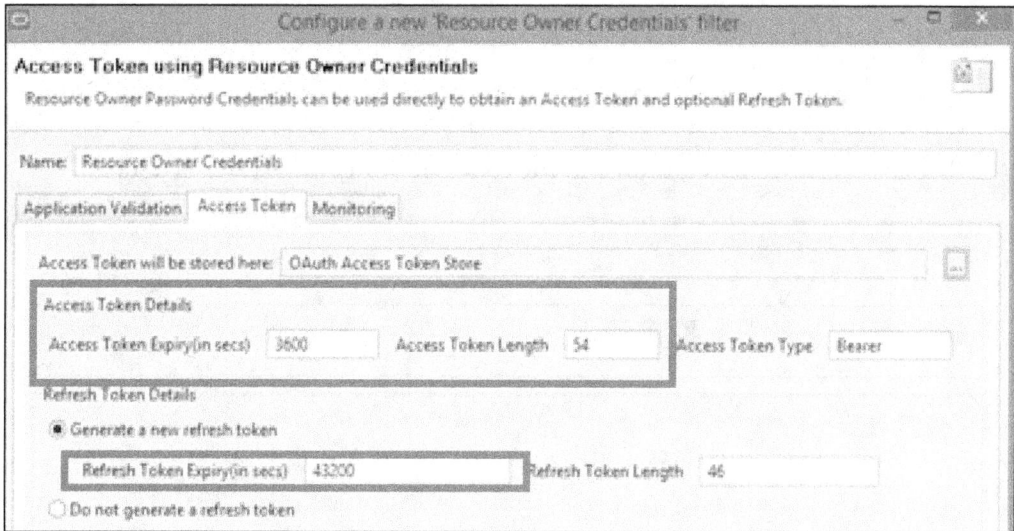

## Oracle API Gateway Implementation Overview

27. Now move to the **Monitoring** tab. From the **Monitoring Options** section, select the options **Monitor service usage**, **Monitor service usage per client**, and enter **authentication.subject.id**, which is the default attribute used for storing the ID of the authenticated subject (for example, the username supplied by the client). Also, select **Record Outbound Transactions**.

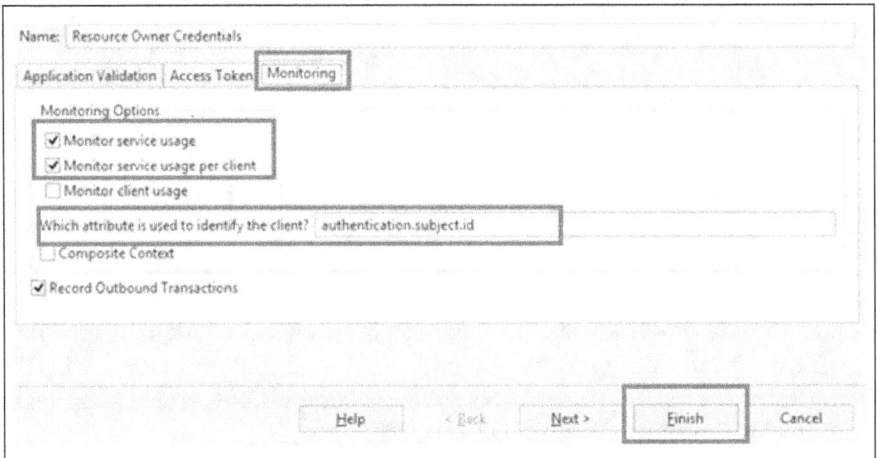

 The information provided in this tab is very important to enable the monitoring of API calls.

28. Click on the **Finish** button and the configuration of this filter is done.

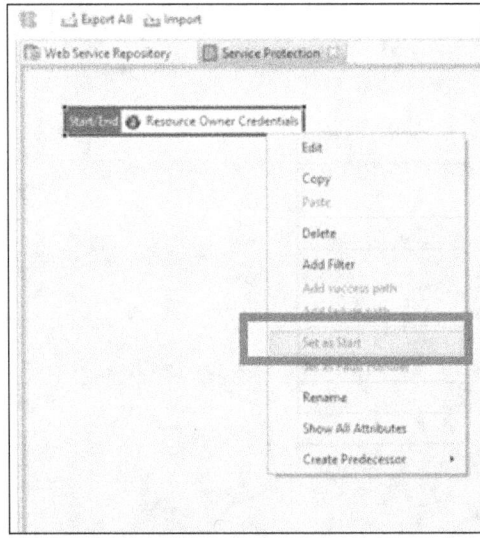

[ 210 ]

*Chapter 5*

# Adding throttling filters to an existing policy

This newly created policy can now be used to authenticate users against an LDAP directory and authorize applications for use of the exposed APIs via OAuth. However, it cannot yet protect the underlying services against other threats such as denial of service (DoS) attacks and malicious code, to name a few.

In the steps that follow, the previously created policy (Service Protection) will be extended to also provide throttling capabilities. This will provide protection against DoS attacks.

1. Open **Policy Studio**. Expand the **Policies** tree node and then the **WBCV** container. Double-click on the **Service Protection** policy:

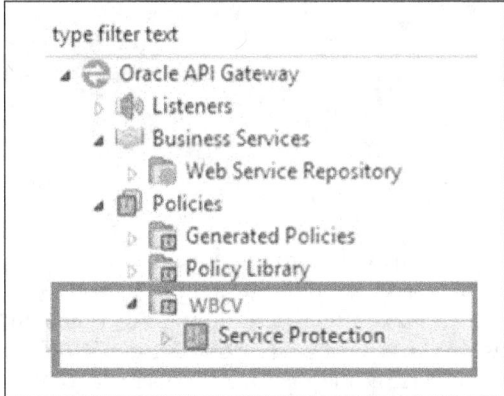

2. Using the textbox above the policy filter palette, located on the right side of the screen, search for **Throttling**. The search should return the **Throttling** content filter. Drag and drop it onto the canvas.

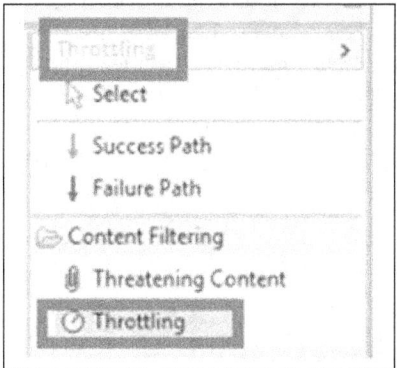

3. A window will appear that allows the user to configure **Throttling** properties. In the **Allow** field, enter the number of calls that will be allowed in a given period before OAG starts blocking. In this case, it is set to 10 every second.

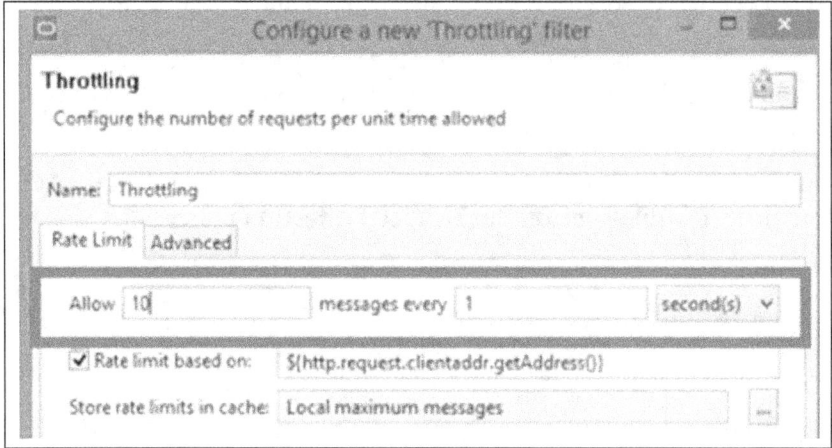

> It is important for the reader to understand the concept of throttling. Throttling is the ability to limit throughput to a specified threshold value. By predefining a maximum throughput, OAG is able to block any call that exceeds this threshold value. For example, WBCV decided to allow a maximum of 10 API calls a second in this instance. Should a DoS attack against this API result in the number of calls increasing beyond 10 a second, OAG will discard any additional calls.
>
> While this functionality is very useful in preventing DoS attacks, it is clearly essential that organizations calculate usage levels accurately to ensure that access is not denied to known, high volume customers. This calculation is called a volumetric analysis. Inaccurate calculations will risk OAG rejecting genuine calls (which is far from ideal). It is therefore highly recommended that organizations conduct a detailed volumetric analysis before applying this policy to any API.

4. Then click on **OK**. The **canvas** should look like this

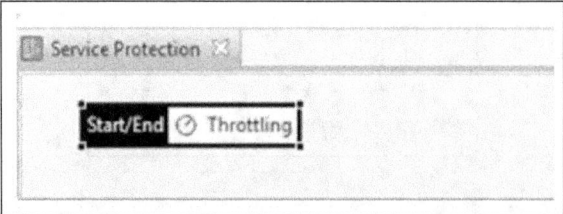

*Chapter 5*

5. Join the two filters, as follows:

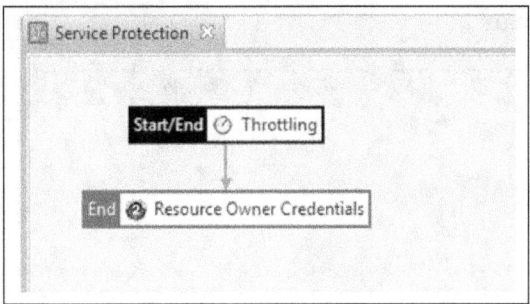

6. Save the policy.

## Applying a policy to a web service

Now that a policy has been created to handle authentication, authorization and an additional level of threat protection, the next step is to secure the previously registered web service (Subscriber Service) using a policy. In this scenario, not only will the service be exposed using REST, but also as a secured SOAP web service therefore providing the developers with two interface options.

1. From the **Policy** node tree, expand the policy group **Generated Policies** and then go to **Web Services | SubscriberService** and finally double-click on the **SubscriberService** policy. This will place the user in edit mode.

2. Open **Service Handler for 'SubscriberService'** and filter by double-clicking on it. This will open a **configuration** window.

*Oracle API Gateway Implementation Overview*

3. Click on the **Message Interception Points** tab and then click on the **Request from Client** tab. Click on the dialog button for option **A)** to select the policy previously created.

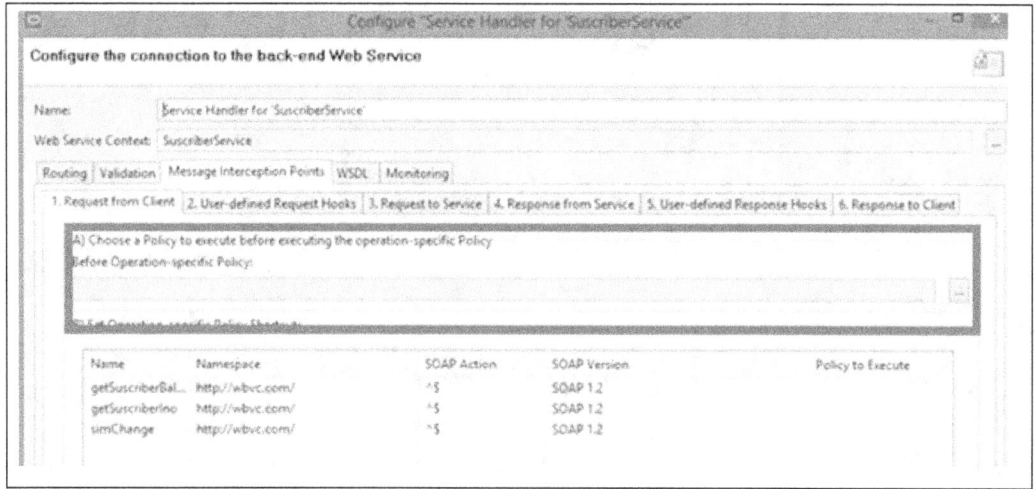

 By adding a message interception point, OAG will make sure that the selected policy is applied to all service requests made to the operations listed in section **B)** of the screen.

4. Another window will appear. From this window, select the **Service Protection** policy previously created.

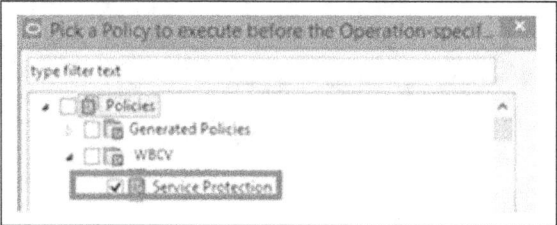

 This policy can be applied to different service operations or even REST URIs. In this case, the policy will be applied to all three operations of the service that was registered in previous steps.

5. Click the **OK** button and then the **Finish button** on the **Configure Service Handler** window.

# Deploying a policy

Now that the policy has been built and applied to a service, the next step is to deploy it to the runtime gateway instance group. This process is very simple and performed using **Policy Studio** as described next:

1. Open **Policy Studio** and then from the **Policy** node tree, expand the policy group **Generated Policies** and then **Web Services-the SubscriberService** policy and finally double-click on the **SubscriberService** policy. This will take the user into edit mode.

2. Once the policy opens in the canvas, click on the Sync button which is located in the upper right hand side of the editor. This will take us to the deploy window in order to select to which OAG instance this policy will be deployed.

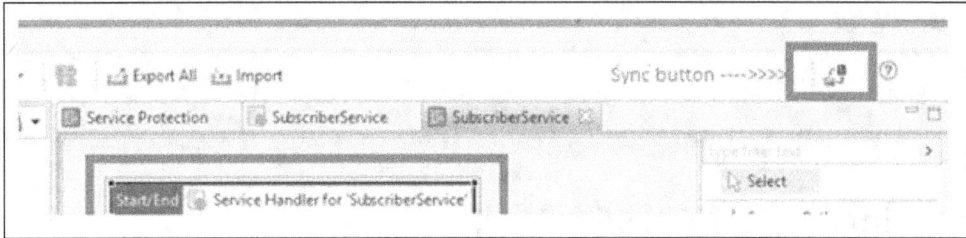

3. Once the **Deploy** window opens, select an OAG gateway group from the **Group** drop-down and then select the specific gateway instances onto which you wish to deploy these policies. Then click on **Deploy**.

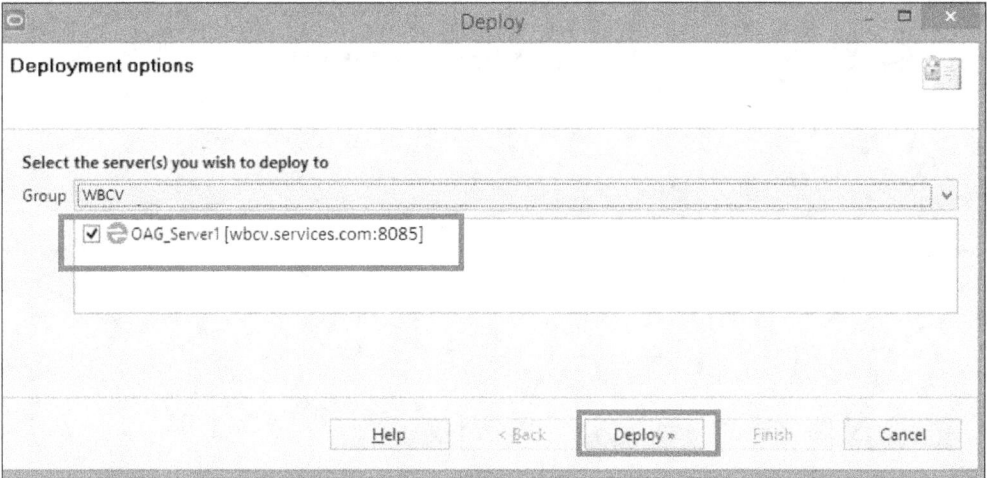

*Oracle API Gateway Implementation Overview*

4. The **Deploy** window will now show the **deployment results**; if the deployment is successful the **Status** should be set to **Completed. Deployment successful**. If this is the case, click on **Finish**.

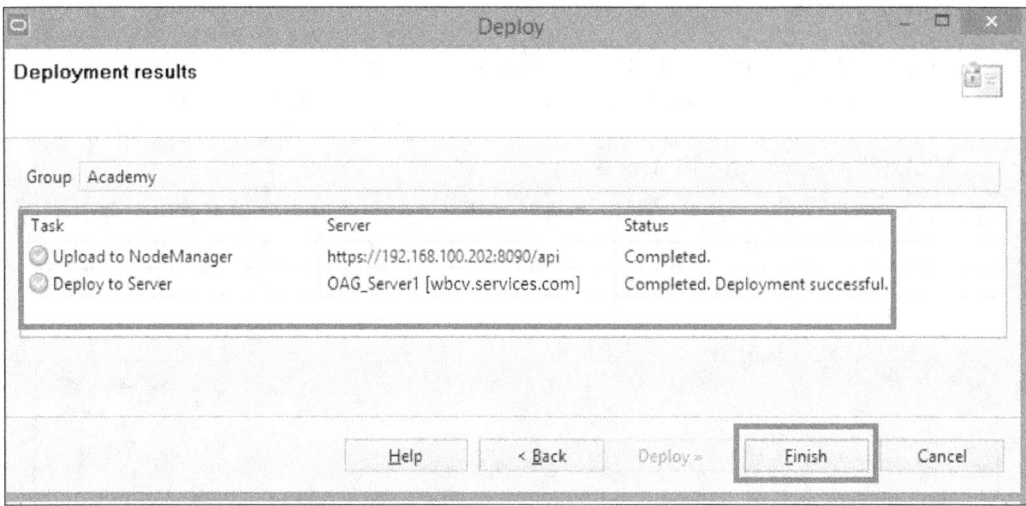

## Creating a REST/JSON API

Up to this point, WBCV has registered an internal web service and applied a custom policy to handle authentication, authorization, and a level of threat protection. The policy has been deployed into an OAG server group and tested. However, up to this point, a web API hasn't yet been created, so mobile and/or web developers cannot consume it using REST and JSON in order to build applications. For this purpose, a new web API has to be created that will expose all service operations as REST/JSON resources and facilitate JSON to SOAP conversations and vice-versa.

The high-level steps are the following:

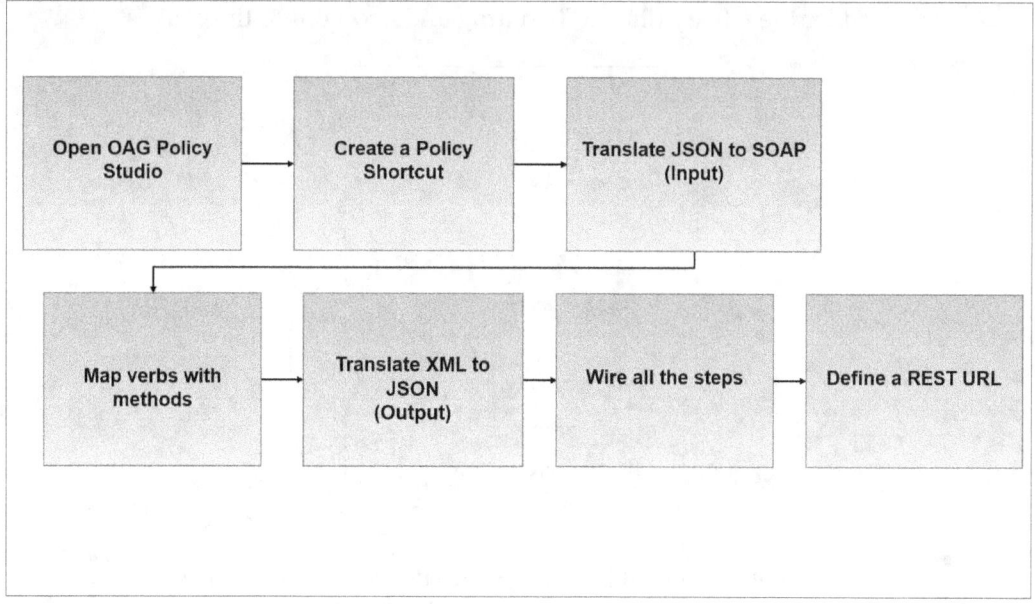

The following detailed steps describe how to achieve this:

1. From **Policy Studio**, and as described in previous steps, create a new **policy** with the following details under the **WBCV container** option. Once all the details are entered, click on **OK**.
    - **Name**: Include a meaningful name (for example, Subscriber REST)
    - **Category**: Choose **MVNO**
    - **Description**: Type a meaningful description

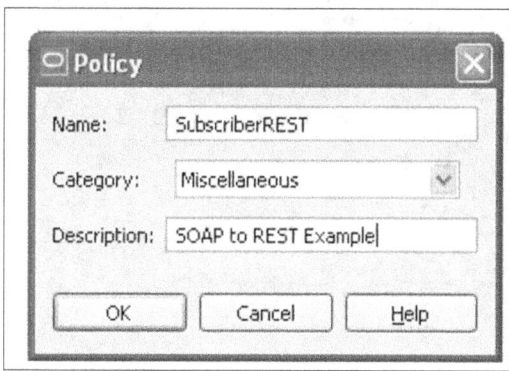

## Oracle API Gateway Implementation Overview

2. The next step is to add and configure a number of filters for this policy. Search for the **Policy Shortcut** filter from the filters menu or select it from under the **Utility** filters. Then drag and drop it into the **canvas**.

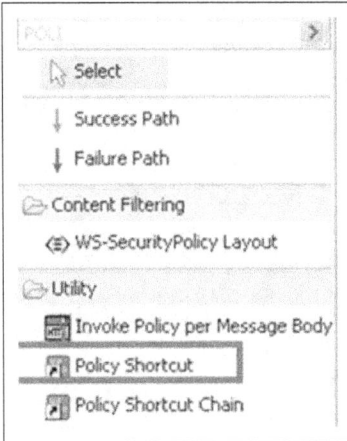

> A **policy shortcut** is a type of filter that enables users to create a link from one policy to another. For example, one could create a policy that inserts security tokens into a message and another that adds HTTP headers. A third policy can then be created that calls the other two policies using a policy shortcut filter.

3. Once the policy shortcut is dragged onto the canvas, double-click on it. A new window will open to configure the filter. Select the policy that was previously created (**Service Protection**) and then click on **Next**.

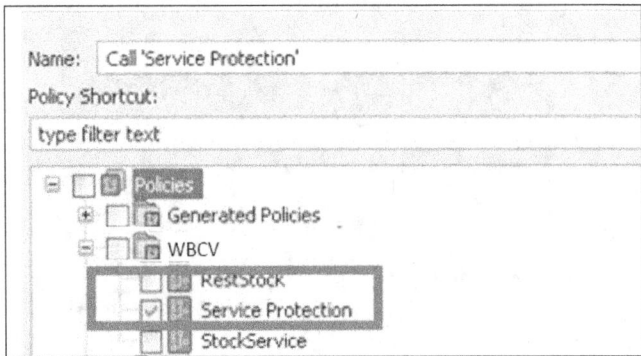

4. Accept the remaining default values and click on **Finish**.

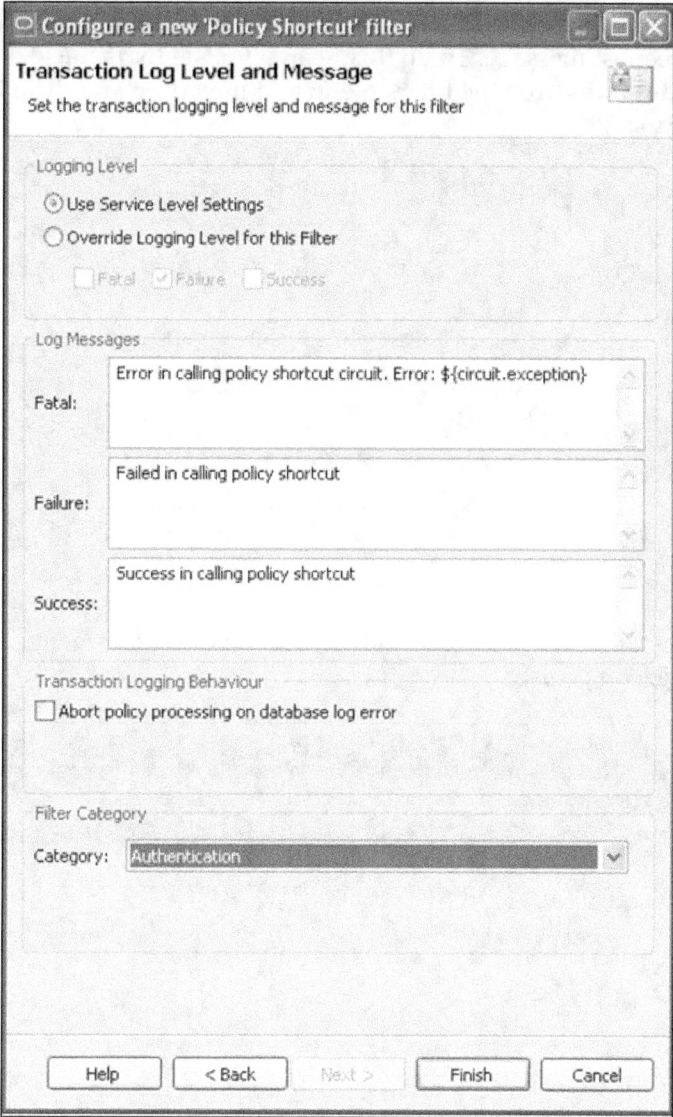

*Oracle API Gateway Implementation Overview*

5. In this example, the APIs will be invoked via **GET** requests, which means that the attributes can be either in the **Headers** or **Query Strings**. For this reason the user must add a filter that extracts all **REST attributes** from the HTTP request message. To do this, search for the **Extract REST Request Attributes** filter from the filters menu and then drag and drop it into the canvas.

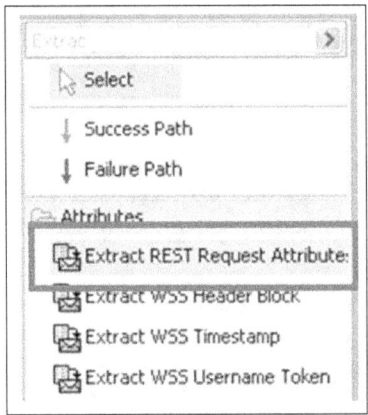

6. From the canvas, double-click on the filter to change its name, if desired. Then click on **Finish**.

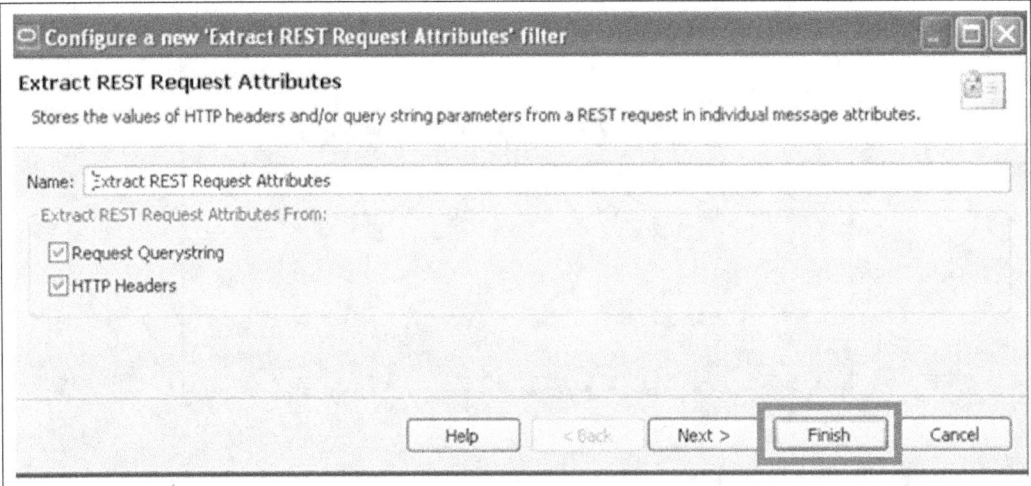

7. The next step is to add a filter that basically creates a SOAP envelope, which is needed to create a clearer API Rest service for our federated partners. From the filters menu, search for the **Set Message** filter and then drag and drop it into the canvas.

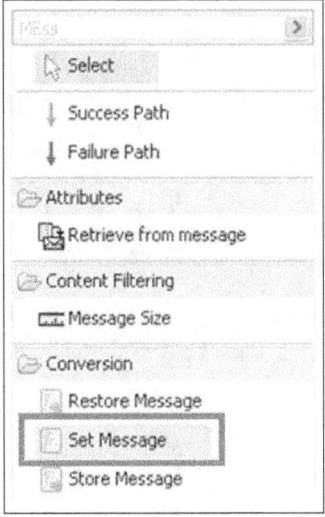

8. From the canvas, double-click on the filter to change its name and set the values as per the following example:
    - **Name**: `Set Message`
    - **Content-Type**: `test/xml`
    - **Message Body**:

    ```
    <soapenv:Envelope xmlns:soapenv="http://schemas.xmlsoap.org
    /soap/envelope/" xmlns:nmp="http://servicios.
    montedepiedad.com.mx/NMP/Schema/NMPStandardHeader">
        <soapenv:Body>
          <wbcv:getSubscriberBalance>
          <subscriberID>${http.querystring.attribute}
          </subscriberID>
          </wbcv:getSubscriberBalance>
        </soapenv:Body>
    </soapenv:Envelope>
    ```

9. Click on the **Finish** button to save the changes made to the filter.

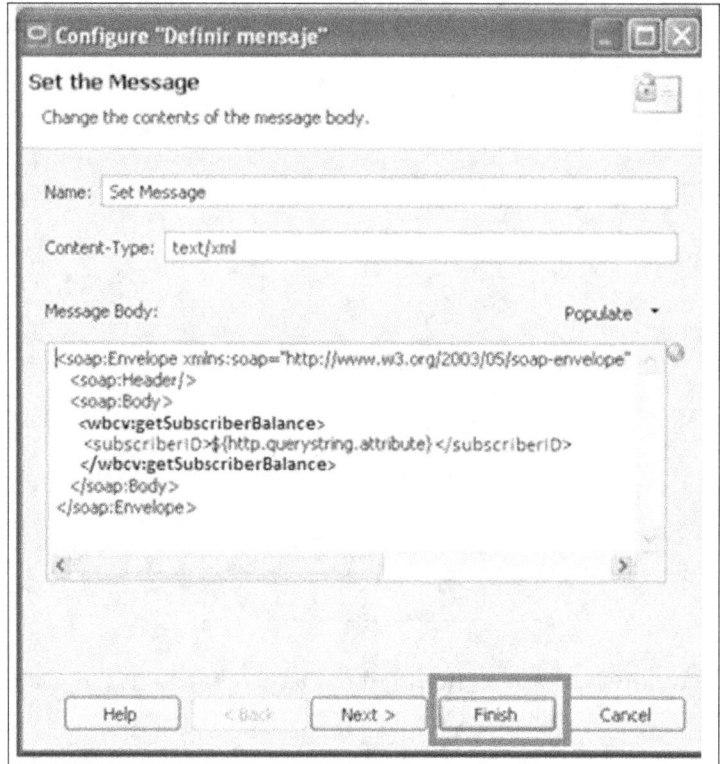

 The variable ${http.querystring.attribute} refers to the HTTP query string attribute that was previously defined. This then injects values into the SOAP message. This example shows how SOAP elements can be constructed based on the REST attributes extracted from an incoming message.

10. Since we are routing the message to the original web service we need to make proper and literal use of HTTP verbs when performing different operations—for example GET, POST, PUT, DELETE. It is necessary to always default the HTTP verb to POST during a REST to SOAP message protocol conversion. To do this from the filters menu, search for the **Set HTTP Verb** filter and then drag and drop it into the canvas.

11. On the canvas, double-click on the filter and add details as per the following example:
    - **Input Name**: A meaningful name. In this case, Set HTTP verb.
    - **HTTP Verb**: POST.

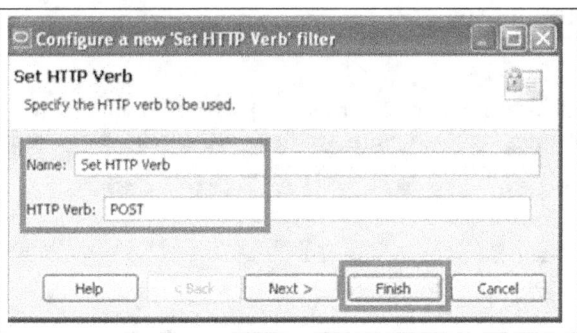

12. Click on the **Finish** button to save the changes made to the filter.

*Oracle API Gateway Implementation Overview*

13. The next step is to forward the created SOAP message to the endpoint of the service that was previously registered (**SubscriberService**). To do this from the filters menu, search for the **Connect to URL** filter and then drag and drop it into the canvas.

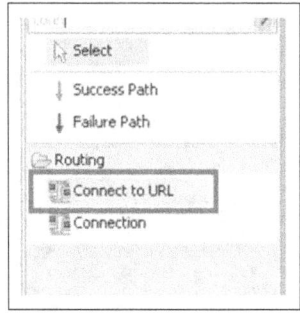

14. On the canvas, double-click the filter and add details as per the following example:
    - **Name**: Enter a meaningful name
    - **URL**: The endpoint of the previously registered service (for example `http://10.8.0.22:7001/MVNO/Subscriber/SubscriberSoap12HttpPort`)
    - **Method**: `${http.request.verb}`

 The `${http.request.verb}` variable contains the verb of the message. Note that we have previously defaulted this to POST.

    - **Request Body**: `${content.body}`

 `${content.body}` contains the SOAP message previously created.

    - **Request Protocol Headers**: `${http.headers}`. This will insert the headers, if needed

 The `${http.headers}` variable, whilst not really required, contains all HTTP headers in use.

*Chapter 5*

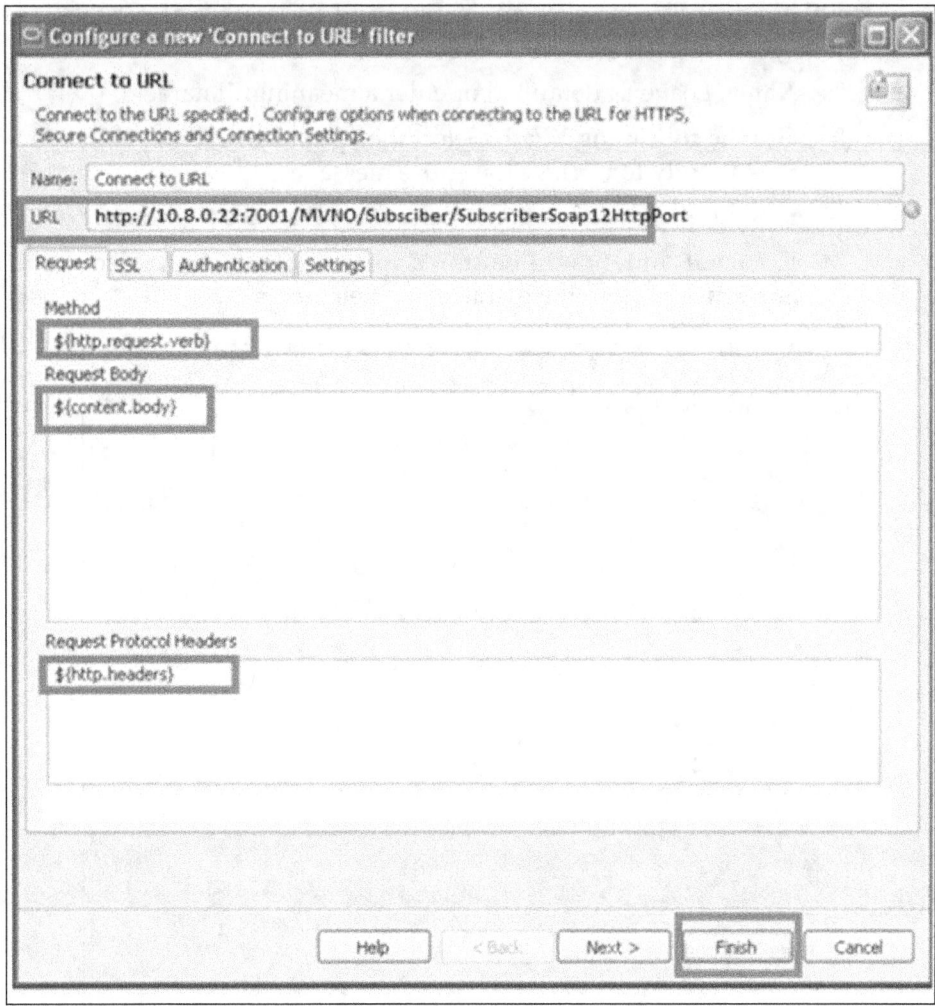

15. Click on the **Finish** button to save the changes made to the filter.
16. Filters have now been added to convert a request (incoming) message from REST into SOAP. The next step is to convert the response message from SOAP back into REST/JSON. To do this, search for the **Retrieve from message** filter from the filters menu and then drag and drop it onto the canvas.

*Oracle API Gateway Implementation Overview*

17. From the canvas, double-click on the filter and add details as per the following example:
    - **Name**: Leave as defaulted or enter a meaningful name
    - **Use the following XPath**: Select the option **All Elements inside SOAP Body** to retrieve the entire message
    - **Store the extracted content**: Select **for all nodes found as text**
    - **Extracted content will be stored in attribute named**: Select **content.attributes** to store the extracted text elements

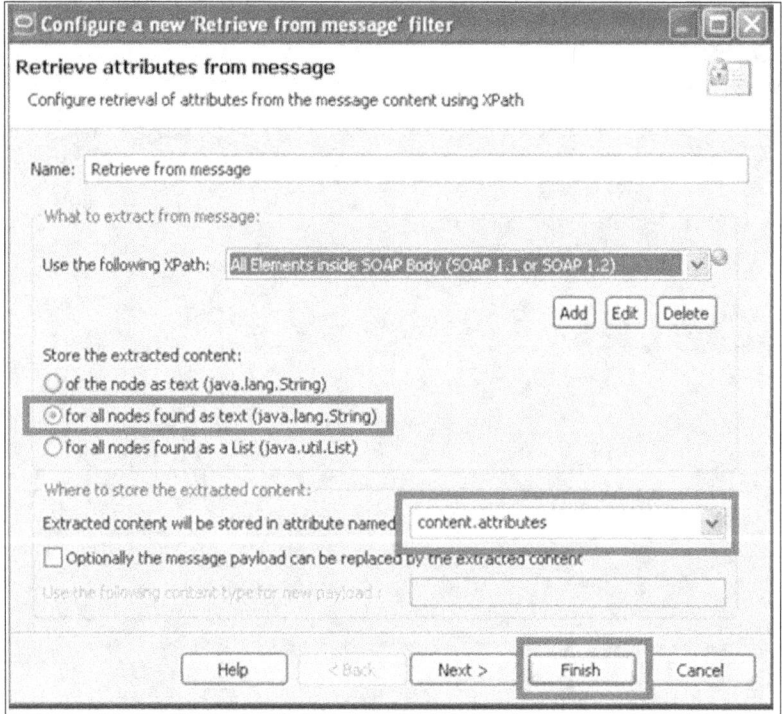

18. Click on the **Finish** button to save the changes made to the filter.
19. Now that the SOAP response message has been extracted and stored in the variable content.attributes, the next step is to inject this into the HTTP response which is converted into JSON. To inject content.attributes into the HTTP response, search for the filter **Set Message to JSON** and then drag and drop it to the canvas.

[ 226 ]

20. From the canvas, double-click on the filter and add details as per the following example:
    - **Name**: Leave as default or enter a meaningful name
    - **Content-type**: `test/xml` as the content is still in XML
    - **Message Body**: `$content.attributes` since it contains the full SOAP message

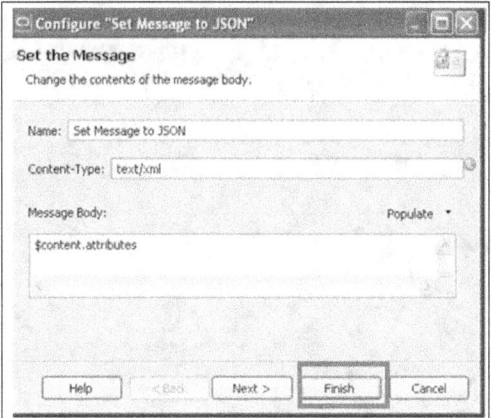

 This step simply injects the SOAP message contained in the variable `content.attributes` into the HTTP response. The next step is to transform the response from SOAP/XML into JSON.

21. The next step is to convert the HTTP response to JSON from its current SOAP/XML format. To do this, search for the **XML to JSON** filter from the filter menu and then drag and drop it to the canvas.

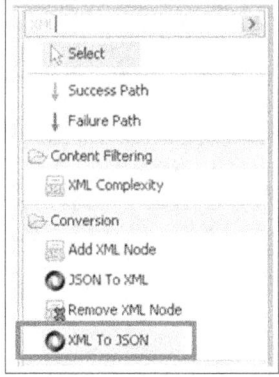

## Oracle API Gateway Implementation Overview

22. From the canvas, double-click on the filter and add details as per the following example:
    - **Name**: Leave as defaulted or enter a meaningful name
    - Select options **Automatically insert JSON array boundaries** and **Convert number/boolean/null elements to primitive**
    - In the **Use the following XPath to convert** dropdown, select the option **All elements inside SOAP Body**

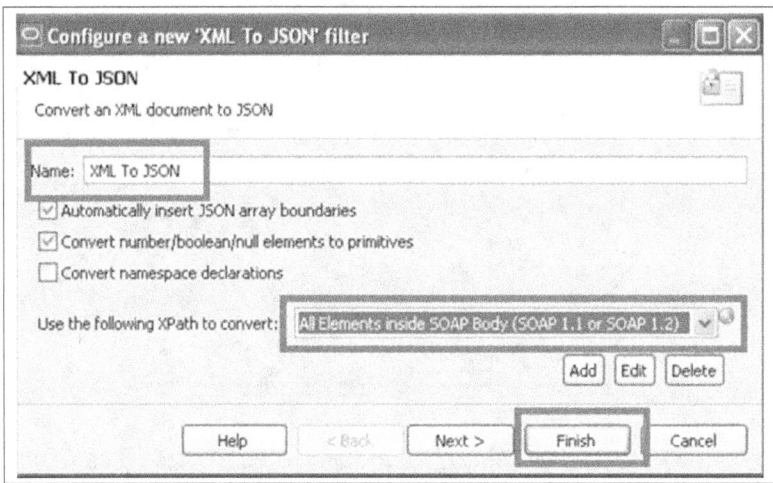

23. The next step is to set the REST attributes that were received in the incoming message as part of the HTTP response. To do this from the filter menu, search for the **Reflect Message & attributes** filter, and then drag and drop it to the canvas.

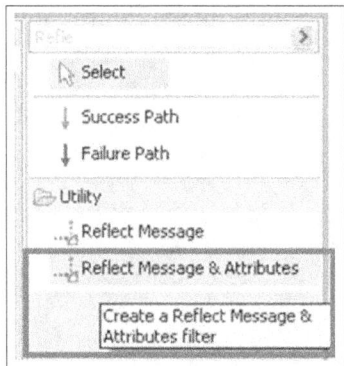

24. From the canvas, double-click on the filter and modify the name, if desired, otherwise leave as default and click on **Finish**.

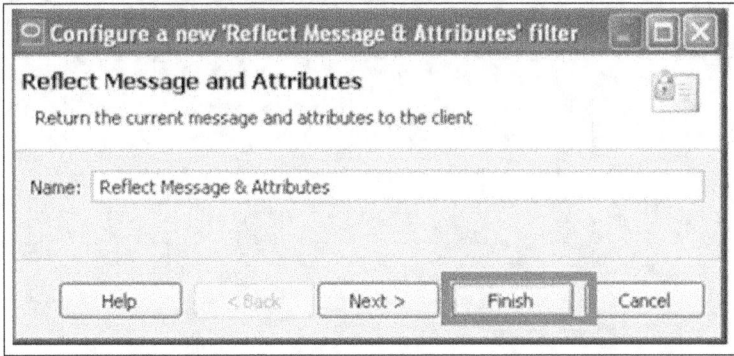

25. At this point, all the necessary filters have been added and configured. The next step is to wire everything together in the correct order and also to add **success** and **failure** paths to the circuit. First we need to specify the start of the circuit. To do this, locate the filter **Call Service Protection**, right-click on it, and then select **Set as Start**. This will make this step the first step of the circuit. Remember that this filter was created in earlier sections to handle authentication, authorization and also protect against DoS threats.

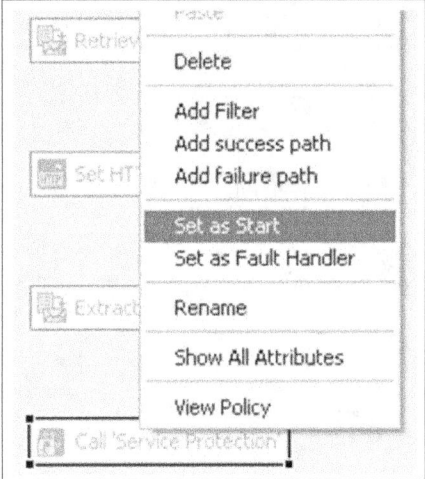

26. To add a success and path to the circuit, search or select the filter **Success Path** and/or **Failure Path**.

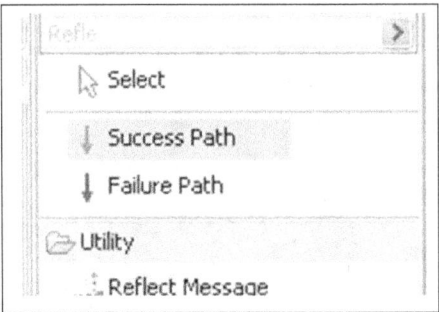

27. Once a **Success Path** and/or a **Failure Path** filter has been selected, simply connect the filters in the same order as they were created, as illustrated in the following sample. Note that, in this sample, a **JSON Error** filter was added as the failure path.

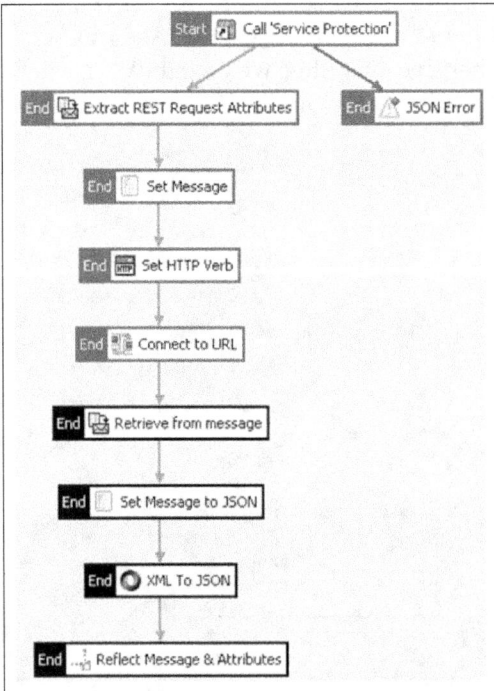

*Chapter 5*

28. The last step before deploying and testing the API is to define the **REST URI** and the resource path that the API will respond to. This can be done by double-clicking on the **Path** item located in the relevant **service groups** and **OAG server** instance.

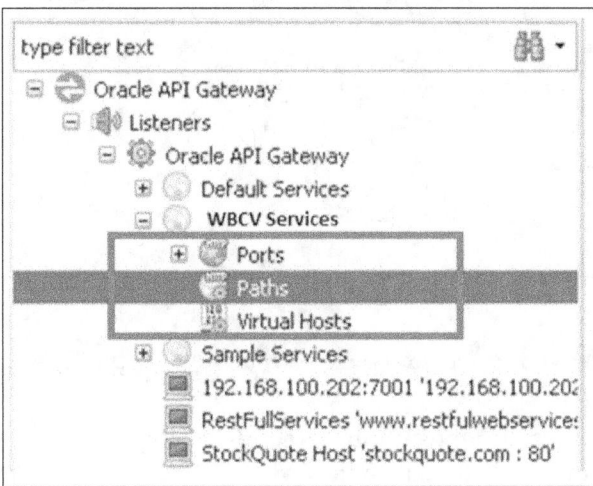

29. Once the path **Resolver** window opens, click on the **Add** button on the right-hand side of the window and then select **Relative Path** so that a URI can be provided.

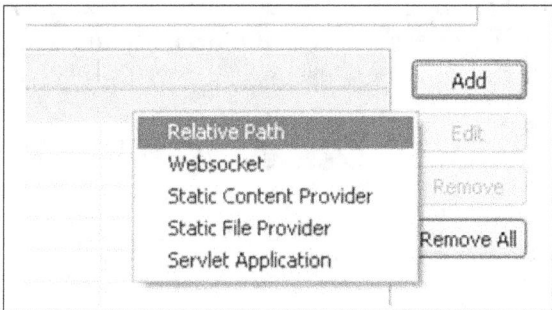

[ 231 ]

30. A new window will appear from which you can select the policy that will be associated with the specified path. Select the relevant policy, in this example it would be **SubscriberREST**, and then click on **OK**.

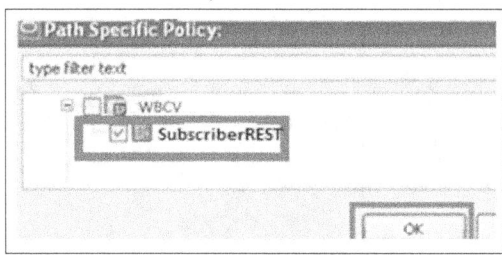

31. Once the **Resolve path to Policies window** opens, enter the details as follows:
    - **When a request arrives that matches the path**: `/MVNO/REST/Subscriber`
    - Select the options **Global Request Policy**, **Path Specific Policy**, and **Global Response Policy**

     It is considered good practice to invoke **global request and response policies**.

    - For the **Path Specific Policy** option, select a specific policy that should be associated with this path (in this example `SubscriberREST`)

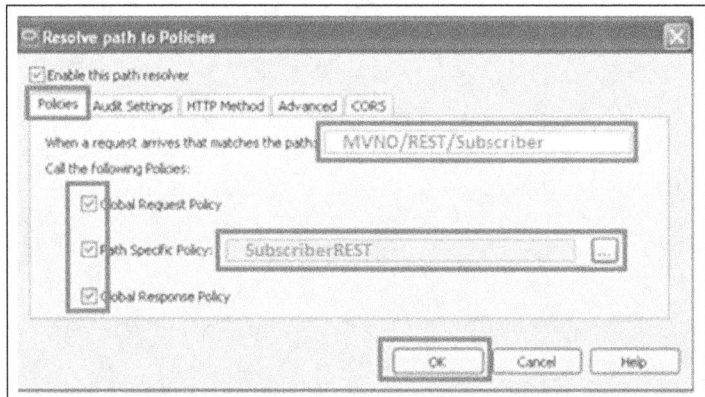

32. Now that all the steps have been completed, the policy can be deployed and tested in a similar way to that described in the section *Deploying a Policy*.

## Summary

This chapter started by providing a complete overview of OAG. The fundamental OAG concepts, the component architecture and the different capabilities and features of the product were described.

The chapter continued by elaborating on the importance of implementing an API gateway in order to apply security policies to APIs that are publicly accessible. This provides critical protection against different external threats. We presented a typical use case with a brief description of why implementing OAG, along with different policies, would be beneficial for WBCV telecom rather than keeping their existing web security set up.

The later sections of the chapter provided hands-on and step-by-step instructions on how SOAP resources can be exposed as web APIs in a secure fashion, using different policies and by making use of policy filters. The chapter also provided steps on how to deploy and test the policies.

 This chapter did not cover the installation and basic configuration steps of OAG as this has already been summarized in the *Chapter 6, Installation Tips and Techniques*.

# 6
# Installation Tips and Techniques

This chapter provides tips and techniques for those performing a full installation of **Oracle API Catalog**, **Oracle API Gateway**, and **Oracle API Manager**. It is not our intention to provide a full installation guide for each product as these can be obtained from Oracle via their website. Instead, we provide some useful pointers gleaned from past experience gained from installing the product set.

Oracle provides software installers that guide the user through the installation process. The installer can be run in graphical, console, or silent mode. In graphical mode, the user is presented with a rich GUI that guides them through the process in a wizard-driven manner. Console mode provides an interactive text-based mode for command-line installation. Silent mode, which requires the use of XML configuration files, is a non-interactive method of installation and can run from the command line or as part of a script. The following sections assume that the user is using the full graphical installation process.

*Installation Tips and Techniques*

# Explaining the installation topology

The following diagram shows the installation topology of the SOA Governance Suite, as prescribed by this book:

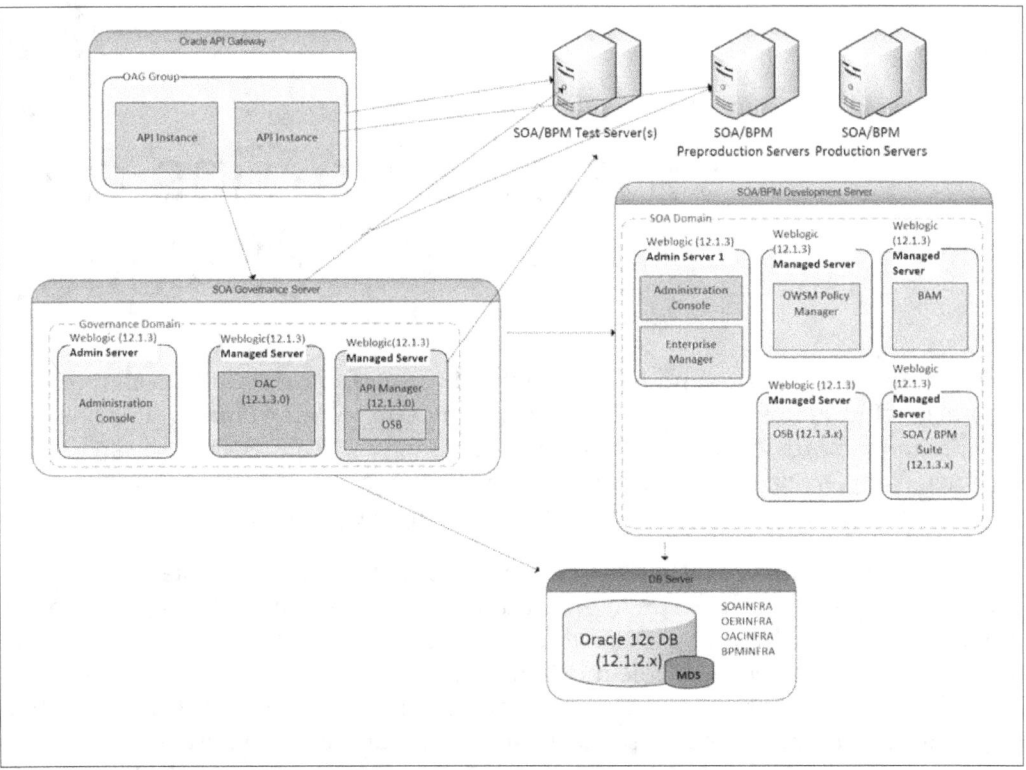

Since OAC and API Manager are meant to be the single source of truth throughout the entire development lifecycle, WBCV made the following considerations when defining the SOA Governance Solution environment strategy:

- A shared instance of the SOA Governance Server (OER and API Manager) to support the development lifecycle stages: development, test, pre-production, and production
- A sandbox instance of the Oracle API Gateway for the purpose of trying out new patches and configuration changes
- A sandbox instance of the SOA Governance Server (API Manager and OAC) for the purpose of trying out new patches and configuration changes
- A separate passive instance of the Governance Server for Disaster Recovery

With regards to Oracle API Manager, WBCV made the following considerations when defining the API Management strategy:

- Create a single instance of Oracle API Manager together with Oracle Service Bus. This instance will manage the federated OSB domains that are aligned with eTOM domains
- This topology is replicated in the different environments:
    - Production
    - DR
    - Pre-production
    - Testing
    - Development

# Installation overview

The overall installation process is summarized in the following diagram:

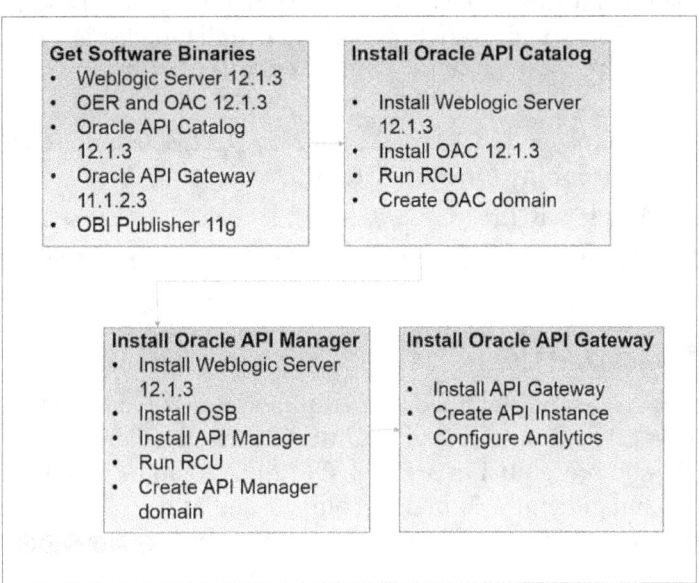

This chapter will follow the process described in the diagram to install the installation topology outlined in the previous section.

*Installation Tips and Techniques*

The Oracle binaries can be obtained from Oracle eDelivery, the **Oracle Technology Network (OTN)** website or from Oracle support through a service request. The general recommendation is to get the software through eDelivery as this is the official download site. It will require registration, and software is protected by a username and password that is obtained as part of the registration process. OTN should only be used for conducting trials of software or for general proof of concepts.

The following installation binaries are required. If you wish to try the installation, you may also use the OTN links provided next. For production or testing installation, download binaries from Oracle eDelivery.

- `http://www.oracle.com/technetwork/middleware/weblogic/downloads/index.html` for WebLogic Server 12.1.3.
- `http://www.oracle.com/technetwork/middleware/repository/downloads/index.html` for Oracle API Catalog *12c* R1 (12.1.3.0). This is included in the download of OER.
- `http://www.oracle.com/technetwork/middleware/weblogic/downloads/index.html` for Oracle API Manager *12c* R1 (12.1.3.0).
- http://www.oracle.com/technetwork/middleware/api-manager/downloads/index.html for Oracle API Manager *12c* R1 (12.1.3.0). This installation link is necessary to be able to install Oracle Service Bus: `http://www.oracle.com/technetwork/es/middleware/service-bus/downloads/index.html`.
- Oracle API Manager *12c* (12.1.3.0). Patches: 20225320 and 20311552 (to be downloaded from My Oracle Support).
- Oracle API Gateway (`http://www.oracle.com/technetwork/middleware/id-mgmt/oeg-300773.html?ssSourceSiteId=ocomen#download`)

# Installing OAC

Once the Oracle binaries are obtained, the administrator is ready to begin the installation process. The first step is to read the Oracle-supplied installation guide and to ensure that all prerequisites are met. OER/OAC can be installed in 32 or 64 bit environments but generally 64 bit is recommended as the 32 bit architecture is limited to addressing less than 4 GB of RAM. With 64 bit architecture, all system memory can be addressed and there are consequently more options available for JVM tuning.

 For this *12c* release, only Oracle DB is certified.

# Installing the database

Before installing the middleware components, the installer must create a database that will be used to house the Oracle schemas necessary to support the SOA Governance Suite of products. This book assumes installation into an Oracle *12c* database. Once a database is created, the WebLogic installation can be continued followed by the OER/OAC software itself. In *11g*, there were some manual steps that had to be performed in the database, but now, in *12c*, **Repository Creation Utility** (**RCU**) is used to create the schemas and database objects needed to install both OER and OAC.

Oracle provides an OER sizing guide that can be used as a guide for sizing environments and is located at the following URL:

```
http://www.oracle.com/technetwork/middleware/repository/overview/
oer12sizingguidelines-2347802.pdf
```

# Temporary disk space requirements

The Oracle installer uses temporary disk space during software installation. A temporary directory should be allocated by the server administrator. During the installation process, the temporary space must be sufficiently sized to hold the compressed JRE bundle and the uncompressed JRE. The default temporary directory is dependent on the platform; for Windows, it is the directory pointed to by the TMP (temporary) environment variable, whereas in Unix it will vary dependent on the flavor adopted. We would recommend allocating a temporary directory of suitable size and specifying this as part of the command line for the installer program using the –D command line switch.

> For further details, please refer to the OER/OAC installation guide at
> ```
> https://docs.oracle.com/middleware/1213/oer/install-
> oer/toc.htm.
> ```

*Installation Tips and Techniques*

## Installing WebLogic 12c

The OAC software will execute in a Java runtime environment. This book assumes that Oracle WebLogic will be used to host OAC. Prior to installing OAC, the administrator must first obtain the WebLogic binaries and install WebLogic. WebLogic installation requires a JDK1.7 install or above. To install WebLogic, log into a Unix Shell console as the Oracle user and change directory to the directory into which the WebLogic download has been installed. Follow the given steps; this will execute the Oracle Installer for WebLogic:

`PATH=<JAVA_HOME>/bin:$PATH`

`export PATH`

`java -jar fmw_12.1.3.0.0_wls.jar-log=$HOME/logs/fmw_12.1.3.0.0_install.log`

When installing WebLogic in a new environment, choose to create a new Middleware Home Directory.

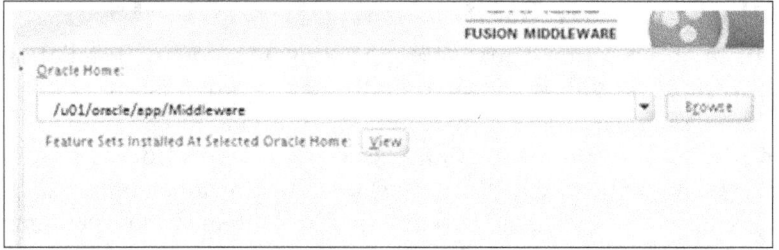

This directory will act as a repository for all installed middleware products for a given machine. When prompted, choose a WebLogic installation.

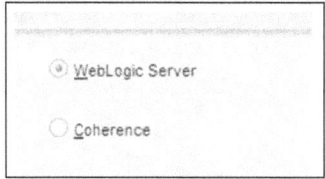

*Chapter 6*

Hit the **Next** button and the system validations will be initiated. After the validation has occurred, hit the **Next** button and the installation will commence. Ensure that you wait for it to finalize before clicking on the **Finish** button.

## Installing OAC Software

Log into a shell console using the Oracle user and change directory to the location where the installation binaries are located. Then, follow the given instructions to start the Oracle installer program:

```
PATH=<JAVA_HOME>/bin:$PATH
export PATH
java -jar oer-generic.jar -log=$HOME/logs/OER_install.log
```

 The installation binaries for OER are the same for OAC. There is no specific download for OAC.

When running the installer program, the user will be initially asked to specify a Middleware Home Directory. The user should opt to use the existing middleware home into which the WebLogic server was installed.

Hit **Next** and the user will be prompted to specify a product type installation. Choose **Enterprise Repository**.

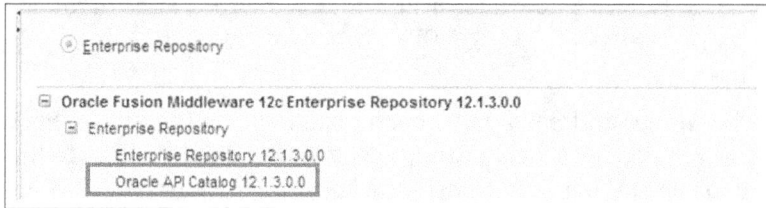

*Installation Tips and Techniques*

This will install both OER and OAC. Then click on the **Next** button and the installer will validate the platform requirements (Operative System and Java version).

After the system prerequisites validation has completed, click on the **Next** button which displays a summary of the specified installation.

Click on the **Next** button and the installation will start. Ensure that you wait for it to finalize.

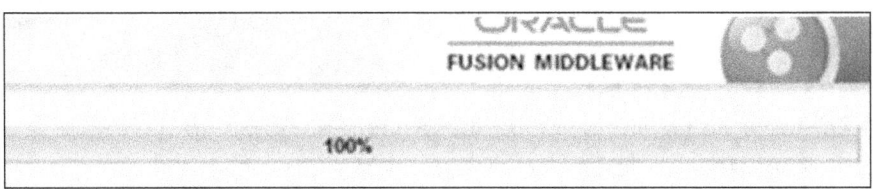

Once at 100%, just click on the **Finish** button and the OER and OAC software will be installed.

Before creating the WebLogic domain for OAC, it is necessary to apply a patch for RCU. Basically this patch will add the option for OAC.

The patch number is: 18718889 and can be downloaded from My Oracle Support.

After downloading the patch, install it using the OPatch utility.

 To use OPatch follow these instructions at `http://docs.oracle.com/middleware/1213/core/OPATC/toc.htm#OPATC101`.

Once the OAC binaries and patch have been installed, run the RCU. This will generate the required OAC schemas and objects in the database. To do this, start a Unix Shell console and log in with the Oracle user. From the Middleware home directory, execute the following command:

`<ORACLE HOME>/oracle_common/bin/rcu.sh`

The RCU welcome page will appear; hit the **Next** button.

The second screen will prompt you for the method of schema creation. Select **Create Repository** and the sub-option **System Load** and **Product Load**.

*Chapter 6*

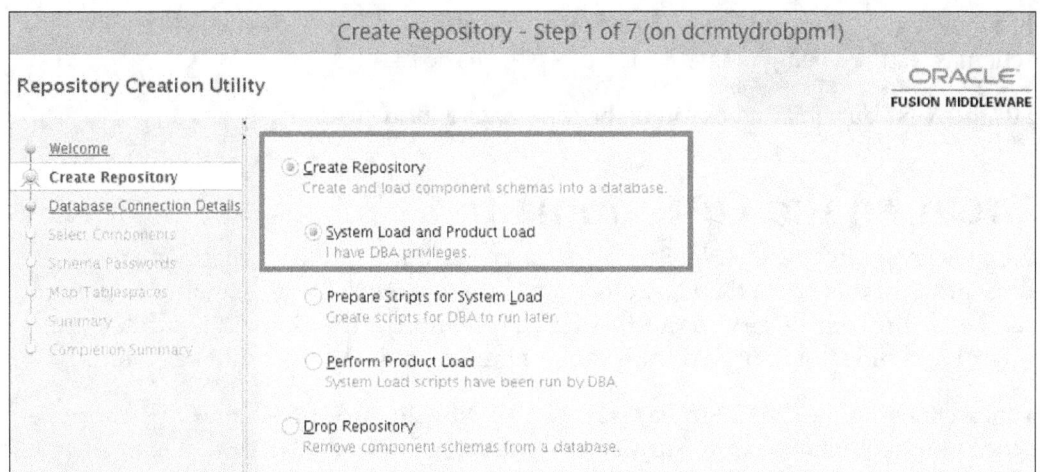

Then, provide the database connection details and click on the **Next** button. Enter a custom prefix when prompted, choose: WBCVGOV.

Choose the following components:

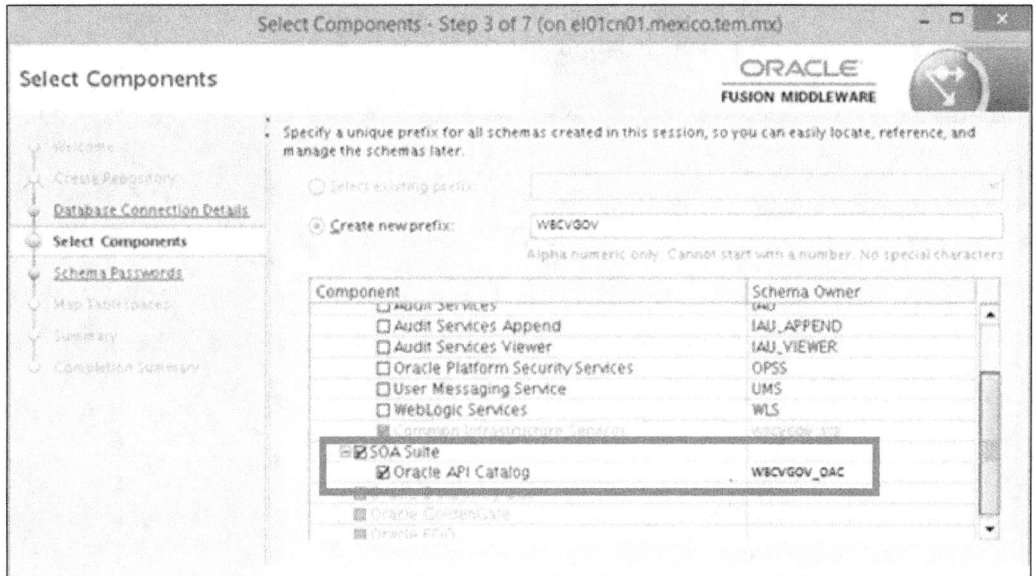

*Installation Tips and Techniques*

Hit the **Next** button and, when prompted, specify the schema passwords for the schemas that are being created, for example, welcome1.

Hit the **Next** button and complete the schema creation.

## Creating the OAC domain

Next, we need to create a WebLogic domain containing OAC. As mentioned previously in this book, there is going to be one centralized OAC instance to govern the whole lifecycle of services and APIs. The creation of this domain is similar to any other WebLogic domain: an admin server and a managed server will be created.

When choosing the OAC template it is not possible to also choose the OER template within the same domain. For further information, please refer to this: https://docs.oracle.com/middleware/1213/oer/install-oer/config.htm#BABGJGHI.

To create the OAC domain, start a Unix Shell console and log in with the Oracle user and, from the Middleware home directory, execute the following command:

`<ORACLE_HOME>/wlserver/common/bin/config.sh`

When the WebLogic configuration wizard opens, select **Create a new domain**, browse to a location, and then click on **Next**.

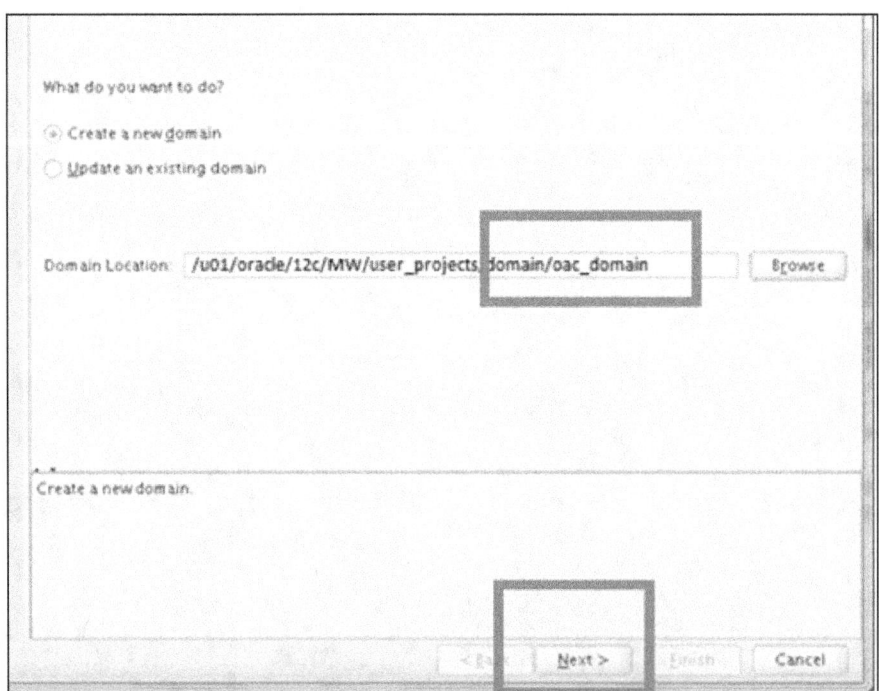

On the next screen, select **Oracle API Catalog 12.1.3.0.0** and click on **Next**:

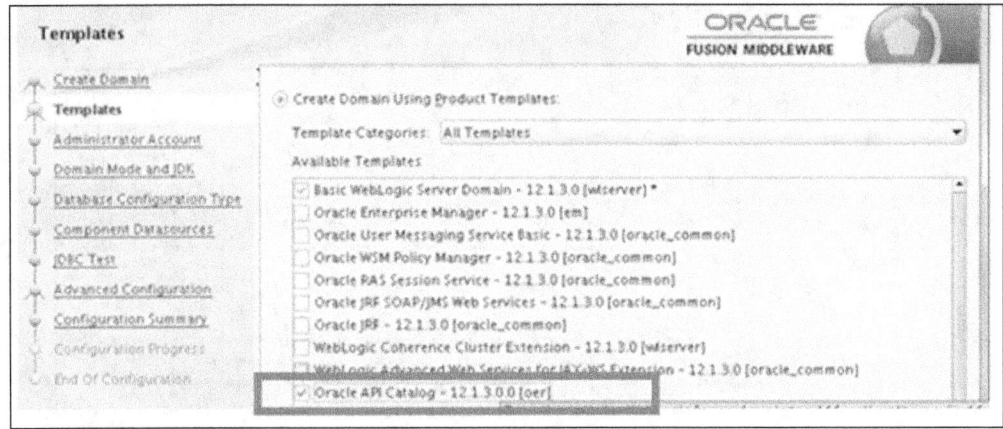

On the next screen, enter the desired username and password for the WebLogic domain administrator. Select **Next**, once completed.

Now we can configure the server JDK. Here, we are installing a development environment, so select Development Mode with the Oracle Hotspot JDK. Then click on **Next**.

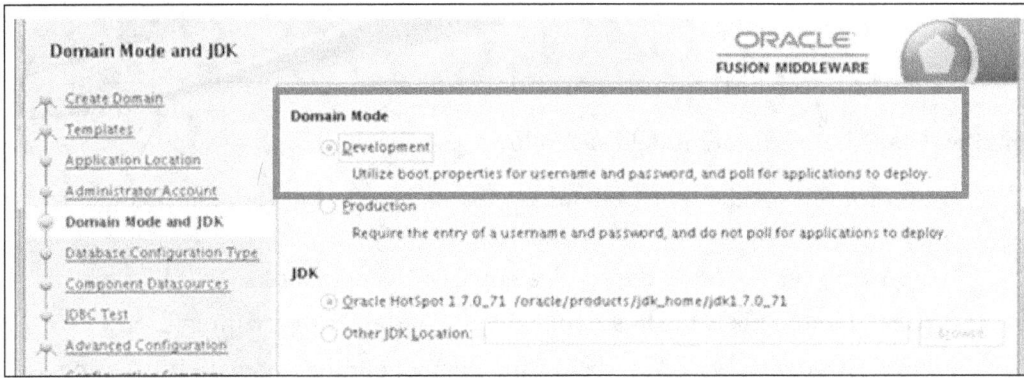

*Installation Tips and Techniques*

On the next screen, enter the database details — the one that was created in the previous step. Recall that the name of the prefix has been set to WBCVGOV, as shown here:

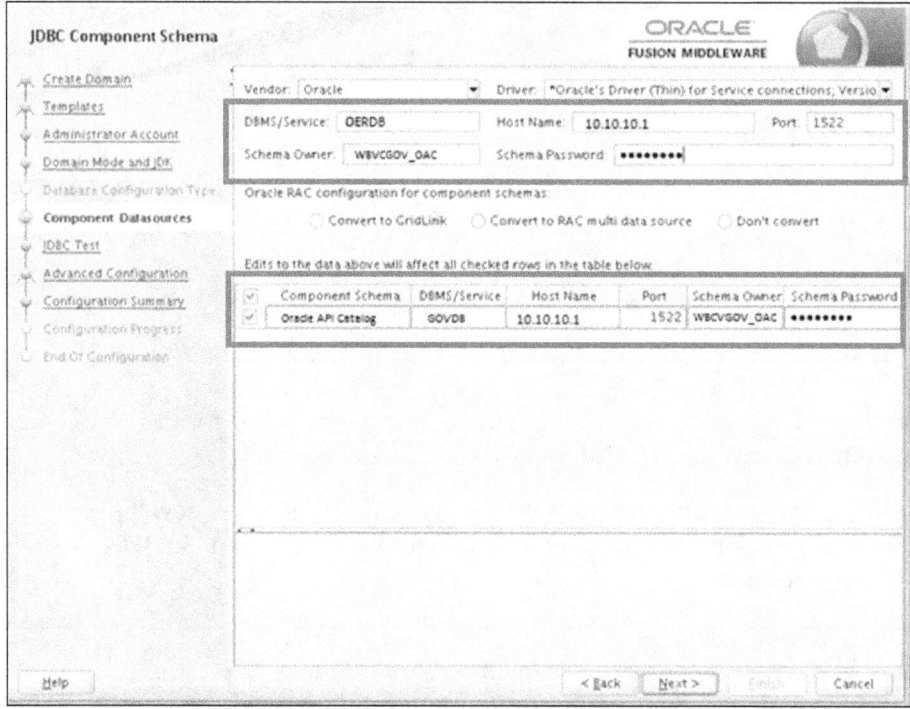

Fill the details in the different fields as follows:

- **Vendor**: This is the type of database that is being used for the MDS repository. In this case, it is Oracle.
- **DBMS/Service**: This is the service name of the database.
- **Host Name**: This is the hostname where the database is running.
- **Port**: This displays the number of the port where the database is listening.
- **Schema Owner**: The database schema owner that is being used for this installation. In this case: WBCVGOV_OAC. This was created while executing the RCU.
- **Schema Password**: This field concerns with the password of the schema owner.

>  In the case of a production environment, it is recommended that the database is installed as an Oracle RAC. If that is the case, then the options of Grid Link and Multi data sources are used.

Hit the **Next** button and the database connections will be tested.

On the next screen, select **Administration Server** — this is very important and must be done; otherwise the domain will be installed without an *Admin server*. Also, select the **Managed Servers, Clusters, and Coherence** link to create the OAC-managed server, as shown here:

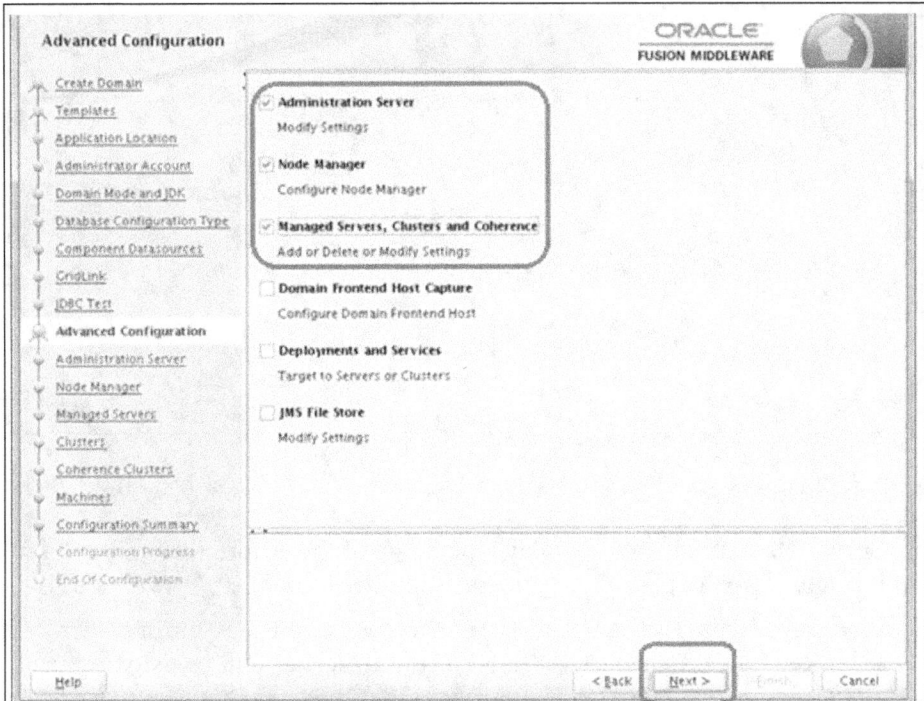

Once all the required selections are made, hit **Next**.

*Installation Tips and Techniques*

On the following screen, enter the Administrator Server and listener port.

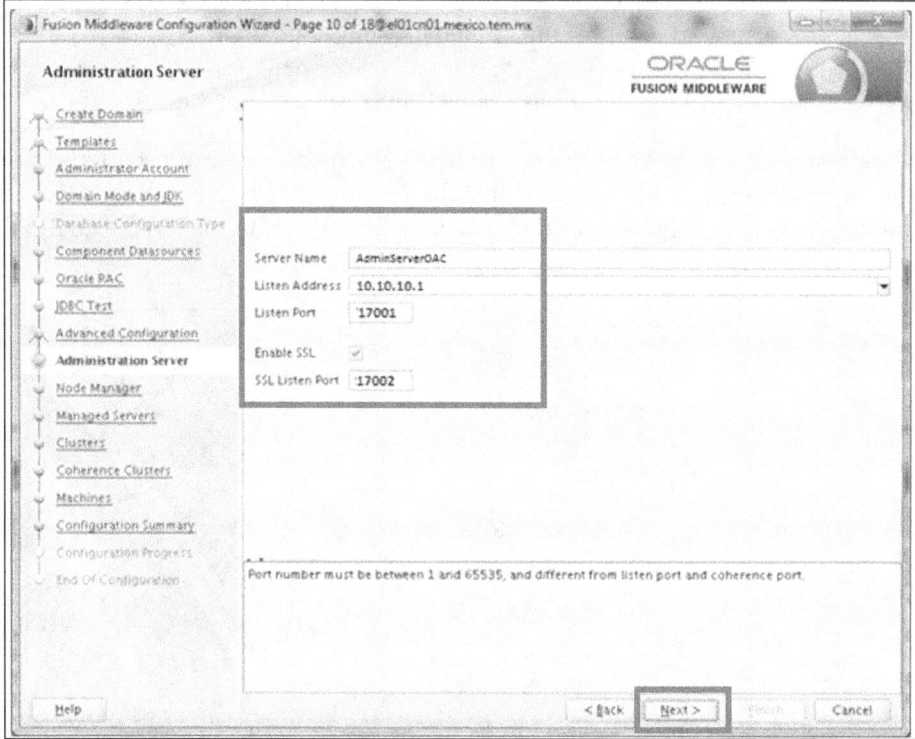

Here are the fields:

- **Server Name**: This field displays the name of the admin server. By default, it is AdminServer. For OAC we are renaming it to AdminServerOAC.
- **Listen Address**: This is the address where we want the admin server to be listening. If it is not selected, then the admin server will be listening in all the available addresses/network interfaces that the host provides.
- **Listen Port**: This is the port where the admin server will be listening.
- **Enable SSL**: This is to have the admin server listening in a secure port.
- **SSL Listen Port**: This is the SSL port we would like to use.

On the next screen, review the details for the OAC0managed server and hit **Next**. The following screen appears, which is used to configure the managed server that will host OAC:

*Chapter 6*

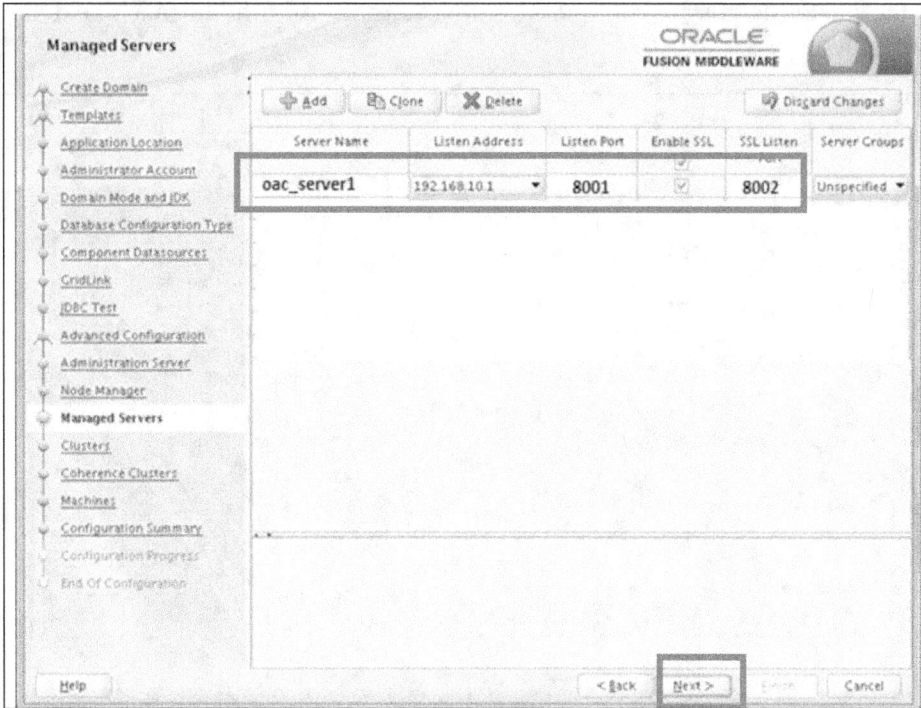

Here are the fields under Managed Servers:

- **Server Name**: This is the name of the managed server where OAC will be running, in this case `oac_server1`.
- **Listen Address**: This is the address where we want `oac_server1` to be listening. If it is not selected, then the admin server will be listening in all the available addresses/network interfaces that the host provides.
- **Listen Port**: This is the port where `oac_server1` will be listening.
- **Enable SSL**: This is necessary if we want to have the OAC listening on a secure port.
- **SSL Listen Port**: This is the port to be used for SSL purposes.

Enter the name of the managed server and the required listener port and hit **Next**. The next couple of screens allow the user to configure the cluster details.

 For more information on installing OER in a clustered environment, please refer to the OER installation Guide at `https://docs.oracle.com/middleware/1213/oer/install-oer/toc.htm`.

*Installation Tips and Techniques*

Once the cluster details are configured, hit **Next** and configure the machine details, as shown here:

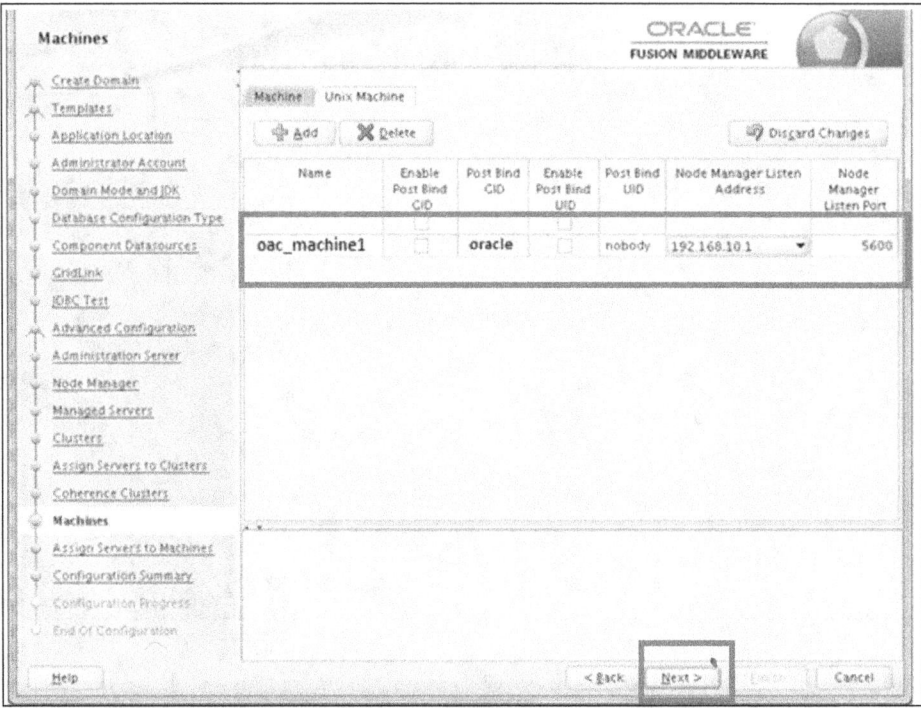

Here are the fields:

- **Name**: This is the name of the Unix WebLogic machine that will host the admin server and the OAC managed server
- **Node Manager Listen Address**: This is the node manager listen address
- **Node Manager Listen Port**: This is the port where the node manger will be listening

>  For more information about Node Manager, go to the official Oracle documentation at `http://docs.oracle.com/cd/E24329_01/web.1211/e21050/overview.htm#NODEM112`

*Chapter 6*

In our case, we have created a machine call `oac_machine1`. Hit **Next**, and then add the servers to the machine created in the previous step, as illustrated here:

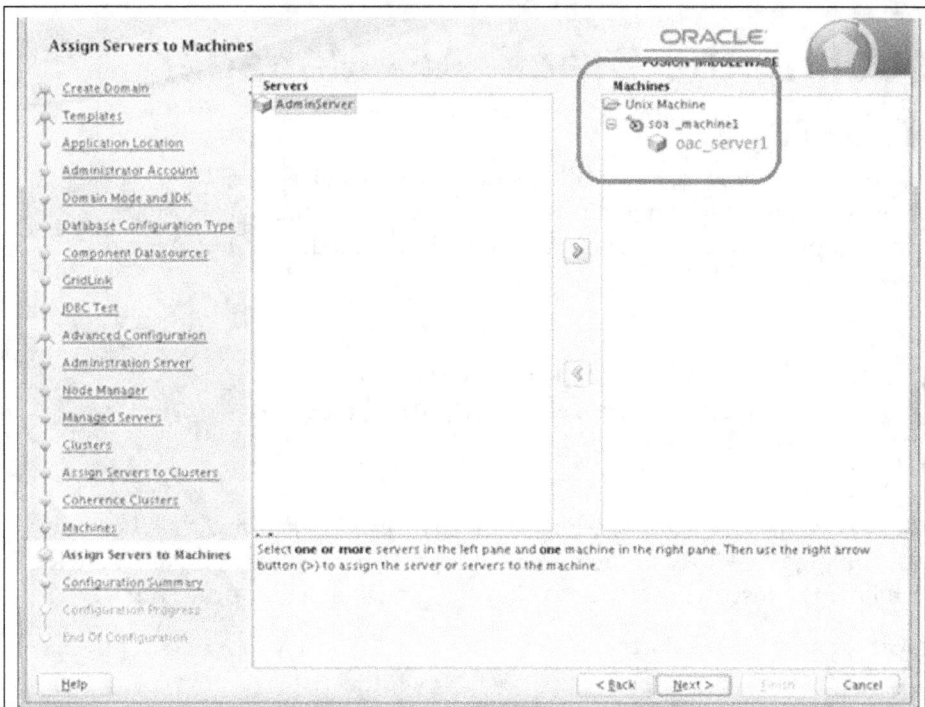

 In our installation topology we deployed the Admin and OAC-managed servers onto the same machine. However, it is possible to have the Admin server and OAC-managed servers located on different machines for more complex topologies such as a cluster.

Finally, review the entered installation details using the summary screen and hit the **Create** button when you are happy. Review the creation details to make sure that the domain is created properly. Should any errors be encountered, check the log files, correct any problems and repeat the preceding process.

Verify that the installation was successful by starting the Admin and OER-managed servers and access the OER console.

Verify that the installation was successful by starting the Admin and OAC-managed servers and access the OAC console (http://machine:8001/oac).

# Installing the Oracle API Manager software

Oracle API Manager is installed alongside **Oracle Service Bus**. The first step is to install WebLogic: the steps that WBCV followed to install WebLogic are described in previous steps. Once WebLogic is installed, the Oracle Service Bus needs to be installed.

> Details on how to install WebLogic are here:
> http://docs.oracle.com/goldengate/1213/gg-monitor/GMINS/prepare.htm#CHDBFIIH

In order to install Oracle Service Bus, log into a Unix shell console as the Oracle user and change directory to the location where the installation binaries are located. Then, follow the instructions here to start the Oracle installer program:

**PATH=<JAVA_HOME>/bin:$PATH**

**export PATH**

**java -jar fmw_12.1.3.0.0_osb.jar -log=$HOME/logs/OSB_install.log**

When running the installer program, the user will be initially asked to specify a Middleware home directory. The user should opt to use the existing Middleware home into which the WebLogic server was installed. This directory will act as a repository for all installed Middleware products for a given machine. When prompted, choose a **Service Bus** installation and hit the **Next** button. The prerequisites validation step will then commence. This will validate the operative system and JDK versions. Once this has completed, click on the **Next** button. The installation summary will be displayed, hit the **Next** button. The installation process will start. Once completed, click on the **Next** button. Finally, click on the **Finish** button to dismiss the installer.

> For complete details on how to install OSB *12c*, refer to the following Oracle documentation at https://docs.oracle.com/middleware/1213/core/INOSB/installing.htm.

After installing the software, there are a couple of patches that need to be installed before a WebLogic domain can be created to host Oracle API Manager and Oracle Service Bus 12c. These are:

- Patch number: 20225320
- Patch number: 20311552

Both patches need to be downloaded from My Oracle Support. Once downloaded, apply them using OPatch.

The first patch is for the RCU. Once this patch is applied, the **SOA Infrastructure** option within the RCU will include the necessary schemas and objects for API Manager.

The second patch is the Oracle API Manager itself. The software for API Manager is included in that patch.

After applying both patches, run the RCU. To do this, start a Unix Shell console and log in with the Oracle user and, from the Middleware home directory, execute the following command:

`<ORACLE HOME>/oracle_common/bin/rcu.sh`

The first step is to select the **Create Repository** option followed by the **System Load** and **Product Load** sub-options:

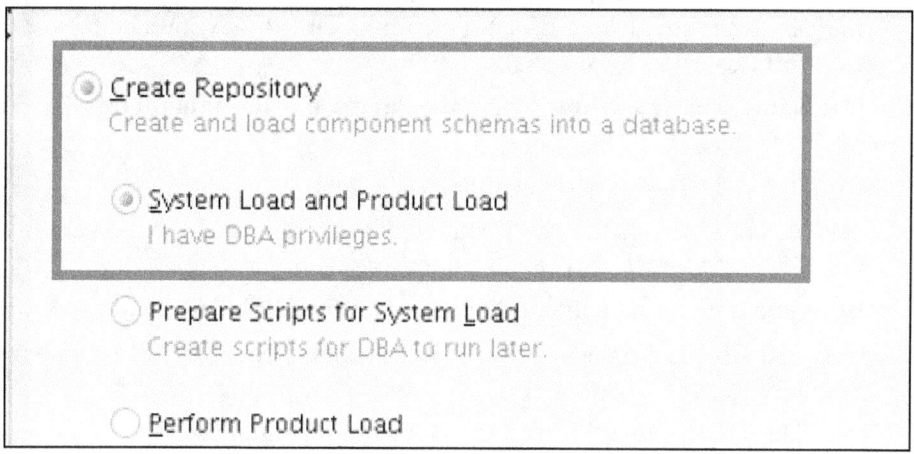

*Installation Tips and Techniques*

Click on the **Next** button and enter the database connection details.

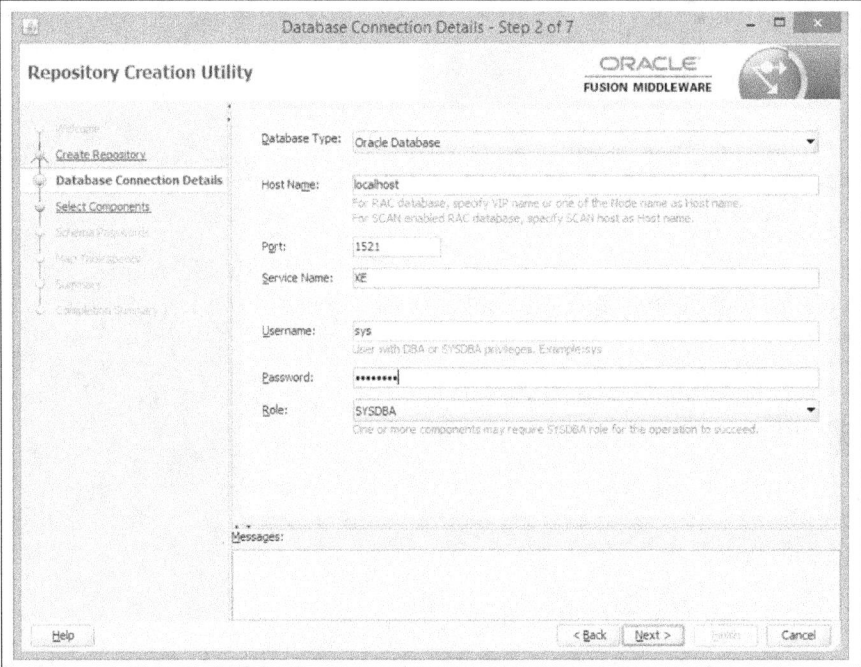

- **Database Type**: This is the type of database to be used as the repository. There are different alternatives, for example, Oracle, MySQL, and Microsoft SQL.
- **Host Name**: This is the host where the database is running. In this case, `localhost`.
- **Port**: This is the port where the database is listening.
- **Service Name**: This is the service name of the database. In this case, WBCV is using Oracle Express Edition (XE).
- **Username**: This is the name of the user with the SYSDBA role.
- **Password**: This is the password of the user that is being used to connect to the database.
- **Role**: This is the role to be used to connect to the database, in this case, **SYSDBA**.

Once the details have been entered, hit the **Next** button.

When prompted for the schemas and prefix to be used, choose **WBCVAPI**.

Select the SOA Infrastructure component; this is just like a normal Oracle Service Bus 12c installation.

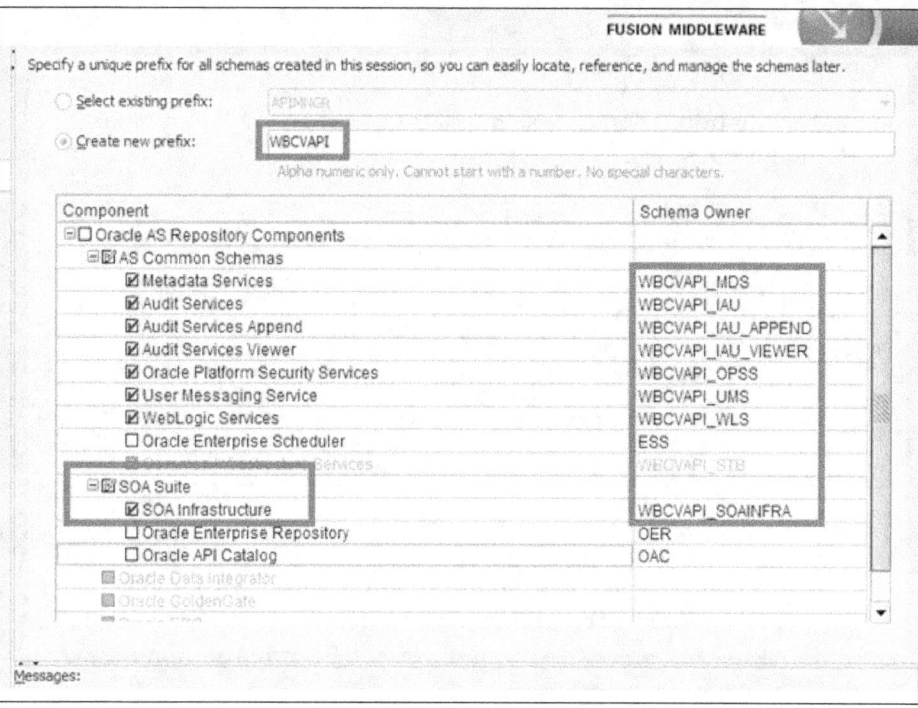

After this, choose a password for the schemas that will be created. Choose: `welcome1`.

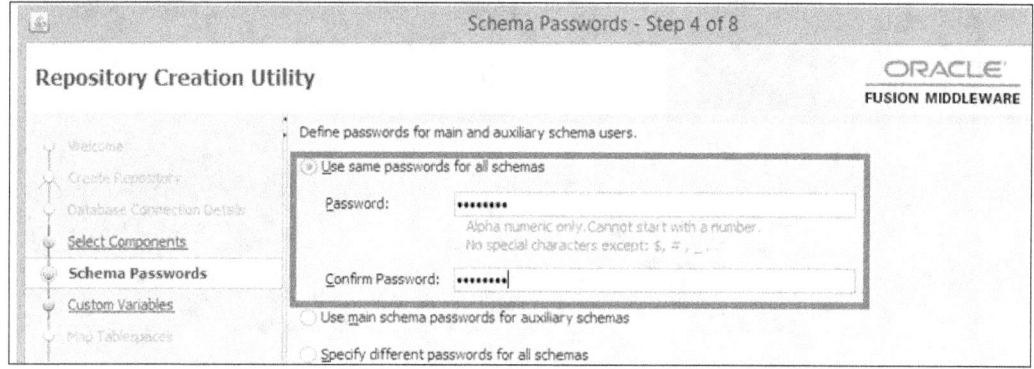

*Installation Tips and Techniques*

These are the password-related fields:

- **Password**: This takes in the password for all the schemas that the RCU will create
- **Confirm Password**: This confirms the previous password

Click on the **Next** button. Then choose the option of **SMALL** deployment, since this is for development purposes:

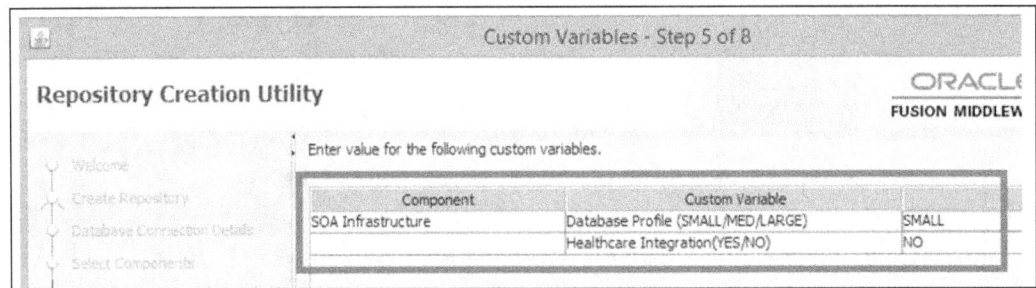

 The available options for the database profile depend on the type of deployment. For more information, go to the Oracle official documentation at https://docs.oracle.com/middleware/1213/core/RCUUG/rcu_screens.htm#RCUUG383.

Click on the **Next** button and complete the schema creation:

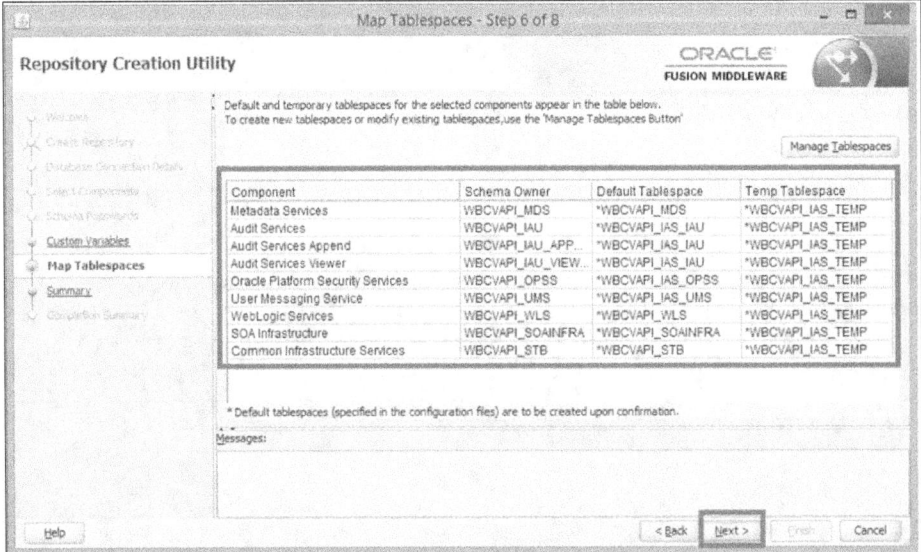

[ 256 ]

Review the tablespace names. If needed, there is an option to manage tablespaces. By default, the values can remain as in the image. Just click on the **Next** button to review the summary. After this review, hit the **Create** button.

After the creation of the repository, the following summary will appear:

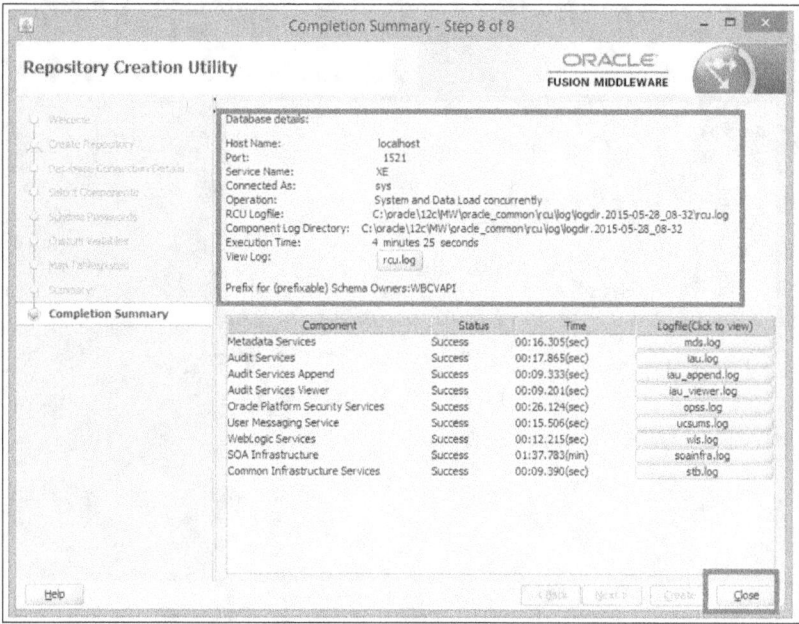

With this, the **Repository Creation Utility** (**RCU**) has finished and a repository for API Manager is ready to be used. Click on the **Close** button.

# Creating the Oracle API Manager 12*c* WebLogic domain

The Oracle API Manager WebLogic domain is created together with Oracle Service Bus.

> For complete details on how to create an Oracle API Manger *12c* domain, follow the official Oracle documentation at `https://docs.oracle.com/middleware/1213/apimgr/using-apimgr/GUID-318F00C2-1CFB-4797-91C3-2860004B0985.htm#OSBAM280`.

*Installation Tips and Techniques*

To start the configuration wizard, log into the server as the Oracle user. Change directory to the following, `$ORACLE_HOME/oracle_common/common/bin` and execute `./config.sh`.

The following screenshot will appear:

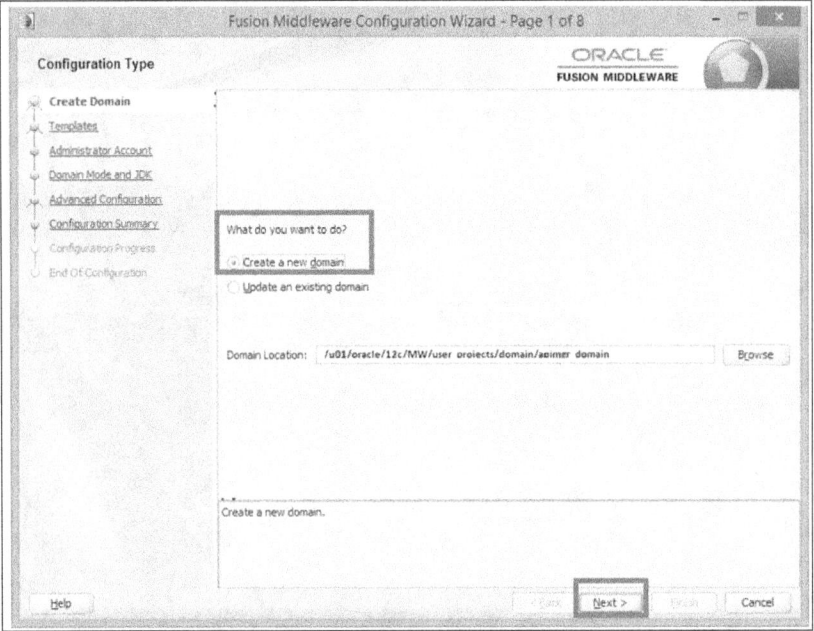

Now perform these actions:

1. Choose the **Create a new domain** option.
2. Use `/u01/oracle/12c/MW/user_projects/domain/apimgr_domain` in the **Domain Location** field. This is the location where the domain will be created.

*Chapter 6*

An important thing to highlight is that, in this release of Oracle API Manager (12.1.3.0), you must install the OSB and Oracle API Manager in separate domains.

 For further details on the preceding content, please refer to the following document at `http://docs.oracle.com/middleware/1213/apimgr/using-apimgr/GUID-394545CC-387E-4BF1-AA37-B1E6B6B84F19.htm#OSBAM416`.

3. Click on the **Next** button and then select the following template options:

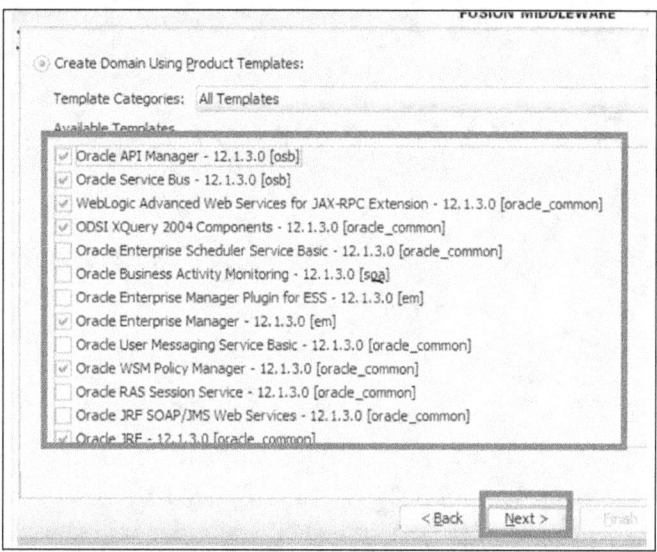

[ 259 ]

*Installation Tips and Techniques*

4. Hit the **Next** button and, when prompted, choose the application home for the domain.

>  For further details on the key WebLogic domain directories, refer to the official Oracle documentation at `https://docs.oracle.com/middleware/1213/core/ASCON/terminology.htm#ASCON11233`.

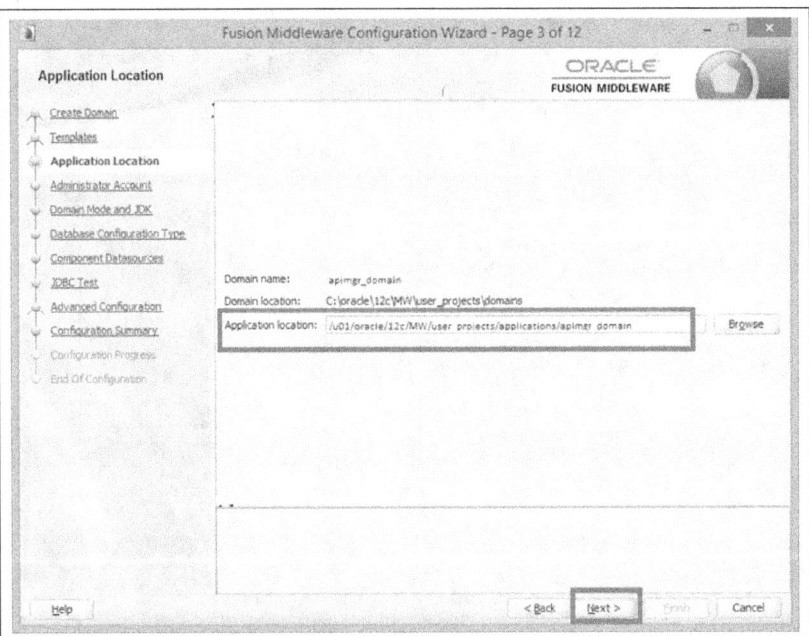

5. Click on the **Next** button and configure the administrator account for this domain. Have **User**: `weblogic` and **Password**: `welcome1`.

*Chapter 6*

6. Click on the **Next** button and select the JDK location and the **Development** domain mode:

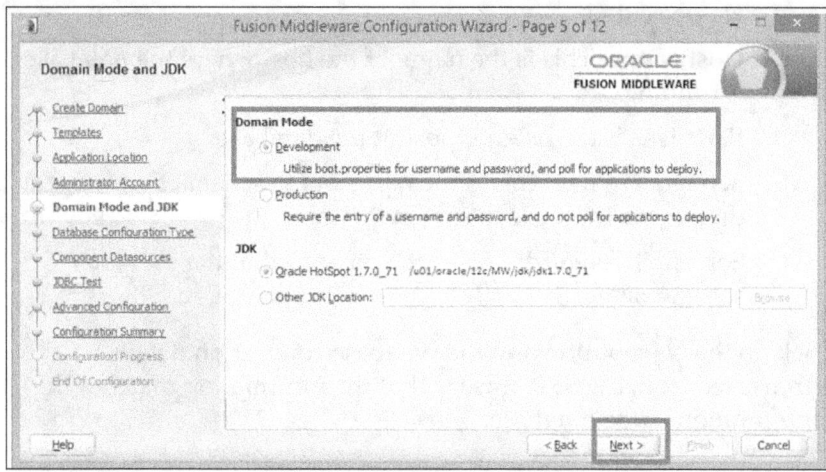

7. Click on the **Next** button and enter the database connection details to obtain the RCU configuration via the **Service Table (STB)**.

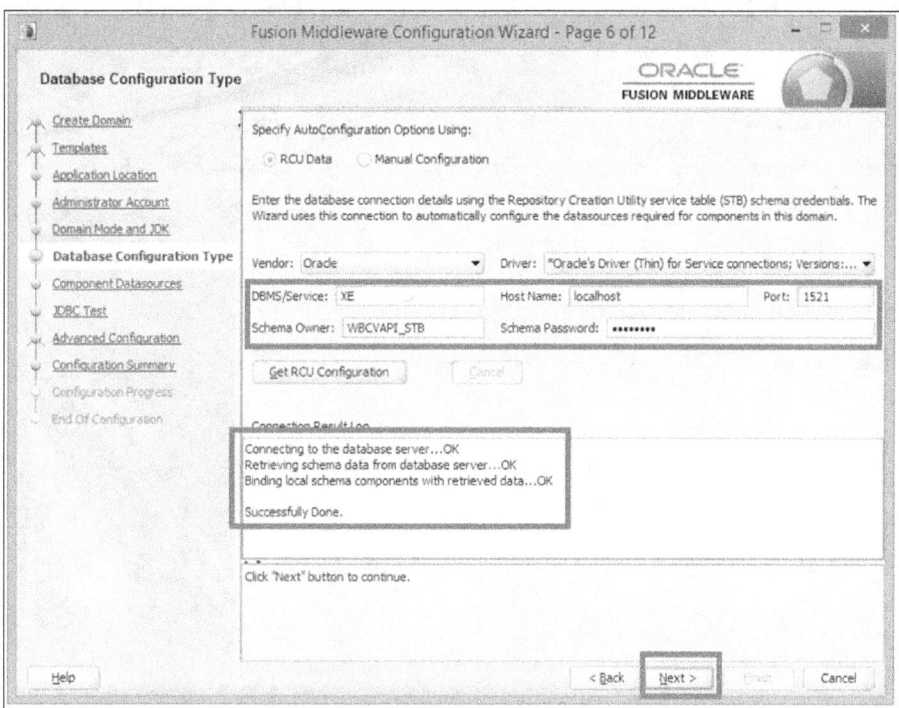

*Installation Tips and Techniques*

Here are some of the fields in this dialog:

- ○ **DBMS/Service**: This is the name of the DB service where the RCU was executed.
- ○ **Host Name**: This is the name of the host where the database is running.
- ○ **Port**: This is the listener port of the database.
- ○ **Schema Owner**: This is the name of the schema that was created during the RCU execution. In this case, the prefix is `WBCVAPI`.
- ○ **Schema Password**: This is the password of the previous schema owner.

8. Click on the **Next** button and the database connection details will be retrieved from the STB. Ensure that the information matches the configuration of the database.

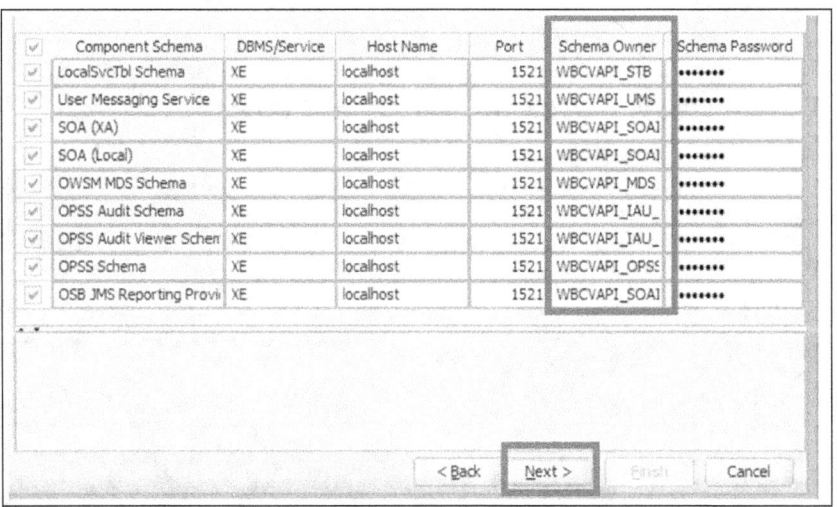

[ 262 ]

*Chapter 6*

9. Hit the **Next** button and test the data sources, if one or more of them fail, review the connection details and try them again. Once all the data sources are correct, click on the **Next** button.

10. In the advanced configuration screen, select the following options:
    - **Administration Server**
    - **Node Manager**
    - **Managed Server, Cluster and Coherence**

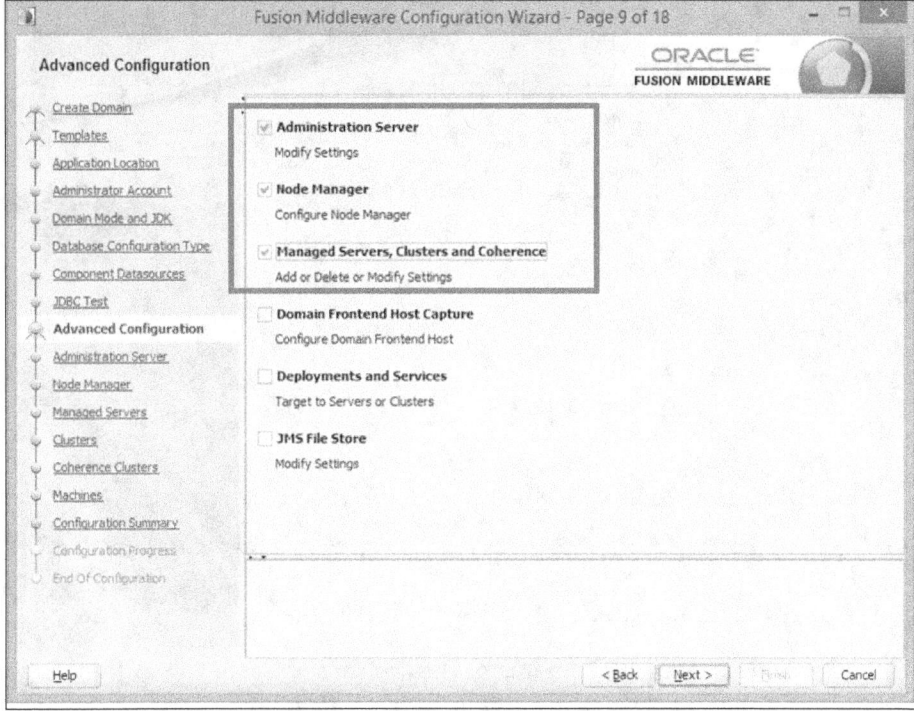

*Installation Tips and Techniques*

11. Click on the **Next** button and, in the **Administration Server** screen, select the port where the administration server will be listening for connections, for example `47001`. For the **Server Groups** field, do not select anything. If there is a need to deploy AdminServer in SSL mode, select the checkbox and choose **SSL Listen Port**.

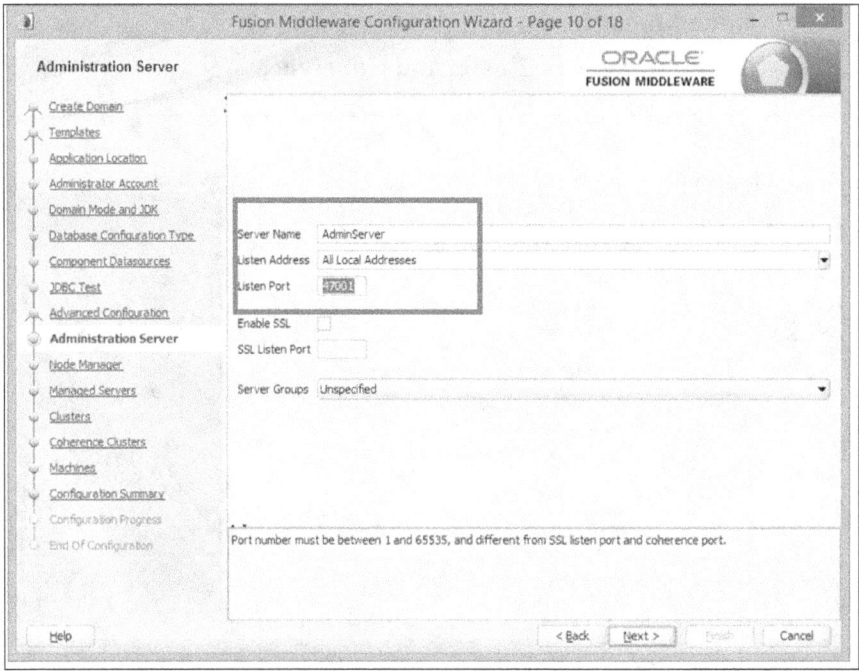

Here are the options under **Administration Server**:

- **Server Name**: The name of the admin server for this API manager domain. Let's use the default: `AdminServer`.
- **Listen Address**: The address where the admin server will be listening. Choose all local addresses, in this case the admin server will be listening on all the available addresses the server provides.
- **Listen Port**: The port where the admin server will be listening.
- **Enable SSL**: If SSL is desired, this checkbox needs to be selected.
- **SSL Listen Port**: The secure port where the admin server will be listening.

12. Click on the **Next** button and configure the Node Manager. Choose **Per Domain Default Location** as the Node Manager type and define the credentials.

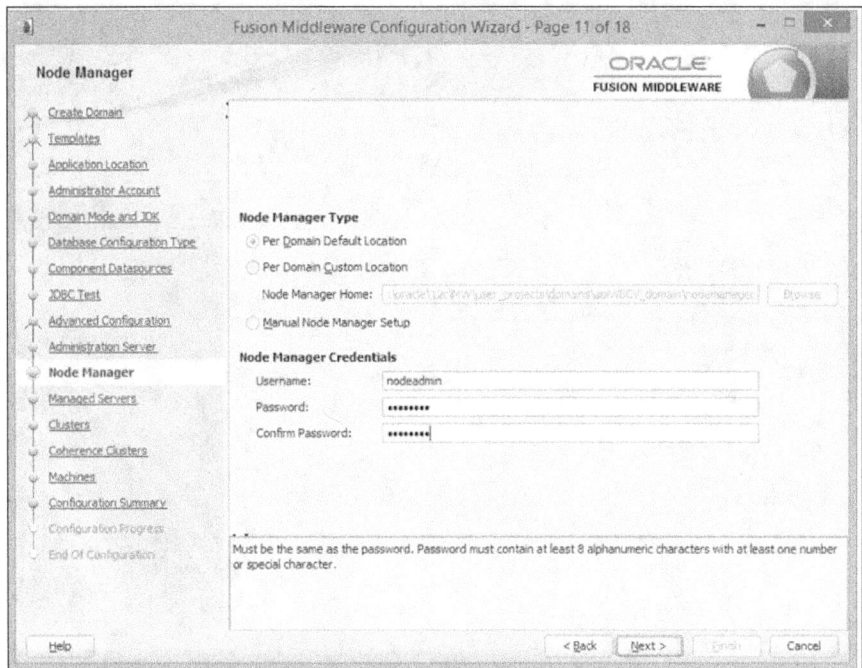

Here are the fields in **Node Manager Credentials**:

- **Username**: Here, the username of the Node Manager that will be used to start and stop this service is entered
- **Password**: Here, the password of the Node Manager user is entered
- **Confirm Password**: This field is used for the confirmation of the previous password

Under **Node Manager Type**, select **Per Domain Default Location**. With this selection, the nodemanager location will be under the domain directory that will be created after the domain is installed.

*Installation Tips and Techniques*

13. Hit the **Next** button and configure a managed server. Choose the name, for example, osb_server1. Define the port where this server will be listening, for example, 47003. For the server groups, select: OSB-MGD-SVRS-COMBINED.

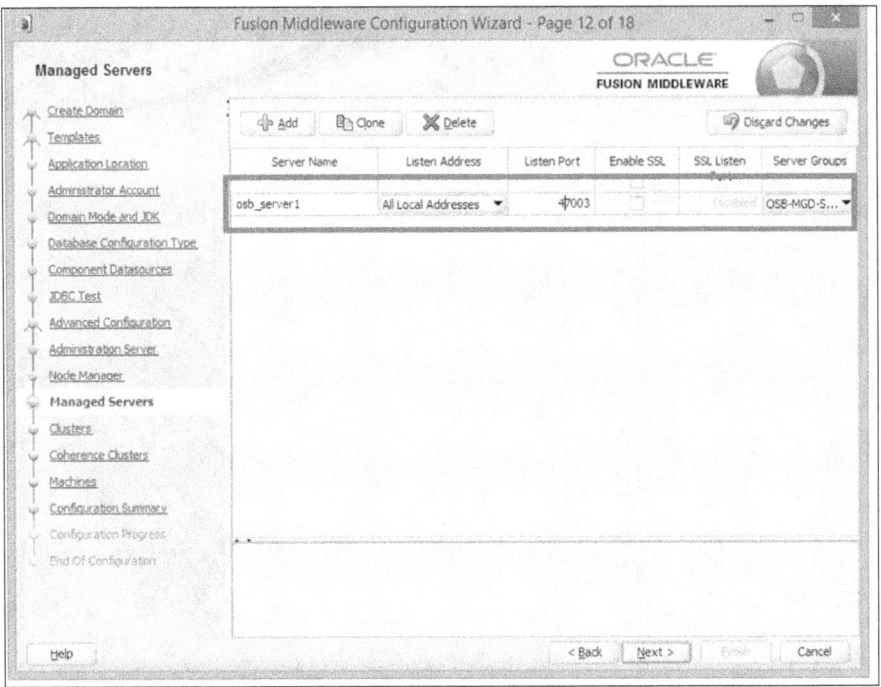

The following are the fields:

- **Server Name**: This deals with the server name for the managed server that will host the API Manager.
- **Listen Address**: This is the *listen address* where the managed server will be listening. If **All Local Addresses** is selected, the managed server will be listening on all the server available addresses.
- **Listen Port**: This is the *listen port* where this server will be listening.
- **Enable SSL**: If this option is selected, the managed server will be also listening on a secure port.
- **SSL Listen Port**: This is the secure port where this server will be listening.

14. Click on the **Next** button. Do not configure a cluster; this is a development environment that will not include clusters. Production environments will definitely need a cluster configuration.

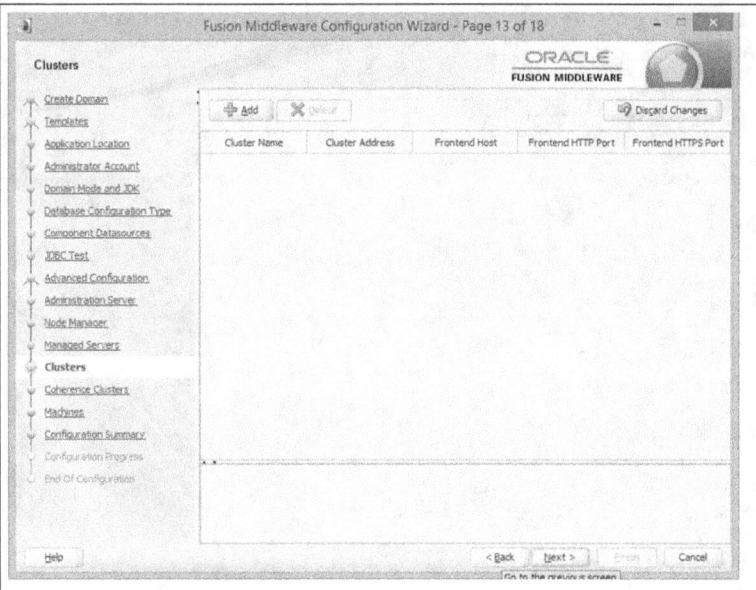

15. Click on the **Next** button and configure the **Coherence** cluster. Leave the default port as **0**.

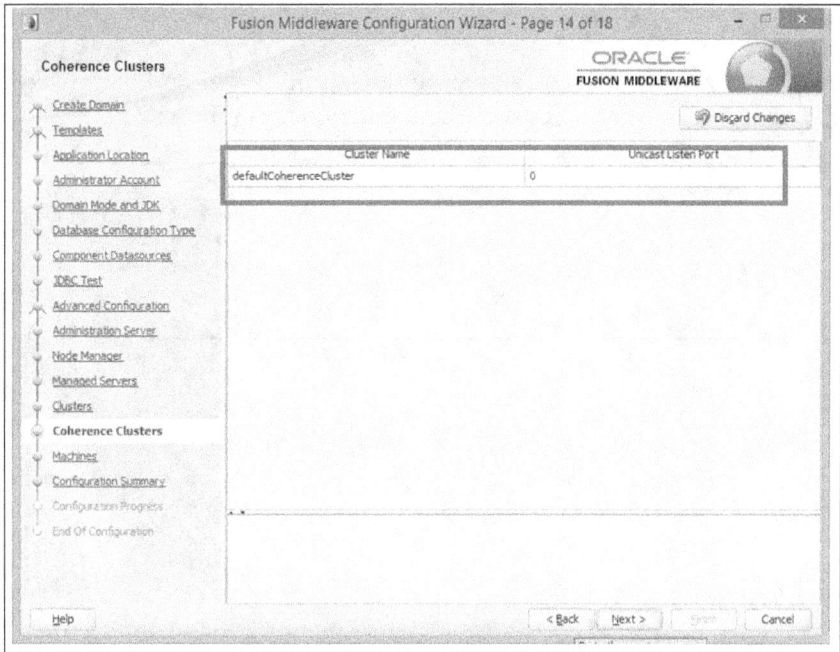

*Installation Tips and Techniques*

16. Hit the **Next** button and configure a Unix machine. Create a machine with the name `apimgr_machine`.

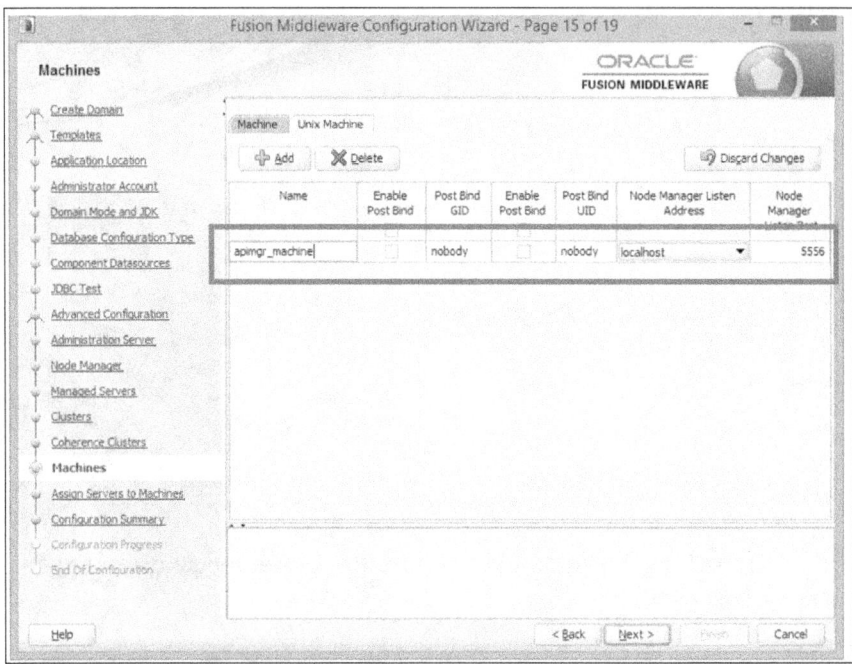

17. Hit the **Next** button and assign both the admin server and the managed server to the previously created Unix machine, as follows:

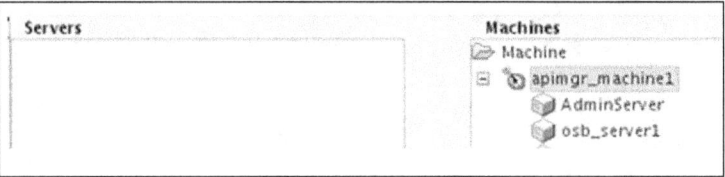

18. Click on the **Next** button and review the configuration. Hit the **Create** button and wait for the domain to be created.

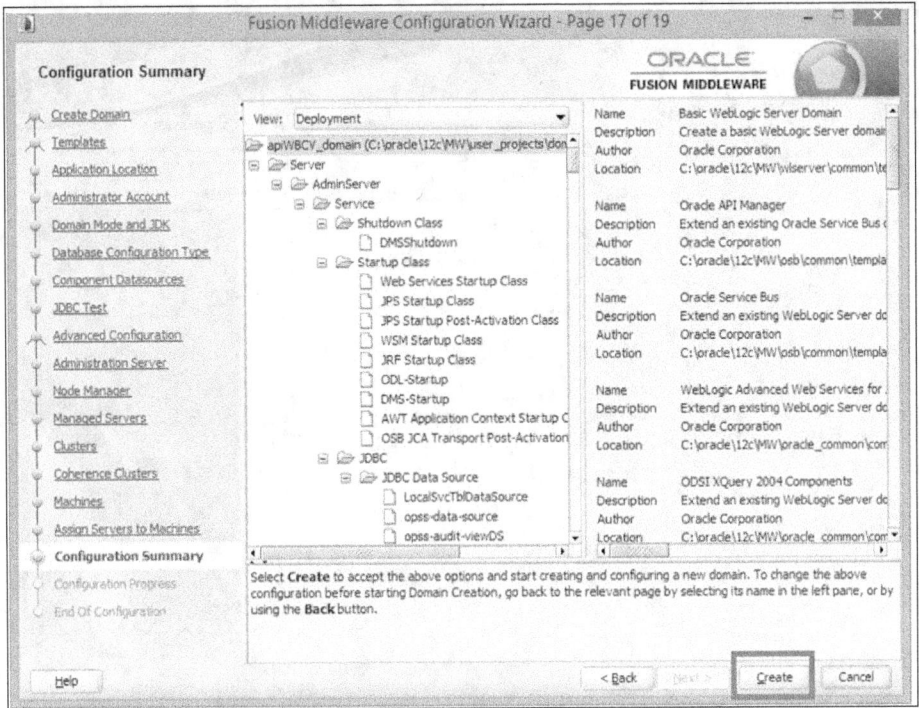

*Installation Tips and Techniques*

19. While the domain is being created, the following progress bar will appear. Just wait until it reaches 100%. Once it hits the 100%, click on the **Next** button.

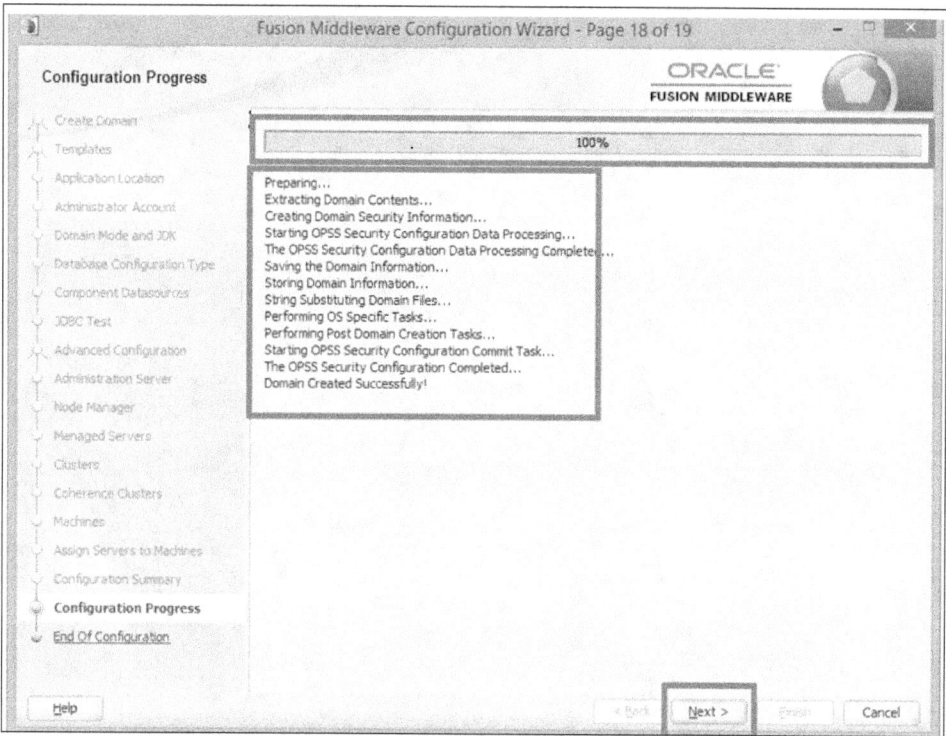

20. After clicking on the **Next** button, a summary window will appear. Review the relevant information such as:

    o **Name of the domain:** `apiWBCV_domain`
    o **Domain location:** `/u01/oracle/12c/MW/user_projects/domains/apiWBCV_domain`
    o **Admin server URL:** `http//api.wbcv.com:47001/console`
    o It is possible to use the checkbox to start the admin server right away.

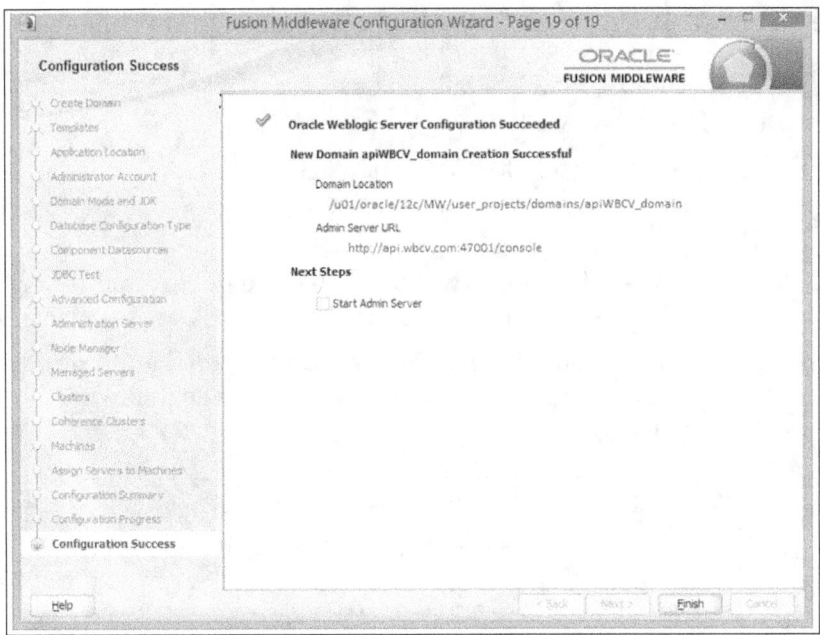

Validate the domain starting the node manager, admin, and managed server. Ensure that the API Manager is running by entering the URL: `http://machine:47001/apimanager`.

# Installing Oracle API Gateway

The next steps demonstrate how to install an instance of Oracle API Gateway. This section should circumvent the need to read the official Oracle documentation.

 For more information on this configuration please refer to section *16 Configuring Reporting with BI Publisher* of the *OER Configuration Guide* at the following link:
`http://docs.oracle.com/cd/E28280_01/admin.1111/e16580/bipub.htm#sthref868`

*Installation Tips and Techniques*

There are three installation pieces that will be described in the upcoming pages:

- Oracle API Gateway Core Server
- Oracle API Gateway Analytics
- Database schema creation for OAG analytics

Now, follow these steps:

1. Go to the machine where OAG will be installed, and create a directory like this: `/u01/app/oracle/product/OAG_11gR2`. This will be the `OAG_HOME` instance.

2. Locate where the installation package was downloaded and execute: `./OAG-11.1.2.2.0-linux-x64-installer.run`. The following screenshot will appear:

3. Hit the **Forward** button and the following screenshot will appear. Choose the path where OAG will be installed. This will be `OAG_HOME`. Hit the **Forward** button after selecting the path.

*Chapter 6*

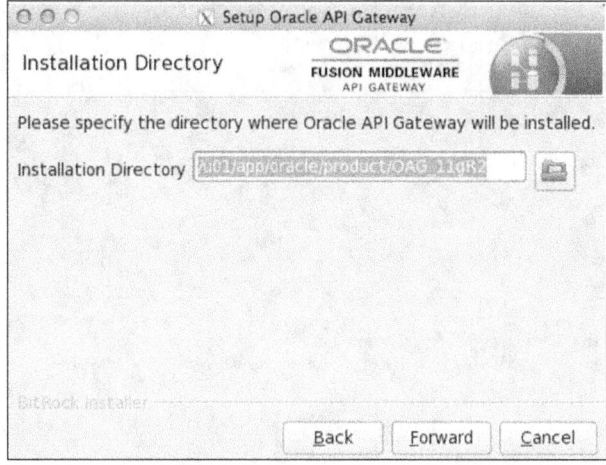

4. After hitting the **Forward** button, the following screenshot will appear:

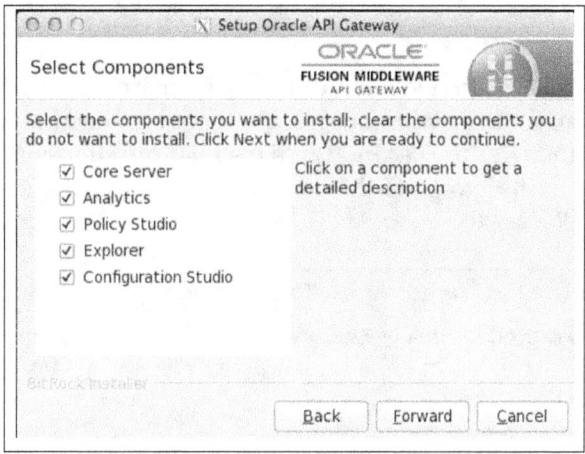

5. Select the following options (refer to *Chapter 5*, Oracle API Gateway Implementation Overview, for details of these components):
    - Core Server
    - Analytics
    - Policy Studio
    - Explorer
    - Configuration Studio

*Installation Tips and Techniques*

6. After selecting the different components, click on the **Forward** button. The following screenshot will appear:

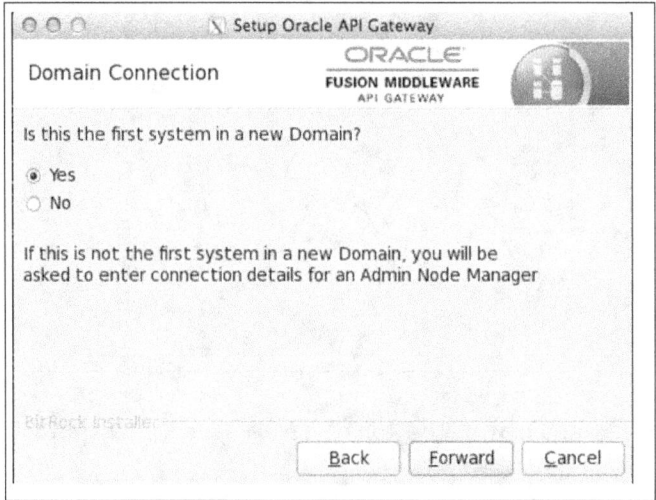

7. When asked, **Is the first system in a new Domain**, choose **Yes** as this will be a single instance installation. Should there be a need to install OAG in a cluster then, for the second node installation, choose **No**. Click on the **Forward** button to go to the next step. The following screen will be displayed:

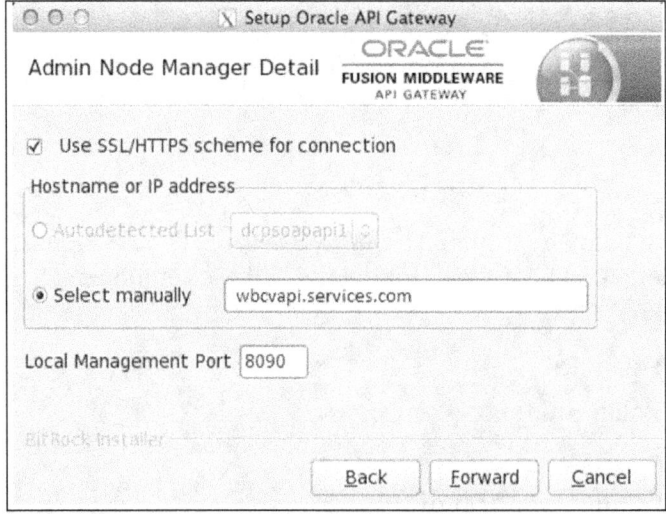

[ 274 ]

8. Use the SSL/HTTPS scheme for connection. This means that connections will use HTTPS and SSL. Also, select the hostname or IP address where the node manager will be receiving requests. Finally, choose a value for the listener port which accepts requests.

9. Hit the **Forward** button and the following screenshot will appear. To start the installation, select the **Yes** option and hit the **Forward** button.

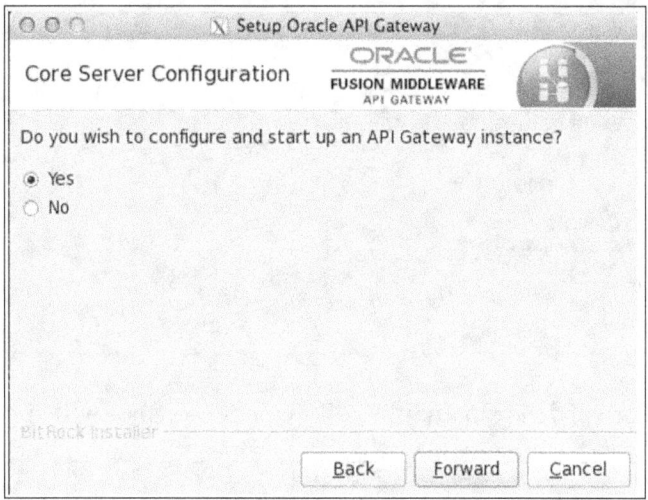

10. The next screen (see the preceding screenshot) prompts the user for the following details:
    - **API Gateway Name**: This is the name that we will use for our API Gateway.
    - **API Gateway Group**: The Gateway Group name, as described in *Chapter 5*, Oracle API Gateway Implementation Overview, is an instance that belongs to a group.
    - **SSL/HTTPS**: This specifies whether we want our gateway to listen on HTTPS or not
    - **Local Management Port**: This is the management port for this specific gateway

*Installation Tips and Techniques*

- **External Traffic Port**: This is the port where this gateway will be receiving the external traffic:

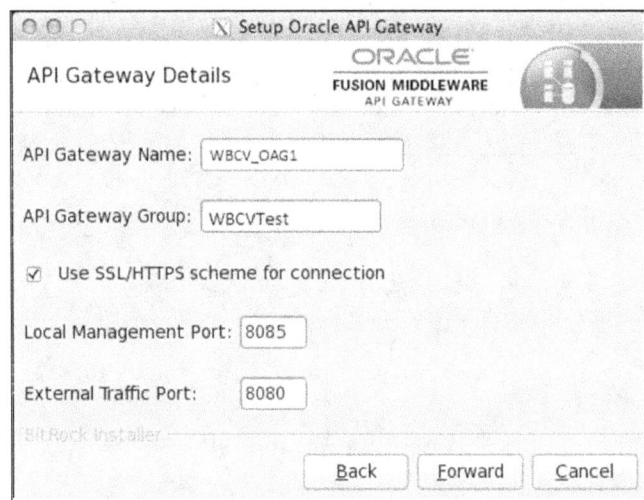

11. Hit the **Forward** button and the following screenshot will appear:

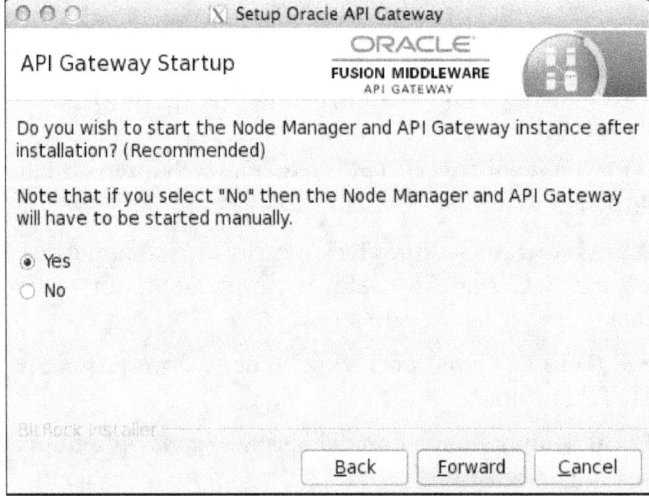

12. The preceding prompt asks if the install process should start the Node Manager and API Gateway instance after the installation. Select **Yes** and hit the **Forward** button.

*Chapter 6*

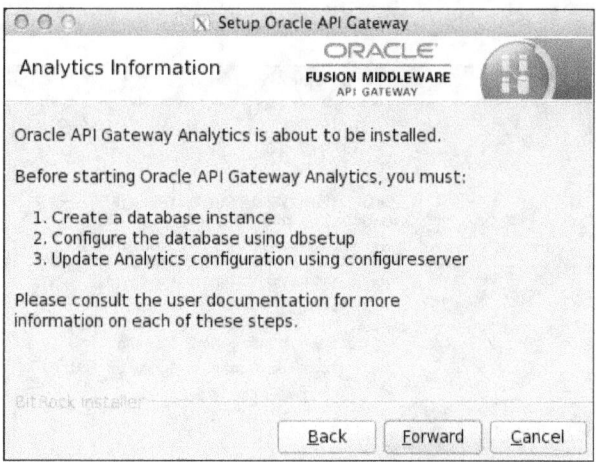

13. The next step is to install API Gateway Analytics. This requires an Oracle database to be already in place. For details on installing a database, follow the Oracle official documentation at `https://docs.oracle.com/cd/E39820_01/doc.11121/gateway_install_docs/content/reporter_config.html`.

14. Hit the **Forward** button and go to the next step.

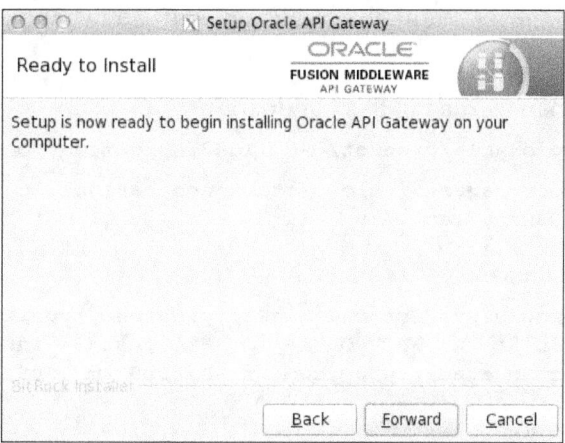

15. Oracle API Gateway is now ready to be installed. Just click on the **Forward** button and a progress bar will appear.

# Installation Tips and Techniques

Once the installation is complete, the following screenshot will appear:

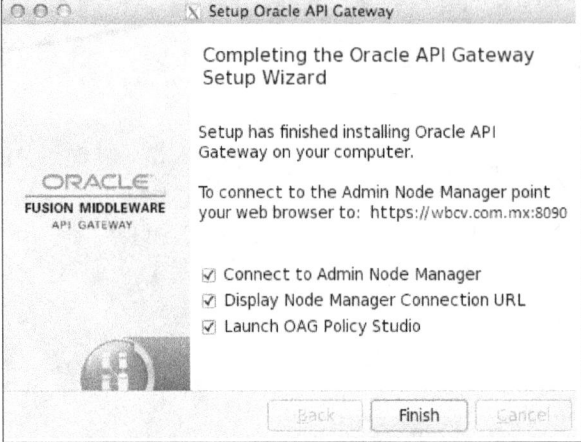

It is possible to open up OAG Policy Studio and open a browser to connect to the Admin Node Manager. Should you wish to do so, select the options (refer to the preceding screenshot).

After clicking on the **Finish** button, the installer will close.

To start the Node Manager manually, create and start an instance, following the given steps:

1. Start node manager using this command:

   ```
   cd /u01/app/oracle/product/OAG_11gR2/apigateway/posix/bin
   nohup ./nodemanager > . logs/start_nodemanager.log 2> ../logs/start_nodemanager.err./ &
   ```

2. Create an instance:

   ```
   /u01/app/oracle/product/OAG_11gR2/apigateway/posix/bin/
   managedomain -c -n "WBCV_OAG1" -g "WBCVTest" --instance_scheme https --instance_host wbcv.com.mx -s 8080 -m 8085
   ```

3. Start an instance:

   ```
   cd /u01/app/oracle/product/OAG_11gR2/apigateway/posix/bin/
   nohup ./startinstance -g "WBCVTest" -n "WBCV_OAG1" > ../logs/start_OAG1.log 2> ../logs/start_OAG1.err &
   ```

# Summary

This chapter started by describing a typical topology employed for a SOA Governance implementation that utilizes the main products of the Oracle SOA Governance Solution. It went on to detail numerous considerations made by WBCV when defining an environment strategy suitable to support their development lifecycle.

The chapter provided steps, tips and techniques to install WebLogic Servers, Oracle API Manager, Oracle API Catalog, and BI Publisher.

Throughout the chapters of this book, the authors have set out to illustrate how WBCV embarked on its SOA Governance journey and the different challenges they faced along the way. Each chapter started by describing the business problem that tools, processes, and people are meant to address and continued by providing practical steps on how to implement the relevant Oracle SOA Governance tools to achieve this.

In summary, this book is a one-stop shop for SOA practitioners that want to succeed in the implementation of Oracle SOA. The book provides many use cases that deliver invaluable insights into how tools, processes, and people must be realigned to address the challenges that prevent organizations from getting the most out of their SOA solutions and investments.

# Index

## Symbol

**4APPmigos**
　about 47
　API Management capabilities, lacking 42
　recommendations 39-46

## A

**Active Directory (AD)** 72
**administrative tasks**
　performing 149-154
**Administrator's Guide, for OAC**
　URL 59
**aggregation interval, for Service/API**
　URL 163
**Ansible**
　URL 27
**Ant Harvester**
　URL 95
　used, for SDLC harvesting 91
**Apache Ant**
　URL 92
**API Blueprint**
　URL 5
**API catalog** 42
**API curator**
　APIs publishing,
　　from OSB Console 155-158
**API economy** 6
**API gateway** 42
**API Keys**
　URL 172

**API Management**
　and SOA Governance, convergence 8, 9
　concluding 6, 7
　defining 4-7, 140, 141
**API Management product**
　　evaluation model 43
**API Management website, Oracle**
　URL 48
**API Manager**
　used, for working with
　　JSON/REST-based APIs 177-179
**API metadata**
　editing 99-103
　viewing 99-103
**API rating**
　defining 104-106
**APIs**
　about 140
　defining 104, 105
　discovering 97
　publishing from OSB Console,
　　as API curator 155-158
**API security**
　with OAG 183, 184
**Application Programming**
　　**Interface (API)** 4
**architecture, OAC**
　OAC application 53
　OAC core platform 52
　OAC roles 64, 65
　user interfaces 64, 65

**architecture, OAG**
  defining 184
  Design-time management 185
  Personas 185
  Runtime execution 186
  Runtime management 186
**ASG**
  about 1, 10, 32, 40
  framework 12
  framework scope 13, 14
  implementing 11
  URL 44
**ASG design-time**
  ASG design standards 23
  ASG information standards 23
  ASG programming standards 23
  ASG SDLC 23
  key deliverables 23
  logical reference architecture 23
  monitoring and SLA standards 24
  physical reference architecture 23
  security standards 23
  service and APIs catalog 24
**ASG framework scope**
  ASG design-time 22-24
  ASG runtime 24-26
  defining 13, 14
  Development Operations (DevOps) 26, 27
  people 17-20
  strategy 14-17
  tools 28
**ASG runtime**
  defining 24
  features 24-26
**ASG strategy**
  about 140
  defining 14
  objectives 14-16
**Assets** 2

## B

**BelTelecomm** 166
**binaries, from Oracle eDelivery**
  references 238
**bootstrapping** 77
**business as usual (BAU)** 26

## C

**case study**
  defining 29-33
  discovery 34-37
  implementing 29
  readiness assessment 34-37
**Chef**
  URL 27
**Chief Security Officer (CSO)** 189
**Chief Technology Officer (CTO)** 189
**Coherence cluster** 267
**command-line Harvester**
  Oracle Service Bus,
    bootstrapping with 86-89
  Oracle SOA Suite,
    bootstrapping with 82-86
  WADLs, bootstrapping manually with 90
  WSDLs, bootstrapping manually with 90
**Community Management** 6
**components, OAC engine**
  Harvester 62
  OER subsystems 63
  REX API 62
**configuration and assets, OAC**
  exporting 118
  importing 118
**configuration, OAC**
  defining 68
  departments, setting up 69-72
  logging, into OAC 68
  users, setting up 72-75
**content management system (CMS)** 80
**Conway's law**
  about 17
  URL 18
**cross-site scripting (XSS)** 184

## D

**Demilitarized Done (DMZ)** 42, 183, 187, 190
**denial-of-service (DoS)** 184
**Development Operations (DevOps)**
  about 7, 26, 27, 42
  key deliverables 27
**disk space requirements**
  defining 239

WebLogic 12c, installing 240, 241
distributed denial of service (DDoS) 191

# E

Enterprise Architecture (EA) 66
enterprise information systems 140

# G

gap analysis
  defining 37, 38
GET requests 220
global request and response policies 232
governance framework 12

# H

hardening process 185
Headers or Query Strings 220
high volume customers 212
Hudson
  URL 27
Hypertext Transfer Protocol (HTTP) 4

# I

Identity and Access Management 184
Import/Export utility
  URL 118
  used, for exporting assets 119, 120
  used, for importing assets 121
Infrastructure as a Service (IaaS) 45
installation process
  defining 237, 238
installation topology
  defining 236
Internet of Things (IoT) 10

# J

JavaScript Object Notation (JSON)
  about 4
  URL 4
Java Web Start
  URL 60

JDeveloper
  URL 107
JDeveloper plug-in, for OAC
  setting up 106
  using 106
Jenkins
  URL 27

# L

Logging, exception handling and auditing frameworks (LEAF) 25

# M

Managed Servers
  fields 249
Master OSB 145
mobile risks, OWASP
  URL 189
Mobile Virtual Network Enabler (MVNE) 148
Mobile Virtual Network Operators (MVNOs) 148

# N

Node Manager
  starting, manually 278
  URL 250

# O

OAC
  about 51, 66
  architecture, defining 52
  bootstrapping 77-82
  configuration 68
  database, installing 239
  functional overview 52
  implementing 67
  installing 238
  OAC domain, creating 244-251

OAC software, installing 241-244
settings, defining 57-60
system settings, changing 76
temporary disk space requirements 239
**OAC application**
OAC engine 62, 63
OAC web console 53-61
**OAC configuration**
URL 73
**OAC console**
used, for discovering APIs 98, 99
**OAC Harvester**
reference 86
**OAC web console**
URL 60
**OAG**
about 183
active functionality 188
API registration 193-198
API security, performing with 183, 184
architecture overview 184-186
defining 181, 182
features 182, 183
implementing 192
key security-related capabilities 184
passive functionality 188
service discovery 193
**OAG policies**
implementing 198
**OAG server 231**
**OAPIM 143**
**OAuth**
about 206
URL 206
**objectives**
defining, for 4APPmigos 32, 33
**OER Binaries 52**
**OER functionality**
Harvester 65
JDeveloper OER plug-in 65
REX API 65
Web console 65
**OER installation**
URL 249

**OER JDeveloper plug-in**
installing 106-109
using, with OAC 110-118
**OER/OAC installation guide**
URL 239
**OER Oracle**
URL 52
**OER sizing guide**
URL 239
**OER template**
URL 244
**OFM control**
URL 150
**OPatch**
URL 242
**Open Web Application Security Project (OWASP)**
about 7, 189
URL 7
**options, database profile**
URL 256
**Oracle API Catalog.** *See* **OAC**
about 193, 235
URL 238
**Oracle API Gateway.** *See* **OAG**
about 235
URL 238
**Oracle API Management 44**
**Oracle API Manager**
about 139, 235
architecture overview 144, 145
capabilities 145, 146
case study background 148, 149
components 145, 146
defining 142, 143
functional overview 144, 145
Oracle API Manager Portal 146
Oracle Service Bus Console 146
prior administrative tasks, performing 149-154
roles 146
URL 148
working, as consumer 166-176

Oracle API Manager (12.1.3.0)
    URL 259
Oracle API Manager 12c R1 (12.1.3.0)
    URL 238
Oracle API Manager software
    installing 252-257
    Oracle API Gateway, installing 271-278
    Oracle API Manager 12c
        WebLogic domain, creating 257-270
Oracle API Manger 12c domain
    URL 257
Oracle API portal
    accessing, as administrator 159-165
Oracle Cloud Services, for PaaS
    URL 45
Oracle documentation
    URL 154
Oracle Enterprise Repository (OER) 52, 106
Oracle Fusion Middleware (OFM) 150
Oracle Service Bus
    about 252
    bootstrapping, with command-line
        Harvester 86-89
Oracle SOA Suite
    about 44
    bootstrapping, with command-line
        Harvester 82-86
Oracle Technology Network (OTN) 238
Oracle Unified Directory 199
OSB 12c
    URL 252
OSB Ant Harvester
    using 95-97
OWASP top 10 mobile risks
    URL 7

# P

PACE layer application strategy
    URL 30
perimeter security 183
personas 6
phases, roadmap
    foundation 48

implementation 48
inception 48
policy containers 198
policy enforcement point (PeP) 42
policy shortcut 218
private access 5
public access 5
Puppet Labs
    URL 27

# Q

questionnaire, 4APPmigos
    results 36, 37

# R

RACI model
    defining 21
recommendations
    for identified gaps 39-46
Repository Creation Utility (RCU) 239, 257
Repository Extensibility Framework (REX)
    about 122
    URL 124
Representational State Transfer (REST)
    about 4
    URL 4
REST APIs, creating
    URL 177
RESTful API Modeling Language (RAML)
    about 77
    URL 5
REST URI 231
REX API
    about 122, 123
    used, for finding API 123-136
    used, for updating API 123-136
roadmap
    about 47, 48
    phases 47
role-based access control (RBAC) 64
roles, OAC
    Admin 65
    Curator 65
    Developer 64

**roles, Oracle API Manager**
  API administrator 146
  API consumer 147
  API curator 146
  defining 146-148

**roles, SOA and API software development lifecycle**
  ASG designer 20
  ASG developer 20
  ASG middleware engineer 20
  ASG Solution architect 19
  ASG testers 20
  C-Level executive sponsors 18
  DevOps engineer 20
  DevOps manager 21
  enterprise architect 19
  Functional/Business analyst 18

## S

**SDLC**
  harvesting, Ant Harvester used 91

**service gateway 187**

**service groups 231**

**Service Oriented Architecture (SOA) 181**

**Service Table (STB) 261**

**SOA Governance**
  and API Management, convergence 8, 9
  challenges 3
  defining 1-4
  principles 4

**SOA Governance 11g implementation**
  URL 16

**SOA Governance requirements**
  references 63
  URL 63

**SOAPUI**
  URL 172

**SOA Suite Ant Harvester**
  using 91-95

**software as a service (SaaS) 30**

**success and failure paths**
  adding 229

**Swagger**
  URL 5

## T

**TOGAF**
  about 37
  URL 37

**TOGAF enterprise architecture frameworks**
  URL 34

## U

**uniform resource identifiers (URIs) 4**

**use cases**
  implementing 66, 67, 189-191
  policy, applying to web service 213, 214
  policy creation, for handling authentication 199-210
  policy creation, for handling authorization 199-210
  policy, deploying 215
  REST/JSON API, creating 216-232
  throttling filters, adding 211, 212

## V

**volumetric analysis 212**

## W

**WADLs**
  bootstrapping manually, with command-line Harvester 90
  URL 5

**warnings (WARN) 85**

**WBCV architects**
  inventory 78-80

**WBCV implementation**
  URL 31

**WBCV low score**
  reasons for 38

**WBCV Telecom 29**

**WBVC**
  business model 149
**WebLogic**
  URL 252
**WebLogic domain directories**
  URL 260
**WebLogic Server 12.1.3**
  URL 238
**Web Service Manager (WSM) 192**
**workshop, 4APPmigos**
  business 34
  creating 34
  DevOps 35
  enterprise architecture 34
  People and Organization 35
  SOA 35
**WSDLs**
  bootstrapping manually,
      with command-line Harvester 90
**WSM policies, applying**
  URL 192

## Thank you for buying
## Oracle API Management 12c Implementation

# About Packt Publishing

Packt, pronounced 'packed', published its first book, *Mastering phpMyAdmin for Effective MySQL Management*, in April 2004, and subsequently continued to specialize in publishing highly focused books on specific technologies and solutions.

Our books and publications share the experiences of your fellow IT professionals in adapting and customizing today's systems, applications, and frameworks. Our solution-based books give you the knowledge and power to customize the software and technologies you're using to get the job done. Packt books are more specific and less general than the IT books you have seen in the past. Our unique business model allows us to bring you more focused information, giving you more of what you need to know, and less of what you don't.

Packt is a modern yet unique publishing company that focuses on producing quality, cutting-edge books for communities of developers, administrators, and newbies alike. For more information, please visit our website at www.packtpub.com.

# About Packt Enterprise

In 2010, Packt launched two new brands, Packt Enterprise and Packt Open Source, in order to continue its focus on specialization. This book is part of the Packt Enterprise brand, home to books published on enterprise software – software created by major vendors, including (but not limited to) IBM, Microsoft, and Oracle, often for use in other corporations. Its titles will offer information relevant to a range of users of this software, including administrators, developers, architects, and end users.

# Writing for Packt

We welcome all inquiries from people who are interested in authoring. Book proposals should be sent to author@packtpub.com. If your book idea is still at an early stage and you would like to discuss it first before writing a formal book proposal, then please contact us; one of our commissioning editors will get in touch with you.

We're not just looking for published authors; if you have strong technical skills but no writing experience, our experienced editors can help you develop a writing career, or simply get some additional reward for your expertise.

## Oracle APEX Cookbook
### Second Edition

ISBN: 978-1-78217-967-2    Paperback: 444 pages

Create reliable, modern web applications for desktop and mobile devices with Oracle Application Express

1. Explore APEX to build applications with the latest techniques in AJAX and JavaScript using features such as plugins and dynamic actions.

2. With HTML5 and CSS3 support, make the most out of the possibilities that APEX has to offer.

3. Part of Packt's Cookbook series: Each recipe is a carefully organized sequence of instructions to complete the task as efficiently as possible.

## Oracle ADF Enterprise Application Development – Made Simple
### Second Edition

ISBN: 978-1-78217-680-0    Paperback: 432 pages

Successfully plan, develop, test, and deploy enterprise applications with Oracle ADF

1. Utilize best practices for real-life enterprise application development.

2. Plan and estimate your very own ADF project.

3. Successfully organize your code and your team for maximum efficiency.

Please check www.PacktPub.com for information on our titles

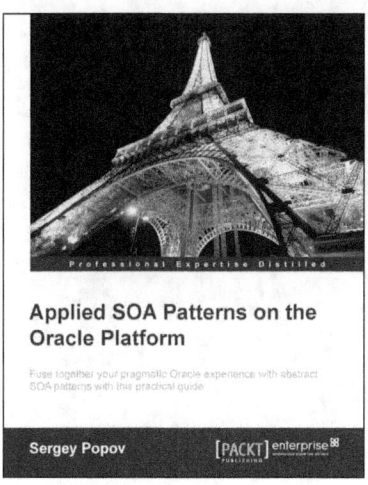

## Applied SOA Patterns on the Oracle Platform

ISBN: 978-1-78217-056-3 　　　Paperback: 572 pages

Fuse together your pragmatic Oracle experience with abstract SOA patterns with this practical guide

1. Demonstrates how to approach the Big Problem, decompose it into manageable pieces and assess the feasibility of SOA methodology to build the entire solution using real-life examples.

2. Explores out the links between SOA Principles, Open Standards and SOA Frameworks with clear standards implementation roadmaps.

3. A collection of "lessons learned" from various implementations undertaken over the years, but the book can also be used as a textbook of preparation for SOA Professional/Architect exams (from SOA school).

## Oracle Coherence Quickstart

ISBN: 978-1-84969-494-0 　　　Duration: 01:43 hours

Build dynamic next-generation applications using the market leading in-memory datagrid

1. Step-by-step, and easy to follow instructions to leverage Coherence and provide real-time updates to client applications.

2. Detailed demonstrations with suggested best practices to build scalable websites and Enterprise applications using a tried and tested data grid product.

3. Structured examples and projects, with hands-on exercises and guidance.

Please check www.PacktPub.com for information on our titles

www.ingramcontent.com/pod-product-compliance
Lightning Source LLC
Chambersburg PA
CBHW062318220526
45469CB00008B/2552